SUPPORT SYSTEMS AND MUTUAL HELP

Multidisciplinary Explorations

SUPPORT SYSTEMS AND MUTUAL HELP
Multidisciplinary Explorations

Edited by
Gerald Caplan and Marie Killilea
Laboratory of Community Psychiatry
Department of Psychiatry
Harvard Medical School

Contributors

Ruby B. Abrahams
Gerald Caplan
Ruth B. Caplan
Matthew P. Dumont
Mark Dyer
Marie Killilea
David E. Richards
Phyllis R. Silverman
David Spiegel
Henry Wechsler
Robert S. Weiss

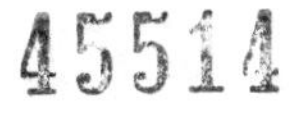

Grune & Stratton
A Subsidiary of Harcourt Brace Jovanovich, Publishers
New York San Francisco London

Library of Congress Cataloging in Publication Data
Main entry under title:

Support systems and mutual help.

Bibliography: p.
Includes index.
1. Mental hygiene – United States. 2. Self-help groups – United States. 3. Helping behavior.
I. Caplan, Gerald. II. Killilea, Marie Lyons.
III. Abrahams, Ruby B.
RA790.6.S9 362.2'04'25 76-7473
ISBN 0-8089-0927-4

Grune & Stratton, Inc.
111 Fifth Avenue
New York, New York 10003

Library of Congress Catalog Card Number 76-7473
International Standard Book Number 0-8089-0927-4
Printed in the United States of America

This book is dedicated to the memory of Erich Lindemann, 1900 - 1974, pioneer in the multidisciplinary approach to community mental health.

CONTENTS

CONTRIBUTORS

Ruby B. Abrahams, M.A.
Robert Wood Johnson Foundation Fellow
Radcliffe College – Radcliffe Institute Programs in Health Care
Cambridge, Massachusetts

Gerald Caplan, M.D., D.P.M.
Professor of Psychiatry and
Director, Laboratory of Community Psychiatry
Department of Psychiatry
Harvard Medical School
Boston, Massachusetts

Ruth B. Caplan, Ph.D.
Lecturer
Department of English Literature
The Hebrew University of Jerusalem
Jerusalem, Israel

Matthew P. Dumont, M.D.
Assistant Commissioner for Drug Rehabilitation
Department of Mental Health
Commonwealth of Massachusetts and
Lecturer on Psychiatry
Department of Psychiatry
Harvard Medical School
Boston, Massachusetts

Father Mark Dyer, S.T.L.
Missioner to Clergy
Episcopal Diocese of Massachusetts
Boston, Massachusetts

Marie Killilea
Associate in Psychiatry (Health Administration) and
Assistant Director (Development and Special Projects)
Laboratory of Community Psychiatry
Department of Psychiatry
Harvard Medical School
Boston, Massachusetts

Bishop David E. Richards, M.Div.
Director, Office of Pastoral Development
Episcopal Church of the United States
Coral Gables, Florida

Phyllis R. Silverman, Ph.D.
Lecturer on Social Welfare in the
Department of Psychiatry
Harvard Medical School
Boston, Massachusetts

David Spiegel, M.D.
Assistant Professor of Psychiatry
Department of Psychiatry and Behavioral Sciences
Stanford University School of Medicine
Palo Alto, California

Henry Wechsler, Ph.D.
Director of Research
The Medical Foundation, Inc., Boston and
Lecturer on Social Psychology
Harvard School of Public Health
Boston, Massachusetts

Robert S. Weiss, Ph.D.
Professor of Sociology and Chairman
Department of Sociology
University of Massachusetts at Boston and
Lecturer on Sociology in the Department of Psychiatry
Laboratory of Community Psychiatry
Harvard Medical School
Boston, Massachusetts

Gerald Caplan

Introduction and Overview

This is the third publication of our Harvard Laboratory of Community Psychiatry dealing with support systems. We first emphasized the importance of this topic in the book, *Helping the Helpers to Help* by Ruth B. Caplan et al.[1] That book described a program that started out as a traditional mental health consultation project in the Episcopal Church conducted by our community mental health specialists; that then moved on to my training bishops to offer skilled consultation to their peers; and that eventually developed unanticipated features of a self-energized and maintained mutual support system, which has begun to permeate the entire structure of this religious denomination. It was our analysis of the potential theoretical and practical significance of this latter development that brought us to the conceptual model of support systems as a valuable addition to our previous theories.

In the second book in this series, *Support Systems and Community Mental Health* by Gerald Caplan,[2] the new model was further developed, and was brought into articulation with the basic concepts that our Harvard group has developed over a twenty-year period in guiding our research and practice in community mental health.

The present volume is the next step. Like its predecessors it is not intended as a definitive or systematic statement, but as a report on work in progress that shares with others our theoretical and practical explorations

[1]Ruth B. Caplan, *Helping the Helpers to Help: The Development and Evaluation of Mental Health Consultation to Aid Clergymen in Pastoral Work* (New York: Seabury Press, 1972).

[2]Gerald Caplan, *Support Systems and Community Mental Health: Lectures on Concept Development* (New York: Behavioral Publications, 1974).

of this new idea, and that we hope will stimulate many of our fellow community mental health workers to try out variations of it for themselves. Marie Killilea's review (Chapter 2) of part of the vast literature that seems relevant shows that many people are already working in some part of this field and that complicated and exciting vistas are being opened up by them at every turn in the road. Our Harvard group is not re-discovering the wheel. What we are advocating is an attempt to develop a *coherent framework* that will bring together into a meaningful whole a body of ideas, research findings, and practice principles that may be used to guide our program planning and techniques, and thus make us more effective in raising the level of mental well-being and competence in populations.

Advisedly, at our present stage we are trying not to be too restrictive in bounding the topic on which we are focusing, but our intention in this book is nevertheless to narrow our field somewhat by concentrating on one of the elements that our previous publications have revealed to be crucial, namely the mutual-help aspect of support systems.

The book consists of three parts: First is a group of five theoretical chapters that are mainly devoted to the further development of the concepts of support systems and mutual help. This is followed by three chapters that report empirical studies of the detailed operation of natural societal or organizational support systems that involve mutual help. The book ends with a group of five chapters that describe recent attempts by members of our Laboratory to make use of support system concepts in organizing helpful intervention programs. The contributors to the book are drawn from many disciplines: psychiatry, psychology, social work, sociology, religion, moral theology, intellectual history and English literature, adult education, and administration. We hope that readers will agree with us that the picture that emerges from bringing their manifold viewpoints and methodological approaches to bear on our topic not only enriches, because of their varied interests, but also improves our understanding. It certainly broadens our view of the multifactorial nature of the field. We hope that it also brings into focus the significant threads that appear to weave a common meaningful pattern across the boundaries of the different settings.

The first conceptualizing section opens with my chapter on the family as a support system. This is a direct continuation of the first chapter of *Support Systems and Community Mental Health,* and is my attempt to explore in greater depth an important segment of the field discussed in that book and to derive from my theorizing some guidelines for action. I do not emphasize in this chapter, mainly because I dealt with it in the prior publications, that a major feature of the supportive operations of healthy families is *mutuality* and *reciprocity* in need satisfaction. Each time an individual or the family as a unit guides, controls, or nurtures another family member, this action personally benefits the givers as much, if not more, than the receiver. Helping activity within the family circle may involve sublimated elements of altruism, but the importance of self-interest is not hard to identify. A parent has a basic urge to nurture, and profits from satisfying this drive just as much as his child may benefit from being guided, supported, and loved.

This reciprocity is so much part of the air we breathe in families that it is usually invisible. Its significance obtrudes when the pattern is upset, as when a psychosocial disorder leads to one individual or group within a family exploiting another by seeking personal gain through manipulating him as an object and not through the medium of satisfying his needs. The results are usually harmful to both parties in ways that are well known to us in our clinical practice. The frequency of such problems among patients tends to prevent our realizing that ordinary families, with healthy interpersonal relationships where the members are sensitive and respectful of each other's current needs, are the norm in the population; and this is not only in itself a source of support for many people, but probably also provides a model for non-family supportive groups and organizations.

My theoretical analysis of the elements of the supportive structure in an ideal-type healthy family therefore has possible implications that go beyond the family to a wide range of other support systems.

The second chapter in this section is the literature review by Marie Killilea. This is more than a summary of previous work. It attempts to document and classify the many meaningful factors involved in mutual support groups and organizations, both in regard to the forces involved in their development and maintenance, and in relation to how they operate and how they help their members. Writers have usually focused on particular aspects of this field, whether in line with their theoretical interests or because of their wish to develop interventive systems within their own professional domains. Many of these have clear validity in their own right. What Marie Killilea does is show how the various approaches highlight elements in a very complicated multifactorial field; she then derives implications for future theoretical and practice explorations that may provide a systematic framework for increasing our understanding and interventive skills.

The third chapter, by Mark Dyer, focuses on religious aspects of support systems and on supportive aspects of religious denominations, particularly the neo-pentecostal groups. Marie Killilea's literature review has already emphasized the importance of spiritual and religious concepts in the developmental history of the mutual-help movement; even superficial experience with such typical mutual-help organizations as Alcoholics Anonymous, Recovery Incorporated, or TOPS, emphasizes the similarity of many of their practices to the traditions and rituals of religions. Mark Dyer clarifies some of the common elements as he responds to questions posed by the staff of our Harvard Laboratory of Community Psychiatry. We have felt it worthwhile to publish this chapter in the form of a transcript of one of the weekly sessions of a staff seminar that we established in 1973 to enlarge our understanding of salient issues in this field. Many of the chapters of this book were originally presented as papers to this seminar. The transcript of the discussion with Mark Dyer has been edited only to delete confidential material, and to clear up ambiguities of the oral interchange. We feel that although it is possibly more burdensome to read and develops some of its points less effectively than if we had invited Father Dyer to write the more usual kind of chapter, it does have the advantage of presenting a vivid picture of the atmosphere of intellectual enthusiasm and wide-ranging inquiry of our multidisciplinary group. It also raises many significant questions about the interface of religion and the mutual support field, to which currently we have no adequate answers; and the format of the chapter perhaps allows us to do this more comfortably than if we had solicited a systematic presentation from a single authority.

Chapter 4 is the reprint of a position paper originally written for the American Journal of Psychiatry by Matthew P. Dumont. We include it here because it makes some important points in developing our thesis, and because in its original form of publication it possibly escaped the notice of many of our readers. Dumont deals first with the sociopolitical forces that have led to the recent popularity of mutual-help and self-help organizations. He then develops the thesis that this movement should primarily be considered a political phenomenon, a rebellion of the hitherto powerless consumers against the privileged position of the professional community, and eventually the manifestation of a power-to-the-people drive of the weak, whose needs have for too long been neglected. He writes with the fervor and intellectual passion of an ideologically committed person, and in this he speaks for many who have studied and worked in this field.

Chapter 5, "Going Public and Self-Help" by David Spiegel, is the report of a study that throws further light on questions raised in the two previous chapters. First, it deals with the significance of confession and public testimony that characterize ritual behavior in many religions as well as in many mutual-help organizations, particularly of stigmatized persons; and then the author links such practices with political action. He defines "going public" as "making an open declaration about a personal attribute" – usually one that would be socially condemned and that the person has previously hidden as a shameful secret.

Spiegel then uses a study of person–group interactions in three mutual-help groups of stigmatized persons to develop the thesis that there is a meaningful parameter that leads from keeping a shameful attribute secret to divulging it within the setting of a small supportive group of people who share this attribute and who band together to strengthen each other against the hostility of society, to making a public declaration to the wider society. The members of the mutual-help organization then form themselves into a political pressure group to force society to reduce its stigmatizing attitudes and behavior, and to re-admit them as members in good standing.

Spiegel interprets this process within the conceptual framework of existential psychiatry and speculates "that groups as well as individuals go through a development from private to public to political activity" that has profound meaning for improving their personal competence and mental health.

Chapters 6 – 8 form the next section. Each of these chapters describes an empirical study of a society or an organization that enriches our view of the central topic. The chapter by Spiegel might have been included in this section. It, too, uses empirical data in developing a thesis. The difference is one of relative emphasis. Spiegel appears to have arrived at his concepts about "going public" from existential psychiatry and from his experience in the mutual-help field, and then he seems to have planned a study to illustrate and enrich his ideas. The writers of the next three chapters, in contrast, appear to have initiated their studies with a relatively open mind and to have arrived at their theoretical conclusions, if any, mainly on the basis of analysis of their data. In Chapter 6 the writer does not even explicitly relate her findings to our field of interest; we have to derive the links ourselves. But, of course, no researcher begins a study without prior biases and preconceptions that mold his selection of data and his approach to analysis. So the division between this section and its predecessor is really a matter of degree. I believe, however, that although both approaches are valid and of potential value such a division is not unimportant because the more attention we pay to studies at the "open-minded, empirical" end of the parameter, the more we are likely to avoid early closure and arbitrary constriction in our theorizing, and the richer will be the fund of ideas on which we base our interventions.

Chapter 6, "Deathbed Scenes and Graveyard Poetry" by Ruth B. Caplan, is most interesting from this point of view. It uses textual analysis of English literary productions of the eighteenth-century to develop an understanding of certain aspects of that society. Unlike many psychohistorians whose studies may be familiar to community mental health workers, and who make use of modern psychological theories to interpret the literature and the personalities of literary figures of the past, Ruth Caplan analyzes the content of texts in order to speculate about the systems of psychology that were current at that period, upon which their writers must have relied in molding their literary material. She also uses the texts and other contemporary data to build a picture of dominant values, attitudes and practices that must have been part of the culture of these writers and their readers. The potential value to community mental health workers of such a contribution is not that it may validate our theories by using past literary texts as though they were present-day clinical material we collect from our patients, but that by comparing the ideas and experience of earlier times with those of today we may observe similarities and differences that may increase our sophistication and draw our attention to certain issues that might otherwise be obscured by the structure and blind spots of our own culture.

The impression that emerges from Ruth Caplan's study is the tremendous psychosocial sophistication of some of the experts in human nature in eighteenth-century England and America, the philosophers, religious leaders, poets, and novelists. I find particularly interesting their understanding of the reverberative reinforcement factor in mutual perceptions, and the importance for personality functioning of the perceptual net within which individuals are enmeshed in a small group or in society at large; their emphasis on multifactoriality in the constitutional, psychological, and social forces that mold behavior; and the importance they apparently ascribed to what we would call support systems in helping people master the inevitable stresses and challenges of life, as well as their skill in utilizing anticipatory guidance. The aspect of their culture that I find of most interest is that which also fascinates the author, namely the centrality of thinking about and preparing for death and the process of dying, not as a morbid or masochistic preoccupation but as a means of equipping people to live an effective life and as a medium for mutual support. The preoccupation of the eighteenth-century writers with this topic must to some extent have mirrored the salient thinking and behavior of their times, and the repeated vivid descriptions in so many literary works of deathbed scenes, in which the dying person and his social circle were bound together in a mutually supportive transaction, must mean that similar scenes frequently occurred in their society. This contrasts painfully with our treatment (or non-treatment) of this issue in present-day western society, and strengthens the hand of those who advocate social change in this regard.

Once again, as in my chapter on the family, the lessons we may learn from this example of eighteenth-century deathbed practices go beyond suggesting ways of improving our own handling of dying to deriving principles for organizing potent mutual supports in dealing with other life crises for those involved, and for the people around them. The crucial issue here is that of detail, and the meticulous detail describing social interaction that characterized eighteenth-century writers such as Richardson, as highlighted by Ruth Caplan, provide us with many new leads in trying today to design ways to recapture certain of the spontaneous benefits of a bygone culture.

Chapter 7, "The Contributions of an Organization of Single Parents to the Well-being of its Members" by Robert S. Weiss, brings us back to more familiar ground. It reports on a study of Parents Without Partners, which is one of the best known mutual-help organizations in this country. Weiss studies the ways in which this organization tries to respond to the two dominant disabilities of its members: the marital loss problems of divorced or widowed parents, and the burdens of a single parent in taking care of children. He shows how PWP provides an accepting social setting that combats the isolation consequent on the loss of the spouse and the reduced acceptance in usual social activities because the individual is no longer part of a marital couple. He goes beyond the superficial description of opportunities to meet new friends of both sexes and the benefits of belonging to an understanding group of people in the same boat, to an analysis of the deeper contribution of becoming involved in the activities of the organization to the sense of personal worth of the individual, which has been weakened either by the rejective trauma of divorce or by the absence of a spouse who used continually to revalidate one's personal significance.

Weiss also describes the ambivalence of PWP in grappling with the unsatisfied needs of its members for intimacy. It explicitly opposes the role of a "lonely hearts club" that offers an opportunity to find a new mate. And yet the need eventually to replace the lost mate and to satisfy the need for intimacy is not lessened by all the other guidance, friendship, social participation, and support activities of the organization. Moreover, the style of PWP appeals only to a fraction of the large population of single parents, and Weiss discusses some of the factors involved.

This issue is of wider significance than the present example, because it would appear that a mutual-help organization, in order to succeed and maintain itself, must develop a clear and stable ideology and code of behavior. This must appeal to a significant number of people in line with their previous value system and patterns of behavior, or they will not join and maintain their membership. By the same token, it will also not be attractive to others who do not initially share such a sociocultural pattern. Some religious denominations grapple with this issue by involving prospective members in a deeply moving conversion experience that to some extent separates them from their previous mental and behavioral set, and a few of the more "religiose" mutual-help groups mimic this process; but PWP represents a type of mutual-help organization at the more secular end of the parameter, and this restricts its appeal to a narrow segment of the sociocultural pool.

Chapter 8, "The Self-Help Organization in the Mental Health Field" by Henry Wechsler, reports a case study of an organization with a much broader appeal – Recovery, Incorporated – an association of former mental patients that is at the other end of the religious – secular parameter from PWP. Recovery, Inc. incorporates many analogs of a religious denomination: a prophet, disciples, missionaries, a Bible, a dogma, a common language, prescriptions for life behavior, a set of group rituals that include frequent rigidly structured meetings, public confession, testimony, reading the lesson, etc. It draws its members from a group all of whom have shared a common fate – their mental illness and its treatment, and their consequent stigmatization by society.

Henry Wechsler conducted the study before he joined our Laboratory group, and it owes little to our thinking about such issues as support systems, crisis intervention, and the value of nonprofessional person-to-person help. The consonance of many of his findings with our current thinking is therefore impressive. We asked him to contribute his 15-year-old paper to this book rather than write an updated version in order to make this point, but also because we did not believe that he could write anything better than the original article that many of us believe to be the single most productive report dealing with the psychosocial aspects of a mutual-help organization in the entire professional literature.

Wechsler begins with a description of the developmental history of the organization, starting as a group of former patients organized in Chicago as a rehabilitation group by the late Dr. Abraham A. Low, their psychiatrist, budding off local chapters in many parts of the country during his lifetime, and continuing as a rapidly growing self-perpetuating association organized and directed by its own members following his death. Wechsler then gives us a meticulous description of the details of the organization's traditions and ways of operating, as well as of its dominant philosophy. Based on this, he analyzes the roles of members and leaders, and he then discusses the basic functions of the Recovery method and of its stereotyped group practices in relation to their contribution to the well-being of its members. He analyzes the psychological significance to members of their accepting a simple systematic cognitive framework prescribed by the organization that imposes order on their chaotic psychological field; provides them with a routine to counteract anxiety-producing ambiguity or uncertainty associated with their problems; prescribes self-control to strengthen defenses against anxiety and organizes group training for this, as well as group support and ways of mastering backsliding through confession and absolution; offers inspiration; and maintains both activity and the satisfaction of passive dependency needs as a member of the organization. Wechsler then continues his analysis by focusing on the ways the group in Recovery acts as a buttress for its members: It provides them with a primary group of significant others to counteract their isolation and loneliness, a sheltered social environment (in our terminology a "haven"), a source of rewards for conforming behavior and mastering the graded challenges inside the organization to counteract lack of success in the outside world, a direct controller of behavior by group pressure, a reference group whose judgments help self-evaluation (usually more flexible and sympathetic than those of outside society), and a cause with which to identify as an enlargement of self.

After spelling out in some detail these benefits of the organization, Wechsler concludes his chapter by discussing some of the shortcomings of

Recovery and some of the criticisms levelled at it because it "offers magical–omnipotent–authoritarian–unrealistic solutions;" because it "is superficial, limited, and prevents or hinders insight;" because it "is regressive, fixes defenses, forces adjustment at a low level of maturity;" and because it "creates complacency about the problem of mental illness." He sees some of the rigidity of the philosophy and behavioral patterns of the organization as a product of its having been started by a charismatic professional whose death has enshrined his writings as an unchanging "bible," and whose authoritarian prescriptions can not be modified by his lay disciples and those who succeeded them, lest the whole structure collapse. He points out that the rigid application of the Recovery method may have certain advantages in preventing its members straying into areas that would arouse unmasterable anxiety, and that "the feeling that the method is perfect and can help all members is in line with the inspirational aspects of the organization."

What makes Wechsler's paper so useful to us today is that it describes and analyzes the details of a mutual-help and self-help system so that we can understand how it works psychologically; so that we can appraise the price that its members have to pay for the undoubted benefits they receive; so that we can improve our understanding of a system that, although started by a professional, has been perpetuated by nonprofessionals; and so that we can perhaps consider building in some of its elements, although in modified forms, in mutual-help projects that we ourselves may wish to foster.

Chapter 9 is the first of the five chapters of the final section of the book that describe some of the recent attempts by our Harvard group to work out intervention techniques and strategies that are based on the support system and mutual-help approach. "Transition States and Other Stressful Situations: Their Nature and Programs for Their Management" by Robert S. Weiss begins with a short discussion of the theoretical benefit of focusing attention not only on short crisis periods in line with traditional crisis theory, but also on the longer transition states, often ushered in by the crisis of a sudden change, but continuing until the individual and his social environment have worked out a stable new way of life. Weiss emphasizes the contribution of an adequate support system in helping those involved in transition states to work out self-satisfying and socially desirable new patterns of life organization; and the main part of his chapter is devoted to reporting a method that he has developed for providing support to men and women who are separated from their spouses, and that he is in the process of adapting to provide similar help to widows and widowers.

At first sight, the method developed by Weiss in helping the separated seems worlds apart from the method of Recovery, Inc. Instead of an authoritarian dogma enunciated by a charismatic leader and a religion-like setting with all its ritualistic trappings, Weiss organizes an eight session academic-style seminar taught by a professional, who reports on the latest findings of research about the problems of separation and solicits free questions and discussion. The scientific style of the seminar is reinforced by building in an evaluation study that implies that the whole process is open-ended and exploratory, and that carries exactly the opposite message of the Recovery claim of infallibility. In fact, the participants are told in all kinds of ways that the problems of the separated are complex and that they vary idiosyncratically from one person to the next. They are also told that even the most expert researchers still do not feel that they fully grasp the issues involved, and are eager to recruit the separated themselves as co-investigators in achieving a clearer picture.

But as Weiss continues his description of his method, a number of basic similarities to Recovery, Inc. begin to appear. First, the intervention setting is explicitly educational – a time-limited, task-oriented, carefully pre-programmed, and highly structured series of discussions – and not, for example, a free-association, therapy-like group experience in which participants are encouraged to lay down their defenses and allow "the unconscious to become conscious." Second, the implication of the entire exercise is that despite individual variations there are regularly occurring problems in this transition state that most separated people are likely to have to handle, and that probably there may be found a range of more or less effective ways of mastering these problems. In other words, the seminar with its academic trappings is introducing order into a confusing cognitive field just as Recovery tries to do by using its religion-like mode. The seminar approach has the advantage of continually appealing to and fostering the autonomy of the participants, who are invited to make their own contributions to the accumulation of knowledge; but there is little doubt that belief in the professional competence of the seminar teacher is an important reassurance that ordering the field in this way is likely to be feasible and helpful.

Third, Weiss allots double the time at each meeting for group discussion that he devotes to his lecture. And, especially in the early stages of his project, he ostentatiously modifies his lecture material by incorporating what participants have previously reported. In these ways he emphasizes the importance of peer contributions and he fosters peer support by those "in the same boat," not only emotional but cognitive, too. Information and guidance come not only from the authority figure but from those currently grappling with transition state issues. The recognition of the value of these contributions by the seminar leader and by other participants rewards the contributors within the seminar setting and counteracts self disparagement and feelings of impotence related to their previous confusion and frustration as they struggle with issues they have not been able to understand and control.

Experience with the seminars for the separated has now reached the stage that Weiss has been able to write a manual for use by seminar leaders and participants.[3] This is a development of the Outline he includes as an appendix to his chapter, and which he hands out to participants at the beginning of the seminar to help structure their expectations.

In his chapter Weiss also discusses the issues involved in modifying his method for use with widows and widowers. The above principles carry over, but he concludes "that every program intended to help people in transition will have to be responsive both in content and in format to the character of the particular transition with which it deals."

Weiss ends his chapter with some interesting comments about three kinds of helpers that he believes are needed in a successful supportive program for persons in transition: the *expert,* an authority whose knowledge is derived from systematic study of the problems experienced by other persons in a particular transition; the *veteran,* an individual who has been through the transition and can speak from experience and can "demonstrate" in his own person that recovery is possible; and the *fellow participant* who "can offer the immediate understanding that comes only from being in the same boat."

Chapters 10 and 11 should be read as a pair. Chapter 10, "The Widow as a Caregiver in a Program of Preventive Intervention with Other Widows" by Phyllis R. Silverman, describes the development of our Laboratory's earliest program in the mutual-help field, and focuses in particular on the role of the helping widow and her acceptability to the one being helped because the helper is both a veteran and a fellow participant, as defined by Weiss in the previous chapter. Chapter 11, "Mutual Helping: Styles of Caregiving in a Mutual Aid Program" by Ruby B. Abrahams, presents a more intensive analysis of the range of helping styles of nonprofessional widows in this program, on the basis of an intensive study of the details of their operations.

Our Widow-to-Widow program began in 1967, not within the framework of support system theory, which developed several years later and was itself significantly influenced by our experience in that program, but as a logical extension of our crisis theory researches on conjugal bereavement and as an attempt at preventive intervention during a crisis to improve the chances of healthy adjustment and adaptation. At that time we chose nonprofessional widows as our intervention agents because we had found during exploratory studies that widows spontaneously turn for help to other widows, partly because professional helpers are not available and if available are often found not to be effective, and partly because another widow is usually expected to be more understanding since she is in the same boat. The chapter by Phyllis Silverman is mainly a validation of this rationale. It shows that help from another widow who had herself mastered the problems of widow-

[3]Robert S. Weiss, *Marital Separation* (New York: Basic Books, 1975).

hood was usually easily acceptable to a recently widowed woman. It also describes in general terms, but with illustrative detail, the different methods used by the veteran widows in helping the recent widows. The author describes how our experience with this program persuaded us of the special merits of a person-to-person mutual help organization in contrast to the more traditional professional-client approach, how we designed the Widow-to-Widow program in such a way as to safeguard the nonprofessional style of our widow-helpers, and how our program began to take on a life of its own under the leadership of the nonprofessionals after it was initiated and supported for some time by our professional staff. Phyllis Silverman also makes brief reference to the difficulties that many professionals with service responsibilities encounter as they try to foster the entry of nonprofessional caregivers into their field. These difficulties not infrequently lead the professionals to exercise a degree of direction and control, for instance through training and supervisory activities, that curtails the optimal development of the nonprofessional self-help and mutual-help processes.

The chapter by Ruby Abrahams deepens our understanding of the latter process. She has analyzed the details of the work carried out by nonprofessional widows and widowers in helping those bereaved men and women who turned for assistance to a telephone "hot line" organized by our Widow-to-Widow program, in which there was minimal interference by professionals who spent most of their time studying what was happening rather than trying to modify it. By the time this project was begun and Ruby Abrahams carried out her study, the professional staff of our Laboratory had several years of experience in the Widow-to-Widow program and had learned how not to interfere with spontaneous nonprofessional organization and helping approaches, so she had an optimal situation for a study of this kind.

The results are most interesting. Ruby Abrahams shows that there is a variation in the helping operations of different widows; and she categorizes them into four ideal types along a parameter, one end of which approaches the traditional style of professional–client caregiving and the other end of which resembles the reciprocal give-and-take of ordinary friendship. In the first type, which she names "informative supportive, non-self-revealing," the helper maintains significant social distance from the recipient and offers help mainly through giving information and guidance, based partly on personal experience but largely also on having studied community resources. The second type, which she names "emotive supportive, non-self-revealing," is characterized by slightly less social distance, and the helper provides warm emotional understanding based on her own enduring personality attributes in addition to giving some cognitive guidance. In the third type, "emotive supportive, some self-revealing," the outstanding characteristic is that the helper provides emotional support mainly on the basis of revealing to the recipient the details of her own problems with bereavement and emphasizing the "same boat" situation. The fourth type, "integrative friendship, self-revealing," provides a situation in which the helper freely gives and takes, and in which she shares equally with the recipient the emotional and cognitive benefits of their interaction.

In her chapter Ruby Abrahams not only describes and illustrates the details of each of the four helping styles but also discusses the differential inputs and satisfactions associated with each. Her study unfortunately does not cover the other side of the equation, the types of needs and satisfactions of the recipients. In order to have accomplished this she would have had to interact intensively with the recipients, which would have distorted the program by introducing a professional inside the orbit of the helping relationship. But she speculates that such a study might have revealed a range of patterns of need among the recipients, and she ends her chapter by suggesting that if we were to find out more about this we might work out ways of classifying both recipients and helpers and then optimizing the caregiving by matching them.

Here I part company from Mrs. Abrahams, because what she is suggesting is a professional approach that is based on standardizing helping techniques and making diagnostic categorizations of clients which then govern a systematic choice of treatment. Such a pattern would almost certainly upset the natural caregiving process, which leaves such issues to be handled by trial and error in what I might call a "free market" rather than a "planned economy" situation, where each individual behaves freely and unselfconsciously on the basis of his idiosyncratic impulses and attributes. On the other hand, Ruby Abrahams' findings and speculations do point to the possibility of so organizing a mutual-help program that there should be an exploratory phase during which a population of would-be recipients is brought into interaction with a population of would-be helpers; and the matching of needs and styles in giving and receiving might then be left to personal free choice on both sides. A watered-down, but simpler, version of this pattern did, in fact, develop in our widowed hot-line project: Each week the list of all callers was discussed in a meeting of the helpers; and after an attempt to describe each of the callers and their needs, they were divided up among the helpers, who were thus able to choose those recipients with whom they felt they might be comfortable and to whom they sensed they might be most helpful. This appears to be one step in the right direction.

Chapter 12, "Peer Consultation Among Clergy" by David E. Richards, reports another of our professional attempts to stimulate mutual-help activities, which, after we have initiated them, continue and maintain themselves by their own momentum and because of the personal benefits to the participants. The project described by Bishop Richards was a sequel to our bishop-to-bishop consultation program in the Episcopal Church. In the Diocese of Massachusetts we had for several years been conducting traditional group consultation with parish priests and other practicing clergymen. The new project consisted of choosing a number of experienced consultees who had for years received consultation from our Laboratory mental health specialists, training the clergymen in consultation techniques, pairing them off, and then establishing them as consultation couples who would meet at regular intervals and help each other by alternating the role of consultant and consultee.

Since this book is dedicated to the memory of Erich Lindemann, it may be of interest to mention that he and I first worked out this pattern as a way of supporting each other during the years 1954 – 1964, when he was the Head of the Department of Psychiatry of Harvard Medical School at the Massachusetts General Hospital and I was his successor as the Head of the Community Mental Health Program at Harvard School of Public Health. Each week we would escape to a phone-free situation in a French restaurant and spend a couple of hours together. On each occasion I would ask him for consultant help with some of my work problems, and he would consult me about some of his. Despite the difference in age and experience, this never turned into supervision, and even though we knew each other's personal idiosyncracies quite well our discussion never dealt psychotherapeutically with personality issues but was restricted to analyzing the complications and options in our work settings. The only tension between us related to who got the first chance to be consultee, because sometimes a problem would turn out to be so complicated that it would take up the entire lunch hour, and the other person would miss the chance to ask for help with his pressing problem until the following week.

Our bishop-to-bishop consultation program was originally established as a "one-way" program; I trained senior bishops to offer consultation to newly appointed bishops. This pattern continues to this day; but it has begun to change spontaneously as consultant bishops, once they have developed relationships of mutual trust and respect with their consultees, have begun to spend part of their visit asking for consultation about problems in their own diocese. The Massachusetts project formalizes this pattern with parish clergy; and Bishop Richards in his chapter describes how it is working out.

From the point of view of our overall interest in the field of natural support systems based on mutual help, the role-alternating consultation dyads of Massachusetts clergy are of special significance because a standardized technique has been worked out by a mental health specialist, taught to a group of caregiving professionals who are not mental health specialists, and then utilized by them as a vehicle for coordinate mutual support. What we have here is an interesting mixture of professional and nonprofessional modes. The mutual help of peers, based on personal experience and a sharing of needs and burdens, is essentially not a professional matter. In effect, the clergymen should not be fundamentally different in this than the widows who help each other, particularly as the widows offer and receive help not just as people with general problems but as persons whose social role and situation are structured by their widowhood. On the other hand, in this project we have trained the clergymen to operate within the discipline of a particular consultation technique, and this is clearly a well-defined professional mode involving social distance and clear role constraints. The fact that the helper and recipient roles alternate prevents the development of a fixed professional–client relationship; but once again, even this aspect of role alternation is a carefully structured part of the program and is a kind of "professionalized nonprofessional" pattern. Two such experienced mental health professionals as Erich Lindemann and I did not need outside reinforcement to maintain such a pattern for many years. I doubt, however, whether the same will hold true in the clergy program; and we may eventually discover that the continued utilization of a highly professional technique as a mode of mutual support requires not only that the persons using it should be themselves accustomed to a professional role, although not necessarily that of a mental health specialist, but also that the initiators of the program – in this case Bishop Richards or I – should continue from time to time to meet with the participants and reinforce them. Up to the time that Bishop Richards wrote his chapter this was more or less the case, but since then both he and I have withdrawn from this project; and it will be most interesting to see if and how it survives.

Chapter 13 is my report about my experience in Israel during and after the Yom Kippur War, when I acted as a community intervenor in helping organize support systems for the civilian population. This is not only the final but to some extent the culminating chapter of this book. My work in Israel was an attempt to put into practice the ideas discussed in the rest of the book; and what I report is in a way "the state of the art" of support system intervention, as of 1973. I have continued this work since that time, and have participated in the implementation of many of the organizational recommendations I made in the last part of the chapter, which I hope to report in a future publication; but I do not believe that I have changed many of the fundamental ideas expressed in the chapter as a result of my experience during the last two years.

Since the essence of this chapter lies in its detail, I will not attempt here to summarize its main messages, but merely to list a few of the major issues it addresses: First, it is clearly based not only on support system theory, and particularly on the notion of organizing mutual help, but also on the entire body of community mental health and community organizational theory and practice that my colleagues and I have been developing over many years. Second, and in line with this, a major target of my efforts was the stimulation of existing community organizations, institutions, and networks to collaborate across their normal boundaries in identifying salient needs of individuals, families, and groups, and then in providing immediate feasible assistance. Third, I helped mobilize those mental health professionals who had no current institutional affiliation in order to bring them inside the emergency system we were organizing. Fourth, I helped the professionals reach out and draw into their system the organized and unorganized nonprofessional volunteers who were mobilized by the emergency to offer their services. Fifth, I provided specialized information and cognitive guidance to all the different groups, based on my previous research findings and practice skills, but continually being updated by our experience of the current unfolding situation, much as Robert Weiss does in his seminars for the separated. Sixth, I used my special position as a high status outsider to support the supportive individuals and groups emotionally, to help them evaluate positively their contributions to our program, and to convene them in groups so that they could support each other emotionally and cognitively.

The final point I wish to make is that this chapter, like several others in this book, illustrates ideas, approaches, and techniques that have wider applicability than the setting it describes – it deals with issues that are probably of importance in all community intervention and in organizing support systems in peacetime as well as in war – but one of its most important messages is that successful intervention can not be crystallized and transferred as a stereotyped package from one situation to another. It must be, as was my work in Israel, sensitively tailored to the local situation, and energized by personal relationships built up between the intervenor and local formal and informal influentials that were developed prior to the intervention or that grow while it is ongoing. From the latter point of view it is just as well that the reality-based demands for quick action during the widespread arousal of a community emergency are accompanied by a lowering of organizational and institutional boundaries, an increased readiness to build relationships with a relative stranger who seems helpful and comes well recommended, and a willingness of all parties to set aside personal and professional prejudices and work together in the common cause.

I hope that my rather detailed discussion of some of the issues raised in this book will help to build a cognitive framework that will make the reading of it more meaningful. I hope also that this introduction will not be confusing since it necessarily deals with matters that may only be clarified after reading the chapters concerned. Perhaps my discussion should rather have been written as a concluding section. Some readers may find it valuable to re-read it after they finish the other chapters, and in this way to compare their own impressions with my editorial comments. Whether or not they agree with me, I hope that the comparison may help to stimulate community mental health workers to undertake their own explorations of a field that they, too, will feel to be of great importance.

Gerald Caplan
October 1975

Gerald Caplan

1

The Family as a Support System[1]

THE SUPPORT SYSTEMS MODEL

In a recent book,[2] I proposed a conceptual model that focused on the health-promoting and ego-fortifying effects on individuals of what I called "support systems." I defined these as "continuing social aggregates (namely, continuing interactions with another individual, a network, a group, or an organization) that provide individuals with opportunities for feedback about themselves and for validation of their expectations about others, which may offset deficiences in these communications within the larger community context." I linked this definition with the epidemiologic and ethological researches of Cassel,[3] who has demonstrated that subpopulations influenced by such aggregates have a lower incidence of mental and physical disease than their neighbors, especially under conditions of acute and chronic stress associated with rapid physical and social change.

I postulated that "the characteristic attribute of these social aggregates that act as a buffer against disease is that in such relationships the person is dealt with as a unique individual. The other people are interested in him in a personalized way. They speak his language. They tell him what is expected of him and guide him in what to do. They watch what he does and

[1]A lecture delivered on October 24, 1974 in Providence, Rhode Island, at the Butler Hospital Fall Symposium on "The Family: Dynamics and Treatment."

[2]Gerald Caplan, *Support Systems and Community Mental Health* (New York: Behavioral Publications, 1974). See also Ruth B. Caplan, *Helping the Helpers to Help* (New York: Seabury Press, 1972).

[3]J. C. Cassel, "Psychiatric Epidemiology," in *American Handbook of Psychiatry*, vol. II, ed. G. Caplan (New York: Basic Books, Inc., 1974) pp. 401-411.

they judge his performance. They let him know how well he has done. They reward him for success and punish or support and comfort him if he fails. Above all, they are sensitive to his personal needs, which they deem worthy of respect and satisfaction.

"Such support may be of a continuing nature or intermittent and short-term and may be utilized from time to time by the individual in the event of an acute need or crisis. Both enduring and short-term supports are likely to consist of three elements: (a) the significant others help the individual mobilize his psychological resources and master his emotional burdens; (b) they share his tasks; and (c) they provide him with extra supplies of money, materials, tools, skills, and cognitive guidance to improve his handling of his situation."[4]

In my recent book, I discussed how support systems seem to operate in our current social life through kith and kin groups and networks, via the informal operations of individual nonprofessional caregivers, and through such organizations as religious denominations, fraternal associations, and mutual assistance and self-help groups. I used this discussion as a basis for proposing some innovations in mental health and human services practice which stimulate the development of nonprofessional support systems to augment on a community-wide scale the capacity of individuals to master their environment in mentally healthy ways, particularly individuals made vulnerable because they are involved in acute crises, life transitions, or chronic privations. My main thesis was that we professionals must learn to appreciate the fortifying potential of the natural person-to-person supports in the population and to find ways of working with them through some form of partnership that fosters and strengthens nonprofessional groups and organizations. I wish now to focus on one segment of this field by examining how the concept of support systems illuminates a particular aspect of the functioning of family life and to use this in developing some preliminary guidelines for helpful community action.

TODAY'S FAMILY AS A SOCIAL UNIT

Until recently, I, like many other caregiving professionals, maintained three beliefs about the modern American urban family. First, I believed that, in contrast to the extended family of traditional rural America, the modern urban family is mainly a small, nuclear unit of two parents with one to three children, relatively cut off from grandparents and other close relatives. A corollary of this was my second belief that most older people lived isolated lives, effectively separated from their children and grandchildren. Third, I believed that a large proportion of people over the age

[4]Caplan, *Support Systems,* pp. 5-6.

of 65–70 are chronically sick, dependent, and ineffectual, which I linked with their having been extruded from the labor force and separated from their children so that they have neither public nor private roles that satisfy them. Since advances in public health and clinical medicine have led to an increase in the proportion of our growing population who are over 65[5] I felt that the two-pronged problem of isolation of family units and of the older generation would lead to the need to provide specialized public care-giving services to both on a large and increasing scale.

I now realize that all three of my fundamental beliefs are false. A series of empirical researches – particularly those of Sussman[6] – has demonstrated that the modal family of present-day urban America is still an extended family in which grandparents and often great-grandparents, although they may live in separate households, remain active participants in the primary kin network. Ethel Shanas[7] has shown that not only in the cities of the United States but also in England, Denmark, Yugoslavia, Poland, and Israel, the majority of older persons live either in the same household or within 10 minutes of one of their children. From 70 to 80 percent of the elderly persons studied by Shanas and her collaborators had personal contact with at least one of their children within the previous week.

And, finally, my third belief – that most people over 65 are sick, ineffective, and dependent – is as false as the others. Two of our recent Harvard studies on different populations have revealed that 80 to 85 percent of men and women over 65 are, and feel themselves to be, active and in good health, irrespective of current age[8] – findings that are consonant with those of several other researchers. In other words, the elderly are about as healthy and potentially as active as younger people. Their life expectancy is, of course, shorter; but until they fall ill and die, they remain capable of playing an active role in public and family affairs.

The findings of such studies reveal that the modern American family, far from being a small, isolated, nuclear unit of parents and their children,

[5]"The proportion of the aged population cohort doubled from approximately 4% to 6% between 1900 and 1950. Projections into the next three decades anticipate a further increase to about 12.9% ...." G. S. Rosenberg, "Implications of New Models of the Family for the Aging Population," in *The Family in Search of a Future,* ed. H. H. Otto (New York: Appleton-Century-Crofts, 1970), quoted by Sylvia Claven and Ethel Vatter, "The Affiliated Family: A Device for Integrating Old and Young," *Gerontologist,* vol. 12, Winter 1972, p. 408.

[6]Marvin B. Sussman, "The Isolated Nuclear Family: Fact or Fiction," *Social Problems,* no. 6, 1959, pp. 333-339. Marvin B. Sussman and Lee Burchinal, "Kin Family Network: Unhearalded Structure in Current Conceptualizations of Family Functioning," *Marriage and Family Living,* vol. 24, 1962, pp. 231-240. (Contains an extensive research bibliography on this topic.)

[7]Ethel Shanas, "Family-Kin Networks in Cross-Cultural Perspective," *Journal of Marriage and the Family,* vol. 35, no. 3, August 1973, pp. 505-511.

[8]Carol Ryser and Alan Sheldon, "Retirement and Health," *Journal of the American Geriatrics Society,* vol. 17, no. 2, 1969, pp. 180-190.

is in the majority of cases an interdependent network involving parents and their siblings, children, grandparents, and increasingly great-grandparents living under one roof or in nearby households.

I will now examine the average family's operation as a support system, with the understanding that there are many deviations from the ideal-type pictured, which will entail supplementation of social policies and service programs that we plan on the basis of the modal patterns.

SUPPORT SYSTEM FUNCTIONS OF THE FAMILY

The Family as a Collector and Disseminator of Information About the World

This is a fundamental support system function. Traditionally, most people have thought of it mainly in connection with the socialization of children, and surely it is important that parents share their store of information about the outside world with their children so that the latter are not forced to collect all this knowledge themselves, even though there is a limit to what a person can learn vicariously from the experience of others. In a multigenerational family, information from grandparents helps their adult children learn the parental roles, and grandparent-child interaction provides a situation where the giving and acceptance of information may often be easier because the usual tensions produced by the reality-based obligations of the parent-child relationship are absent or reduced.

It is important to realize that a multigenerational family also provides a vehicle for information to flow in the reverse direction, so that the younger members, from their own unique age-linked experiences of the current world, tell their elders what is actually happening "out there." This is particularly significant at the present time when the speed of change is such that knowledge about the world quickly gets outdated.

The Family as a Feedback Guidance System.

The researches of Cassel alert us to the crucial importance for physical and mental health of the capacity of individuals to make valid assessments of feedback cues in their environment, especially in new and therefore potentially bewildering situations. In animal population experiments, this is shown by the increase in morbidity and mortality produced, apparently by nervous and hormonal depletion, when the size and density of the population are increased so that animals are not able to differentiate friends from foes and are therefore forced continually to be on guard to fend off possible attacks. An analog in humans is the personality disorganization resulting from culture shock. A family provides a continuing training ground for members to learn how to adjust to immediate feedback about what other people feel regarding their behavior, because signals in the family are usually obtrusive and easily understandable. It also provides a receptive group where members can relatively undefensively report what they have done and how people have reacted to their actions, so that the rest of the family can help them understand what went on.

From this we can see the significance of what occurs in most families where, shortly after members come home, they give detailed reports on their behavior at school, work, or in social situations, together with how others reacted to them, especially if these reactions were upsetting, surprising, or incomprehensible. In some families, such discussions take place regularly at mealtimes and have almost a ceremonial aspect. During these discussions, the other members of the group help the person evaluate not only his own reported behavior in the light of the family value system but also the meaning of the reactions of the people with whom he was involved.

The Family as a Source of Ideology

The family group is a major source of the belief systems, value systems, and codes of behavior that determine an individual's understanding of the nature and meaning of the universe, of his place in it, and of the paths he should strive to travel in his life. Together with the stream of cumulative information about the concrete nature of the real world, these systems of belief and values provide the individual with a map of his universe, and with a set of goals and missions, as well as a compass in finding his way. Part of this information comes from explicit teaching, part comes from introjection of assumptions and meanings that characterize family culture with its traditions, memories, and myths, and part comes from conscious copying, or unconscious identification, with family role models and with relationships among family members and between them and outsiders.

These processes are buttressed by the expectations of the social milieu that individuals will naturally conform to the dominant views, beliefs, motivations, and practices of their family. This is well illustrated by the usual reciprocal reinforcement of family units and religious denominations. Most denominations recruit their members from family units. Religious rituals focus on developmental incidents and transitions of family life, from dealing with which the denomination derives much of its potency as a power for social integration, while at the same time it strengthens the family as a social unit. Religious denominations are the leading social institution that deals with the entire family as a unit throughout its developmental history. Conversely, families inculcate and foster among their members the value and belief systems and code of ethics of their religious denomination and strive to recruit the marital partners of their children to the same beliefs, as well as to ensure that grandchildren follow a similar path.

The strengthening power of these internalized systems of beliefs and values as well as the abstract and concrete maps of the world, and the prescriptions for wise conduct that go with them, can be seen in operation whenever a family member, even in geographical isolation, is faced with an acute crisis. At such times, the individual is faced by novel problems that he is not able to solve quickly with his usual problem-solving and coping mechanisms, and he is inevitably frustrated and confused because he is not able to predict the outcome of the predicament – he cannot, as it were, see round the corner. At such times, it is very hard for him to choose what path to take, and he usually feels weak and helpless. That is just the time when he may derive particular benefit from the traditions of his family. They may tell him, for instance, to stay with the problem and to keep struggling to find its solution by trial and error, with the expectation that eventually something constructive will emerge, rather than to quickly admit defeat and give up the struggle, as he may naturally be inclined to do. If, in addition, his family code is part of a larger religious tradition, he will feel a deeper faith that he is moving in a wise direction by continuing the struggle, and he will feel buttressed by the multitudes of his coreligionists. Moreover, by relying on the accumulated wisdom of his family and of the previous generations of members of his religion, whose trials and errors in the past have led to the traditional action prescription, he is likely, in reality, to be acting more wisely than if he has to choose his path based only on his own individual wisdom, particularly during the confusion of crisis.

Years of crisis research have given me many illustrations of the advantage of individuals who conform to family and religious traditions over the nonconformists, the rebels, and the irreligious – except, of course, for "rebels with a cause" who are strengthened by the ideology of their social or political movement, even though it may be explicitly antifamilial and antireligious. This was brought home once again to me when I was in Israel during the Yom Kippur War, helping to organize services for the relatives of casualties. I was much impressed by the steadfastness of those with a strong family, religious, or other ideological identification compared with those who lacked these internalized supports, even though the nature of the situation was such that it evoked for all of the sufferers an outpouring of loving concern and concrete help from the entire population. Time after time I heard from religious and social leaders when they returned to report to me on their visit of condolence to a bereaved family, "We came to offer them our consolation in the name of the community, and instead they consoled and comforted us, telling us how much they appreciated the good work we were doing and reassuring us that our efforts were worthwhile and that we were earning God's blessing." Such bereaved families were invariably either deeply religious or members of the ideological elite, the heroic Israelis who had a long family tradition of national service and sacrifice. In contrast, the irreligious and those without a strong family culture or Zionist ideological commitment were expectedly distraught and dispirited – they had less of an internalized structure to hold them together, and their poise had to come from their constitutional ego-strength plus the active support and help of their families and neighbors. When any of these factors was deficient, they tended to collapse, at least for a while.

The Family as Guide and Mediator in Problem Solving

In addition to the incorporation within individuals of cognitive maps and codes of conduct derived from their participation over many years in family patterns of organized behavior, members benefit from here-and-now guidance when they become involved in crises or long-term burdens. Most families encourage members to communicate freely about their personal difficulties, many of which are likely to involve some or all of the other members of the group. In either case, the family shares the problem, and other members offer advice and guidance either as an organized group or as individuals, in accordance with family tradition and the respective talents and roles of its members.

An important element in a family's helping a member with a problem is not only telling him how to find external sources of care and assistance, such as health and welfare agencies, but actually helping to make the arrangements for the relevant caregivers to take action. This may mean calling them in or actually going with the person in distress to the community institution. Most families over the years accumulate a list of dependable community professional and nonprofessional caregivers and agencies and build up a network of relationships with key individuals in the health and welfare field to whom they can turn when a family member is in need.

The problems and challenges of life emerge not only from acute mishaps and long-term disabilities but also from the necessity to alter attitudes, skills, and perceptual patterns with the changing roles demanded by a changing social and physical world. What characterizes our era historically is the quantum leap in the rapidity of social change linked with our technological accomplishments that have revolutionized communication, transportation, and energy control. The adaptive challenge for most individuals in our times demands a flexibility, readiness, and speed in giving up old roles and acquiring new roles that may be historically unique. The multigenerational family unit provides its members with important help in this matter.

Boulding,[9] in a recent paper, expressed this very well:

> The family as a unit is continually in transition from one stage of the family cycle to the next, so that it can never be in a static condition. Family life is a swiftly

[9]Elsie Boulding, "The Family as an Agent of Social Change," *The Futurist,* vol. 6, no. 5, October 1972, pp. 186-191.

moving series of identity crises as members of various ages are socialized into new roles. . . . In addition to the identity crises that stem from aging and individual pathologies, there are externally-triggered crises that may result in unemployment, separation, injury, and death of family members. . . .

Fortunately, the identity-crises that people go through do not make them unrecognizable to each other. There are constants as well as variables, and the group culture created by every family unit that lives together through time . . . provide[s] some security and stability for individual members . . . we can see the family as a workshop in social change.

Since people are undergoing similar role changes in the non-family settings in which they perform daily, the fact of individual growth and change is not a unique property of the family. What is unique about the family is that only in this setting are people intimately confronting role changes in other people who are much older or much younger. Thus the family setting continually prods individuals into a better understanding of themselves.

I would add that, in addition to its long-term training in the skills of role changing, living in a family setting necessarily inculcates the expectation and acceptance by individuals of a series of inevitable personal role changes; and the family group actively assists members in dealing with their cognitive and emotional difficulties during periods of role transition.

Leadership inside many family groups in alerting individual members to the need for adjustment and adaptation to social change is not fixed but varies in relation to the presenting problem. In particular, younger members who are actively in touch with specific changes in the outer world and whose perceptions may be less distorted than those of their elders by preconceptions, may sound the alert and suggest novel paths for exploration, as symbolized by the story of "The Emperor's New Clothes." But in our society that so downgrades the effectiveness and wisdom of the old, I feel it is worth emphasizing that grandparents and great-grandparents often have a very special contribution to make in the area of encouraging readiness and flexibility in the altering of roles to conform to social and physical environmental change. Meierowitz[10] has recently pointed out that, contrary to our usual stereotypes, many older people are likely to be better prepared than young people to change their attitudes and acquire new skills in adjusting to new conditions. Youth and early adulthood is often a period of dogmatism and rigidity because limited experience causes the individual to oversimplify and to cling uncritically to a newly learned system of ideas and skills. After putting in so much time and effort in learning these, it is hard for the young person to give them up or even to accept their limitations, especially as he has been promised that they will assure him continuing rewards, and he still has not learned about possible alternatives. Old people, on the other hand, have discovered the hard way that their learned ideas and skills do not in fact lead to the wonderful results promised by their teachers; and

[10]Joseph Meierowitz, Personal communication, Jerusalem, September 9, 1974.

they have also been forced to learn how to compensate for waning personal capacities in one area by developing in others – for instance, the old tennis player who wins his points by outwitting his opponent rather than by his strength, speed, and agility of the past. Eventually, of course, the old man may become too frail to play tennis at all; but, as I mentioned previously, most old people are not in fact as weak as we used to believe, and until that eventual stage is reached, many of them can not only play well themselves, but, of special importance in the present context, they can coach others in the flexibility and adaptive skills that their own personal development has forced them to master.

The Family as a Source of Practical Service and Concrete Aid

Until recently, few studies dealt with the practical assistance given by the family group to its members as long-term contributions or in responding to acute need. In the past 15 years, however, there has been a rapidly growing research literature dealing with this topic. Sussman and Burchinal[11] have written a comprehensive review of empirical studies. They showed that most families studied, irrespective of social class, reported giving aid to relatives and receiving aid from them. Assistance included continuing and intermittent financial aid, sometimes disguised as gifts of money or valuable goods at times of marriage, birth of children, birthdays, Christmas, or to help with hospital or funeral expenses. It included help with shopping and care of children, physical care of old people, performing household tasks, and practical assistance at times of crisis, such as hospitalizations because of illness or accident, or during transition ceremonies such as weddings and funerals.

A particular significance of these contributions of resources and services is that during crises and periods of transition an individual is usually preoccupied with his current predicament and not only pays scant attention to the demands of ordinary life tasks but also has little personal energy available to deal with them. Either the household runs down or he must exert special effort to maintain it – and this is at the expense of energy and attention needed to deal with his predicament.

During the Yom Kippur War, I was impressed by the acute need of many families of wounded or fallen soldiers for help in shopping, doing household chores, getting lifts to a distant hospital, and taking care of young children or elderly relatives. The timely mobilization of the family network to accomplish these tasks enabled those most centrally affected to devote all their energies to visiting the wounded or mourning the dead. I felt that in addition to the benefit of the concrete help, the fact that it was immediately available as needed, usually without having to be asked for, was a

[11]Marvin B. Sussman and Lee Burchinal, "Kin Family Network: Unheralded Structure in Current Conceptualizations of Family Functioning," *Marriage and Family Living,* vol. 24, 1962, pp. 231-240.

source of great strength at a time when people felt particularly weakened by their sense of vulnerability and increased dependency. When a person knows that he is receiving what he needs as his right and not at the price of having to ask or beg for it, his pride in his own autonomy and his self-respect are likely to be maintained even though he is actually a dependent recipient.

The other thing that impressed me over and over again was the specially strengthening effect of giving material help in maintaining the household, doing the shopping and cooking, and caring for children and aged parents and grandparents. These actions seemed to convey more powerfully than any words of consolation and solidarity the message that the helper was an effective and involved participant in the tragedy and was automatically sharing its burdens.

The Family as a Haven for Rest and Recuperation

In most healthy families, every member knows all the other members very well and feels himself equally known and understood. Within the boundary of privacy that surrounds this group, he usually feels free to relax and "be himself." As a lifelong member of the family group from which he knows he will not be extruded except for some enormous transgression, he can feel confidence in revealing aspects of himself that he would hide even from his friends. This is probably linked with the fact that the fate of all members of the family group are to a considerable degree connected, so that inescapably one member's problems must to some extent be shared by the others and vice versa. If we add to this that every family member is being continually observed at first hand from many points of view over a very long period – in the case of children from their earliest beginnings – we realize that the family group is without equal as a reservoir of developmental personality data about each member.

All this adds up to the family being a group in which each member has the possibility of being understood and dealt with as his own unique self, and in which his idiosyncratic needs are recognized, respected, and satisfied to the degree that this is possible within the limits of available resources.

It is these aspects of family life that make the family a sanctuary or haven, namely a place where it is safe to relax and be oneself, where despite continual changes, the other people are well known, where one can speak one's own language and be readily understood, and, most important, where one can set aside the burdens and demands of the outside world for as long as both the person and the family consider appropriate. Since we now know that what is particularly hazardous about prolonged strain is the possibility that it will have an unremitting character that leads to an inexorable buildup of toxic metabolites which have no discharge routes, so that they rise above the capacity of the organism to bear them, with resultant disorganization and disintegration, this haven function of the family can be understood to be most significant in protecting its members from morbidity.

Another relevant function is the operation of the family group as a monitor of fatigue when a member is grappling with crises. The confusion and frustration of crisis, together with the pressure of prolonged emotional arousal and of efforts to master these emotions as well as to cope with the crisis tasks, lead inevitably to fatigue. When this rises above a certain threshold, the individual's efficiency and effectiveness begin to fall. A vicious circle may be produced as the individual mobilizes more and more effort to overcome his fatigue and only becomes more tired and ineffective. At such times the family may play an essential role by telling the individual that he is tired and that he should rest, advice which they make possible for him to accept by temporarily taking over certain essential aspects of his crisis tasks, such as caring for a sick child or parent. When they feel that he is sufficiently rested, they call him back to continue his struggle. Of particular significance in this sequence is the legitimation by the family of the need for a rest period, since many people in crisis feel that the crisis tasks are so essential and urgent that if they put them aside even for an instant it must be because they are lazy or selfish and unwilling to put up with the personal burden. Left to themselves this guilt might drive them to wear themselves out.

The Family as a Reference and Control Group

Because an individual's fate is so bound up with his family and because he realizes that they know him so well, he is likely to be quite sensitive to their opinions about his attitudes and behavior, and especially to their judgment of how well he adheres to the family code. This is likely to be consolidated by his trust that they have his best interests at heart, since such trust, which is hard to build in a relationship with a nonkin counselor or therapist, comes naturally inside the circle of a family, where the reputations and interests of all members are inextricably intertwined.

In an era when the dominant philosophy of clinicians is nonjudgmental, it may be well to emphasize that a nonjudgmental approach inside the family in our culture is not necessarily of value. The essential element of an effective reference group is that it does judge; and if it is also to control and mold the behavior of its members, it must also reward success and punish failure in adhering to its code. Types of reward and punishment vary from family to family in accordance with social class and subculture, but even punishments that might seem savage to outsiders are usually well tolerated within a family because members are used to them and feel that, unless they have committed an offense so terrible that they will be expelled, whatever punishment they incur is designed to foster their acceptance by the group – they are being punished for what they did – but regardless of this they will continue to be accepted for what they are, namely lifelong members of the family.

The Family as Source and Validator of Identity

The clarity and security of a person's self-image and his confidence in the stability of his own identity are a major source of his fortitude in grappling with life's problems. In particular, they provide the foundation upon which he bases his courage in facing the complexities of the unknown and his tolerance of frustration during periods of struggling with the temporarily insurmountable problems of crisis, or in coming to terms with the long-term privations of loss. It is, therefore, an irony of fate that there is a natural tendency of individuals during crisis and role transition to become vague and confused about their identity, just when they are most in need of clarity and confidence in this area. Another characteristic of persons in crisis is that they usually become more open and more susceptible to the influence of other people, particularly significant figures in their social milieu. The result is that a person in crisis or in a period of life transition normally relies in large measure on the messages he receives from his social environment in appreciating his own identity. This is one of the major features of his increased dependency at such times.

His family, which in any case is a primary source of the ingredients that molded the individual's identity in the first place, therefore often has a crucial role to play in buttressing it during the confusion and uncertainty of crisis and transition by reminding him of those elements, particularly his abilities and strengths, about which he is temporarily in doubt or which he has entirely forgotten. In other words, during the frustration and confusion of struggling with an at-present insurmountable problem, most individuals feel weak and impotent and tend to forget their continuing strengths. At such times, their family reminds them of their past achievements and validates their precrisis self-image of competence and ability to stand firm.

The Family's Contribution to Emotional Mastery

This topic is so well known that I need only make brief mention of some of the main issues:

1. Short-term crises and long-term challenges and privations inevitably evoke a complex of negative emotions – anxiety, depression, anger, shame, guilt, and the like. Not only are these painful in themselves but they also reduce effectiveness in grappling with the problems of external physical and social reality because of the energy needed to control and contain them and because they distract attention. A major contribution of the family is to augment the efforts made by the individual on the basis of his ego capacities to master and control these emotions.

2. I have repeatedly referred to the feelings of frustration that characterize crises and periods of life transition. In addition to the pain they engender, these feelings press the individual toward premature closure in his adaptation work, and this is one of the main causes of failure. The family can add to a member's ego-derived capacity to tolerate such frustration by expressing solidarity and by offering love, affection and comfort.
3. Families can help individuals accomplish their "worry-work" and "grief-work" during crises and the much longer periods involved in adjusting to loss and deprivation. They do this not only by offering guidance on the basis of past experience of family members but also by counteracting despair and feelings of helplessness through their continuing presence and expressions of love, and through maintaining hope in an eventual triumph.
4. A person who loses a love object by death or desertion, his bodily integrity by illness or crippling, or his major role by unemployment often feels a debilitating loss of personal worth. His family can counteract this and help him see his loss in realistic perspective by continuing to treat him with love and respect and by providing him with transitional objects or roles in the family circle until such time as he can rebuild his life once more. Sometimes, the family may provide him with a permanent replacement for the objects or roles lost in the outer world or with a permanent source of alternative emotional satisfaction.

LIMITING FACTORS

Most of these support system functions depend on a significant level of intactness, stability, and integration in the family. Of particular importance is a common language and free communication among family members, especially between the generations. During a period of rapid sociocultural change, such as we are currently experiencing, the generation gap is a major factor that impedes essential aspects of this communication – many young people today speak a quite different language from their parents, let alone their grandparents. Among immigrants and in upwardly mobile families, this will be exaggerated because of the greater gap between their sociocultural world of today and that of their past.

Another element that is clearly a precondition of most of the supports I have discussed is that the interpersonal relationships in the family should be healthy; namely, that individuals should be dealt with in their own right and not as symbolic manifestations of other objects or personality attributes. Since disordered relationships, based on unconsciously linking another family member with the actors in some past psychological conflict, are so commonly found in the families of psychiatric patients, we clinicians are often prone to see families in general as potentially pathogenic rather than as supportive, especially in dealing with family members with emotional burdens who are so much in need of the kind of support I have been discussing. I have no empirical research on which to base this statement, but it is my impression that unhealthy relationships of the type commonly encountered in clinical practice do not occur in more than about 10 to 15 percent of families in the general population. We clinicians should therefore not exaggerate the prevalence of this factor.

A third factor that is possibly of greater frequency is related to the fact that a family is likely to be optimally supportive only if its members accept its ideology and code of behavior, including the obligations of mutual concern for each other, as well as the social mission of the family in monitoring and controlling individual behavior. This, in turn, depends on consonance, or lack of dissonance, between the culture of the family and that of the ethnic, religious, and community systems of which it is a part. Whenever these outer cultural circles become disorganized, or where for a variety of reasons the family culture gets out of line with them, certain members are likely to be partially or totally unlinked from the family group, and what they gain by their freedom to move easily in the outside world may be offset by loss of the personalized benefits of the internal family support system.

IMPLICATIONS FOR PLANNING AND SERVICE

Social Policy

Social planning should promote the intactness, integration and mutuality of extended families:

1. Income maintenance programs should direct funds into family coffers; and the family as a group should be responsible for their disbursement to individuals.
2. Housing programs should provide residential accommodations so that old people and their families can choose to live in the same household or in the immediate vicinity. Housing for the aged should be distributed throughout the community and not be segregated far away; the same applies to housing designed for young married couples.
3. Priority of installation of telephones and special low rates should encourage all old people to acquire and use telephones to communicate regularly with children and grandchildren. Similarly, public transportation should be free or very cheap for old people so they can visit their families easily.
4. The Census Bureau should alter its definition of a family from kin living in the same residential household to kin who interact frequently and are bound together by positive concern. This will provide us with readily available demographic data about families as a valid basis for planning and evaluating social policy and services, which we do not have at present.

Health and Welfare Services and Community Institutions

1. Services should avoid, wherever possible, segregating and isolating family members. For instance, old people who are sick should be cared for at home or in day hospitals; full hospitalization should be avoided with them, just as we have learned to do with children. If hospitalization is unavoidable, it should be as short as possible; we should encourage visiting by the entire family group, and the family should be actively involved in plans for convalescence and rehabilitation. Also, diagnosis and therapy of individuals should actively involve the personal participation of the total multigenerational family group – once upon a time in child guidance clinics we treated the child in isolation, then we included the mother, and eventually also the father; we should henceforward regularly include the rest of the family, including grandparents. I am not here advocating specific family therapy, useful as this certainly is at times, but I am suggesting that we actively promote family cohesion in relating to a member with difficulties.
2. We should involve the total family unit in all crisis intervention. Professional and nonprofessional caregivers should exploit every opportunity for convening family groups and facilitating the organization of family action projects. Crises, which naturally excite human interest and mobilize energy and motivation to help others, provide us with an excellent opportunity to promote family support systems. Not only can the caregiver make use of the family supports to help the individual in crisis but also, perhaps more important, by an educational and communication bridge-building approach the caregiver can use this as an opportunity to train the family group to improve its problem-solving and mutual help skills.
3. Community recreational and religious institutions should modify their facilities and patterns of organization to cater to total family groups, as was done years ago at the Peckham Health Center in London and as is done in some community centers and settlement houses today.

Development of Programs to Bridge the Generation Gap

What is involved is bringing the older and younger generations together in situations where each can learn to respect the other, can learn each other's language, and can discover and appreciate the other's capacities and potential helpfulness. Examples include the Foxfire Project[12] in rural Georgia where a group of high school students went into the countryside with tape recorders and cameras and recorded for subsequent publication the personal

[12]Eliot Wigginton, *Foxfire Book* (New York: Anchor/Doubleday,1972).
Brooks E. Wigginton, *Foxfire Two* (New York: Anchor/Doubleday, 1973).

accounts of old people of their traditional crafts and country lore, such as hog dressing, log cabin building, spinning and weaving, wagon making and other affairs of plain living. As Pete Seeger says in the book that emerged, the project "proves that old folks and kids can be great allies. May it show young people in thousands of other communities how they too can link up with the oldest and youngest generations and be proud of our country, not for its power and production, but for its many different ways of living, and how to make do with what we have."[13]

Other examples include numerous volunteer programs in which retired persons are brought into school systems to act as counselors and to tutor children with learning difficulties; "foster grandparent" projects in which old people act as friendly helpers in institutions for retarded or emotionally disturbed children or in community programs for delinquent youth; and work-study and volunteer programs in colleges in which students volunteer to help in institutions and community services for the aged.[14]

Development of Educational Programs that Promote Ethnic Pluralism

These go beyond such projects as Foxfire. What is intended here is to break from the tradition of the American "melting pot" and to replace it by building knowledge and respect among young and old for the rich traditions and folk wisdom of their ethnic group subculture, as well as an appreciation, tolerance, and respect for the different heritage of other ethnic and religious groups in our pluralistic society.[15,16] Such programs not only promote intergeneration identification and communication but also contribute to reducing dissonance between second and third generation immigrant families and the culture of the large heterogeneous general American society by locating within the latter a subculture with which the family can meaningfully articulate and from which it can draw external support, guidance, and sanction for its own ways of life.

[13]Ibid.

[14]Jaques Lebel and Maureen Lebel, The First Retrospective Evaluation of One Significant Intergenerational Experiment. Lecture to 25th Annual Meeting of the Gerontological Society, San Juan, Puerto Rico, December 17-20, 1972.

Janet W. Freund, "The Meaning of Volunteer Services in Schools – to the Educator and to the Older Adult," *Gerontologist,* vol. 11, no. 3, part I, 1971, pp. 205-208.

[15]Sally Wendkos Olds, "Young Class in Growing Old," *McCalls,* July 1973, p. 26.

Howard H. Bede, Community Volunteer Programs. Winnetka Public Schools, Illinois. Lecture to National Association of Welfare Workers, Chicago, Ill., February 9, 1970.

Edith M. Sherman, Margaret R. Brittan, and Ira Friedelson, eds., *A Plan to Span.* U.S. Dept. of Health, Education, and Welfare. School and Rehabilitation Service, Administration on Aging. June 1970, Publication No. 190.

[16]Joseph Giordano, *Ethnicity and Mental Health: Research and Recommendations.* National Project on Ethnic America of the American Jewish Committee, New York, 1973.

Development of Neighborhood Educational Programs

Neighborhood programs should be developed to emphasize the importance of family life, to provide detailed information on the ways families can help individuals deal with short-term and long-term challenges and burdens, and to promote the idea of volunteerism and mutual support. We should produce manuals and audiovisual aids to help in this public education campaign, and we should also experiment with short-term residential institutes where family units can be trained by being involved on action projects.

Use of Retired Persons

We should train and utilize retired men and women to act as family educators and we should use them also as counselors to offer guidance to families that are currently trying to support their members during a life crisis or in adjusting to a permanent burden or disability. These elders should also be used as liaisons between the professional caregivers and the families of the population. They will thus help keep the focus of the professionals on the total family unit and prevent a return to the old individual focus.

Use of Family Units

We should experiment with innovative methods for training and utilizing family units as corporate caregivers, not only for their own members but also for other families. I am advocating a family-to-family mutual help approach. This is being tried at present both in Boston and in Israel in poverty-stricken populations where families who, despite their poverty, are living a rewarding life are linked as groups of volunteer counselors and role models to families that are failing. In Israel, a similar pattern has also been suggested among new immigrants, using families that have successfully worked through their adjustment phase to help those who have just arrived and are still floundering.

Development of a Multigenerational Family Structure

We should find ways of rebuilding a multigenerational structure for those families that are incomplete in this regard. A most promising example has been described by Claven and Vatter.[17] They describe a pattern that they call the Affiliative Family, which they have discovered to be a rapidly

[17]Sylvia Claven and Ethel Vatter, "The Affiliated Family: A Device for Integrating Old and Young," *Gerontologist,* vol. 12, Winter, 1972, pp. 407-412.

Sylvia and Ethel Vatter "The Affiliated Family: A Continued Analysis," *The Family Coordinator,* vol. 21, no. 4, October 1972, pp. 499-504.

developing phenomenon in a number of communities. They define an affiliative family as "any combination of husband/father, wife/mother, and their children, plus one or more older persons, recognized as part of the kin network and called by a designated kin term. They may or may not be a part of the residential household. Monetary remuneration may or may not be involved. Voluntary commitment to responsibility for one another within the unit is the single basic criterion." What is involved is an analog of the foster family or adoptive family in the case of childless parents and parentless children. In affiliative families, we are dealing with old persons who currently lack children and grandchildren, and nuclear or one-parent family units without grandparents nearby. The two incomplete units team up to produce a multigenerational unit of adopted kin, which then develops a role pattern that takes better care of household tasks and operates as an integrated support system to produce reciprocal rewards for all concerned.

Marie Killilea

2

Mutual Help Organizations: Interpretations in the Literature[1]

There is a substantial and growing body of literature on self-help and mutual help groups which has been quietly accumulating over a period of some years. Despite this, these groups, as an object of professional study, have received relatively little systematic attention conceptually and methodologically. This is changing concurrent with shifting emphases in scholarship in other fields, such as the recent work on folk art in relation to savant art (126), on popular culture and high culture (58), and in the field of literary criticism, on sentimental romance as a secular Scripture (56).

Self-help and mutual help[2] groups exist in our society amidst a growing number of peer-oriented helping networks and associations, such as peer counseling (76, 78) and children teaching children (59), elders helping elders (147), modern communes (133, 134) – including an old-agers commune: a community of grandmothers (87–89), consciousness-raising groups (112, 176), and some of the activities loosely categorized as the human potential and growth movements (109, 125, 131). Much of this activity can be seen as part of a search for what Vickers, discussing institutional and personal roles, calls "an appreciative system sufficiently widely shared to mediate communication, sufficiently apt to guide action and sufficiently acceptable

[1]I would like to acknowledge the contributions of Diana Wainman Bitan to the bibliographic research, and the contributions of our colleagues by their helpful comments when some of this material was presented to the Support Systems Seminar at the Laboratory of Community Psychiatry, Harvard Medical School on February 28, 1974.

[2]The terms self-help and mutual help are often used interchangeably in the literature and therefore in this review. My preference is for the phrase "mutual help" because it more clearly delineates the most salient aspect of these groups, programs, and organizations.

to make personal experience bearable" (203:439). The form this search takes need not only be in face-to-face encounters but can also occur through letters (31), hot lines (3), radio talk shows and the print media, including newspaper reader exchange pages such as the "Confidential Chat" of *The Boston Globe* and advice columns (46, 83).

This chapter will focus on reports on more or less formal, more or less structured, not-professionalized, mutual help organizations which are problem or predicament focused, such as La Leche League, Gay A's, Parents Without Partners, Al-Anon, The Little People of America, Synanon, Overeaters Anonymous, and person-to-person programs such as Widow-to-Widow and heart-wife counselors, from the point of view of the categorizations of these groups used by the authors to interpret what they saw to themselves and to others.[3]

Mutual help organizations are not simple phenomena nor am I sure we are dealing with a single movement. Some explanations in the literature appear to be contradictory, if considered in isolation to one another. For example, self-help groups are seen as alternative caregiving systems, e.g., Vietnam Veterans rap groups versus Veterans' Administration psychotherapy groups (175); and they are seen as adjuncts to the professions by which access to the population groups to be served is controlled by the professions, e.g., hospital visitation by an ostomate from the Ostomy Association to the person about to undergo ileostomy or colostomy can be done only with the surgeon's permission (120). Mutual help groups are viewed as part of the phenomena of the service society in which macroeconomic forces are at work which impose new forms of service with a necessarily different division of labor to accommodate the demands of a postindustrial era (64); and they are viewed as an expression of the democratic ideal, as a model of consumer participation (202). Gartner and Riessman resolve this ambiguity by seeing a convergence of "the service society and the consumer vanguard" (61). Mutual help groups are categorized as growth-promoting and helpful support systems (32); and they are also seen as agencies of social control (7, 52, 77, 170, 214) which may have some repressive features which are psychologically and sociopolitically undesirable. These organizations are seen alternatively in the literature as societies of deviants (164), peer self-help psychotherapy groups (93), and as groups of people sharing a common problem or predicament who band together for mutual support and constructive action toward shared goals (106).

The literature on self-help and mutual help groups, while numerous,

[3]Although each is important in its own right, this review will not be concerned primarily with group psychotherapies, encounter or sensitivity groups, growth groups, consciousness-raising groups, companionship therapy, reevaluation or co-counseling, lay therapy (self-directed or otherwise), affiliative therapy, buddy systems, network therapy, informal caregivers, personal influence networks, the more usual formal voluntary and fraternal associations, nor cooperative economic development groups.

is of uneven quality in both scope and depth. As in any situation, what is reported (including what is covered in this review) necessarily goes through a filtering process of selectivity, determined by interests, discipline and training, and the methodology used. Because of its unfashionable nature, much of the work by professionals in this field has had to be done with few resources of time, staff, and funds. This review of the literature will move from categories of interpretation which offer characterizations of a more global explanatory nature, to categories which focus on the relationship of these groups to the formal caregiving systems, on the kinds of communal solidarity offered, and on the nature of the functions of various groups. A separate section will indicate the characteristics of a group or its processes which are emphasized in the literature.

Categories of Interpretation

Social assistance – A factor in evolution
Support systems
A social movement
A spiritual movement and A secular religion
A product of social and political forces which shape the helping services
A phenomenon of the service society
An expression of the democratic ideal – Consumer participation
Alternative caregiving systems
An adjunct to the professions and A solution to the manpower problem
An element in a planned system of care
An intentional community
A subculture – Way of life
A supplementary community
A temporary/transitional community
Agencies of social control and A resocialization process
Expressive/social influence groups
Organizations of the deviant and stigmatized
A vehicle to aid coping with long-term deficits and deprivations
A vehicle to aid coping with life-cycle transitions
A therapeutic method

Characteristics of the Group

Common experience of members
Mutual help and support
The helper principle
Differential association
Collective willpower and belief
Importance of information
Constructive action toward shared goals

These *Interpretations* and *Characteristics* will be illustrated with quotations from the literature linked to the bibliography. The review will conclude with a brief description of the typologies available in the literature and with a section on work for the future.

It is the intention of this review to provide a guide to the literature, to encourage additional case studies and comparative surveys, and to offer bibliographic data to aid in the development of curricula on support systems and mutual help. From all of this future work, together with what has already been reported in the literature, may come the needed integrative conceptual framework which will increase our understanding of mutual help groups and the important services they provide their members.

CATEGORIES OF INTERPRETATION IN THE LITERATURE

Social Assistance — A Factor in Evolution

The primary proponent of this interpretation is Prince Petr Kropotkin, a nineteenth-century Russian scientist and revolutionary, who wrote a series of articles in England in the 1890s, the essence of which was that man as a social animal could survive the evolutionary process only within a form of group life – tribe, family, mutual benefit groups – in which mutual aid was the dominating influence. He wrote this series of articles to counteract directly the attention given certain Darwinists, particularly Huxley and his struggle for life manifesto of 1888. The articles he wrote were collected into a book, *Mutual Aid*, which has seldom been out of print since. Kropotkin states:

> In the animal world we have seen that the vast majority of species live in societies, and that they find in association the best arms for the struggle for life: understood, of course, in its wide Darwinian sense – not as a struggle for the sheer means of existence, but as a struggle against all natural conditions unfavourable to the species. The animal species, in which individual struggle has been reduced to its narrowest limits, and the practice of mutual aid has attained the greatest development, are invariably the most numerous, the most prosperous, and the most open to further progress. The mutual protection which is obtained in this case, the possibility of attaining old age and of accumulating experience, the higher intellectual development, and the further growth of sociable habits, secure the maintenance of the species, its extension, and its further progressive evolution. The unsociable species, on the contrary, are doomed to decay (113:293).

Kropotkin concludes that "in the practice of mutual aid, which we can retrace to the earliest beginnings of evolution, we thus find the positive and undoubted origin of our ethical conceptions; and we can affirm that in the ethical progress of man, mutual support – not mutual struggle – has had the leading part. In its wide extension, even at the present time, we also see the best guarantee of a still loftier evolution of our race" (113:300).

This thesis of cooperation is given new attention today in the emerging field of sociobiology (215).

Support Systems

As defined primarily by Caplan, "Support *System* implies an enduring pattern of continuous or intermittent ties that play a significant part in maintaining the psychological and physical integrity of the individual over time" (32:7). Caplan states that many professions and formal community institutions as well as natural systems (such as the family; nonprofessionalized and informal social units, particularly mutual aid organizations; and person-to-person caregiving efforts, both spontaneous and organized) can be elements in support systems:

> Support Systems are attachments among individuals or between individuals and groups that serve to improve adaptive competence in dealing with short-term crises and life transitions as well as long-term challenges, stresses and privations through (a) promoting emotional mastery, (b) offering guidance regarding the field of relevant forces involved in expectable problems and methods of dealing with them, and (c) providing feedback about an individual's behavior that validates his conception of his own identity and fosters improved performance based on adequate self-evaluation (33:2).

A Social Movement

Toch includes self-help groups such as TOPS, Recovery, and Alcoholics Anonymous in a social movement which aims to produce changes within its members rather than in society, in which "community of membership is the *chief means* to the movement's goals." He sees these self-help groups as movements "which collectively promote individual change" (197:71). Consequent on the nature of self-help movements,

> *each individual's efforts to solve his own problems become part of his efforts to solve a social problem* – one with which he is intimately familiar, and about which he has reason to be concerned. Since the member has learned to see himself as an example of a general problem, he can view his efforts as directed at both the particular and universal goal (197:84).

In a prospectus to study self-help health organizations, Gussow and Tracy state that "the emergence of such consumer-initiated services constitute a social movement. Such phenomena arise when a hiatus exists between felt need and the existence of available services, representation, or social benefits adequate to meet such need" (74:3).

Vattano says that self-help groups are a power-to-the people social movement which has clinical applications (AA, Integrity Groups, Synanon, encounter groups, etc.) and social applications (community organization groups such as welfare rights groups, Mobilization for Youth, etc.):

The movement has caused non-professional self-help groups to emerge as a potent force in the design and delivery of health and welfare services. Whether these groups are indeed manifestations of a single movement or independent phenomena is a moot question. The author believes that both clinical and social self-help groups are products of the general cultural revolution described by Reich[4] and Revel[5] (202:9).

A significant element in all social movements is the search for order and meaning to reality. Cantril wrote about the Oxford Group Movement (a major influence in the formative years of Alcoholics Anonymous) in the depression and war-fearful atmosphere of the 1930s when Buchmanism, as he calls the OGM after its founder Frank Buchman, flourished as an international social movement:

> The essential secret of Buchman's more recent success is that he provided for many people a meaningful interpretation of events which, at the same time, implicitly preserved their security and their self-regard. The Four Absolutes and the method of attaining them gave certain people a new frame of reference which conformed to their basic values and was itself so general that almost every situation could be judged in terms of it. By increasing their range of acquaintances, mixing freely with other believers, and doing good deeds that they thought important, many followers found a place for themselves in a new social world, their behavior became more directed and purposeful (30:166).

Glyer, in a study of natural and health food movements, finds diet healing groups are attractive to followers because they are based on a socially shared set of assumptions about illness and healing: "The groups ... have become disillusioned with the medical world. They turn to leaders who provide a system of health compatible with their own beliefs. In this way, they strive for an important health reward, a self-consistent assumptive world which offers them validation" (67:166).

This search for order occurs not only in the individual's relations to the larger external environment but also in the individual's immediate psychosocial situation. Wechsler, in a case study of Recovery, Inc., states that the "Recovery method is characterized by a search for order amidst a labyrinth of complex psychological problems and processes. Personal experiences are restructured within the cognitive framework provided by Recovery so that events which may be anxiety-promoting and unfamiliar may be translated into a more familiar and understandable form" (207:305).

A Spiritual Movement and A Secular Religion

In the literature on mutual aid groups which help people to deal with such stigmatizing problems as obesity, alcoholism, gambling, and "nervous-

[4]C. A. Reich, *The Greening of America* (New York: Random House, 1970).

[5]J. F. Revel, "Without Marx or Jesus," *Saturday Review,* July 24, 1971.

ness," one frequently finds an interpretation of the organization as a secular religion and as part of a spiritual movement.

Allon, in her study of a commercial weight-reducing organization, which she calls Trim-Down, says:

> My data suggest that the weight-losing groups have qualities of a secular religion; it seems fruitful to draw religious analogies when speaking about the groups. Lecturers and members constantly use religious terminology. They refer to cheating on the diet as "sinning". Some call themselves and others "saints" or "angels," if they have stuck to the diet, and not cheated. Members often talk about how important it is to "confess" cheating or "sinning"; they say that lecturers have the power to grant "absolution" for cheating. Lecturers and members refer to the card with the basic diet written on it as the "diet Bible."
>
> Such usages of religious terminology along with some religious analogies seem to be fruitful for capturing much of the spirit of the diet groups (7:8–9).

Scodel refers to Gamblers Anonymous as inspirational group therapy: "Since religion of a generally accommodating and vaguely specified variety is part of the group's official ideology, weather reports [member's testimonials] will also refer to the spiritual nature of the program and frequent mention is made of a newly acquired religiosity which is incorporated into the person's pronouncement of a reformation of character" (169:116).

Gellman (63), Jones (98), and Ritchie (158), along with many other writers, share perceptions of Alcoholics Anonymous both as a sectarian religion and as a spiritual movement. Gellman states that "... A.A. denies it is a religious movement. It steadfastly maintains that it is a *spiritual* and not a *religious* program" (63:159). He goes on, however, to say, "Our object, rather, is to describe those characteristics of Alcoholics Anonymous which justifiably establish it as a religious movement" (63:164). "It has emerged as a church which may be defined as the formal organization of a group of worshipers who share common and defined beliefs and rituals concerning the sacred objects and entities they revere" (63:168–169). Ritchie, on the other hand, while recognizing that AA is based on the tenets of the Christian religion, sees AA as a spiritual movement which has avoided "entangling alliances" with existing religions or emerging movements of religious reform. He thinks that "it is possible to discern in Alcoholics Anonymous traces of the emergence of a new type of institution – a socioreligious group in which the primary goal is the 'good life' here and now" (158:152).[6]

Wechsler notes that "the Recovery method and its practice at panel meetings is clearly reminiscent of various elements characteristic of certain organized religions. The method involves faith and acceptance of regulations handed down by a higher authority." In further elaboration of the "semireli-

[6]Reprinted with permission from the *Quarterly Journal on Studies of Alcohol* 9:119-156, 1948. Copyright by Journal of Studies on Alcohol, Inc., New Brunswick, NJ.

gious nature of Recovery" Wechsler says, "Recovery has a bible, the textbook of Dr. Low. Hero worship of Low sometimes assumes the proportions of making him almost appear a god-figure. The leaders assume the role of disciples. In certain Recovery groups, the desire for expansion and for national recognition is analogous to the missionary zeal in religious groups. In addition, the repetitive ritual-like panel meetings resemble certain forms of religious ceremonies" (207:307).

Mowrer, the leading exponent of Integrity Groups which are small therapy groups with strong elements of peer support, says

> There are indications that the Small Group may largely replace the Established Church. Christianity started as a small-group movement . . . with great "therapeutic" power; but it has evolved institutionally in such a way as to become increasingly "irrelevant" for many modern men and women.

Mowrer then goes on to say that "Integrity Groups, while non-theistic, are highly *religious* in that they are vitally concerned with human reintegration, reconciliation or reconnection (which is what religion means ...) There is more than one reason for thinking that the Small Group may be the emerging 'church' of the 21st Century" (138:45).

A Product of Social and Political Forces Which Shape the Helping Services

At the macroexplanatory level, mutual aid and self-help organizations can be seen as products of many forces which shape them as helping services – historical, social, intellectual, political, and economic. In a book written about the historical development of services for children, a pertinent and relevant statement of this thesis is made by Murray and Adeline Levine: ". . . social and economic conditions and the intellectual and political spirit of the times exert profound influences upon the particular mental health problems which concern us and upon the particular forms of help which develop and flourish. As a corollary of this thesis, one can argue that changes in the forms of help are shaped at least as much by the predominant social forces of the times as they are by thoroughly supported developments in the science of human behavior" (121:8).

Glaser, in a paper on the historical and theoretical development from many sources (used both deliberately and unconsciously) of Gaudenzia, a self-help addiction treatment program, states a variation on this theme:

> Preliminary investigation indicates that self-help programs such as Gaudenzia, Incorporated did not simply materialize out of nothingness. Rather, they have a definable, if not fully defined, historical and theoretical background. From a general viewpoint there are significant similarities between their basic principles and the thought of such men as Alfred Adler and Kurt Lewin. More particularly there is

a direct line of descent which is well documented from Alcoholics Anonymous, founded in 1935 to Gaudenzia, Incorporated, founded in 1968. From participant observation of the Gaudenzia program and other self-help programs it appears that there are close similarities between the basic ideas of these programs and current thought in at least the areas of existential philosophy and learning theory. As indicated, this is almost certainly not an exhaustive compilation of the theoretical sources of the program. But it may be sufficient to demonstrate that such programs are grounded in substantial thought and are not purely idiosyncratic. Their originality, and their promise, lies in their ability to combine several such strands into a unique and meaningful whole (66:625).[7]

Devall presents "an overview of the preconditions, precipitating factors, and development of gay liberation as a social movement in America after 1950," focusing on male homosexual organizations in San Francisco and Los Angeles. He specifies the development of a more tolerant political and social climate, especially with the rise of the counterculture and alternative life-styles, which provided collateral support, and made change and organization for action possible; the availability of successful role models and strategies in the civil rights and other social change movements; the emergence of a cadre of leaders; the segmentary and decentralized organizational nature of gay groups which permitted the development of local strategies, and which strengthened the movement making it less vulnerable to the internal development of conservatism and to the concerted action of external attacks; the development of communication media such as gay periodicals which promoted a collective ideology and provided a means of sharing strategies and tactics for action among declared and potential members; the provision by gay groups of alternative services which drew in recruits who helped in forging a new positive collective identity which permitted the development of new individual homosexual life-styles, and who provided the manpower to work to change society's traditional definitions of and responses to homosexuals. Devall does not attempt to explain the recruitment of some, and not other, homosexuals to the movement, nor to compare the development of gay liberation in other American cities and in other cultures (45:24–35).

A Phenomenon of the Service Society

Gersuny and Rosengren offer economically based formulations on the service society which could include mutual help organizations. They see "our society ... marked by the emergence of secularized services rendered outside the family. A service revolution has, in fact followed on the heels of the industrial revolution. This service revolution brings with it not only great new markets for the distribution of intangibles, but a new and highly signifi-

[7]Reprinted from the *International Journal of Addictions,* with permission from Marcel Dekker, Inc.

cant dimension in the division of labor – the active participation of the consumer in the production of many services" (64:ix). Gersuny and Rosengren focus on the quinary section of the economy which includes health care, education, and recreation. They state that services in the quinary sector "are intended to produce alterations in the customer, in his behavior patterns, and hence in the division of labor itself." With the consumer as coproducer, this sector of society offers life-cycle services, occupational opportunity services, alteration-of-self services (often literally "selves for sale") and problem-oriented services (64:5-6).

Gartner and Riessman also address, within broad political and economic frames of reference, the service society and the consumer as producer, emphasizing the convergence of the service dynamic and the consumer dynamic "producing the service-society ethos, the value syndromes, and the interpersonal revolution that emerged in the sixties and continue into the seventies" (61:25). They say that "in addition to those services offered in a formal setting by members of the work force, there are similar services provided outside of such settings in alternative institutions, by the self-help movement, the women's movement and others" (61:4).

> This new direction provides a whole new agenda for services – both their production and consumption. It should lead to a tremendous broadening of the growth and development services – lifetime education, new forms of interpersonal recreation, new therapeutic forms, women's groups, men's groups, marriage encounters, sex therapy, new religious, mind-expanding forms, special services for the dying, the development of all kinds of groups, family planning services, day care centers, preventive health groups. The services of the future will go far beyond the traditional health, education, and welfare classification and should be far more consumer-involving (61:145–146).

An Expression of the Democratic Ideal — Consumer Participation

There are a number of articles which, in one way or another, say that mutual help organizations are, among other things, an expression of the democratic ideal by which people determine how they view themselves and through which they demand the kinds of services they feel are appropriate to meet their needs. Lenneberg and Rowbotham state that "with the voluntary health agency movement firmly established in America as a means for the public to participate in relieving human suffering, the stage for mutual-aid or self-help groups, was set." They suggest that "the development of mutual-aid groups of patients or parents of child patients should be viewed, (1) clinically as a healthy effort at self-help towards the ultimate goal of rehabilitation – independence, and (2) sociologically as an outgrowth of the increasing participation of the American public in matters of physical and emotional well-being" (120:75–76).

Vattano says:

> A new emphasis on broad democratic participation is motivating clients and other nonprofessional groups to become involved in policy-making and service delivery in many social institutions.... Some interpret these phenomena as manifestations of a growing anarchy; others view them as signs of an evolving, more democratic society.... The challenge is particularly evident in the emergence of self-help groups – groups that emphasize the power of their members to assist one another rather than depend on the help of professionals (202:7).

Dumont makes a vigorous statement about self-help groups as a reification of the aspirations of the Founding Fathers with their concern for individual rights, balance of power, and decentralization of authority within pluralistic structures. He goes on to add that current concern with

> the redistribution of political and economic power is meaningless if the power residing in professionalism is not redistributed as well. In recognition of this, two developments emerged during the last decade that act as countervailing influences on the professionalization of power. These developments, advocacy and consumer control, have largely culminated in the self-help movement (48:633).

In some ways these views are restatements of Tocqueville on American democracy, and of Schlesinger (166) on the United States as a "nation of joiners." There are obvious links to the literature on voluntarism, voluntary associations, citizen and consumer participation, and human and civil rights.

Alternative Caregiving Systems

Traunstein and Steinman, in a survey of self-help organizations in an upper New York State community, found "that a large number of people are being delivered a service by their peers which parallels, complements and in many instances competes with the delivery of the social welfare 'establishment', and that there is a strong tendency toward the 'de-bureaucratization' and 'de-professionalization' of this delivery system" (198:236). They also report that the groups they studied made few referrals to other caregiving systems, thus rejecting the roles of gatekeeping and specialization. Hansell found that the Looking Glass of Chicago, an organization of volunteer young adults, served a population of young persons "not in contact with more formal caregiving agencies. They are half-way between a *folk* care system and a *professional* care system" (78:1). Shatan, in an article describing his work and that of other mental health professionals with the Vietnam Combat Veterans' Self-Help Movement says that, in the Manhattan chapter of Vietnam Veterans Against the War,

> many vets distrusted not only "establishment" psychiatric services, but even the private offices of former combat psychiatrists, themselves VVAW members.... The VVAW membership opted for rap sessions to fill an unmet need – the need to "get their heads together" (175:641).

. . .

> Since the spring of 1972, there has been a deluge of inquiries and ... [many veterans in many places around the country and in Canada] have launched rap groups, and have established contact with the New York chapter. All report that they organized in response to the absence of effective VA treatment services, or to the unavailability of these services due to technicalities (175:643).

The examples of this abound. Berzon and Berman, in writing about Gay Growth Groups, say that "the use of gay non-professionals as group leaders appears to be one viable alternative to the void being created as more and more gay people reject the traditionalist, clinically-oriented services of non-gay mental health professionals" (19:14-15). Ginsberg, in discussing the Mental Patient Liberation Movement says, "Its strength is derived partly from the obvious correctness of the cause, partly from the fact that the groups do not generally seek new public resources or services. More typically, they seek freedom from the mental health system and some activities associated with it" (65:3). Gussow and Tracy take the position that self-help groups represent "a substantial consumer response to a basic inadequacy in the classical medical care system in providing individuals with needed human support in areas interstitial between medical treatment, adaptation and rehabilitation" (74:8).

An Adjunct to the Professions — A Solution to the Manpower Problem

Stunkard (191) in reporting on TOPS, and Dean (44) in discussing Recovery, Inc., see them as adjuncts or potential adjuncts to the formal caregiving systems with an appropriate division of labor, and as solutions to the shortage of professional personnel. Stunkard says that

> if the family physician or internist could confidently turn over to TOPS the jobs of weight monitoring and psychologic support for obese patients, his efforts at controlling obesity could be confined to periodic assessments of their diets and weight goals. We believe such a plan is feasible and that it would result in larger weight losses for obese patients and in conservation of the physician's time and energy (191:147).

Dean states that "it is consistent with the democratic ideal that help for the mentally afflicted should be available to every individual rather than the privileged few. To achieve that goal we professionals must envision a system of outreach that literally permeates every level of society.... Factors peculiar to our complex times have combined to create a veritable psychiatric explosion. To cope with it, the new psychiatric task force will have to expand its horizons. It will have to recruit sergeants and corporals as well as commanding officers.... Already various paraprofessional psychiatric aides have validated their roles in modern treatment, especially psychiatric social workers, clinical psychologists, occupational therapists and psychiatric nurses. But in addition, there are also many informal self-conducted 'therapeutic clubs' within the community – e.g., Alcoholics Anonymous, Synanon, Weight Watchers, Recovery, Inc. – whose potential resources have been largely unexplored by professionals, although they have withstood the test of time and bid fair to become a permanent feature of the socio-psychiatric scene" (44:72–73).

To Lenneberg and Rowbotham, the ostomy groups are a community resource, working in collaboration with the hospital professions as an "adjunct to existing resources." They state that the ostomy groups "possess specific information and knowledge which hospital staffs need," and that consultation can be of the supportive-visiting type to the patient, and also technical to the staff. In the community, ostomy groups can "develop a two-way program: (1) interpretation and referral to other agencies, and (2) supplying assistance needed by other agencies in their work with patients" (120:86–87).

An Element in a Planned System of Care

In only a few instances in the literature are examples given of groups which were seen as elements in a planned system of care. One such program in Seattle, Washington is reported by Pomeroy. The Washington Association for Sudden Infant Death Study initiated the project by obtaining initial funds from the state legislature. Every incident of an unexplained infant death in King's County is referred to the pediatric pathologist of the local children's hospital who performs an autopsy. The findings of the autopsy are reported by the pathologist to the families immediately, usually by telephone. Families are concurrently sent literature about SIDS from the hospital. The family is visited at home in about a week by a nurse who is supportive but, most importantly, also provides cognitive information about "crib death." The parents in the Washington Association, who have experienced SIDS in their own families, act as resource persons: "They have a 'telephone committee' of informed mothers, who are willing to talk to other parents at any time, and they send a letter to each family we [the nurse] visit, telling them they are available and willing to help in any way" (150:1890).[8] The Association has prepared informative literature on "crib death" and has distributed it to the people most likely to be in first contact with the family while the death is still unexplained – the coroners, the police, firemen, and funeral directors. The Association also pursues an educational campaign of the media. A member follows up every news article and radio or TV story which reports an incident of SIDS with incorrect information or in a manner to unfairly and cruelly appear to accuse the parents of abuse.

The first support group as such in the medical field was also part of

[8]Quoted with permission from the *American Journal of Nursing*. Copyright 1969 by the American Journal of Nursing Company.

a planned system of care (153). In 1905, Pratt organized what he called "classes" for tuberculosis patients in Boston. These were poor outpatients who remained at home and took bed rest in their tenements, on roof, balcony, or in the yard. They were called on often by a friendly visitor, sometimes a nurse, who provided information and guidance about bed rest, cleanliness, and nutrition to the patient and his family, and encouragement over the long haul of a TB patient's treatment. Weekly meetings of the patients in small groups were held first in Pratt's offices and later in the outpatient department of Massachusetts General Hospital where Pratt provided medical supervision and inspected the record books kept by the individual patients themselves. These meetings developed many of the mechanisms now seen in Weight-Watchers and Alcoholics Anonymous, such as weigh-ins (in this case, rewards were given for gaining weight), sharing of information about what worked, testimonials from patients who were progressing, visits from former members who had "graduated" and were now working. The financing for this work was provided by the Emmanuel Episcopal Church of Boston and, when they had progressed sufficiently, many patients participated in the church's Wednesday evening meetings known as the Health Class, led by the pastor, Dr. Elwood Worcester. These health classes were part of what came to be known as the Emmanuel Movement, a method of moral control of functional nervous disorders combining what was thought to be sound religion and sound psychology. The church developed a social service department which often found employment for the recovered TB patient.

Stichman and Schoenberg describe a program of care for coronary patients which incorporates heart-wife counselors: "women who have been through it helping women who are going through it, in collaboration with psychologists, cardiac nurses, dieticians, social workers (when involved with a particular patient) – and with reference to the family doctor and/or cardiac specialist" (188:156). In Phase I, the cardiac nurse introduces the new cardiac wife to the heart-wife counselor who uses a questionnaire to obtain needed information:

> ... the questionnaire's most immediate value in the program is the natural and easy way it lets the wife and the counselor meet. By the time it's filled out, conversation between the two is natural and relaxed as it can be, considering the circumstances. The wife is eager for reassurance; a woman whose husband recovered from the same illness is made to order. "Recovery" is the kind of talk she wants to hear. And the counselor offers a special kind of empathy she can't get even from her family. It is heartfelt; more important, it is *knowledgeable.* What the counselor is really saying to the wife is, "I know what you're going through, I know just what it feels like; I have been there, too." Soon the wife has the relief of letting go, letting herself say the words she was afraid to say, expressing the thoughts she was trying desperately not to think. She has a safety valve (188: 157).

During this crisis phase, the heart-wife counselor also provides a role model, gives anticipatory guidance about what's coming next, and offers concrete assistance with problems that must be dealt with immediately, such as placing calls to other members of the family, providing for care of children, and making arrangements about the patient's employment or business. In the meantime, the psychologist is working with the patient in a program of crisis intervention to ameliorate the psychological sequelae of a sudden severe illness. In Phase II, through joint meetings with professionals, other wives of hospitalized cardiac patients in the same boat, and the heart-wife counselors who have successfully been through the experience, the emphasis moves from emergency help with immediate problems and reassurance to education, preparation for homecoming, and problem solving. Throughout the phases, the heart-wife counselors are available by telephone at any time. In Phase III, after homecoming, the program continues with monthly mutual help meetings of ex-patients and their wives, with other members of the family joining from time to time. The meetings give "the families a chance to compare notes on what adjustment problems have come up and explore ways of handling them.... They offer a chance for full, frank discussion among people who share the same basic problem and who, therefore, understand each other's problem as no outsider could" (188:160).

Apart from relationships with the professional caregiving systems, mutual help groups and organizations are also seen in the literature as providing varying kinds of communities.

An Intentional Community

In some respects, utopian communes are viewed as mutual help organizations in the form of intentional communities. One of these is the Bruderhof, which has been described by Zablocki:

> An intentional community is defined as a community whose members have come together purposely, usually to implement certain patterns of social structure which differ from those of the larger society. . . . Its members live in complete economic sharing and community of goods.... It is found that the Bruderhof is designed to be able to take the energy liberated by the collective behavior experience, which is usually volatile, ephemeral, and unpredictable, and to transform this energy in such ways as to make it useful and reliable in holding together a community.... The extraordinarily high degree of commitment to the group makes possible a system of social control which is highly task-efficient but has little regard for individual autonomy (218:1-3, abstract).

The Bruderhof aim for a lifelong commitment and are ambivalent about outreach and contact with the outside world, which is limited and controlled.

Jacobs, in an article on emotive and control groups in America (primarily sensitivity and encounter-type groups but also including AA, TOPS, Synanon) says that in their ideal type, these proliferating groups relate to the utopian tradition in Western civilization, functioning as do all utopias. Utopias compensate for felt difficulties – in this case the lack of personal satisfactions in mass culture and the paucity of emotive, integrative, and control mechanisms. Unlike earlier utopian communities, most emotive and control groups are part time, but their part time nature is consistent with the segmented structure of modern life. Utopias can incorporate recessive cultural genes, enclose deviance or institutionalize it, offer solidarity, catharsis, control, and hope for their members, and sometimes serve as change models. In contemporary America, not only do emotive and control groups serve these ends; in addition, they are effective because they are legitimated by all three types of authority – traditional, charismatic, and legal-rational. The extent of the groups is diagnostic of the crisis in American culture (95:234).[9]

Organizations such as "concept-type" drug programs, while different in some important respects, have many of the characteristics of intentional communities like the Bruderhof. Weppner in a report on Matrix House states that it is representative of ex-addict self-help groups which seem to follow the model of Synanon. He says:

> There is a severance of ties to the outside which serves to strengthen the self-help organization's "primary group nature" (after Cooley).[10] In other words, no member may receive outside communications of any kind for a stipulated period, quite often 90 days. The "newcomer" must totally submerge himself in the activities and philosophy of the group and subscribe completely to its rules, which range from a prohibition on "street talk" to a requirement of long, hard hours of work. He must acquiesce to the fact that his peers will inform "oldtimers" in the house about any deviations (212:74).

Synanon, which started out as a therapeutic method for reform of drug addicts, became a way of life, and now has taken on the characteristics of an intentional community for nonaddicts as well as former addicts. In 1965, Yablonsky says that "Synanon is more than symposiums and seminars. It is a new kind of group therapy; an effective approach to racial integration; a humane solution to some facets of bureaucratic organization; a different way of being religious; a new method of attack therapy; an unusual kind of communication; and an exciting, fresh approach to the cultural arts and philosophy" (217:viii). In 1967, Yablonsky, in an introduction to a new printing of his book, adds that "a part of Synanon's character that has become more articulate is its significance as a social movement. The organization has steadily moved beyond the limited work of treating drug addiction and crime.... Some of these people [who were never addicts, criminals nor had a history of serious character disorder] have become so fascinated and intrigued by the Game, the social movement dimensions of the organization and the Synanon way of life that in growing numbers they have

[9]R. H. Jacobs: Emotive and control groups as mutated new American utopian communities, the *Journal of Applied Behavioral Sciences* 7:234-251, 1971. Copyright by NTL Institute for Applied Behavioral Sciences. Reproduced by special permission.

[10]C. H. Cooley, *Social Organization* (New York: Scribners, 1909).

moved in, some with their families.... Synanon Industries increasingly provides meaningful occupational opportunities for its members and has given Synanon an important source of finances in its movement towards self-sufficiency" (217:v-vi). By 1971, Glaser, in his paper reviewing the evolutionary development of programs for treatment of drug addiction such as Daytop and Gaudenzia, says that

> ... Synanon came more and more to feel that society at large was a dangerous and pathological institution, and that a full life was to be found only within the Synanon organization itself. Thus no one who entered was expected to leave. Synanon became a way of life in itself, rather than a means to the end of re-entering the general society. Daytop, on the other hand, felt that it had an obligation to return its residents to the general society where they might not only lead useful and productive lives but act as agents of social improvement, building upon their Daytop experience (66:618).[11]

In 1975, Ofshe says, "If, during its early period as an organization dedicated exclusively to the resocialization of drug and alcohol dependent individuals, Synanon could reasonably have been conceptualized as a 'total institution' (Goffman, 1961)[12] it might now be properly considered to be an organization in the process of transforming itself into a 'total society'" (143:67).

A Subculture — Way of Life

Shapiro, in writing about communities of the alone as mutual aid societies in single room occupancy hotels, says that

> the SRO population consititutes a subculture with a self-assigned identity, and with mores and predictable norms unique to it. The style of living forms a recognizable pattern in one SRO after another in which a high degree of interconnective and mutual dependency is the rule. Despite the ugly and painful lives of these rejectees of the larger culture, a core of health has emerged; with remarkable ingenuity they have built a private culture which affords them a network of social supports. In their substitute world, some have built stable "quasi-families", have learned to protect each other and themselves from the grossest excesses of their own pathology, and have managed to survive in a situation of extreme deprivation of all forms of material goods. Gleams of altruism, love, help, wisdom and self-knowledge have emerged from deeply embittered and damaged people. The SRO is a survival culture where chronic crises apparently stimulate highly social behavior in many of its members (173: 124).

Very few mutual help organizations have been studied from the viewpoint of organizational theory. Gellman, in an analysis of Alcoholics Anonymous using Parson's[13] suggestions for a sociological approach to the theory

[11]Reprinted from the *International Journal of Addictions,* with permission from Marcel Dekker, Inc.

[12]E. Goffman, *Asylums* (New York: Doubleday, 1961).

[13]T. Parsons, in *Complex Organizations,* ed. A. Etzioni (New York: Holt, Rinehart, Winston, 1961).

of organizations and Bakke's[14] concept of the bonds of organization, finds that AA "is fundamentally 'organization therapy' involving the structure and processes of the total system of the association" (63:135). He says that AA "is essentially a circular system in which the organization is the therapeutic agency and in turn is molded and shaped by the activities and accomplishments of its members" (63:141). "The most important aspect of 'organization therapy' is the socialization process which leads to A.A. as a 'way of life'" (63:142). And this "total involvement in A.A. as a way of life is the principle safeguard against serious breaches in the normative system of the organization. In effect a subculture is created in which the status of alcoholic has positive connotations" (63:172).

Hochschild, in describing life-styles for the old in the subculture of an elderly housing complex, says that

> ... communal solidarity can renew the social contact the old have with life. For old roles that are gone, new ones are available. If the world watches them less for being old, they watch one another more. Lacking responsibilities to the young, the old take on responsibilities toward one another. Moreover, in a society that raises an eyebrow at those who do not "act their age," the subculture encourages the old to dance, to sing, to flirt and to joke. They talk frankly about death in a way less common between the old and young. They show one another how to be, and trade solutions to problems they have not faced before.
>
> Old age is the minority group almost everyone joins. But it is a forgotten minority group from which many old people dissociate themselves. A community such as Merrill Court counters this disaffiliation. In the wake of the declining family, it fosters a "we" feeling, and a nascent "old age consciousness." In the long run, this may be the most important contribution an old age community makes (89:57).[15]

A Supplementary Community

Some mutual help groups offer a supplementary community to their members. In an organization such as Little People of America, which includes opportunities for friendship and dating as well as psychological support, Weinberg cites a range of dependency on the organization by members for social relationships and social activities (209:68). He goes on to say that

> the L.P.A. does not, however, attempt to engulf the life space of its members, entrenching them in a world of little people. The association persuades its members instead to distribute themselves throughout the social structure. They are encouraged to live in a world of both normal and little people and not to hide from either. They should not look primarily to the world of entertainment; they should seek to further their education and seek other employment. The L.P.A. provides social support for their activities. It is attempting an organized attack on social barriers

[14]E. W. Bakke, *Bonds of Organization* (New York: Harper and Bros., 1950).

[15]Published by permission of Transaction, Inc., from *Society,* Vol. 10, No. 5. Copyright ©1973, by Transaction, Inc.

and discrimination, and its social training helps little people to overcome stigma. A source for friends, dates, and mates, it provides an opportunity for its members to lead "social" lives (209:71).

In writing about the contributions of Parents Without Partners to the well-being of its members, Weiss (210, 211) seems to use the concepts of PWP as a supplementary community, as an alternative community, and as a sustaining community interchangeably. The designation of supplementary community is probably congruent with the way most members use PWP. Weiss describes PWP's program as a response to its members' "sources of distress: (a) the absence of a sustaining community; (b) the absence of similarly placed friends; (c) the absence of support for a sense of worth; and (d) the absence of emotional attachment" (210:322). Weiss also indicates some of the organizational difficulties inherent "in an organization attempting, as PWP does, to respond directly to the needs of its members rather than act as an instrument through which the members may achieve goals elsewhere in the society" (210:325–326).

A Temporary/Transitional Community

For those who view modern communes as part of the self-help movement, Marx and Selden's observations may be pertinent:

> ...present-day American communes are seen as transient, age-graded, quasi-therapeutic sheltered workshops. By providing a temporary psychosocial moratorium from competitive conventional society, contemporary communes facilitate individual-psychological reorientation, growth, and reintegration into the non-communal context. This latent function is fulfilled by encouraging interpersonal experimentation in the context of an intimate, permissive, supportive, non-hierarchical (nonprofessional) collectivity of sociologically homogeneous peers (132:39).

In the mental health field, ex-patient groups, also known as therapeutic social clubs, developed to provide the discharged patient with a transitional bridge from the hospital to the community (20). For some, this has been a successful device toward the goal of reintegration; for others, the group/club becomes a substitute community. Organizationally these clubs range in a continuum from essentially self-help organizations to centers dominated by professionals. Grob, in a paper which reviews the rationale, history and varieties of social clubs for ex-patients, says that "the primary goal is to create a social and cultural environment that will help motivate and activate discharged mental patients to return to normal community life and useful employment" (71:133).

Landy and Singer in a study of ex-patient clubs found that

> the club culture may be expressed in terms of what it means to its members (common understandings), and what it is (values and behavior norms). What it means

has been expressed graphically by the members themselves. It is one man's "crutch," which he needs because he is "emotionally crippled." For another, "Maybe this club is my desert island. I'd like to say to hell with society and find me a desert island somewhere." For another, "It's like a cradle. Sometimes one needs a cradle for a while. You might jump into it if you need it." It becomes a place to escape the pressures of a family life which has become pathological for them, or a society which has been intolerable to, and to some extent intolerant of, them. And since each is in his own way a "lonely one," it is a place to socialize without the ordinary pressures of the community's culture (117:39).

Landy and Singer express the reservations and ambivalence many professionals feel toward ex-patient groups: "To the extent that the club is a self-perpetuating group for perennially sick people, it may fulfill the qualifications for such a 'subculture of the sick' of which Parsons speaks. To the extent that the club serves transitional functions as bridge between hospital culture and community culture, and for some it does appear to operate in this way, it becomes a midpoint, so to speak, in the process of shedding the sick role for the well role, and so Parson's 'dangerous potentiality' is circumvented" (117:39).

Houpt et al. describe the formation of successful reentry groups of discharged psychiatric inpatients to bridge the hospital-community gap:

Ex-patients were chosen to be group leaders in order to assist the patients in their task of redefining themselves as competent, by serving as successful role models. That ex-patients were suitable role models and were looked upon by the group as individuals who had successfully negotiated the hospital-community gap was confirmed when one of the group members said to an ex-patient, "Looking at you is like looking at the fat lady after she's lost two hundred pounds. That's inspiration enough to make this program worthwhile" (91:147).

Relative to drug abuse programs, Scott and Goldberg suggest that self-perpetuation by retention of participants as staff members may account for what success residential treatment programs based on the Synanon model have had (170).

Agencies of Social Control and A Resocialization Process

Some mutual help organizations are viewed as agencies of social control. Allon says that "Trim-Down weight-losing groups seem to be a microcosm of a more general public concern over excess pounds. The groups may be viewed as social control agencies to help people lose and keep off weight" (7:258). She observes that

in the contemporary United States, obesity seems to be a central target for human vindictiveness and puritanical zeal. The public condemns and scorns the overweight, who are viewed as handicaps to themselves. Attitudes toward the obese are related

> to several conflicting trends in the American cultural orientation. Americans emphasize the freedom of development as well as compulsion to conform. And, obese people do not conform to statistical averages, or to the standardized beauty ideal. Overweight people are denied the right to please themselves by eating as much as they want. They are reproached for not exercising self-control (7:260).

In a similar study of Weight Watchers, Wernick says "Weight Watchers attempts to make members aware of the liabilities of fatness so that they will be motivated to diet. Thus, the stigmatization of obesity is a frequent theme of lectures and Weight Watchers' publications . . . excerpts from Weight Watchers materials ... provide a vivid picture of stigma as it affects fat people" (213:83).

Volkman and Cressey, in a study of Synanon, found that "in the admission process, and throughout his residence, the addict discovers over and over again that the group to which he is submitting is antidrug, anticrime, and antialcohol. . . . The rules indicate the extreme extent to which it is necessary for the individual to subvert his personal desires and ambitions to the antidrug, anticrime group" (204:133).

In connection with mutual help organizations in total institutions, Wilson, a penologist, says that

> the self-help movement in prisons and reformatories had its beginning in areas such as A.A., religious groups, and various activity clubs. The groups have been recognized as an activity that keeps inmates out of plots against the discipline of the institution. At the same time they have been considered conspiracies against discipline and manipulation movements.
>
> They no doubt can be either of these.
>
> The direction self-help groups take depends on the objectives of the groups and the acceptance by the members of the goals, and also on leadership both of staff and inmate.
>
> The achievement of a self-help group is directly related to a balance of power and cooperative effort reciprocated by inmate and staff. The goals must be in keeping with the institution objectives, as well as those of the group (214:12).

As part of a more general resocialization process, Frederickson, in writing about a smoking withdrawal clinic, says:

> There is evidence that, for some, development of control over cigarette smoking tends to generalize to other areas of behavior bringing, in turn, a renewed sense of one's ability and often, what appears as an actual increase in one's capacity to deal more constructively with other "problems of living." When experienced this phenomenon can serve as a powerful incentive re-inforcing non-smoking behavior. We have observed this generalization of control frequently enough to feel secure in alerting smokers to the possibilities of its occurrence (55:88).[16]

Trice has written extensively about Alcoholics Anonymous over a period

[16]Reprinted from the *International Journal of Addictions,* with permission from Marcel Dekker, Inc.

of many years. He has said that when he looks at AA, "I see it as what we like to call a social device or mechanism whereby a deviant person can reenter acceptable society" (199:160). In a more recent article, Trice and Roman look at the processes of delabeling and relabeling, in which a "stigmatized label is replaced with one that is socially acceptable." They say that one means by which delabeling can occur successfully "is through the development of mutual aid organizations which encourage a return to strict conformity to the norms of the community as well as creating a stereotype which is socially acceptable. Exemplary of this strategy is Alcoholics Anonymous.... [which] provides opportunities for alcoholics to join together in an effort to cease disruptive and deviant drinking behavior in order to set the stage for the resumption of normal occupational, marital, and community roles (Gellman, 1964)" (200:538-539). A variation on the Trice and Roman thesis is found in Petrunik who states that AA like many religious sects or cults is "a model of resocialization as conversion or redemption" (148:30).

In an article on a self-help group in the 1950s at Boys Republic in Michigan, Eglash reports that "effectiveness means more than simply delinquency prevention, important as that is. When the boys at Boys Republic rejected *Delinquents* Anonymous [as a name] in favor of *Teen-agers* Anonymous, they indicated their awareness of stigma. To be stigmatized is to be set apart as different from others. The goal of this program is to enable people whose behavior has set them apart to rejoin their peers. For these juveniles, participation in the program is a beginning and a means; being a teenager in the full sense of the word is the hoped for goal" (50:48).

All of the literature reviewed here refers to studies of mutual help groups as they are found naturally in the community, not to laboratory experiments. In this category in the literature of mutual help organizations as agencies of social control, it may be interesting to look at one such laboratory study. Crosbie, Petroni, and Stitt proposed that already established principles of group dynamics might be used "to facilitate the processes of conformity and social control in corrective groups." They conducted an experiment with smoking cessation groups manipulating, in several groups and in different combinations, (a) experimenter attention, (b) simple group environment, (c) public commitment, and (d) goal interdependence, hypothesizing that "pressures toward conformity and control would increase with the addition of each successive characteristic, and that smoking reduction among the conditions would be ordered along this pressure dimension. The results of the experiment support the hypothesis; smoking reduction increased directly with increasing social pressure" (41:294). Crosbie et al. list several cautions:

> First, there is likely to be some difficulty encountered in adopting some variables that have been established in the small groups laboratory to the more permanent and natural conditions of corrective groups. . . .

Secondly. . . . research is needed to establish the generality of the findings in this experiment to other types of corrective groups.

Thirdly. . . . research is needed to determine whether or not there are effective limits to the magnitude of social pressure that can be used. . . .

Finally, there is the important problem of maintaining change once it has been produced (41:300).

One would add another concern about employing group pressures in the community to induce conformity, that of the ethical, civil, and human rights issues involved.

Expressive/Social Influence Groups

Mutual help organizations can also be seen within the familiar expressive/instrumental, expressive/social influence frame of reference. Groups which can be classified primarily as expressive are concerned principally with the self-interest and satisfaction of their members. Instrumental groups seek primarily to influence the larger society and to bring about change on behalf of the interests of their members. While groups like Alcoholics Anonymous and Synanon more nearly fall into the expressive category and groups like those homophile organizations which focus on combating discrimination in employment, housing and the media more nearly fall into the second category, most groups exhibit characteristics of both.

In a society with many persons haunted by feelings of alienation and isolation, particularly those who are stigmatized, mutual help associations can be vehicles toward the reconstitution of a primary group. Bassin reports on a visit to Synanon some years ago:

In a gravel-tone voice, our bull-necked host [Chuck Dederick] explained his approach in anthropological terms: "We attempt to create an extended family of the type found in preliterate tribes which usually have a strong, almost autocratic, father-figure, who dispenses firm justice combined with warm concern, who is a model extolling inner-directed convictions about the old-fashioned virtues of honesty, sobriety, education and hard work" (14:68).[17]

Shapiro describes the spontaneous mutual aid society formed by the residents of deteriorated single-room-occupancy hotels in New York City. She found that "to cope with this abject material poverty the tenants turn to one another to share scarce material resources and emotional ties. The lives of all but a few of the tenants are actively intertwined, a finding which sharply contradicts the stereotype of the single, poor individual as reclusive. Groups exist whose members give mutual support to each other's deviant or maladaptive behavior, but who also provide the human association, the sense of some help and belonging, which makes physical survival possible

[17]Reprinted with permission of *Psychology Today* magazine, copyright ©1968 by Ziff-Davis Publishing.

and emotional life meaningful. ... Dominant individuals, around whom group life revolves, vary in personality and leadership style. ... A recurrent pattern is the matriarchal quasi-family in which the dominant woman tends to feed, protect, punish, and set norms for 'family' members" (172:645–646).

Ritchie, in his sociohistorical study of Alcoholics Anonymous, says that the success of AA may largely be "due to the fact that members of this fellowship meet on a basis of mutual interest and understanding. They engage in informal face-to-face relationships which lead to the modifications of each other's personality. Inherent in this associative life are the interpersonal contacts which provide opportunities for self-expression. This collective activity is an in-group relationship in which recognition and security may be obtained. It also has primary-group characteristics which are evidenced by informal and personal face-to-face associations. These are important contributing factors in the resocializing process as it operates in Alcoholics Anonymous" (158:150–151).[18]

Allon, in her case study of a weight-reduction organization, found some "members stated that they enjoyed the Trim-Down route to thinness because the group was a close-knit, familial *Gemeinschaft.* Trim-Downers did not have cold and aloof secondary relationships with each other, as did traditional medical healers with their patients: Many appeared to transpose their gossipy morning coffee sessions with the girls to the different time and place setting of the Trim-Down group" (8:37).

In discussing groups of parents of handicapped children, Katz finds that, indeed, the emotional and cognitive help and support the parents receive is therapeutically necessary in order to release energy for constructive social action to benefit themselves and their children. He says that the "self-organization of the parents makes it possible for them to channel their emotional drives into means of bringing about changes in the social environment" (100:2). In another paper, Katz states that

> in the first place, feelings of having been singled out by providence or fate for a special lifelong burden, feelings of isolation and consequent helplessness are overcome. Secondly, even in the absence of professional counselling or guidance, parents get much help from other parents – who they can readily trust. They receive help with practical problems of information, methods of bringing up their children, rates of growth, expectations and problems to be anticipated at different ages; and also in the area of emotion and feelings about themselves and their child. Many of the meetings of the groups have a character similar to that of more formal group counselling and group therapy, with their attendant therapeutic benefits. Finally, for parents, the groups represent an opportunity for constructive social action – which has been demonstrated to be one of the most important ways of overcoming feelings of guilt, anxiety, helplessness and defeat (102:209).

Bender (18), Segal (171), Shatan (175), and Spiegel (186) also point out

[18]Reprinted with permission from the *Quarterly Journal of Studies on Alcohol* 9:119-156, 1948. Copyright by Journal of Studies on Alcohol, Inc., New Brunswick, NJ.

the beneficial effects of self-organization in supportive groups which are also socially and politically oriented.

Organizations of the Deviant and Stigmatized

Barish, in a review article on self-help groups says that "one of the major purposes of a self-help group is to counteract the isolation and alienation that result from being 'different,' by creating a place in which a member can belong. Most self-help groups emphasize that they provide a 'world within a world' where the 'deviant' is given a voice that can be heard and accepted as part of the collective. In this he has the security of finally being one of a majority and a movement, rather than individual and alone" (11:1165).[19]

Sagarin, in a book called *Odd Man In,* is one of the few individuals who have written both extensively across some self-help organizations nationally and in depth about individual groups. He deals with groups he calls societies of deviants, whose members, e.g., alcoholics or homosexuals, "form organizations because they already are in trouble with society or themselves" and "they seek association with others like themselves to assist in the handling of their problem" (164:20). He says that "the deviant always seeks to escape his stigma, but he does so by seeking either (1) to conform to the norms of society, or (2) to change those norms to include acceptance of his own behavior. In the first instance, he renounces his deviant behavior; in the second, he changes not himself but the rule-making order" (164:21).

Alternately, Sweet focuses on homophile organizations as part of a norm-oriented social movement composed of minority Americans facing problems of intolerance and discrimination who engage in collective behavior to effect social change and whose sexual orientation is irrelevant (194:242).

Traunstein and Steinman state that most of the self-help organizations or mutual benefit associations in the United States usually are "established by groups of individuals who share a condition stigmatized by the larger community" (198:230). In their survey of self-help organizations in one city, a criterion for inclusion in the study was that at least one-half of the membership that originated or were now members of the organization share a common problem stigmatized by the larger community. This varied from stuttering to a background of criminal conviction.

A Vehicle to Aid Coping with Long-Term Deficits and Deprivations

Self-help organizations are also viewed as vehicles for coping with

[19] Herbert Barish: Self-help groups. In *Encyclopedia of Social Work* (New York: National Association of Social Workers, 1971). Quoted with permission.

long-term deficits and deprivations, e.g., mutual help groups of stutterers, paraplegics, ostomates, mended hearts, laryngectomees, mastectomees. Caplan, in an article in *McCall's,* analyzed a sample of the 50,000 letters, telegrams, and telephone messages which poured in after Shirley Temple Black announced that one of her breasts had been removed because of cancer. He quotes from one of these letters from the California chairman of Reach to Recovery, a mutual help organization of women who have had mastectomies:

> ". . . . Welcome to the club! Hope your surgeon has okayed a visit for you by one of our screened and trained volunteers. Not only can they offer a psychological boost as one who has had the same experience (doesn't sound like you need that) but they provide some helpful information which you might like to receive. Included in our concern with the quality of life after surgery is education . . ." (31:54).

Borkman, in her sociological survey of active and disbanded stutterers' self-help organizations in the United States, New Zealand, Holland, and Sweden, found evidence which "leaves the strong impression that stutterers' self-help organizations can be effective in helping their members decrease the stigma, shame and fear of stuttering and of talking and increase their willingness to talk in a variety of situations, to admit to others their problem and to develop a more positive constructive attitude toward themselves as persons. There is much less indication that members will increase their fluency to any extent and 'curing stuttering' does not seem to occur by participation in a SHO [Self-Help Organization]." Borkman states that

> the important implication of these findings for the SHO as an organization is that the club which develops modest but attainable goals for its members and does not emphasize increasing fluency or curing stuttering as possible outcomes of participation in the organization is more likely to continue and to satisfy its members than if more ambitious and relatively unattainable goals of fluency or curing stuttering are promulgated in the organization. In the latter case members develop high expectations which are frequently not realized, disillusionment and dissatisfaction are then likely, followed by discontinuation or dropout from participation (23:29).

Lenneberg and Rowbotham say that "ileostomy groups grew up simultaneously in a number of American cities in the early 1950's when ileostomy surgery had been employed with some frequency for five or six years. While good health was being restored to most patients, rehabilitation was lagging behind because hospital personnel were obviously unable to solve the patients' practical problems and were returning them to home and community with many unanswered questions and often unmanageable problems of daily existence. . . . Necessity drove patients to consult one another for advice on keeping one's self clean and functioning in daily pursuits. . . . It was very quickly obvious to surgeons that their patients were not only learning a great deal from mutual exchange on practical matters, they also seemed no longer to feel alone and therefore were less unhappy with their new 'plumbing.' . . .

Surgeons were responsible for bringing these morale boosters into the hospital for visits to new and prospective patients to give visible evidence of the success of rehabilitation through ileostomy to the despondent patient" (120:76).

A Vehicle to Aid Coping with Life-Cycle Transitions

At the other end of the continuum from societies of deviants, mutual help organizations are seen in the literature as vehicles to aid in coping with life-cycle transitions, such as widowhood, becoming a parent, and marital separation.

Hansell, in an informal report on La Leche League, a mutual help group of women who want to learn how to include breast-feeding in their mothering, says that

> the local La Leche League groups are an example of a self-help group useful to its members, usually for several weeks to several months. It is not a type of group in which an individual expects to spend years or a lifetime. It is focused on an important problem in a particular segment of the life-cycle. As such, it is oriented around a discrete body of pertinent information and techniques. It facilitates formation of a small-group support system critical to the success of the transmission and use of the information. It gives encouragement and support to women who would not otherwise take the minority path of breast-feeding in a social context where most friends, neighbors and mothers don't know how to assist (80:5).

Mutual help programs can also provide access to new social roles. In two papers (2, 3), Abrahams describes this element in the operation of a widowed service line, in which the volunteers who provided information and support were themselves widowed: "[Many callers were] looking for new ways to reengage in the social system, find new roles and build a new network of social relationships.... Embarking on such a role [helping] can be a turning point that leads toward the development of a new life-style bringing the satisfaction and care for and commitment to others" (2:57, 61). She found that "the dynamics of mutual helping are constantly fluid and both helper and seeker of help move into new roles and find opportunities for healthy personal growth" (3:246). Harris in a study of Parents Without Partners says, "The *raison d'être* of PWP is the fact that, despite the frequency of divorce, separation, and early widowhood in contemporary America, many single parents and their children find themselves socially isolated. The adults no longer fit into married society.... Neither are they altogether at ease among single people.... All the normal problems of parenthood weigh more heavily on the single parent" (82:93-94). Harris points out that

> as individuals, PWP members are in many different stages of solution of their problem, both emotional and practical. At any given observation point, some will

be in a state of shock at the trauma of the experience which has left them partnerless. Others will be well adjusted to the circumstances of single parenthood, having worked out a satisfactory *modus vivendi* for themselves and their children. The rest will be moving unevenly between these extremes, some heading for a good adjustment, others groping, or at an impasse which may or may not be temporary (82:97).

In a paper presented at a national meeting on emergency mental health services, Silverman and Murrow define a critical life transition as "(1) ... a series of events, which can be disequilibrating, and which can tap the individual's ability to cope. (2) It is a period of time in which a process takes place that has a beginning and an end, and during which the individual does the 'work of transition.' The transition involves a turning point for the individual which usually means a status change necessitating a redefinition of the role he performs in his social network" (183:3-4). Silverman and Murrow propose focusing the limited resources available for the development of emergency services on preventive services at these critical transition points in the life-cycle through the encouragement of the development of mutual aid groups and networks.

A Therapeutic Method

Many mutual help organizations can be viewed as vehicles for the practice of certain methods and techniques which they have developed to deal with specific problems. Members' success in these organizations is often viewed by the leaders of the organization relative to their complete acceptance and practice of these methods. Toch states that

> the social movement's claim that it can help its members is *provable* and frequently *proved.* Although the assumption that the movement's techniques are the best means to this end is usually *false,* it is a *useful* assumption, because it increases the confidence of its members. What could be correctly claimed is that *every social movement which enables its members to solve their problems must incorporate features that are essential to its effectiveness.* Although it may not be the only road to Rome, it does know the way. Possibly *despite* dogmatically defended arbitrary variations, every effective movement provides the necessary support for the efforts of its members (197:83).

Thus AA's Twelve Steps (63, 158) (adopted or amended by other groups such as Gamblers Anonymous, Overeaters Anonymous, etc.), the Recovery method and language (207), the Weight-Watchers' recipe (68, 213) plan, La Leche League's instructions (80, 116, 183), and the Synanon game (184, 217) become the means by which sobriety is achieved, nervousness controlled, weight loss accomplished, successful breastfeeding practiced as an expression of biologic femininity and meaningful parenting, and character reformed.

Adler and Hammett view self-help groups as extensions of the Maxwell Jones concept of therapeutic community "in its broadest aspect, i.e., the utilization of the social milieu as a major instrument of change" (4:862).

They postulate that all therapeutic systems, including psychoanalysis as well as therapeutic communities, build on the individual's needs for attachment to a group system and the change process can be generically stated as:

> ... progression from "disease" through "cure" ... involving first crisis, then conversion, and finally cult formation. We believe that just as the group system may be the generic therapeutic agent, the crisis-conversion-cult formation sequence may be a common therapeutic pattern for a significant attitudinal change (4:863).

Hurvitz, in a paper very sympathetic to self-help groups, sees them, in an ideal type, as a "fellowship or movement which attempts to foster maximum interaction and mutual assistance between peers, which requires complete self-revelation, and which affords the members the opportunity for mobility within their fellowship or movement as they overcome their common problems or inappropriate behavior" (93:43). He focuses primarily on these groups as a form of psychotherapy. Indeed, he calls them PSHPG – Peer Self-Help Psychotherapy Groups. Condensed in part from Hurvitz's material[20] on these groups as a form of group therapy, Dean (44) develops approximate comparisons of self-help group therapy vis-à-vis orthodox psychotherapy:

Orthodox Psychotherapy	Self-Help Group Therapy
1. Professional, authoritative therapist.	Non-professional leaders, group parity.
2. Fee.	Free.
3. Appointments and records.	None.
4. Therapy-oriented milieu (psychiatrist's office, clinic, etc.)	Non-therapy oriented milieu (church rooms, communitty centers, etc.)
5. No family confrontation.	Family encouraged.
6. Psychiatrist is presumed normal, does not identify with patient.	Peers are similarly afflicted, identify with each other.
7. Therapist is not a role model, does not set personal examples.	Peers are role models, must set examples for each other.
8. Therapist is non-critical, nonjudgmental, neutral, listens.	Peers are active, judgmental, supportive, critical, talk.
9. Patients unilaterally divulge to therapist, disclosures are secret.	Peers divulge to each other, disclosures are shared.

[20]N. Hurvitz, "Similarities and differences between peer self-help psychotherapy groups and professional psychotherapy." Presented at the 76th annual convention of the American Psychological Association, September 1, 1968, San Francisco, California.

Orthodox Psychotherapy	Self-Help Group Therapy
10. Patients expect only to *receive* support.	Patients must also *give* support.
11. Concerned about sympton substitution if underlying causes are not removed.	Urges appropriate behavior, not concerned about sympton substitution.
12. Accepts disruptive behavior and sick role, absolves patient, blames cause.	Rejects disruptive behavior and sick role, holds member responsible.
13. Therapist does not aim to reach patient at "gut level."	Peers aim to reach each other at "gut level."
14. Emphasis on etiology, insight.	Emphasis on faith, willpower, self-control.
15. Patient's improvement is randomly achieved.	Patient's behavior is planfully achieved.
16. Therapist-patient relationship has little direct community impact.	Peers' intersocial involvement has considerable community impact.
17. Everyday problems subordinated to long-range cure.	Primary emphasis on day-to-day victories: another day without liquor or drugs, another day without panic, etc.
18. Extra curricular contact and socialization with psychiatrist discouraged.	Continuing support and socialization available.
19. Lower cumulative dropout percentage.	Higher dropout percentage.
20. Patient cannot achieve parity with psychiatrist.	Members may themselves become active therapists. (44:73-74)

Zusman, on the other hand, proposes "no-therapy" as the name for the activities which go on in groups and settings like Alcoholics Anonymous and Synanon, which are not labeled therapeutic but which help people deal with problems of behavior. Zusman says that "no-therapy is essentially a method of suppressing symptoms and encouraging conformity. It does not deal directly with 'inner life' – the thoughts and feelings of an individual. It is useful where the character or severity of symptoms is such that there is a great risk of social disability if symptoms continue, and where a disturbed 'inner life' is either a comparatively minor problem or is not a problem at all" (220:486).

SOME CHARACTERISTICS OF MUTUAL HELP GROUPS IN THE LITERATURE

Some authors provide summaries of some features of self-help groups as distinct entities (11, 15, 18, 44, 81, 93, 94, 96, 106, 125, 138, 164, 181, 197, 202, 220). Some authors, in describing the effectiveness of a self-help or mutual help group in dealing with the problems of its members, give emphasis to the power of one or more of the characteristics of the group or its processes.

Common Experience of Members

Katz says that "the fact of sharing a central problem ... defines membership status in self-help groups, despite many individual differences. A peer in a self-help group thus has a commonality or mutuality of problems with others" (106:54). Silverman believes that among the primary characteristics of self-help groups are "that the caregiver has the same disability as the carereceiver; that a recipient of service can change roles to become a caregiver; and all policy and program is decided by a membership whose chief qualification is that they at one time qualified and were recipients of the services of the organization" (177:547).

Pomeroy writes that "there is one group of people who can talk to parents of the victims of SDS as no one else can. These are people who have experienced this same loss. No one else can say to a parent, 'I *know* how you feel now, but time will help'. The Washington Association for Sudden Infant Death Study is a lay organization, made up mostly of parents who have lost an infant due to SDS and have a keen interest in helping others.... One mother said, 'They made me turn my thoughts outward to others, instead of inward to myself. I knew they understood my feelings – bitter or otherwise' " (150:1890).[21] Bassin states that "the change agent most likely to be effective with a junkie is another addict who has made a commitment to change himself, one who is prepared to use himself as a role model and become *involved* with his 'brother'. When a professional therapist attempts to communicate with the addict, he is simply turned off with: 'This dumb bastard doesn't know what he is talking about. He doesn't know the scene. He's never been there' " (14:49).[22] Ablon, in her study of an organization which was formed to help the families of alcoholics, says, "Many persons come into Al-Anon thinking that they alone have suffered these 'unique' experiences. Recognition of the universality of these problems and the finding of a safe arena in which to talk about their own feelings and modes of handling the problems are of utmost importance in the Al-Anon experience" (1:38).

[21]Quoted with permission from the *American Journal of Nursing.* Copyright 1969 by the American Journal of Nursing Company.

[22]Reprinted with permission of *Psychology Today* magazine. Copyright ©1968 by Ziff-Davis Publishing.

Mutual Help and Support

Wechsler says that "the distinctive philosophy and method of Recovery facilitates establishing a particular type of role for the member. The first aspect of this role relates to the fact that the individual is a member of a group which meets regularly in order to provide mutual aid. Each member has certain obligations toward his fellow members and in return has certain expectations about their behavior toward him. He is expected to show concern about the condition and progress of other members, to provide them with support and acceptance, and to help them in the 'correct' application of the Recovery method. He has expectations that others will act toward him in a similar manner. Because of the mutual aid quality of Recovery, the group feels helped by any individual's successes or harmed by any individual's failures" (207:303). Abrahams, in analyzing styles of helping by widow volunteers in a Widow Service Line, found that "the style of helping that each volunteer may develop varies according to his own needs and the satisfactions he seeks from the mutual helping relationship. Variations in styles of helping range from a style approximating the professional/client type of relationship to a style approximating friendship, as social distance diminishes between helper and recipient of help, and as the area of mutual two-way sharing of emotional input increases" (3:257).

Lenneberg and Rowbotham say that the successful ex-patient can exemplify a good outcome for the patient currently suffering from a hazardous or stigmatized condition:

> Reassurance and goals for both the patient and the caretakers are established when the ex-patient appears in person; his degree of success becomes temporarily the model.
>
> Access to such a model promotes the visualization of the self with the condition, and when the model has been successful, positive identification can take place in the patient. Conversely, if the model has not been successful, negative identification may be established, or the model may not be accepted. This mechanism of the psyche, which happens in all human situations, is the root of mutual aid between troubled and previously troubled people (120:81).

They go on to outline a progression of helping, with mutual exchange at the core of each stage:

> Principle 1. Contact between two individuals with a common problem. Its crux is identification.
>
> Principle 2. Expansion of the identification with another individual into identification with a group: passive acceptance of the program.
>
> Principle 3. Expansion of group identification into identification with its program: active participation (120:81).

People participate in one or more of these stages according to individual need and personal preference.

The Helper Principle

Riessman, recognizing the widespread use of people to help others who share a common problem with them, enunciated the "helper" therapy principle to call attention to the idea that it may be the helper who benefits most from the exchange. He says that "perhaps, then, social work's strategy ought to be to devise ways of creating more helpers! Or, to be more exact, to find ways to transform *recipients* of help into *dispensers* of help, thus reversing their roles, and to structure the situation so that recipients of help will be placed in roles requiring the giving of assistance" (157:28). Skovolt, seeking to describe and explain the helper therapy principle, summarizes the benefits received from helping as: "(1) the effective helper often feels an increased level of interpersonal competence as a result of making an impact on another's life, (2) the effective helper often feels a sense of equality in giving and taking between himself or herself and others, (3) the effective helper is often the recipient of valuable personalized learning acquired while working with a helpee, and (4) the effective helper often receives social approval from the people he or she helps." Skovolt hypothesizes that all four factors, rather than any one, make the helper therapy principle potent (185:62).

Cressey, in discussing the social psychological foundations for using criminals in the rehabilitation of criminals, talks of making the criminal who is the agent of change the *target* of change. In a process he calls "retroflexive reformation," he says that

> it is my hypothesis that such success as has been experienced by Alcoholics Anonymous, Synanon, and even "official" programs like institutional group therapy and group counseling programs is attributable to the requirement that the reformee perform the role of the reformer, thus enabling him to gain experience in the role which the group has identified as desirable (40:56).

Frederickson's report on a smoking withdrawal program states that "the most meaningful reinforcement comes, however, to those ex-smokers who accept assignments as volunteer staff. . . . Smokers seem to intuit that in accepting responsibility for helping others break the habit, they will bring into play a highly effective means of reinforcing their own non-smoking behavior" (55:89).[23]

Weiss, in his study of Parents Without Partners, found that "both men and women sometimes found that contribution to the organization through service in administrative or planning roles supported their own sense of worth. Leaders referred to this phenomenon by saying 'The more you put into PWP, the more you get out of it'." Because PWP seemed to recognize that "helping" was therapeutic, it maintained many divisions and programs responsible for their own activities: "This administrative fragmentation

[23]Reprinted from the *International Journal of Addictions,* with permission from Marcel Dekker, Inc.

made it possible for an administrative position to be offered to almost any member who wanted one, if not as a director of a division, than as a program coordinator or other functionary within one" (210:323-324).

Differential Association

Using Sutherland's theory of differential association[24] and general symbolic interactionist theory, Cressey in a 1955 article (39) elaborated a set of principles for changing behavior by changing the group, and discussed its implications for rehabilitation of criminals. The principles were designed in part to show that sociology could contribute nonpsychiatric theory useful to practitioners in the prevention of crime and the rehabilitation of criminals. In 1963, Volkman and Cressey found Synanon (204) an in-nature example of Cressey's principles in action formulated in the earlier article.

Cressey's principles dealing with the use of anticriminal groups as media of change are:

1. If criminals are to be changed, they must be assimilated into groups which emphasize values conducive to law-abiding behavior and, concurrently, alienated from groups emphasizing values conducive to criminality. Since our experience has been that the majority of criminals experience great difficulty in securing intimate contacts in ordinary groups, special groups whose major common goal is the reformation of criminals must be created. . . .
2. The more relevant the common purpose of the group to the reformation of criminals, the greater will be its influence on the criminal members' attitudes and values. . . .
3. The more cohesive the group, the greater the members' readiness to influence others and the more relevant the problems of conformity to group norms. The criminals who are to be reformed and the persons expected to effect the change must then have a strong sense of belonging to one group: between them there must be a genuine "we" feeling. The reformers, consequently, should not be identifiable as correctional workers, probation or parole officers, or social workers. . . .
4. Both reformer and those to be reformed must achieve status within the group by exhibition of "pro-reform" or anti-criminal values and behavior patterns. . . .
5. The most effective mechanism for exerting group pressures on members will be found in groups so organized that criminals are induced to join with noncriminals for the purpose of changing other criminals. A group in which criminal A joins with some non-criminals to change criminal B is probably most effective in changing A, not B; in order to change criminal B, criminal A must necessarily share the values of the anticriminal members (39:118-119).[25]

Goldwyn, in her study of Weight Watchers, focuses on WW as an

[24]E. H. Sutherland, *Principles of Criminology* (New York: Lipincott, 1947).

[25]D. Cressey: *American Journal of Sociology* 61(1):116–120, 1955. Copyright 1956 by the University of Chicago.

example of joint action with special attention given to the changes in self-concepts of the different types of members. She uses Lofland's[26] concepts of normal-smith groups, pivotal normals, and pivotal deviants: "Lofland is touching upon the process of continual reinforcement of a normal identity through the members' interaction within the group. His description stresses the reinforcement in self-concepts of normality that the relatively recently-arrived members receive from the newest members which hastens their separation from commitment to their previous deviant identities. What completes the circle of reinforcement is that in attributing such normality to everyone else in the setting, the newest members are giving great validity to these others. While this reinforces the latter's definitions of themselves as successful and normal, it also increases the significance of the definitions of normality that the newest members are receiving from them" (68:158-159).

Collective Will Power and Belief

Frank, in roughly dividing group therapies into directive groups (including AA and Recovery) and evocative or free-interaction groups, says that the "persuasive power of therapy groups resides basically in the tendency of each person to look to others for validation of his feelings and attitudes" (53:288).

Hansell found in looking at TOPS that part of its group philosophy is that "everyone can lose weight. With the decision, will power, stick-to-itiveness, concentration of energies on it, with the help of friends and TOPS members, one can achieve and maintain a target weight."

> They constantly correct each other, looking for "hocus-pocus methods" or "blue-sky schemes." They establish "reducing pals" to assist each other. There are rituals in which the members stand in a circle and covenant each other to assist in their purposes. They watch over any person who makes headway and then stops for any reason. They assist each other when an individual waivers in resolve, challenging him to re-commit himself to a decision of extraordinary importance. They give each other what they term "will-power booster shots" (79:4).

Toch, describing a Recovery meeting, says, "The stream of vignettes that pours forth around the table reiterates that Recovery works. And each member, by providing examples, *constitutes an example himself.* His victorious presence contributes to the resolution of his peers and builds the determination of novices and laggards. Conversely, group reactions to examples reinforce the convictions of the narrator. As he is endorsed for having applied the prescribed techniques, he becomes less prone to question their validity."

> The Recovery group is thus a concentrated pep rally, which sustains each member's enthusiasm in solving his problems. Between meetings, the member fights

[26] J. Lofland, *Deviance and Identity* (Englewood Cliffs, N. J.: Prentice-Hall, 1969).

his battles in confidence, knowing that success is almost inevitable. He knows that he is in possession of weapons he can use with *absolute trust.* Although his own goals may be uncertain, and his own experience may deceive him, the unanimity of his group and the univocacy of their reports provide incontrovertible evidence. The ritual has become indistinguishable from spontaneous unanimity (197:80).

Importance of Information

Barish states that, in self-help groups, "the use of education is important. Here education refers to the promotion of greater factual understanding of the problem condition, as opposed to intrapsychic understanding. Education is generally directed at the general public, but it is very often offered to the members of the self-help groups as well. Some groups are formed purely for the purpose of educating the public and themselves about their problem" (11:1167).[27]

Information, including both technical and anticipatory guidance on expectable problems and phases or transitions, is an important element in almost all mutual help organizations. What constitutes "help" is often a new definition of the problem and specific information about practicalities learned through experience and shared with others because it "works." This kind of information is usually not readily available from books, professionals, or formal caregiving institutions. Silverman in describing the Widow-to-Widow Program says that "help comes, not only from understanding but also in being able to give specific directions and have real alternatives available to offer the widowed individual."

> Education for these women is not an academic process. They need concrete direction to find their way out of the house and get involved in new activities. For the younger women this may mean learning to drive and getting a job. For the older women it is finding ways into car pools, learning what resources are available and where their talents and energies can be used. The aide encourages, prods, insists, and sometimes even takes the widow by the hand and goes through the motions with her. . . . The aide, then, is a teacher, a bridge person . . . and is instrumental in helping the widow repeople her life to find new roles for herself (179:101).

Ladas hypothesized that women, with support and information of the type given by La Leche League, would have a better outcome in regard to breastfeeding than those women who lacked them. She found that her hypotheses were confirmed and that "information relates to outcome of breastfeeding. Support relates to outcome. Any combination of information and support relates more highly to outcome than either alone. Some support, even with opposition, is as effective as much support" (115:2). Silverman and Murrow found that LLL gave information and help about preparation

[27]Herbert Barish: Self-help groups. In *Encyclopedia of Social Work* (New York: National Association of Social Workers, 1971). Quoted with permission.

for the birth of the child; handling problems in the hospital; understanding the period of exhaustion following the birth of the baby; preparation and support in facing the difficulties of the sudden, full-time task of motherhood; physical preparation for nursing; physical problems of the mother; physical problems of the baby; social-economic problems of the mother; behavior of the baby; and generalized feelings of guilt and anxiety (183:15–22).

The ileostomy patient, when he is ready to leave the hospital, is informed by his visitor (who is also an ostomate) about the program and services of the ostomy groups. Lenneberg and Rowbotham observe that

> at his first group meeting he will see that not only his model has solved the problems, others have also achieved success. From the group he learns further attitudes with regard to specific problems, and he gets group know-how. Professional speakers come and educate him; the appliance chairman gives him information; he is in ileostomy school (120:84).

Bailey in a study of Al-Anon found that "Al-Anon members most frequently volunteered that they had learned about alcoholism as an illness and had gained some understanding of themselves and their own behavior in relation to their husbands' drinking. Although these responses, especially about alcoholism, also appeared fairly often in relation to the Alcoholism Information Center, their frequency was negligible among the descriptions of contacts with other resources [physician, psychiatrist, clergyman, lawyer, court, family agency]" (10:73). In another study of Al-Anon, Ablon says that "Al-Anon basically is not an interprocess group, nor does it focus on 'here and now' relationships within the group. To the contrary, there is a minimum of direct personal confrontation or conflict between members. Each individual brings up only those issues that she cares to discuss" (1:37).

> My research suggests that the imparting of information in its own specialized form is the most prominent process element in the Al-Anon experience. The sharing and exchange of strategies for and reactions to common problems provides alternatives for the new member to consider, to choose for use if she wishes, or to reject. The very act of consideration of these as presented by others provides a basis for graphic comparison with her own typical modes of operation, and the stimulation for the process of self-examination leading to new insights (1:39).

Ablon sees this process in Al-Anon groups as "education by alternatives" (1:38).

Constructive Action Toward Shared Goals

Barish says that in self-help organizations "the use of activity is common and necessary, whether it is social action, socializing, working, or the like.... These activities help overcome passivity and enhance self-esteem as well as encourage a greater sense of personal responsibility. The emphasis is upon 'doing' rather than upon intellectual pursuits or emotional cathartic release" (11:1167).[28]

Toch states that "one service every self-change movement seems to provide is to build a fire under its members by stressing the intolerability of their fate. By spelling out the undesirable consequences of the member's condition, the movement defines his problem. The result is *to reinforce the member's conviction that he must take action.* The next step is to demonstrate that action is feasible, and that the goal *is attainable.*" He says that self-help groups, as a social movement to collectively promote individual change,

> ... *retain their members on the road toward the goal.* They accomplish this through *incentives* and *encouragement.* Members are made aware of their progress through concrete indicators or achievement (such as weight charts in TOPS, and Recovery endorsement). It is also a general practice to rebuke more or less sympathetically any member who strays. Lastly, the progress of the whole group provides each member with *norms* against which he can gauge his own achievement (197:83-84).

Katz says that "*personal involvement* becomes a requirement in all self-help groups, with activity and personal engagement the keystones in defining membership. Thus, in contrast to most social agencies and many organizations, the concept of membership does not fully include members who are mere passive recipients or financial supporters. Each member is expected to involve himself in and to work for the good of the group to his best capacity at the time. . . . Groups are action-oriented, their philosophy being that members learn by doing and are changed by doing" (106:55). In contrast, Aldrich describes Mensa, an organization of persons of high intelligence, as a sociable organization. He says that "new members come to meetings with a wide variety of interests, and this heterogeneity of interests prevents Mensa from becoming a goal-directed interest group. The process, once begun, is self-sustaining. New members come into a situation defined as a sociable one, and find themselves caught up in the maintenance of sociability. The roles they are required to play constrain their behavior into channels of activity that pose no danger to Mensa's sociable nature" (5:437).

Shatan, writing about the Vietnam veteran's struggle for reintegration in American life, says, "To men who have been steeped in death and evil beyond imagination, a 'talking cure' alone is worthless. And merely sharing their grief and outrage with comrades in the same dilemma is similarly unsatisfying. Active participation in the public arena, active opposition to the very war policies they helped carry out, was essential. By throwing onto the steps of Congress the medals with which they were rewarded for murder in a war they had come to abhor, the veterans symbolically shed some of their guilt. In addition to their dramatic political impact, these demon-

[28]Herbert Barish: Self-help groups. In *Encyclopedia of Social Work* (New York: National Association of Social Workers, 1971). Quoted with permission.

strations have profound therapeutic meaning. Instead of acting under orders, the vets originated actions on their own behalf to regain the control over events – over their lives – that was wrested from them in Vietnam" (175:648-649). Bender, in describing members of self-help groups and their activities, coins the phrase "emotional activists," "signifying a reversal of the means-end relationship of power and politics. Thus politics becomes a means towards self-awareness and a fuller, freer emotional life for themselves and their 'significant others'" (18:7). This is a point also made by Spiegel (186).

TYPOLOGIES OF MUTUAL HELP GROUPS IN THE LITERATURE

While there is a substantial literature on one or another mutual help organization and certain of its characteristics, relatively few contributions in the literature attempt a typology of these groups either within the mutual help group field itself or in relation to other group activities in the broader mental health arena.

One of the earliest classificatory schemes was developed in 1943 by Thomas in an attempt to understand the then emerging phenomenon of group psychotherapy. In Fig. 2-1, Thomas uses Moore's[29] two main types of psychotherapeutic methods as a means of classifying the various types of therapy used by different workers. In Fig. 2-2, he uses the same ana-

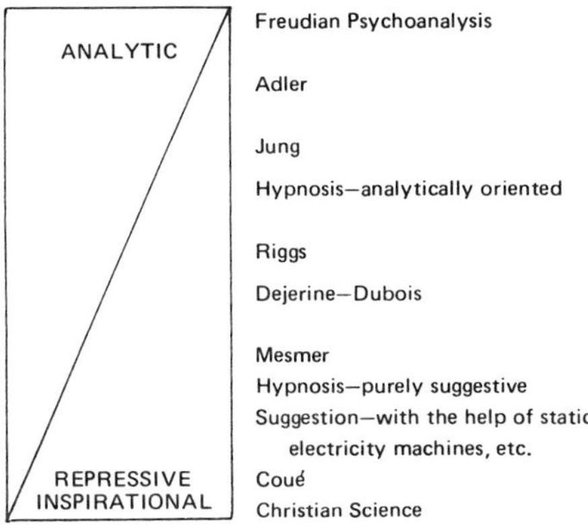

Fig. 2-1. From: G. W. Thomas, "Group Psychotherapy: A Review of the Recent Literature," *Psychosomatic Medicine,* vol. 5, no. 2, April, 1943.

[29] M. Moore, "The Practice of Psychiatry," *Harvard Medical Alumni Bulletin,* vol. 16, no. 53, 1942.

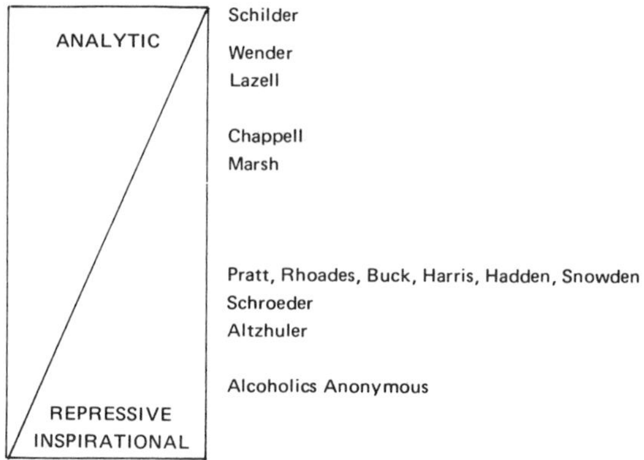

Fig. 2-2. From: G. W. Thomas, "Group Psychotherapy: A Review of the Recent Literature," *Psychosomatic Medicine*, vol. 5, no. 2, April, 1943.

lytic/repressive inspirational schema to classify group psychotherapeutic activities, ranging from AA's organization by the afflicted to help themselves and each other, to Pratt's thought-control classes, to Schilder's more purely psychoanalytic techniques (196:167-168).

More recently, Lieberman suggests four major categories of healing groups:

> At one end of a continuum would be those activities that formally fall within the purview of societally sanctioned, professionally led groups – group psychotherapy. Group therapy has as its avowed public goal the production of mental health and sees as its relevant population those who define themselves as patients experiencing psychological misery. The activities of group therapy operate explicitly within a medical framework. There is emphasis on malfunctioning, defined in terms of "sick behavior," which the client brings into the formally defined system. One implication of this emphasis is that there are individuals within society who would be legitimized as appropriate patients, and those who would be seen as inappropriate.
>
> At the opposite end of the professional continuum are a variety of self-help movements: Alcoholics Anonymous, Synanon, Recovery Inc., etc., up to perhaps as many as 216 separate organizations. By intention these groups are not professionally led. As lay movements, however, they share some notions of appropriate clientele with group psychotherapy. The definition of appropriate clientele is usually much narrower than in group psychotherapy, but there are clear-cut inclusion-exclusion principles. One must be an alcoholic, an abuser of drugs, a child-abuser, a parent of a child who has a particular disease, and so forth. The range for any particular self-help movement's attention is limited to individuals who have a common symptom, problem or life predicament.

A third set of healing groups comes under the rubric of the Human Potential Movement, including such variously labeled activities as sensitivity training, encounter groups, and so on. Although there are many instances of non-professional leaders, these activities usually do involve professionals, whether legitimized by traditional psychological and psychiatric disciplines or by newer types of training institutions. A major distinction between the previously mentioned activities and encounter or growth groups is that the latter view themselves as having universal applicability. Unlike group therapy which emphasizes patienthood, or self-help programs which emphasize a common problem, the encounter movement emphasizes that its activities are relevant to all who want to change, grow, and develop.

Finally, we come to consciousness-raising groups, which share with self-help groups the non-professional orientation and peer control, but, unlike the self-help groups, have broad criteria for inclusion. Although they do not take in everyone, as does the Human Potential Movement, consciousness-raising groups are formed on the basis of certain general demographic similarities: sex, race, ethnicity, age, or sexual behavior. The tie that binds is not a common syndrome but a general characteristic of a large subgroup of people, and permits wide latitude regarding personal particularities (125:101-102).

Within the self-help field itself, Bean and Levy have begun the much needed process of developing typologies which discriminate among the various types of groups. Bean, in a monograph on AA, divides all self-help groups into three categories:

First are the groups that help with a crisis: groups of parents who have retarded children, amputees, mastectomy patients, colostomy and ileostomy groups, widows' groups, Parents Without Partners. They give specific information on how to cope with the problem. . . . Such groups see their activities as limited. The need for help, support, and information is initially acute, but later it may lessen. The member may eventually stop using the group altogether, or may participate in the group's work as a helper.

The second type helps people with a permanent, fixed, stigmatized condition. This includes groups for homosexuals, dwarfs, ex-convicts, and former mental patients. These groups help a person deal with the stigma and improve his image of himself; at the same time, they attack prejudice and try to improve the public image of the condition. . . . These groups expect the person to continue using the group as long as he lives or as long as social attitudes condemn him, although individual needs vary.

The third kind of group helps people trapped in a habit, addiction, or self-destructive way of life. It includes weight reduction groups, such as TOPS and Weight Watchers, Alcoholics Anonymous, Synanon, organizations for stutterers and smokers, and Gamblers Anonymous. These groups all undertake to help a person behave differently, and achieve this by offering a wide variety of techniques and aids to change. The person caught in one of these problems needs to make a sweeping reorganization of his life, how he spends his time, his relationships with people, his personality structure and defenses (17:8).

Levy has been funded by the National Institute of Mental Health to look at self-help groups as mental health resources. In his proposal, Levy hypothesizes a preliminary typology according to function:

> Type I. These groups have as their objective some form of conduct reorganization or enhancement of self-control of their members. . . . Typical of this type of self-help group is Alcoholics Anonymous, Gamblers Anonymous, Synanon, TOPS (take off pounds sensibly), and Gateway Houses. . . .
>
> Type II. Members of these groups share a common status or predicament which entails some degree of stress, and the aim of these groups is the amelioration of this stress through mutual support.... Representative of this type of group are the Golden Age Clubs, Parents Without Partners, Recovery, Inc., and parents of terminally ill children.
>
> Type III. These groups might be thought of as survival-oriented, having as their aim providing mutual support for a particular style of life or subculture generally regarded as deviant or subject to various kinds of negative sanctions by the majority in society. Included in this type are the various kinds of support groups organized by homosexuals, womens' liberation groups, black pride and power groups, and some communes....
>
> Type IV. ... The objectives of these groups tend in one way or another to focus on personal growth, self-improvement, character development, and greater joy and effectiveness in living. In contrast with groups of the first three types, few of these groups have any degree of national representation and their underlying philosophy tends to vary from one locale to another. An exception to this local character of groups of this type are the Integrity Groups, whose development has been fostered by O. H. Mowrer... and Koinonia, a religious fellowship of youth found in some communities and apparently growing in popularity (123:14).

As can be seen from these typologies, boundaries are imprecise between mutual help groups and other kinds of group activities, and criteria for inclusion in one or another subtype of mutual help organization are unclear. As more work is done, it may become possible to classify mutual help groups along such parameters, among others, as expressive/social influence; dominance of professional/peer involvement; opportunities for reciprocity in the helping process; cognitive/affective emphasis; time dimensions of member participation; promotion of dependence/autonomy; emphasis on predicaments or character reformation; types of educational, reconstitutive, and social change processes employed; types of links with the formal caregiving professional and institutional network of services.

WORK FOR THE FUTURE

Conceptual and ideal models of mutual help groups which have a high level of abstraction and are widely generalizable are useful for the delineation and development of a new field of inquiry. I suspect, however, that the most productive work will be accomplished by the accumulation of evidence from intensive case studies of specific groups to add to a growing body of fruitful studies (1, 7, 16, 17, 26, 68, 115, 190, 191, 207, 209, 210). In addition, surveys of different kinds of mutual help organizations, locally, regionally, and nationally, are needed. Among the few such surveys reported are: Wechsler on ex-patient organizations (206, 207); Borkman on a study of twenty stutterers' self-help organizations in the United States and some other countries (23, 24, 25, 26); Grosz on 500 Recovery groups (72); Traunstein and Steinman on an exploratory study of all the self-help organizations they could identify in one medium-sized city (198). Gussow and Tracy have underway a survey of self-help health organizations (73, 74, 75); Levy is studying self-help groups as a mental health resource (123). The National Institute of Mental Health is currently sponsoring a comprehensive survey, under the direction of Marcia Guttentag of Harvard University, of the use by women of mental health services, including AA, Weight Watchers, Recovery, Inc. etc. NIMH is also sponsoring a monograph by Phyllis Silverman of Harvard Medical School on mutual help groups, and possible relationships with professionals and community mental health centers. On the basis of the results of studies such as these, comparative studies between organizations in different parts of this country and in other countries may be possible along typological parameters.

Self-help and mutual help take many forms, and these forms probably change from era to era (69). Perhaps most important is the need for historical studies which would provide us with information about the intellectual traditions, the social and political forces which impinge on specific persons with needs, who take significant action culminating in the development of a particular helping service. For instance, Alcoholics Anonymous is the product of many diverse influences. Glaser[30] has developed a geneology of the drug-free therapeutic community through Synanon to AA, influenced by the Oxford Group Movement. No one has as yet gone beyond this to examine the nineteenth-century evangelical and pietistic traditions, largely lay-directed and anti-intellectual, of American life which developed much of the substantive content and techniques later incorporated into AA via Buchmanism. In addition, the parallel developments of the temperance movement, prohibition, the repeal of prohibition, the emergence of AA, and the Rockefeller family involvement in all four movements are important to elucidate. Maxwell has shown that all of the alcoholism reform movements in the United States and Great Britain – Father Mathew's Movement in the 1840s, the Washingtonian Movement in the 1840s, the Reform Club Movement in the 1870s and 1880s, the Catch-My-Pal Movement beginning in 1909, and AA beginning in 1935 – have common characteristics: testimonials of past experience and recovery; public commitment to total abstinence (modified by AA); reliance upon a power greater than self; organized local groups meeting weekly to provide social support; and in all but Father

[30]F. B. Glaser, "Some Historical Aspects of the Drug-Free Therapeutic Community," the *American Journal of Drug and Alcohol Abuse,* vol. 1, no. 1, 1974.

Mathew's Movement, alcoholics working with other alcoholics (134:98-99). Understanding the factors in the rise and fall of such movements contributes to an appreciation of the factors inherent in the development and organizational maintenance of Alcoholics Anonymous, the most recent manifestation. Other mutual help groups may have developed, and indeed probably did develop, out of other historical conditions. Pratt's TB groups in 1905 (153) and his "thought-control" classes in 1931 (152) emerged, not in the community or in response to a social problem per se, but in a hospital out of a physician's need to use his time efficiently in the development of a new form of service, an outpatient department, and to help poor, chronic patients to help themselves to follow medical advice. These groups were quickly followed by the development of others, organized by other physicians, for patients with hypertension, for diabetes patients, and for malnourished children in schools and their mothers. The support system and mutual help elements of these groups were submerged into, and in some cases lost in, other newly developing, competing systems of care such as the Emmanuel Movement, psychoanalysis, the health education movement, group psychotherapy, and in the burgeoning mental health professions and institutions. In stressing the need for such studies, I am not talking about a *Zeitgeist* view of history, where things seem to happen spontaneously, but a multifactorial analysis which takes into account psychological factors, charismatic leadership, and chance, as well as economic, political, historical, and other social forces.

When all is said and done, what is it that members actually get from mutual help groups? How is what they get different from what professionals offer? Who joins; how do they get there; why do some leave and some stay; how does one move from being helped to being a helper? How many make this move? A journalistic, natural history approach to the study of the ante, present, and post careers of individual members of different types of mutual help groups would be very useful. What is the meaning of money in mutual help groups and the absence of its exchange in most groups? How are the self-labeling, self-reconstitution processes described by Rotenberg (160) and Sarbin and Adler (165) applied? Additional work is needed to amplify the reports on these processes in such studies as Trice and Roman on redefinition and relabeling in AA (200) and Borkman on the emergence of stutterers' self-help organizations as a result of the development of a destigmatizing philosophy of stuttering by a core group of influential professionals (26). Concomitant with the redefinition and relabeling processes, there seems to be a redefinition of what constitutes help and a restructuring of how help is given, through different instrumentalities and by different kinds of helpers. How does this come about? Are people with problems better served?

Organizational analyses which look at constituencies, internal and external communication, finances, committee structure and group processes over time would contribute invaluable information. What are the patterns and phases of organizational development? What is the relationship of charismatic leadership to the functions of the groups and the kinds of help given and received? Work such as Sussman's on groups that fail may be particularly useful (192, 193). More studies, such as Segal's on associations of parents of retarded children, of the impact of some self-help groups on public policy are needed (171).

Studies should be undertaken which use techniques comparable to the textual analysis of literary criticism to look at the records, documents, news releases, newsletters, etc., which most mutual aid organizations produce in abundance, to assess how they view themselves, and what they offer. We may be dealing here not so much with revolution as evolution, with the concern for continuity and the transmutation of the useful past and its traditions as much as with dramatic change.

The rhetoric, of almost mythic proportions, surrounding mutual help groups proclaims independence from professionals and formal caregiving institutions. The evidence may actually be different. For instance, Recovery, Inc., was started by a psychiatrist, Abraham Low (127, 128, 129); Phyllis Silverman, a social worker, organized the Widow-to-Widow program (177); Borkman found that most successful stutterers' self-help organizations were co-founded by speech therapists, some of whom were ex-stutterers, who continued their involvement for some time, and most unsuccessful stutterers' self-help organizations did not have speech therapists involved (23:15; 26:3); in their survey of self-help organizations, Traunstein and Steinman found that approximately 31 percent of the groups they studied were initiated in cooperation with professionals and other nonstigmatized persons (198); the success of AA in its early days depended heavily on publicized endorsements by prominent clergymen, physicians, and psychiatrists. The current interaction patterns between ostomy clubs (120), sudden infant death associations (150), some weight reduction groups (190, 191, 205), and professionals and caregiving institutions such as hospitals are very complex and need to be charted. In regard to life transitions, Gelfand in an article discussing emerging trends in social treatment, including peer helping, says that "a possible future role for the social practitioner may be the identification of groups of persons in the process of 'becoming,' that is, making transition from one role or status to another. By linking these groups to peer helpers who are aware and sensitive to the difficulties inherent in the transitional situation, the social worker will provide a service that should help cushion the shock of change." Gelfand goes on to say that this linkage function by professionals "may be offering the most relevant kind of assistance" (62:157–158). Powell,[31] in offering concrete methods for cooperation, suggests that self-help groups may be viewed by the professional "as self-sufficient programs,

[31]T. J. Powell, "The Uses of Self-Help Groups as Supportive Reference Communities." *American Journal of Orthopsychiatry* 45 (5): 756–764, 1975.

concurrent treatment programs, and as sources of information and users of consultation."

In fact the influence of mutual help groups, and the professions and formal caregiving institutions on each other is probably bidirectional, as occurs in other fields. In reviewing the scholarship on American folk art and its relationship to savant art, Hess says

> . . . folk art does not operate in opposition to savant art, as had been thought, but rather in an intimate, polar relationship, the latter continually feeding and amplifying the folk repertory. And, logically, it becomes evident that the genius of the folk artist does not lie in his creation of new forms from some ideal, uncontaminated source of inspiration, but in how he changes the savant prototype, how he adapts it, simplifying and accentuating its elements to fit new requirements (84:71).

In the field of literature, Northrop Frye in the Norton Lectures (as reported in the *Harvard Gazette,* April 11, 1975:3) describes "a periodic literary cycle that begins when sentimental romance inspires a new development in literature, as 'popular theatre pointed the way to Marlowe and Shakespeare'. The new achievements, however, are 'improved and refined by later traditions until it seems no further improvement is possible. Then the conventions wear out, and literature enters a transitional stage where some of the burdens of the past are thrown off and popular literature, with romance at its center, comes again into the foreground'." Similar processes may be at work in the mutual help and formal caregiving human services field. Along with historical patterns of relationships over time, what is needed are more studies looking at the actual relationship in nature between individual professionals and individual members of mutual help groups; the role of professionals in initiating mutual help groups (2, 3, 91, 179, 188); referral patterns and the kinds of transactions between mutual aid organizations, individual professionals, and formal human service institutions (10, 22, 36, 38, 70, 82, 150, 173, 175). We may then be able to answer Jertson's question, echoing others, "whether direct professional involvement is compatible with the self-help tradition" (96:145). We may also, like Gans in his study of high culture and popular culture (58), come down on the side of pluralism with encouragement for separate, diversified professional and mutual help programs with an appropriate division of resources.

All of these studies should be conducted not in a spirit of colonialism or cooptation but in a manner to promote genuine understanding and to enhance coordinate status collaboration to better help people in need.

SELECTIVE BIBLIOGRAPHY

1. Ablon J: Al-Anon family groups. Am J Psychother 28 (1): 30-45, 1974
2. Abrahams RB: Mutual help for the widowed. Soc Work 17 (5): 54-61, 1972
3. Abrahams RB: Mutual helping: Styles of caregiving in a mutual aid program – The Widowed Service Line, in Caplan G, Killilea M (eds): Support Systems and Mutual Help: Multidisciplinary Explorations. New York, Grune & Stratton, 1976
4. Adler HM, Hammett VO: Crisis, conversion and cult formation: An examination of a common psychological sequence. Am J Psychiatry 130 (8): 861-864, 1973
5. Aldrich HE: The sociable organization: A case study of Mensa and some propositions. Sociol Soc Res 55 (4): 429-441, 1971
6. Alexander J: They "doctor" one another: Recovery, Inc. Saturday Evening Post 225 (23): 31, 182-184, 186, 1952
7. Allon NI: Group Dieting Interaction. Doctoral dissertation, Brandeis University, Waltham, Mass. 1972
8. Allon NI: Group dieting rituals. Trans-Action Society 10 (2): 36-42, 1973
9. Almond R: The Healing Community: Dynamics of the Therapeutic Milieu. New York, Jason Aronson, 1974
10. Bailey MB: Al-Anon family groups as an aid to wives of alcoholics. Soc Work, January 1965, pp 68-74
11. Barish H: Self-help groups, in Encyclopedia of Social Work vol. II, no. 16. New York, National Association of Social Workers, 1971, pp 1163-1169
12. Barr R: "Help houses": Better than doctors for troubled kids? Hosp Physician 7 (3): 63-66, 81-95, 1971
13. Barr R: Doctors ask "help houses": Is coexistence possible? Hosp Physician 7 (4): 83, 87, 90, 93, 1971
14. Bassin A: Daytop Village: On the way up from drug addiction, Stopover or cure? Psychol Today 2: 48-52, 1968
15. Bean M: The healing victim: Peer help groups in America. Boston, Laboratory of Community Psychiatry, Harvard Medical School, 1974 (mimeo), 26 pp
16. Bean M: Alcoholics Anonymous, Part I. Psychiatric Ann 5 (2): 7-61, 1975
17. Bean M: Alcoholics Anonymous, Part II. Psychiatric Ann 5 (3): 7-57, 1975
18. Bender EI: The citizen as emotional activist: An appraisal of self-help groups in North America. Can Ment Health 19 (2): 3-7, 1971
19. Berzon B, Berman S: Gay Growth Groups: A humanistically, peer-directed model. Los Angeles, Gay Community Services Center, 1973 (mimeo), 20 pp
20. Bierer J: Great Britain's therapeutic social clubs. Ment Hosp 13 (4): 205-207, 1962
21. Bluecross and Blueshield of Massachusetts: A Directory of Mutual Help Organizations of Massachusetts, BC-BS, 133 Federal Street, Boston 02106, 1974, 42 pp
22. Boggs EM: Relations of parent groups and professional persons in community situations. Am J Ment Defic 57 (1): 109-115, 1952

23. Borkman T: Ingredients for survival: A profile of stutterers' self-help organizations. Fairfax, Va, George Mason University, 1973 (mimeo), 31 pp
24. Borkman T: Organization of stutterers: Therapeutic benefits perceived by the members of a newly discovered self-help organization. Fairfax, Va, George Mason University, 1973 (mimeo), 31 pp
25. Borkman T: A cross-national comparison of stutterers' self-help organizations. NZ Speech Ther J 29: 6-16, 1974
26. Borkman T: Stutterers' self-help organizations: Emergence of group life among the stigmatized. Alpha Kappa Delta Sociol Res Symp V, Richmond, Va, in press, 1975
27. Borman LD (ed): Explorations in Self-Help and Mutual Aid. Evanston, Center for Urban Affairs, Northwestern University, 1975
28. Buckner HT: Deviant group organizations. Master's thesis, University of California, Berkeley, 1964
29. Bumbalo JA, Young DE: The self-help phenomenon. Am J Nurs 73 (9): 1588-1591,1973
30. Cantril H: The Psychology of Social Movements. New York, John Wiley, 1941, First Science Editions, 1963
31. Caplan G: An outpouring of love for Shirley Temple Black. McCall's, March 1973, pp 48, 50, 52, 54
32. Caplan G: Support Systems and Community Mental Health: Lectures on Concept Development. New York, Behavioral Publications, 1974
33. Caplan G: A study of natural support systems. Boston, Laboratory of Community Psychiatry, Harvard Medical School, 1974 (mimeo), 31 pp
34. Carner C: Now: Clubs for mutual mental help. Today's Health, March 1968, pp 40-41, 72-73
35. Cherkas MS: Synanon Foundation – A radical approach to the problem of addiction. Am J Psychiatry 121: 1065-1068, 1965
36. Clayton PN: Meeting the needs of the single parent family. The Family Coordinator, October 1971, pp 327-336
37. Cohen F: Prescriptive group therapy. J Religion Ment Health 4 (2): 188-194, 1965
38. Cohen SZ: The relationship between Recovery, Inc. and the mental health professions. Chicago, University of Chicago, 1973 (mimeo)
39. Cressey D: Changing criminals: The application of the theory of differential association. Am J Sociol LXI (1): 116-120, 1955
40. Cressey DR: Social psychological foundations for using criminals in the rehabilitation of criminals. J Res Crime Delinquency 2 (2): 49-59, 1965
41. Crosbie PV, Petroni FA, Stitt BG: The dynamics of "corrective" groups. J Health Soc Behav 13: 294-302, 1972
42. Dean SR: Recovery, Inc., Giving psychiatry an assist. Medical Economics, September 2, 1969
43. Dean SR: The role of self-conducted group therapy in psychorehabilitation: A look at Recovery, Inc. Am J Psychiatry 127 (7): 934-937, 1971
44. Dean SR: Self-help group psychotherapy: Mental patients rediscover will power. Int J Soc Psychiatry 17 (1): 72-78, 1971

45. Devall B: Gay liberation: An overview. J Voluntary Action Res 2 (1): 24-35, 1973
46. Dibner SS: Newspaper advice columns as a mental health resource. Community Ment Health J 10 (2): 147-155, 1974
47. Driscoll CB, Lubin AH: Conferences with parents of children with cystic fibrosis. Soc Casework 53 (3): 140-146, 1972
48. Dumont MP: Self-help treatment programs. Am J Psychiatry 131 (6): 631-635, 1974
49. Eglash A: Adults Anonymous. J Criminal Law Criminol Police Sci XLIX: 237-239, 1958
50. Eglash A: Youth Anonymous. Fed Probation, June 1958, pp 47-49
51. Egleson J, Egleson JF: Parents Without Partners. New York, Ace Books, 1961
52. Enomoto JJ: Participation in correctional management by offender self-help groups. Fed Probation 36 (2): 36-37, 1972
53. Frank JD: Persuasion and Healing: A Comparative Study of Psychotherapy. Baltimore, Johns Hopkins University Press, 1973, Revised edition
54. Frank JD: An overview of psychotherapy, in Usdin G (ed): Overview of the Psychotherapies. New York, Brunner-Mazel, 1975, pp 3-21
55. Frederickson DT: The community's response to substance misuse: New York City smoking withdrawal clinic. Int J Addictions 3 (1): 81-89, 1968
56. Frye N: The Secular Scripture: A Study of the Structure of Romance. Cambridge, Charles Eliot Norton Lectures, Harvard University, April 1975
57. Gaddis V, Gaddis M: The Curious World of Twins. New York, Hawthorn Books, 1972
58. Gans HJ: Popular Culture and High Culture: An Analysis and Evaluation of Taste. New York, Basic Books, 1974
59. Gartner A, Kohler M, Riessman F: Children Teach Children. New York, Harper and Row, 1971
60. Gartner A: Consumers as deliverers of service. Soc Work 16 (4): 28-32, 1971
61. Gartner A, Riessman F: The Service Society and the Consumer Vanguard. New York, Harper and Row, 1974
62. Gelfand B: Emerging trends in social treatment. Soc Casework 53 (3): 156-162, 1972
63. Gellman IP: The Sober Alcoholic. New Haven, College and University Press, 1964
64. Gersuny C, Rosengren WR: The Service Society. Cambridge, Schenkman, 1973
65. Ginsberg LH: The mental patient liberation movement. Soc Work 19 (1): 3-4, 103, 1974
66. Glaser F: Gaudenzia, Incorporated: Historical and theoretical background of a self-help addiction treatment program. Int J Addictions 6 (4): 615-626, 1971
67. Glyer J: Diet healing: A case study in the sociology of health. J Nutr Educ 4 (4): 163-166, 1972
68. Goldwyn EN: Weight Watchers: A case study in the negotiation of reality. Doctoral dissertation, University of California, Berkeley, 1970

69. Gosden PHJH: Self-Help: Voluntary Associations in Nineteenth-century Britain. London, B. T. Batsford, Ltd., 1973
70. Gould EP: Special report: The single-parent family benefits in Parents Without Partners, Inc. J Marriage Family XXX (4): 666-671, 1968
71. Grob S: Psychiatric social clubs come of age. Ment Hyg 54 (1): 129-136, 1970
72. Grosz HJ: Recovery, Inc.: A Survey of 500 Groups. Chicago, Recovery, Inc., 1973
73. Gussow Z, Tracy GS: VSHHO (Voluntary Self-Help Health Organizations): A study. Paper presented at SAA, Montreal, April 1972 (mimeo), 10 pp
74. Gussow Z, Tracy GS: A prospectus: Voluntary self-help health organizations: A study in human support systems. New Orleans, Louisiana State University, June 1972 (mimeo), 16 pp
75. Gussow Z, Tracy GS: Voluntary self-help health organizations: A study in human support systems. Progress Report, January-May, 1973 (mimeo), 15 pp
76. Hamburg B, Varenhorst BB: Peer counseling in the secondary schools: A community mental health project for youth. Am J Orthopsychiatry 42 (4): 566-581, 1972
77. Hannum TE, Warman RE: The use of inmate "counselors" in the orientation of new inmates. Corrective Psychiatry J Soc Ther 9 (2): 95-99, 1963
78. Hansell N: Explorations of service methods of a volunteer counseling group. Chicago, Department of Psychiatry, Northwestern University School of Medicine, 1971 (mimeo), 6 pp
79. Hansell N: Study of activities of self-help groups: Take Off Pounds Safely. Chicago, Department of Psychiatry, Northwestern University School of Medicine, 1972 (mimeo), 4 pp
80. Hansell N: Study project on self-help groups: La Leche League, International. Chicago, Department of Psychiatry, Northwestern University Medical School, 1972 (mimeo), 6 pp
81. Hansell N: Reemergence of confidence in mutual help groups, in The Person-in-Distress. New York, Behavioral Publications, in press, 1976
82. Harris ET: Parents Without Partners, Inc.: A resource for clients. Soc Work 11 (2): 92-98, 1966
83. Heming J, Proops M, Rayner C: Agony aunties and their contribution to health education. R Soc Health Educ 92 (5): 246-254, 1972
84. Hess T: Art. New York, February 25, 1974, pp 70-71
85. Hill EJ: Buchman and Buchmanism. Doctoral dissertation, University of North Carolina at Chapel Hill, 1970
86. Ho MK, Norlin JM: The helper principle and the creation of therapeutic milieu. Child Care Q 3 (2): 109-118, 1974
87. Hochschild AR: Community of grandmothers. Doctoral dissertation, University of California, Berkeley, 1969
88. Hochschild AR: The Unexpected Community. Englewood Cliffs, NJ, Prentice-Hall, Inc., 1973
89. Hochschild AR: Communal life-styles for the old. Society 10 (4): 50-57, 1973
90. Holzinger R: Synanon through the eyes of a visiting psychologist. Q J Studies Alcohol 26: 304-339, 1965

91. Houpt JL, Astrachan B, Lipsitch I, et al.: Re-entry groups: Bridging the hospital community gap. Soc Psychiatry 7 (3): 144-149, 1972
92. Humphreys L: Out of the Closet: The Sociology of Homosexual Liberation. Englewood Cliffs, NJ, Prentice-Hall, Inc., 1972
93. Hurvitz N: Peer self-help psychotherapy groups and their implications for psychotherapy. Psychother: Theory, Res Practice 7 (1): 41-49, 1970
94. Hurvitz N: Peer self-help psychotherapy groups: Psychotherapy without psychotherapists, in Roman PM, Trice HM (eds): The Sociology of Psychotherapy. New York, Jason Aronson, 1974, pp 85-141
95. Jacobs RH: Emotive and control groups as mutated new American utopian communities. J Applied Behav Sci 7 (2): 234-251, 1971
96. Jertson JM: Self-help groups. Soc Work 20 (2): 144-145, 1975
97. Jones M, Bonn EM: From therapeutic community to self-sufficient community. Hosp Community Psychiatry 24 (10): 675-679, 1973
98. Jones RK: Sectarian Characteristics of AA. Sociology 4 (3): 181-185, 1970
99. Kanter RM: Commitment and Community: Communes and Utopias in Sociological Perspective. Cambridge, Harvard University Press, 1972
100. Katz AH: Therapeutic aspects of parent associations for the handicapped. 2 pp
101. Katz AH: Parents of the Handicapped. Springfield, Ill, Charles C. Thomas, 1961
102. Katz AH: The role of parent groups in services to mentally retarded. Proc Second Int Congr Ment Retardation, Vienna, 1961, Part II, Basel, S Karger AG, pp 208-211 (1963)
103. Katz AH: Self-help in America. New Society, 45, 8 August 1963, pp 13-15
104. Katz AH: Application of self-help concepts in current social welfare. Soc Work 10 (3): 68-74, 1965
105. Katz AH, Husek J, Macdonald CJ: Self-Help and Rehabilitation: A Selective Annotated Bibliography. Los Angeles, University of California School of Public Health, October 1967 (mimeo), 41 pp
106. Katz AH: Self-help organizations and volunteer participation in social welfare. Soc Work 15 (1): 51-60, 1970
107. Katz AH: Self-help groups. Soc Work 17 (6): 120-121, 1972
108. Kessler S: Treatment of overweight. J Counseling Psychol 21 (5): 395-398, 1974
109. Keyes R: We, The Lonely People: Searching for Community. New York, Harper and Row, 1973
110. Kinzer NS: Fatties unite: The sociology of the diet club. Westville, Indiana, Purdue University, 1974 (mimeo)
111. Knapp VS, Hansen H: Helping the parents of children with leukemia. Soc Work 18 (4): 70-75, 1973
112. Knoepfli HE: The origins of women's autonomous learning groups. Doctoral dissertation, National Library, Ottawa, 1972
113. Kropotkin P: Mutual Aid. Boston, Extending Horizons Books. Reprint of 1914 edition
114. Kuehn WC: The concept of self-help groups among criminals. Criminologica 7 (1): 20-25, 1969

115. Ladas AK: The relationship of information and support to behavior: The La Leche League and breastfeeding. Doctoral dissertation, Columbia University, New York, 1971
116. Ladas AK: Information and social support as factors in the outcome of breastfeeding. J Applied Behav Sci 8 (1): 110-114, 1972
117. Landy D, Singer SE: The social organization and culture of a club for former mental patients. Human Relations 14 (1): 31-41, 1961
118. Lee DT: Recovery, Inc.: Aid in the transition from hospital to community. Ment Hyg 55 (2): 194-198, 1971
119. Lefknowitz N: A case study of a mutual aid society among slum dwellers: Analysis of a therapeutic community. Doctoral dissertation, Columbia University, 1970
120. Lenneberg E, Rowbotham JL: Mutual-aid groups for ileostomy patients, in The Ileostomy Patient. Springfield, Ill, Charles C. Thomas, 1970, pp 74-87
121. Levine M, Levine A: A Social History of the Helping Services: Clinic, Court, School and Community. New York, Appleton-Century-Crofts, Meredith Corporation, 1970
122. Levy JH: A study of parent groups for handicapped children. Except Child 19 (1): 19-26, 1952
123. Levy LH: Self-help groups as mental health resources. Bloomington, Indiana, Indiana University, 1973 (mimeo)
124. Lieber L: Mothers Anonymous: A new direction against child abuse. Paper presented to the 1st Biennial Conference of the Society for Clinical Social Work, San Francisco, 1971
125. Lieberman M: Group therapies, in Usdin G (ed): Overview of the Psychotherapies. New York, Brunner-Mazel, 1975, pp 92-117
126. Lipman JH, Winchester A: The Flowering of American Folk Art 1776-1876. New York, Viking Press, 1974
127. Low AA: Lectures to Relatives of Former Patients. Boston, The Christopher Publishing House, 1943
128. Low AA: Recovery, Inc.: A project for rehabilitating postpsychotic and long-term psychoneurotic patients, in Soden WH (ed): Rehabilitation of the Handicapped. New York, Ronald Press, 1949, pp 213-226
129. Low AA: Mental Health through Will-Training: A system of Self-Help in Psychotherapy as Practiced by Recovery, Inc., Boston, The Christopher Publishing House, 1950
130. Lurie A, Ron H: Self-help in an aftercare socialization program. Ment Hyg 44 (4): 467-472, 1971
131. Madison P: Have grouped, will travel. Psychother: Theory, Practice Res 9 (4): 324-327, 1972
132. Marx JH, Seldin JP: Crossroads of crisis: I. Therapeutic sources and quasi-therapeutic functions of post-industrial communes. J Health Soc Behav 14 (1): 39-50, 1973
133. Marx JH, Seldin JE: Crossroads of crisis; II. Organizational and ideological models for contemporary quasi-therapeutic communes. J Health Soc Behav 14 (2): 183-191, 1973

134. Maxwell MA: Social factors in the Alcoholics Anonymous program. Doctoral dissertation, The University of Texas at Austin, 1949
135. Mcdonald JR: Schizophrenics anonymous: An experiment in group self-help. Master's thesis, St. Patrick's College, University of Ottawa, 1967
136. Mowrer OH: The New Group Therapy. New York, Van Nostrand Reinhold Co., 1964
137. Mowrer OH (ed): Morality and Mental Health. New York, Rand McNally, 1967
138. Mowrer OH: Peer groups and medication, the best "therapy" for professional and laymen alike. Psychother: Theory, Res Practice 8 (1): 44-54, 1971
139. Mowrer OH: Autobiography, in Lindzey G (ed): The History of Psychology in Autobiography. New York, Appleton-Century-Crofts, 1972
140. Mowrer OH: Integrity groups: Basic principles and objectives. Counseling Psychologist 3 (2): 7-32, 1972
141. Murphy A, Pueschel SM, Schneider J: Group work with parents of children with Down's Syndrome. Soc Casework 54 (2): 114-119, 1973
142. Nidetch J: The Story of Weight Watchers. New York, W/W Twenty-First Corporation, 1970
143. Ofshe R et al.: Social structure and social control in Synanon. J Voluntary Action Res 3 (3-4): 67-76, 1974
144. Palmer MB, Hoffman EL: A study of the membership and program of a club for ex-patients of mental hospitals. Ment Hyg 48 (3): 372-379, 1964
145. Parsell S, Tagliareni EM: Cancer patients help each other. Am J Nurs 74 (4): 650-651, 1974
146. Patrick SW: Our way of life: A short history of Narcotics Anonymous, Inc., in Harnus E (ed): Drug Addiction in Youth. London, Pergamon Press, 1965, pp 148-157
147. Patterson SL, Twente E: Older natural helpers: Their characteristics and patterns of helping. Public Welfare 29 (4): 400-403
148. Petrunik MG: Seeing the light: A study of conversion to Alcoholics Anonymous. J Voluntary Action Res 1 (4): 30-38, 1972
149. Phillips J: Alcoholics Anonymous: An Annotated Bibliography 1935-1972. Cincinnati, Central Ohio Publishing Company, Public Library of Cincinnati and Hamilton County, 1973
150. Pomeroy MR: Sudden Death Syndrome. Am J Nurs 69 (9): 1886-1890, 1969
151. Poremba CD: Group probation: An experiment. Fed Probation, September 1955, pp 22-25
152. Pratt JH: The use of Dejerine's methods in the treatment of the common neuroses by group psychotherapy, in Rosenbaum M, Berger M (eds): Group Psychotherapy and Group Function. New York, Basic Books, 1963, pp 123-130
153. Pratt JH: The tuberculosis class: An experiment in home treatment, in Rosenbaum M, Berger M (eds): Group Psychotherapy and Group Function. New York, Basic Books, 1963, pp 111-122
154. Rau N, Rau M: My Dear Ones, Englewood Cliffs, NJ, Prentice-Hall, 1971

155. Ricker GA: The Little People of American. Personnel Guidance J 48 (8): 663-664, 1970
156. Riessman CK: The supply-demand dilemma in community mental health centers. Am J Orthopsychiatry 40 (5): 858-868, 1970
157. Riessman F: The "helper" therapy principle. Soc Work 10: 27-32, 1965
158. Ritchie OW: A sociohistorical survey of Alcoholics Anonymous. Q J Studies Alcohol 9: 119-156, 1948
159. Rosenthal MS, Biase DV: Phoenix Houses: Therapeutic communities for drug addicts. Hosp Community Psychiatry 20: 26-30, 1969
160. Rotenberg M: Self-labeling: A missing link in the "societal reaction" theory of deviance. Sociol Rev 22 (3): 335-354, 1974
161. Rubin B, Eisen SB: The Old Timers' Club: An autonomous patient group in a state mental hospital. Arch Neurol Psychiatry 79: 113-121, 1958
162. Ryback RS: Schizophrenics Anonymous: A treatment adjunct. Psychiatry Med 2: 247-253, 1971
163. Sagarin E: Structure and ideology in an association of deviants. Doctoral dissertation, New York University, 1966
164. Sagarin E: Odd Man In. Chicago, Quadrangle Books, 1969
165. Sarbin TR, Adler N: Self-reconstitution processes: A preliminary report. Psychoanalytic Rev 57 (4): 599-616, 1970-1971
166. Schlesinger AM: Biography of a nation of joiners. Am Historical Rev 1 (1): 1-25, 1944
167. Schwartz EK: Self-help organizations: Lessons to be learned for community psychology, in Reiss BF (ed): New Directions in Mental Health, vol. II. New York, Grune and Stratton, 1968, pp 46-56
168. Scimecca J: Gamblers Anonymous. Master's thesis, New York University, 1965
169. Scodel A: Inspirational group therapy: A study of Gamblers Anonymous. Am J Psychother XVIII: 115-125, 1964
170. Scott D, Goldberg HL: The phenomenon of self-perpetuation in Synanon-type drug treatment programs. Hosp Community Psychiatry 24 (4): 231-233, 1973
171. Segal RM: The associations for retarded children: A force for social change. Doctoral dissertation, Brandeis University, Waltham, 1969
172. Shapiro J: Dominant leaders among slum hotel residents. Am J Orthopsychiatry 39 (4): 644-650, 1969
173. Shapiro JH: Communities of the Alone. New York, Association Press, 1971
174. Sharaf MR: Phoenix House: An interview with Mitchell S. Rosenthal. Seminars in Psychiatry 3 (2): 226-244, 1971
175. Shatan CF: The grief of soldiers: Vietnam combat veterans self-help movement. Am J Orthopsychiatry 43 (4): 640-653, 1973
176. Sheehan VH: Unmasking: Ten Women in Metamorphosis, Chicago, The Swallow Press, 1973
177. Silverman PR: The widow as a caregiver in a program of preventive intervention with other widows: I know what is is like. Let me help you. Ment Hyg 54 (4): 540-547, 1970

178. Silverman PR: Factors involved in accepting an offer of help. Arch Foundation Thanotology 3: 161-171, 1971
179. Silverman PR: Widowhood and preventive intervention. Family Coordinator, January 1972, pp 95-102
180. Silverman P, Mackenzie D, Pettipas M, et al.: Helping Each Other in Widowhood. New York, Health Sciences Publishing, 1973
181. Silverman PR: Preventive Intervention and Mutual Help. NJ, Behavioral Science Tape Library, Signia Information, 1975
182. Silverman PR: Mutual help, in Hirschowitz R (ed): Changing Scene in Community Mental Health. New York, Spectrum Publications, in press, 1976
183. Silverman PR, Murrow HG: Caregivers in critical transitions in the normal life cycle. Paper presented at NIMH Continuing Education Seminar on Emergency Mental Health Services, Washington, DC, June 22, 1973 (mimeo), 31 pp
184. Simon S: The Synanon game. Doctoral dissertation, Harvard University, Cambridge, 1973
185. Skovholt TM: The client as helper: A means to promote psychological growth. Counseling Psychologist 4 (3): 58-64, 1974
186. Spiegel D: Going public and self-help, in Caplan G, Killilea M (eds): Support Systems and Mutual Help: Multidisciplinary Explorations. New York, Grune & Stratton, 1976
187. Spotnitz H: Comparison of different types of group psychotherapy, in Kaplan HI, Sadock BJ (eds): Comprehensive Group Psychotherapy. Baltimore, Williams and Wilkins, 1971 pp 72-103
188. Stichman JA, Schoenberg J: Heart wife counselors. Omega 3 (3): 155-161, 1972
189. Strugnell C: Mutual help groups, in Adjustment to Widowhood and Some Related Problems: A Selective and Annotated Bibliography. New York, Health Sciences Publishing, 1974, Section J, pp 183-195
190. Stunkard A, Levine H, Fox S: A study of a self-help group for obesity: TOPS, in Exerpta Medica International Congress Series #213. Proceedings of the 8th International Congress on Nutrition, Prague, August-September, 1969, pp 223-225
191. Stunkard AJ: The success of TOPS, a self-help group. Postgrad Med, May 1972, pp 143-147
192. Sussman M: The Calorie Collectors: A study of spontaneous group formation, collapse and reconstruction. Soc Forces 34: 351-356, 1956
193. Sussman MB: Psycho-social correlates of obesity: Failure of "Calorie Collectors." J Am Dietetic Assoc 32 (5): 423-428, 1956
194. Sweet RBT: Political and social action in homophile organizations. Doctoral dissertation, University of California, Berkeley, 1968
195. Taft R: A note on the characteristics of the members of MENSA, a potential subject pool. J Soc Psychol 83: 107-111, 1971
196. Thomas GW: Group psychotherapy: A review of the recent literature. Psychosomatic Med 5 (2): 166-180, 1943
197. Toch H: The Social Psychology of Social Movements. New York, Bobbs-Merrill, 1965

198. Traunstein DM, Steinman R: Voluntary self-help organizations: An exploratory study. J Voluntary Action Res 2 (4): 230-239, 1973
199. Trice HM: Evaluation of Alcoholics Anonymous, in Eighth Southeastern School of Alcohol Studies, Center for Continuing Education, 1968, pp 158+
200. Trice HM, Roman PM: Delabeling, relabeling, and Alcoholics Anonymous. Soc Problems 17 (4): 538-546, 1970
201. Van Stone W, Gilbert R: Peer confrontation groups: What, why, whither? Am J Psychiatry 129 (5): 583-589, 1972
202. Vattano AJ: Power to the people: Self-help groups. Soc Work 17 (4): 7-15, 1972
203. Vickers G: Institutional and personal roles. Human Relations XXIV (5): 433-447, 1971
204. Volkman R, Cressey D: Differential association and the rehabilitation of drug addicts. Am J Sociol 69 (2): 129-142, 1963
205. Wagonfeld S, Wolowitz H: Obesity and the self-help groups: A look at TOPS. Am J Psychiatry 125 (2): 249-252, 1968
206. Wechsler H: The ex-patient organization: A survey. J Soc Issues XVI (2): 47-53, 1960
207. Wechsler H: The self-help organization in the mental health field: Recovery, Inc., A case study. J Nerv Ment Dis 130 (4): 297-314, 1960
208. Wechsler H: Patterns of membership in a self-help organization in mental health. Ment Hyg 45 (4): 613-622, 1961
209. Weinberg MS: The problems of midgets and dwarfs and organizational remedies: A study of the Little People of America. J Health Soc Behav 9 (1): 65-72, 1968
210. Weiss RS: The contribution of an organization of single parents to the well-being of its members. Family Coordinator 22 (3): 321-326, 1973
211. Weiss RS: Parents Without Partners as a supplementary community, in Loneliness: The Experience of Emotional and Social Isolation. Cambridge, The MIT Press, 1973, pp 212-224
212. Weppner RS: Some characteristics of an ex-addict self-help therapeutic community and its members. Br J Addiction 68: 73-79, 1973
213. Wernick S: Obesity and weight loss in Weight Watchers: A study of deviance and resocialization. Doctoral dissertation, Columbia University, NY, 1973
214. Wilson A: Self-help groups: Rehabilitation or recreation. Am J Correction, November-December, 1969, pp 12-13+
215. Wilson EO: Sociobiology. Cambridge, Harvard University Press, 1975
216. Wyden P: The Overweight Society. New York, William Morrow, 1965
217. Yablonsky L: Synanon: The Tunnel Back. Baltimore, Penguin Books, 1967
218. Zablocki BD: Christians because it works: A study of Bruderhof communitarianism. Doctoral dissertation, The Johns Hopkins University, Baltimore, 1967
219. Zeitlin DI: Synanon: Life style/Learning style. Learning 2 (5): 71-77, 1974
220. Zusman J: "No-Therapy": A method of helping persons with problems. Community Ment Health J 5 (6): 482-485, 1969

Note:

No attempt has been made here to cover the vast literature put out by the mutual help organizations themselves.

There is a separate professional literature of several hundred items on Alcoholics Anonymous. Except for a few articles, the bulk is not listed separately here; a comprehensive annotated bibliography on AA (1935–1972) is provided by Phillips (see 149).

There is also a large literature, mainly sociological and anthropological, which is very relevant to a study of support systems and mutual help groups, although not dealing directly with them. Of particular interest at the conceptual level are the works of Cooley, Durkheim, Simmel, and Sorokin.

The literature on religion is especially useful – particularly that part of it dealing with faith and healing, small groups in the primitive churches, rituals, confession and restitution, and even "positive-thinking and mind cure."

Also pertinent is the sociological and social psychological literature on the psychology of affiliation, personal influence networks, utilization of community services patterns, and the sociology of professions.

Relevant material can also be found in the descriptive and historical literature on the cooperative movements and other economic self-development efforts, trade unionism, fraternal and mutual benefit associations.

The literature of experimental psychology on altruism, friendship, and the like does not seem to have great relevance. Because of their laboratory setting and controlled conditions, most of these studies have little applicability to the community setting of most mutual help groups.

The current general clinical literature – psychoanalytic, psychiatric, psychologic, and social work – on the whole does not seem to be very pertinent to a study of mutual help organizations.

Segments of the legal and political science literature on democratic pluralism and consumer participation are useful.

Dialogue Between Father Mark Dyer and Members of the Support Systems Seminar

3

Some Religious Aspects of Support Systems: Neo-Pentecostal Groups

Some of the multidisciplinary staff and Fellows of the Laboratory of Community Psychiatry met regularly during the 1973 – 1974 academic year to study together the operations of informal caregivers, social networks, and mutual help groups in fostering support systems to aid people in dealing constructively with the problems of crisis, life transitions, and long-term stress and privation. On occasion we invited an outside specialist to discuss with us, from his vantage, some aspects of our study which we were struggling to understand from our generalist viewpoint. Many of us had been struck by the importance of religious metaphors in certain mutual help groups. We thought the more we knew about religion and religious concepts and how they operate in people's lives, the better we might understand about the nature of such things as conversion processes, including brainwashing, persuasion, healing, the giving up of one way of life and the taking on of a new way of life; the meaning for a group of a sacred idea or ideal; the importance of ritual in worship ceremonies and in the normal life cycle; the significance of public confession before others; the processes of restitution (penance/helping others); the role of the charismatic leader; the re-emergence of such phenomena as communes, interest in the occult, and the heavy involvement of some churches and clergy in the human potential movement. What follows is a transcript of our meeting with Father Mark Dyer on December 13, 1973. Although we had not met before as a group with Father Dyer and had no preset agenda, two members of the seminar, Bishop David Richards and Dr. Margaret Bean, had briefed him on our interests and we knew about his educational and spiritual work in Massachusetts through our ongoing consultation activities in the Episcopal Diocese.

MARGARET BEAN: We mentioned last week that you have experience in living in a religious community and also a wide erudition in theology. At present you're working as Missioner to Clergy for the Episcopal Diocese of Massachusetts.

GERALD CAPLAN: What does missioner mean?

FATHER DYER: When I was invited by Bishop Burgess to begin this work as a support person for our clergy in the area of prayer, spirituality and their own ministry, we struggled with precisely what I would be called. The first word that came up was Chaplain. Bishop Burgess said that in his mind that conjured up images of someone who walks in front of an Archbishop with a ceremonial cross and he wasn't interested in that type of image. The second title was Spiritual Director. This conjured up all kinds of images from the past that weren't very favorable about the fellow who goes around directing people spiritually, although this is essentially what I do. The third title, that we agreed on, was Missioner to Clergy, from the concept of mission: that the apostolic community found itself commissioned by the Lord, to live and to preach the Gospel of Jesus Christ in the fellowship of the church. That's simply all it means. I'm someone who's set loose in the Diocese of Massachusetts to be that person who relates to the clergy as one who lives and preaches the gospel and develops their living of it, primarily, so that from the living of it they might be able to preach it so it comes out of them as lived experience not a functional experience. There is an identity of life and preaching and not a disparity. That's what I would understand a missioner is – it's a freeing title. It doesn't tie me down to any one specific task; it makes all of them available and it's up to me to decide just what I do on a concrete occasion. My basic work thus far has been centered in group work. The clergy of the Diocese are invited to and do participate in groups throughout the State weekly or twice a month, discussing and sharing areas of prayer and spirituality specific to themselves and for themselves so that they may share these better with others. Meeting with these groups I am put in contact with unique or individual pastoral problems which I either minister to myself or refer to another. I don't see myself as being all things to all men; I can't possibly be. So that when I hear of a particular pastoral problem of a clergyman, I more often than not will look for another clergyman in the particular geographical area and put them in touch with one another. So the support system grows that way. I would like to set up support systems where there is mutual help and my mission in the Diocese ceases to be.

MARGARET BEAN: One reason we were interested in having you as a resource is that many of us have noticed the religious aspects, or analogs, of support systems or groups that we work with. I think probably as a group we are less interested in fine theological distinctions and more in some basic understanding of the situations in which we see these analogs. I don't know whether people would like to begin with, say, something like confession, or ritual, or rites of passage. Those are three that I think would be of special interest to me.

GERALD CAPLAN: Can I add something, just to put you on the wavelength some of us are on. We've been impressed by the fact that a number of the supportive groupings that we're studying are rather meticulous in having a kind of dogma or set of beliefs and practices which are made explicit, many of them, some of them implicit, but they are enjoined on the faithful. If you want to remain a member of this group in good standing you must keep this dogma. In Alcoholics Anonymous there are things you must do and must not do. It's not left to your own individual choice. This seems to be large in some of these groups and not in others. There seems to be some analogy between this and religious dogma and the code which binds together members of a religious denomination or cult; there's an orthodoxy. Then there are those who feel rebellious; they get thrown out and then they don't get the benefit, etc. Perhaps you could talk about this from what I suppose, historically, are the movements which have most made use of this, which are religious movements.

FATHER DYER: I'll speak from the Christian tradition. From the viewpoint of contemporary Christian groupings, or Christian communities, whatever you want to call them, this is a very important concept, the concept of dogma or law, and they are somewhat equivalent. What dogma is for most Christian bodies is a set of beliefs that the people who adhere to this community must accept to be members, to benefit from the support system that the community is, and in the end to partake of eternal life. What the dogmas offer someone who belongs to a particular group is a set of beliefs upon which he can base his life, which gives him a vision of life, an ethical mode of operation, and an eternal reward. They give substance to his life and meaning to his life. He makes his ethical choices in relationship to this. I would say that this could either be oppressive or generative of a man's religious experience, and that's why I would like to contemporize it somewhat. There is abroad in the Christian experience today what are known as pentecostal groups or movements. I find certain elements in these movements dangerous, dangerous because the leader of these groups often assumes to himself or herself, a certain charisma, the gift of infallibility. These are persons who speak the dogmatic truth. The community surrounds itself around this pentecostal father or mother. There can be teams of infallible teachers who do dialogue teaching on the scriptures. Sometimes the direct object of one's faith is not God, nor the understanding of God which dogma should be, but the teacher or teachers. Now these groups are highly intense; they speak in tongues which is a phenomenon I admit I just do not understand, either clinically (which I would never pretend to understand) or even theologically, where I have some expertise. They speak in tongues; they are baptized in the Holy Spirit, which is their rite of initiation. Flowing from the baptism in the Holy Spirit are the gifts of the Holy Spirit, one of which is tongues.

PHYLLIS SILVERMAN: What does that mean?

FATHER DYER: I've heard it and for me it sounds at times like a semitic language, at times it sounds like Roumanian – I can pick up a few words but cannot understand what they're saying. These people have no knowledge whatsoever of the language which they're speaking, but some linguists have been able to analyze what they're saying and sometimes they can translate it.

GERALD CAPLAN: There's usually some change of consciousness at the time of the speaking in tongues?

FATHER DYER: I've seen it happen in what we might call an ecstatic change of consciousness, and I have also seen it happen when the person was as rationally conscious as I am at this moment. It's an eruptive sort of thing. It breaks through. It's a strange phenomenon which I don't pretend to understand. But this is one of the signs that you can be a member of the community: Baptism of the Holy Spirit, which is distinct from Christian baptism and an added ritual; the gift of tongues; and then adherence to a community of pentecostals, with a teacher. The teacher is often given the charisma of infallibility, which is very fundamentalistic reciting of the New Testament. An interesting phenomenon of this group is its lack of social consciousness. It's turned in; it's not turned out. There's a great turning in to one another. This offers its people a vision of life. Another phenonenon that is readily measurable about this group is smiling all the time. Everything is wonderful, praise the Lord, everything is beautiful. Literally, and I'm not exaggerating, if I smashed my hand in the window, the community would say isn't that wonderful, God has given him some sign as to what he has to do. Then the interpreter will tell me what it is.

PHYLLIS SILVERMAN: Could you give us, those of us who are coming on this for the first time, some names of groups. Are there groups around?

FATHER DYER: They're called pentecostal communities.

PHYLLIS SILVERMAN: Are the "Jesus Freaks" part of this?

FATHER DYER: Not necessarily, they have a lot of the same phenomena attached to them but "Jesus Freaks" are not the same; they're different.

PHYLLIS SILVERMAN: So there's not a popular name?

FATHER DYER: Pentecostal is their name.

MARIE KILLILEA: Yesterday, or the day before, I had occasion to look in the Yellow Pages under Churches. I thought all the Churches would be listed under one heading but they're not. They're listed under Episcopal, Methodist and then there's Pentecostal.

PHYLLIS SILVERMAN: But that's been around for a long time. The Black communities have had pentecostal churches for a long time. Is this the same?

FATHER DYER: No, what I'm talking about are not the traditional Pentecostal churches that have existed from the time shortly after the Reformation. Now within Roman Catholicism, within the Episcopal Church, within the Presbyterian Church, within the mainline Christian churches there are springing up subcommunities of pentecostal groups which are growing rapidly throughout the United States.

GERALD CAPLAN: How do they link with the enthusiastic religions of the eighteenth century?

FATHER DYER: Not historically. This has sort of erupted without a measurable historical link although what they do is equivalent to what the enthusiasts did. There is no direct line with the Holiness churches, and the Assembly of God churches which are the old pentecostal communities, but they do have that kind of enthusiasm.

PHYLLIS SILVERMAN: The ones that are listed in the phone book.

DIANA BITAN: Does this have any relationship to the traveling revival meeting which you get in the South?

FATHER DYER: The only relationship is that the preacher, the traveling preacher, is preaching the same doctrine, but the preacher goes from place to place and leaves people. After he's gone, it's up to them – they do or they don't; it's haphazard whether they come into the community. The new pentecostal movements have community and strong support systems, incredibly strong support systems.

GERALD CAPLAN: Why do you use the word support systems there? What do you mean by it?

FATHER DYER: I mean basically a community that's gathered together with an end in mind, with dogma to achieve the end, and various economic, religious, and, for better or for worse, psychic support in the sense that they offer a vision of something to adhere to and they struggle to obtain that vision. In some communities they have virtually their own medical health program. The community will pool all its funds, its income for the sake of someone who's ill and needs hospital care.

DIANA BITAN: Are these communities self-supporting, in the sense that an Amish community is self-supporting?

FATHER DYER: No. These communities are self-supporting in the sense that their self-support comes from the professional people in the community who seek outside work and whose income goes into the common fund.

DIANA BITAN: They live together?

FATHER DYER: Yes.

MARIE KILLILEA: How does the idea of salvation enter into this? I would think that it's different from a vision of life. Salvation usually means some sort of sin and redemption.

FATHER DYER: You go there as a sinner. That's the first step. You come there seeking conversion, as a sinner. Once you have heard the teaching you repent your sins, and with prayer and contrition you are forgiven.

GERALD CAPLAN: Publicly?

FATHER DYER: Yes, more often than not. There might be the possibility of private confession but they don't like private confessions. It's usually a public confession: "I've done all of these things and now I see the light."

PHYLLIS SILVERMAN: Such as?

FATHER DYER: Whatever it might be – I'm a drunk, I'm an addict, I steal money.

PHYLLIS SILVERMAN: Oh, these are not subtle phenomena. It's very obvious.

FATHER DYER: There's very little subtlety in what they do. At least I haven't come across it yet.

PHYLLIS SILVERMAN: It's not the kind of "I offended an individual" type of sinning. It's gross sinning.

FATHER DYER: No, "I've been cruel to my wife," that might come up, and also sometimes they mention details. Then the community prays for this person, which is another support system that you might say is offered them in prayer. They all pray after hearing the teaching and they all get into this – they'll pray in tongues and the phenomenon starts again.

GERALD CAPLAN: It's not just organized prayer, group vis-à-vis God. It's praying for this individual?

FATHER DYER: It's praying to God for this individual. Often it is with the laying on of hands. The community gathers around. For example, if we were a community of pentecostals and I came seeking help, after teaching, some very intense teaching, you'd say, "Are you ready? Do you want your sins forgiven? Do you want to be saved?" And I would reply, "Yes, I need this." I would kneel here or sit in a chair in the middle of the floor, you would all gather around me and place your hands upon me and then there would be speaking in tongues of those who have been baptized in the Holy Spirit. It's a very emotional experience.

PHYLLIS SILVERMAN: How did you get in, apropos of entry into a system?

GERALD CAPLAN: Do they actually proselytize?

FATHER DYER: Christians, yes. Other Christians.

GERALD CAPLAN: If I wanted to go in to observe, they wouldn't let me in. But if they saw me and I was a Christian and they thought I would be an appropriate soul for them, they would let me in?

FATHER DYER: Yes, they'd ask you to come and visit them.

MARGARET BEAN: They're not interested in non-Christian souls?

FATHER DYER: Not really, not significantly.

PHYLLIS SILVERMAN: To some extent I can't evaluate this totally, but as I hear you I would say that it is a very interesting phenomenon. It sounds a little bit like a kibbutz. It sounds a little like a lot of things all of us know, a new communal thrust. And they work. You are obviously very critical. On what level and how does this come out? What happens to the people who do join in terms of their long-range life-styles and the way they function and the kind of consequences it has for them?

FATHER DYER: There are a lot of questions there. Why am I critical may be the best place to start. Maybe I've given sufficient description of the process – it's believing in what the teachers say the Word of God is in the Scripture and living the life-style as interpreted by the teachers.

GERALD CAPLAN: The teachers are lay people?

FATHER DYER: Often.

GERALD CAPLAN: Is there a priesthood usually?

FATHER DYER: They have priests who perform the ritual sacraments of the Church living in the community.

GERALD CAPLAN: So that it's an egalitarian group. Anyone could become a teacher?

FATHER DYER: This is one of the problems. I don't know what would happen to them once the teacher passes on.

MARGARET BEAN: This raises the whole question of authority and its sources.

FATHER DYER: My basic criticism is the appropriation of the gift of infallibility. I really do not believe that any human being should follow another human being to the bitter end just because that human being always and in every instance says he is relating truth about God – I really have trouble there.

PHYLLIS SILVERMAN: You feel that way about the Pope?

FATHER DYER: Any human being.

DIANA BITAN: In that context, have you any thoughts about the types of individuals who would follow that kind of teacher? Also about how public confession operates and how it binds the community together; how the rituals they have would function to produce cohesion in the community?

FATHER DYER: The type of people: there's a cross section of people – professional people such as lawyers, many college graduates and people who have had a fairly good education plus some middle-class working people. It's a middle-class, upper middle-class type of community. My feeling about this, and my feeling as a teacher about the Christian tradition as a whole, is that we seem to be unable to teach an intellectual Christianity, a Christianity that appeals to each one of us on the level that we are in our professions, such as doctor, psychiatrist, sociologist. I think our grasp of the religion we live should have an equivalent amount of intellectuality, an equivalent amount of life to it. What has happened is that our religion, or at least our grasp of religious concepts, is for the most part adolescent to preadolescent, but yet somehow or another we've got to hold on to these religious concepts because they are ultimately our salvation. For a Christian or someone who has been trained in a Christian community, there is that nagging, nagging, nagging that unless I live as a Christian I'm going to hell, literally. There is a continuation on an adolescent level of living the ritual, subject to the dogma, of going through the motions of Christian community for the end, if not for the present. There hasn't been too much real experience of God; I mean the real emotional experience of God. Well, what a pentecostal community offers is an incredible emotional experience of God and some form of teaching. Certainly still adolescent I think; that's my judgment. But it's more than many people ever had in their lives. Here is something that really works. They have never experienced community support to any significant degree in a parish of 1000 people with three priests. The pentecostal community is living community, they're living an experience and they're offering a belief system that people really don't have to bother that much about intellectually.

GERALD CAPLAN: Now, what about this belief system. What you just said last was very important, connected with things in AA, for instance. I mean some of the beliefs for the upper-middle-class person would sound a little bit absurd if he thought of them in connection with his normal intellectual life and yet he's got to grab hold of them. This implies a suspension of judgment that a lawyer would never permit in his ordinary life. What is this transition between that and the other and how does this suspension of judgment work so that I now adhere to this.

FATHER DYER: This is the area in which I really wish I knew the answer because here is something I've been trying to study and trying to analyze without sufficient data or a clinical way of doing it. I don't know, because I can't do this. For the people I've talked to who have done this, I would say they have been sufficiently moved by the emotional element in experiencing the Lord, by the legitimate outpouring of love and concern of the community, for them to suspend judgment in the other areas. Somehow or another they've been able to accept belief, ritual, community support, and a continued reminder to praise the Lord. They are always reminded, to a point of nausea from my viewpoint, to praise the Lord. Literally, "I put my hand through the window today, praise the Lord." It's so generative of the presence of God that I think, and it's only a thought on my part, that this has allowed the person in that one element of his life to opt out.

GERALD CAPLAN: You know, I was in Jerusalem about a year ago and we visited the Sisters of Zion Convent in the Old City. We went there, my daughter and I, because we were interested in the fact that they were running a program of teaching the Arabs Hebrew and Jews Arabic. We met either with the Mother Superior or the Deputy Mother Superior, a very nice lady from Scotland. She was taking us around, showing us some of the very interesting archeological sites in the cellar where Jesus was the day before He was crucified. She showed us the marks on the pavement where the soldiers had marked out some game they were playing with Him and the crown of thorns, etc. As we were visiting, she got a message and said that there was a group of visitors there that "I'm afraid I'm going to have to deal with." A group of U.S. midwestern people turned up, sort of middle-class men and their wives. So while she was telling us, she was also telling them at the same time. It was almost a tourist kind of thing, telling where you could see the marks and how that fit in with the Bible story, etc. Then, I can't remember exactly what she said, I think it was the word Glory that she used. When we got to this part of the cellar where Jesus was crowned and where the soldiers had played their game she noted that this was "where He got His presentiment of Glory." And suddenly she had used a cue word. This whole group of middle-class people who were behaving in a completely rational way and listening to her rationally, suddenly their eyes began to turn up and they were saying "Praise the Lord" and "Glory be to God." The Mother Superior knew what she'd done although she hadn't done it on purpose, so she quickly said, "Maybe it's time for a prayer; would one of you lead the group in a prayer." And she trundled my daughter and me out of this place as fast as possible while these people were almost going into trances. All she had done was use a cue word and all these "Praise the Lords" began to come out, mainly from the men, very interestingly. All these stolid middle-class businessmen suddenly changed character and moved onto a different plane. I think she, as a Roman Catholic, didn't have too much patience with this. She's very much a rational religious woman. She knew what was going on there and she wanted us out of the way; she didn't want us to see what she may have considered the shame of Christianity being portrayed there in front of us Jews.

MARIE KILLILEA: Isn't all religion based on faith? Isn't all faith to some extent a suspension of judgment, because you cannot in many instances prove what you're believing in. It is an act of will; that's why it's good, because you individually make an act of will. Is that not so?

FATHER DYER: It is an act of faith, but I would make a distinction between rational and irrational acts of faith.

PHYLLIS SILVERMAN: Could you explain that? I think you made a very good point about the adolescent stage. I heard this before from a Rabbi who was commenting on a group of Harvard students who had not gone past their adolescent stage. As he talked, I had a particular problem that puzzled me and which relates directly to this issue. A very rational, adult Jewish lady's daughter was killed in a very tragic automobile accident. At that point the family stopped lighting candles, stopped believing in God, and stopped observing; this kind of shocked me. She said there is no God and if there is a God, He's bad and in some ways He's not worth bothering about. I could not connect this kind of one-to-one relationship with the rational person in the Jewish tradition that I understood. Then she said, "Well, my mother taught me that and I taught my children this literal faith. It abandoned me, and therefore I will do nothing and I will not participate or be part of that community by volition." The concept of the adolescent somehow ties in here in a way with the rational and irrational. If you're fixed at an adolescent point emotionally, is that one of the keys in relation to authority?

FATHER DYER: I guess what I'm going to say to that is a bit of an exaggeration. But in some way or another, it's helpful to believe in Santa Claus even if I do work every day as a physician. There's some reason or other that it's good to have a mythical element to my life.

GERALD CAPLAN: What does the word "good" mean? You mean it's effective?

FATHER DYER: Yes, it gives you solace, comfort, and support and is effective in reaching some kind of end.

MARIE KILLILEA: This is why I don't see (maybe in degree but not in quality) a difference in a belief in the Roman Catholic religion, the Episcopal religion, or a pentecostal religion. It's not qualitatively different, just different in intensity, because there's a supension of belief in all.

FATHER DYER: As I understand it from the Catholic tradition, I would say there's a strong qualitative difference. There's one thing the Roman tradition has steadfastly contributed to the Christian communities of all faiths and that is a strong intellectual understanding of Christianity. Without the 2000 years of that Roman analysis, the great works of Aquinas, and the great theologians who are alive today, I don't think Christianity would have survived. It would have blown out emotionally or something. God would have let it survive, but I'm just saying on a human level it might not have survived. The Roman church has offered through the 2000-year period a strong substantive intellectual input and many of the great minds through the history of the Christian church have been in the Roman tradition.

DAVID SPIEGEL: I'm very interested in the rational and irrational pattern, because a number of the phenomena we have been talking about remind me very much of what I have seen in the use of clinical hypnosis. A trance induction is simple; it could be a word repeated over and over again. A phenomenon seen regularly in hypnosis is what is called the compulsive triad: there is a cooperation with a signal no matter how irrational it is; an amnesia as to how it was planted; and a rationalization for it that is extraneous to reason. I don't wish to reduce all faiths to this, but I think your distinction between rational and irrational faith fits in very nicely. In this irrational component is the kind of community trance induction that seems to occur over and over again, where people will suspend their critical judgment and cooperate for the sake of pleasing the leader. It involves a giving up of some of their rational best interest.

GERALD CAPLAN: Well, for the sake of something they're expecting to get in return.

FATHER DYER: To get to that distinction because it seems pretty critical, I'll give two examples of what I would call irrational faith. At a conference last year, a person (for whom I have tremendous respect: he's a great intellect, he's put the intellect to work, and he's a very good man) walked in with a hymn book in his hand instead of a prayer book. This person is somewhat into the pentecostal movement. He said to me, "The Lord must have wanted us to sing today because when I walked by the pew I picked up the hymn book instead of the prayer book." I said, "Nonsense, you just picked up the wrong book." The other example is the rather facile way that pentecostals can say, "The Lord has told me to do this." A family is going on a vacation and the telephone rings offering something interesting for the husband to do for the summer. He tells the family that they can't go on vacation now because he just got a call from the Lord and has to go out and work on this project. I've seen that happen; that to me is rather irrational. Rational faith is for me . . . let's take the most difficult dogmatic belief of Christianity, namely the theology of the Incarnation in Christianity, namely that Jesus of Nazareth is both God and man. That is a fundamental belief. I cannot intellectually or rationally chart that; I can't clinically analyze it and prove it; I must believe. That is the essential dogma of Christianity. Without that, everything fails; it doesn't make sense. How do I approach that? Do I walk around, suspend intellectual judgment and say, if I'm going to be saved and be part of the group, enjoy all the support systems, but also sacrifice myself because of that, then I'll just say that Jesus is God and man. A lot of people do just say it. Or do I (as I have to do because my life is basically an intellectual life as a teacher) analyze the historicity of the New Testament documents? Do I go to the New Testament with the best of my ability and say "I have the faith that Jesus is both God and man, that He died on the cross, and in His resurrection is offering the way of life and salvation to mankind." I believe that personally. Now what do I do with that? Do I just suspend my brain when I go to church, or suspend my brain when I teach? Well, I can't – especially when I teach. So the first step for me would be to study the historicity of the New Testament documents. If you've ever attempted something like that or ancient documents you know what I'm talking about: deep study – linguistically, the use of languages, archeology, etc. Then there's a mass of rational evidence that this man existed and that He said the things that He did say, He did the things that He claimed were done. Next, for me, was the study of the reflections of a community over a 2000-year period. So I have given an intellectual base to my faith even though I do have to suspend intellectual understanding in the act of belief.

GERALD CAPLAN: Yes, but it's an intellectual framework, underpinning, surround, etc. The central core issue is not being touched by your intellect. On what basis is that accepted? Is it on a basis that your parents told you; that the community says you must believe it if you want to be a member (like AA, if you want control of your alcoholism, you better jolly well believe in these steps and do these things); on the basis of a teacher? Whichever way it is, whether you believe it because the leader says, whether you believe it because your parents brought you up that way, whether you believe it because this is in the air in your community, there is some external force that says believe because we believe. At that level I suppose, from where I sit, I see this as a minor distinction as to how you got to that stage of believing: whether you believe it because one man said it, or because three men said it, or because ten men said it, or because you better jolly well believe or you get thrown out of the community.

FATHER DYER: All of what you say is correct except I would like to add another. I would say there is a developmental stage . . .

GERALD CAPLAN: May I just add one other, the conversion experience, emotional experience . . .

FATHER DYER: Well, not simply emotional; I think that's part of it. The person reaches a point one way or another, through one process or another, where he says (and this comes out of a strong experience – St. John of the Cross, for example, calls it "a dark night of the soul," where one can no longer be in the community, with the parents, or any sort of support system) I *believe,* I believe, not because of the Bishop, or teacher, or the community and I accept the radical consequences of that belief in my life. Now does one, after that, suspend intellectual judgment and just tiptoe through life or does one continue to use the power of one's intellect after that step of belief? One must seek to understand the faith as God's pure gift.

GERALD CAPLAN: I'm very sorry, I'm not following you here because you suddenly deviated. We're talking about that central belief and all your examples of the nonsuspension of your intellect and judgment do not relate to that. They relate to the trimmings, the trappings, the historicity, was there a Jesus or wasn't there a Jesus . . .

FATHER DYER: That's certainly part of it.

GERALD CAPLAN: . . . not about the central issue, which is where you, as an individual came for reasons that I think are very interesting (not just you, the individual), to a personal acceptance of that element of faith. I don't hear you using your intellect on that: I hear you using it on this, this, and this, on all the surroundings, on the history of it, how other people came to it, but not on that.

FATHER DYER: On that, I would say the past leads you to it, the future intellect supports it, but I would have to say that the moment of belief in a God and in his Son as Jesus Christ is the critical threshold where one believes, and that is beyond rational analysis, it is a gift from God.

MARIE KILLILEA: I don't see that that is any different from that same point in the pentecostal groups. I'm reading at the moment about the Bruderhof community and the analysis of it discusses this business of "the dark night of the soul." When they come out of "the dark night of the soul," they have somehow stripped themselves of a strong ego, in the way the author puts it, and their commitment is now to the community. It's referred to as an intentional community, and interestingly enough, the children who are born into that community do not automatically become Bruderhof. They as individuals have to go through the same process, and about 50 percent do remain in the Bruderhof community and 50 percent leave. Marvelous examples are given of this stripping process, marvelous examples are given of the later commitment, but nobody, including the individual himself, can describe what goes on in "the dark night of the soul."

GERALD CAPLAN: At the moment when the dark night becomes the day . . .

FATHER DYER: I still hold to my qualitative difference, Marie, because of what I see. For example, what happens after conversion. Everybody has a conversion; the essential thing is the same, but the quality of what happens, I would say, is radically different.

GERALD CAPLAN: Can you spell it out?

FATHER DYER: Yes, I think, with myself and with the theological approach to faith, there's always an element of doubt, there's always an element of questioning. It's sort of the faithless believer all the time, or the restless believer may be a better way of putting it. My mind is always challenging, always questioning, always trying to deepen that which I've received. I don't have a community saying, believe, believe, believe . . . An example of this might be being alone in a car at midnight when your lights go out and you're in the middle of a fog. Someone once said to me, "That's how I understand the theological process of Anglicanism." I looked at him and said, "You're right." But that means three things for me: if we take the car to be the church, it means that I, the driver, have to have a lot of faith in myself to get through that fog; I've got to have an incredible faith in the vehicle; and above all, I better know that God is there through the midst of it. But the fog is always there for me.

GERALD CAPLAN: Do you consider, with pentecostals, that it's not there?

FATHER DYER: No fog; everything's beautiful.

DAVID SPIEGEL: So what you describe is an article of belief. Where you say, I don't know, I believe, they would say I know Jesus Christ is the Son of God. They assign a different kind of knowledge to that belief.

FATHER DYER: I would say I believe and they would say I know; that's a good way of putting it.

MARIE KILLILEA: It's an experience rather than . . .

FATHER DYER: It is experiential.

PHYLLIS SILVERMAN: Well, it has to be for you too.

FATHER DYER: Yes, it is experiential for me too.

PHYLLIS SILVERMAN: For someone from my tradition, I can't see how you can suspend belief. I think that's a very important difference, in terms of understanding people's capacity to suspend belief.

JOYCE BRINTON: But you have to suspend belief if you want to believe in a God at all.

PHYLLIS SILVERMAN: I'm always questioning whether that's there too. I think one has to take it back to the matter of a commitment of faith, which one has to respect in people who need to have some sense of order in the world.

FATHER DYER: I have trouble living humanly without bringing to bear that element of faith. You might call it irrational, if you want.

PHYLLIS SILVERMAN: There's nothing wrong with it being irrational.

FATHER DYER: No, but I have trouble, after having the conversion, not having to think any more; or being told I don't have to think any more.

MARGARET BEAN: It seems two qualities of a religion which are inherently congruent with intellectual involvement in religion are self-consciousness and internalization. It doesn't necessarily rely on the external community; it has been taken up as part of the person and if the person is removed from the community he can continue on his own. There is the awareness that this is what you are doing. It's not I know, but I believe.

FATHER DYER: I would agree with this precisely. Ten or 11 years of my background was living the monastic life as a Benedictine monk. The teaching of Benedict is to reach that point, that you just spoke of, where the monk becomes the Abba, the Father, and he can go and be a solitary. He has it all together and doesn't need community. The community is always there in case he should need it. He should reach a point when he becomes Father or Abba when he can support others, so there's always a generative process going on and not a regressive process.

GERALD CAPLAN: But in your community are you a collection of individuals?

FATHER DYER: Well, you're a collection of persons; you have personally appropriated your faith, grown into your own strength and your own support of the faith, and you support one another that way. I guess you're a community of mutually supportive, independent people, rather than mutually supportive, dependent people.

GERALD CAPLAN: I think that what you're talking about now is tremendously important. Part of your criticism about the pentecostals, and some of the criticism of some people about Alcoholics Anonymous and the reason that some people can't fit in, is that one set of people are quite confortable about accepting a setting in which they are not independent but are constantly immersed in a community and thus don't need to be independent. This is the way many children are brought up in the communal settlements of Israel. They're constantly immersed in their peer group. They don't have to internalize, and I think some of them don't. Now, someone who feels the need for internalization is going to feel a little uncomfortable by the redundancy here. I think you're talking about a community in which there is a collectivity that supports people who are themselves autonomous and independent; nevertheless they get something from one another in that situation. That's very different from a collectivity which provides a matrix in which you don't need to be independent because there's no need to; they're with you all the time. One of your criticisms of the pentecostals is that I think you feel that it is the latter.

FATHER DYER: I do, precisely; you put it in better words than I could. The Rule of Benedict (547 A.D.), studied through its antecedents, not through what followed, is an incredible document of a genius of community life. I would say that if you're interested in a community rule, read the Rule of St. Benedict, which isn't very long, but don't read it through any commentary from the sixth century on, please. Read it through his sources, it's the only way to do it. You'll understand how he came to what he had to say. If you read him later, so much is centered around the Abbot in later Benedictine tradition. He becomes the infallible teacher. I think Benedict rolls over in his grave to see what has happened to his teachings.

MARGARET BEAN: I'm curious whether what you're talking about is the difference between dependence and interdependence?

GERALD CAPLAN: I think that you can be interdependent even though you're independent. I think what we're dealing with here is an issue that patients often have difficulty with. They are aware that if they are linked to another human being, that very link makes them in some way vulnerable. They then say, they equate being linked with being dependent. But it's not the same thing, and patient after patient that we see have hang-ups over that.

PHYLLIS SILVERMAN: In turn, sometimes *we* make that mistake. I've noticed that psychiatrists say that for a person to be really cured he has to work out all of his problems, so no one needs AA. I think there's another side, of having to be more and more aware of people's need to be interdependent and have these kinds of experiences which provide them with a community, which doesn't necessarily strip them of identity.

GERALD CAPLAN: It doesn't necessarily, but if you've got enough of a community, you can manage without independence.

PHYLLIS SILVERMAN: What I'm wondering about, is there a recognition that comes with time of one's need for this kind of dependence, this kind

GERALD CAPLAN: If you've got a personal problem about dependence/interdependence, you may not be able to put up with it.

FATHER DYER: There seems to be the amazing phenomenon of people who otherwise can use the best of their skills – physicians, lawyers, architects, and creative people – who can go outside the community, have a vital and tremendous life, somehow or other (and that's what I don't know yet) swing back into that community with this kind of adolescent dependence.

PHYLLIS SILVERMAN: What I'm wondering about,is there a recognition that comes with time of one's need for this kind of dependence, this kind of community? Some people can have it in the family, and some people find a more extended community necessary; but we don't know who those people are. We don't appreciate that need of people. It might not be so terrible to have this tremendous need, though one may argue with how this person resolves it. I still have the feeling that we don't have enough respect (and that's where support systems are very important) or give enough acknowledgment of this as an important need that people have.

GERALD CAPLAN: That *some* people have.

DAVID PARADISE: We should look at it in functional terms; how it helps them. At times suspending judgment may be helpful so that it maintains the equilibrium for the other 24 hours or whatever. People can choose to suspend judgement because it helps them maintain their "independence" in other roles.

GERALD CAPLAN: You mean, you go, you pay for a shot in the arm, and then go back to your everyday work and manage OK. I've got a feeling that many of these middle-class or successful businessmen operate along that line. They can do very well as captains of their industry, generals, etc., etc., as long as every now and again they go back for replenishment.

MARIE KILLILEA: I would suspect that this fact that they are successful businessmen is a reinforcement of their belief system. I think the success idea is part of the tradition. The fact that they're successful means that their prayer is working.

DAVID RICHARDS: Does this carry with it a certain ethical pattern? That is, do these people abstain from having cocktails, etc., which you would expect from a fundamentalist group, or is there a blending of some of the social sophistication that you associate with the head of a corporation and a very fundamentalistic Biblical position?

MARIE KILLILEA: This raises a more general question for me. There are probably varying kinds of commitments to religions. In committing yourself to a fellowship, the dogma and the belief system may demand a total commitment in your way of life, including all of the various ways that one might behave. Then there are other religions which may only require a statement of adherence to the belief system, but your behavior is independent of this.

FATHER DYER: The pentecostal demands a life-style, an ethical response. But I can't understand how or why their ethical life style remains unrelated to society as a whole and the political order.

BOB KAGEY: I wonder exactly what happens in the group that enables them to go back into business and do the same, perhaps, unethical things?

FATHER DYER: Well, they support one another that it's all right: that this is the American Way; this sort of wholesale capitalism and consumerism is the American way, which is the God-given way, which is the right way. They do say this to one another in their publications. God owns my business now so it's all right.

BOB KAGEY: Why somebody accepts a faith or joins a religious group could be for a variety of reasons. The important thing to me is why the person remains in the group. What happens to keep him there? Evidently there are positive consequences which increase the likelihood of a person remaining in the group and being a "good" group member. Group behaviors such as attending meetings and giving testimonials are reinforced by the group members. The reinforcers vary from one "religious" group to another and may include such activities as "laying-on-the-hands," praising each other's beliefs, and obtaining status positions in the group. Reinforcement of behaviors accepted by the group may perpetuate and validate, within the group, certain behaviors which others may consider unacceptable. Studying the consequences of behavior appears to be extremely important in understanding how some businessmen could be members of a religious group and continue to behave in a manner that appears to be inconsistent with traditional religion.

PHYLLIS SILVERMAN: I wonder about the quality of the family life these people have, if anyone could ever evaluate that, in terms of how much support, comradeship, or understanding they found in their homes. I was thinking in terms of the Hasidic movement in Jewish life, which also has these qualities where people take on a much greater commitment and become much more involved in a much more dependent way with the Rebbe. I'm trying to think this through in terms of the closeness these movements allow. Now the pentecostal movement allows for a real touching and closeness, which may not come anywhere else. I don't know what they have in their families and perhaps this is their way of doing it in an institutional setting. This is a need people have. These businessmen may do it in a way which is acceptable to them because they're not getting it anywhere else. In Jewish life, one has family traditions that prescribe that you must do certain things within the family which tends to strengthen the supportive function the family plays; so you get less of these institutionalized arrangements.

DIANA BITAN: Isn't the Hasidic movement also an ecstatic movement?

PHYLLIS SILVERMAN: Oh, sure, it has all those qualities. I'm not trying to separate it out in terms of that. The thing that impresses me here, which is an issue which we're struggling with and with which I've struggled in my own personal life, is the amount of commitment and involvement one allows oneself to have in real community. And the demands that you allow yourself to respond to and give in turn. I don't know what the differences are, but I think we have to start to appreciate this as almost a fundamental human need.

FATHER DYER: I do appreciate that. My criticism of, say, the pentecostal groups or that type of community is that it lets people stay where they are without challenging them to grow. The person who comes in for an emotional need, falls back into that state, and then goes off and does his normal everyday life. He's not challenged; he's not helped to grow; he's supported in being regressive.

DAVID SPIEGEL: I think you've raised an important point; that support systems like a lot of other things are neutral and can be used in all kinds of ways. I mean, the Mafia is a support system; they get a lot of help from one another. You see the self-righteousness of a man who, because he doesn't drink, thinks that everything he does is right. Again, this raises the issue that not just any support system (simply because it gives support) can produce things that we would be comfortable with.

GERALD CAPLAN: As you look at the various religious groupings (and you've spent a good deal of time today on the pentecostal, which I think is tremendously interesting), do they divide in any way in regard to the significance of dogma, from the point of view of beliefs and the code of behavior. I mean, is there a division between certain cults or groups, etc. which not only prescribe belief but also a relatively detailed list of how you have to behave. If you are going to be in, you've got to not only believe, but you have to behave; you've not only got to have the faith, you've got to have the experience, you must in fact not only eat and drink this way, but there is a whole variety of prescriptions for living. This on the one hand versus those which just have part of it. They say these are our beliefs, this is our view of the world, this is what we have to have faith in, and as for the rest, you just go off and do what you can within that.

FATHER DYER: To speak specifically to the pentecostals, I would say that they have all of the things you mentioned; the way one lives; the ability to trigger off a response. There's an amazing ability to transfer from location to location, across denominational lines. Let's say I'm an Episcopalian, I could go to a Roman Catholic pentecostal community anywhere in the U.S. and in a very short time be at home there.

GERALD CAPLAN: And to tell the truth, a Hasidic Jew might find the same. In fact, some of the most religious Hasidic Jews go to Jesuit colleges; they feel more comfortable there than in nonreligious institutions.

FATHER DYER: I could understand that very easily.

MARIE KILLILEA: But they're moving from community to community. What happens if they move to a place where there's no community?

FATHER DYER: They go looking desperately. There's a desperate search to form one. There's a catalog that charts out every little whistle-stop in the country that has any kind of a group; it's listed there with a person's name and telephone number. Who put this together, I don't know.

MARGARET BEAN: There's the same thing with AA.

FATHER DYER: The reason I bring up the pentecostals is that it is not a phenomenon that we can look at from a religious viewpoint as something nice to deal with. I mention it because it is a significant phenomenon. In all of the mainstream churches, it's on the upswing. It's by no means declining.

GERALD CAPLAN: What about the second part of my question? What about those who require just a belief? Are there groups that don't do all this and that still hold together?

FATHER DYER: That don't do either one?

GERALD CAPLAN: No, I imagine if they don't do either one, they don't do anything. But are there some that do one and not two, and two and not one?

FATHER DYER: Well, I would say that there is a possibility in a Christian community to grow to what I spoke of earlier. In Benedict's vision you have the teacher, because we do have to learn; we do start out as adolescents no matter where we are in the faith. If one has a conversion experience, and wants to learn about the faith, there should be a teacher or director whose end goal is to make the person self-sustaining, independent and autonomous with a community of like-minded people. That's a possibility and I do see that occurring in some communities. I do see that throughout the tradition of the 2000 years of the Church. I sometimes think about the possibility of writing a religious history of Christianity from that viewpoint, to show that this is where the tradition has been kept alive around the circle, which I call the heart of Christianity, and people have lived it. For me anyway, if I remain on the periphery, I'd go mad. If I remain at the heart, I have some substance to live by. This is possible, and has happened, and is happening in all traditions – "the church must always be renewing itself."

GERALD CAPLAN: Now what about the third possibility, a code of ethics without the dogma. They have that too?

FATHER DYER: Not that I'm sure of.

MARIE KILLILEA: What about the Ethical Culture Society? Is that something which has a code of ethics without dogma?

FATHER DYER: It's just that it's inconceivable to me to have an ethical life without *some* dogma. Although the Unitarians maintain they don't have a dogma, I would say humanitarianism of some sort is the dogma.

GERALD CAPLAN: You mean a value system?

FATHER DYER: I can't conceive of some stated, canonized value system that can grow and develop but that there's something there under which they operate, making choices: this is so or not so; I do or I don't do this. Something has to be behind it.

MARIE KILLILEA: Well, this raises a point that David Spiegel raised last time and that we haven't discussed today. Is it essential in all of this to have a consciousness of the sacred, an ideal of the sacred? I could imagine that there are ethical systems in which there is no ideal of the sacred.

FATHER DYER: On the surface, yes, I will agree. At least they wouldn't claim the sacred. But from my vantage point over Christian community, the element of the sacred is most important and essential.

GERALD CAPLAN: You mean the link with God?

FATHER DYER: The link with God and the participation in that. For the monk at least, or someone trained in that tradition, he sees the universe as sacred because the universe participates in the life of God. There's a very close link, by the way, at the heart of the mystical tradition of Christianity and the mystical tradition of the Orient and of Israel. I've done a comparative study based on other authors: there are seven elements that are essential in all great religions: (1) the transcendence of God; (2) the presence of God in the universe; (3) the nature of this God is love; (4) the way to this God is first negation, purgation, or self-denial; (5) the continuation of self-denial is found in prayer and vigil; (6) a relationship to neighbor or love of neighbor, however one defines neighbor (some being more universal than others, but most of them being almost universalistic about who neighbor is – everybody); (7) the final way to God after self-negation, prayer and the neighbor, is love, ending in a consonant relationship of love with God. The seven elements are consonant within the great religions of the world, from the time that we can analyze comparatively.

GERALD CAPLAN: How does that differ when you get down to the cults and the gnostic sects, etc., I suppose the main problem there is neighbor. Neighbor is only your neighbor within the elite.

FATHER DYER: These are essential elements. For example, in the presence of God, the Indian would say that man is at one with the Brahma, the Brahma is present; St. Paul, in the Christian tradition, said your body is the temple of the Holy Spirit; the Holy Spirit dwells within you. God, who is the holy Other, in the sacredness of the transcendent; is also the sacredness of the presence; the sacredness of God who is love for mankind is found in the sacredness of purgation (because that's bringing you in closer contact with the sacred); the sacredness of prayer (because here is a dialogue of listening and response to God); the sacredness of my neighbor because of all of this; and finally the sacredness of the consonant love in relationship with God. So there's sacredness through all of this, everything then becomes sacred.

GERALD CAPLAN: Can you focus a moment on this purgation. What about the individual aspect of purgation versus the small group aspect versus the large group? I want to link that with the other question. Marie last week went to visit a Christian Science meeting, with a thousand people present. From the point of view of your view of Christianity, what's the significance and the difference of the relatively small face-to-face group, personalized, and the large congregation; how does that link with the purgation idea? Because whether you're talking about brainwashing, support systems, or whatever, confession (individual confession, confession in a two-party situation, and then doing it in a group) is terribly important.

FATHER DYER: First, the purgative way is a more generalized statement than simply confession. It involves personal asceticism. It involves fasting, which isn't confession; it involves vigils, long hours of prayer; it involves much more than confession. But in dealing with confession in both the purgative way and the continuing way, the confessor, the hearer, the absolver, the one who stands for God in the Christian community absolving the sin, was originally the spiritual father. I would say this was the case in Christianity in its most healthy tradition. What he's helping the person to do when the person confesses his or her sins is to identify not so much with sin, but with the process of growth and decline which calls for further growth. Maybe the less healthy way of doing it is: I come in and I have sinned against my husband. This has broken my sacred relationship with God and with my husband. I report that I've been evil in this way and that way. There is a ritualistic way of saying that I will give you absolution and you must say so many prayers in satisfaction for what you've done. The satisfaction element now has been ritualized. The healthy way to promote growth is to say all right, we'll pray over this, but there is an analysis going on here – an asking of why did you do what you did. What's going on here between you and your husband is deeper than this particular incident from the viewpoint of your relationship with God and with yourselves. And then by way of satisfaction, why don't you go home and bake his favorite supper tonight. That's promoting further reconciliation. This is a very simple way and is a helpful way and this person is not only returned to the intimate community of husband and wife in some sort of symbolic way by prayer but the relationship with God is renewed, the sacredness has been reestablished, and the entrance back into the community of so-called saintly sinners, or sinners who are saints, is accomplished at the same time. This I find is probably the most healthy process. The ritualistic way doesn't usually help too much, but it does help somewhat.

GERALD CAPLAN: How does it help; what does it help?

FATHER DYER: Well, it's helped me over the years, when I have done something that I feel tremendously guilty about. Let's say, as a young boy, I stole the farmer's apples and, as a young boy, I felt guilty over stealing because I had been trained that it was a bad thing to do. I feel very guilty over this, and I have to live with the guilt, but I know that my guilt is about my relationship with God, the farmer, my family, and the church. How am I going to get healed? Am I going to have to live with that guilt? Am I going to have to try to suppress it and try to live as if it didn't happen? I go to a priest; I kneel down with a great deal of struggle (because for a boy that is a very big thing; later on in life, other things are big) I spurt it out and say, "Father, I ask God to forgive me for this." The priest would be my vehicle for forgiveness and I could, in a sense, be restored to a relationship with the farmer, my family, and the church. I walk out, and even if it's just to say three Hail Marys or say an Our Father as a ritual satisfaction, I have left the confessional free of my guilt, absolutely free. The guilt is gone. And that's very helpful.

GERALD CAPLAN: And it's gone suddenly.

FATHER DYER: Yes, because I've spoken it out to somebody.

MARIE KILLILEA: It's gone because you've gone through the ritual.

FATHER DYER: Yes, and had the reassurance of the father confessor that it's gone, and the community's dogma that it is gone. I've not only got his assurance that it's gone; I've got thousands of years of teaching and tradition that it's gone.

GERALD CAPLAN: And a very primitive communication system which gets you in the gut.

DIANA BITAN: Is there a vehicle that helps you as a child to understand? You walk in, you confess your guilt, you say three Hail Marys, and you walk out, and you're absolved of your sins and you feel fine. But it doesn't seem to me that there's any vehicle which helps you understand why what you did was wrong – besides the fact that you've been told it's wrong.

FATHER DYER: This is the distinction I am making. Although this is helpful, it's not as helpful as it should be. The director, the one who is trained in spiritual direction and the dogmatic tradition of the church, etc., should be able to take more time with the person and personalize it and also do some things with motivation. Why are you stealing, etc.? This is where I think the Laboratory of Community Psychiatry is and could be extremely helpful. The father confessor might have a great ability to say, "Hey, there's something here that needs clinical help but I'm not capable of doing it," and then the whole support system gets wider. That's super.

DAVID PARADISE: Well, it is but it also diminishes the power of authority of the absolving capacities.

FATHER DYER: Not if it's handled correctly.

PHYLLIS SILVERMAN: Are the roles so specialized? Why couldn't the absolver also be the understanding other?

FATHER DYER: Maybe he could; I'm not saying he can't. I'm just saying there could be clinical help.

GERALD CAPLAN: If you have to mass produce them, it would be much easier to mass produce a ritualistic situation.

FATHER DYER: Well, that's what's happened; a mass production of the ritualized. But it's been helpful to many.

MARIE KILLILEA: In the very early days of the church, confession was public and now there is a movement as in the pentecostals toward a return to public confession with a different idea of restitution. It's not three Hail Marys or an Our Father.

FATHER DYER: From that individual type of thing to the group type of confession, somewhat along the line of AA, in the pentecostal groups the person has been prayed over and has received the gift of the Spirit, then the gift of tongues. It's eruptive tongues; after the period of baptism of the Spirit, the person could be driving home and all of a sudden tongues start, or it could be two days later and the tongues start. These are clinically tested cases that have happened. It doesn't have to happen right after the prayer. Now once this happens, the person sometimes returns to the community and says, "Here is my past life," and gives an exposition of his sins. He says he really wants to be forgiven and to start with a clean slate, etc., etc. It's said to the community and usually with the leader present. The leader and the community then offer the absolution. Now for the pentecostal, the penance (the satisfaction element or reparation) is leading the life of the community. There's no specific penance for sins. In the early church, in early Christianity, there were specific penitentials which told the priest what sort of public repentance was to be assigned to a penitent in a private confession. For example, a murderer had to stay 5 years outside the church, or sometimes 15 years, in sack cloth as a public sinner who had murdered somebody. He had to kneel there and ask the community to forgive him. But in the pentecostal movement, this isn't part of it: it's coming into the community and being forgiven by God.

JOYCE BRINTON: In your description you're talking about sins prior to the conversion. What about sins after? It is assumed that they can no longer sin?

FATHER DYER: No it isn't, and this gets into two areas we certainly don't have time for. When anybody who comes into the community disagrees with the dogmatic teaching or teachers, there is a readiness on the part of the community to tell him that he is possessed by the devil. Now this is where the dogma is sustained in an incredibly terrible way.

GERALD CAPLAN: You're excommunicated because some devil has gone into you?

FATHER DYER: Well, first they pray over you for exorcism and, if that doesn't work and you continue to disagree with the teaching, then you're out. A friend of mine had to go to a community in the South because some church members had become involved in pentacostalism. A number of pentacostal rejects were told that the devil had got them. Their husbands, who were doctors and lawyers, called the Superior to get somebody down there to straighten the situation out – "our wives are convinced they're possessed." The other way is not to identify the devil in the person, but to just excommunicate. In my ministry I've met some pentacostal rejects who have been excommunicated just because they do not agree. Their sin – it's not a moral thing, that can be forgiven – the biggest sin is apostasy.

GERALD CAPLAN: What if they believe, they agree, they say the dogma is right, but they backslide?

FATHER DYER: Then they can be forgiven by the community – 70 times 7 as the Gospel says. They take the Gospel literally.

MARIE KILLILEA: You know that's an essential element of brainwashing; you can always be forgiven and accepted so long as you confess that you committed the sins.

GERALD CAPLAN: Now what about the other part of my question? We've talked a good deal about community, meaning face-to-face community, laying-on-of-hands community, talking-to-other-people community, etc. Now what about the large congregations? What about Marie's observations of 1000 people who came in, mostly as individuals, not with each other and hardly knew each other. When it came to confession time, they stood up in different parts of the hall and spoke out to the whole congregation.

FATHER DYER: In respect to Marie's experience as I would understand Christian Science, these people have been sent from smaller communities. That's the first thing. The great gathering on Sunday at the Mother Church is the bringing in from the subchurches.

MARIE KILLILEA: This was the Wednesday night testimonial meeting.

GERALD CAPLAN: A representatives' meeting?

FATHER DYER: It doesn't have to be official representatives but they are representatives from the local churches who come to the Mother Church for these great meetings of testimony. In the local small communities, testimony is part of the life of the Christian Science church. It's a facile operation, it's not very difficult. The pilgrimage to the Mother Church is great and the people who go there have been formed in little groups, looking forward to the pilgrimage to the Mother Church, where they can stand before everybody and make their testimony. That's the greatest thing possible.

PHYLLIS SILVERMAN: That would account for the fact that they don't know each other.

FATHER DYER: They don't know each other but they know the dogma.

MARIE KILLILEA: In a church like that, isn't an essential element of the feeling of belonging the knowledge that you are aware of the dichotomy between the fact that you're a believer and the rest of the world is not?

FATHER DYER: Yes, that's very much part of it. My wife and I were walking down Charles Street, when we first moved into Boston. We were living on Beacon Hill at the time and we were introduced to a lady who, we found out, was a pentacostal. We were talking to her and she said, "Praise the Lord!" and I said, "What for?" (that's one of my responses when I hear that), and she said, "I have found two other Christians living on Beacon Hill; isn't that wonderful?" I said, "What about the Bishop; his office is right down the street?"

GERALD CAPLAN: Everybody who says "Thank God" doesn't have this meaning. You don't have to become ecstatic when you say it, you just say it.

MARIE KILLILEA: When I hear, "Praise the Lord," I think of a popular song I grew up with when I was an adolescent in the war years: "Praise the Lord and pass the ammunition." And that's not so funny when you start thinking of it in terms of American life. There seems to be a *zeitgeist* in the use of religious metaphors as explanations of phenomena in contemporary life. There seems to be this feeling that formal religious expression is disappearing – that "God is dead"; religious feelings are being expressed in nonreligious ways and we interpret these expressions in terms of the models of religion. You keep finding this explanation of facets of contemporary life; but, in a way, it's a negation of religion as something formal...

GERALD CAPLAN: Religious terminology?

MARIE KILLILEA: Yes, religious terminology, but also using religious concepts as metaphors, as Margaret has said, without the "religion" of religion.

FATHER DYER: Yes, this opens up something, namely the media's use of religious concepts in its advertising – it's incredible. My last year of teaching at a University (I was Chairman of the Department of Theology) I was being bombarded with professors who wanted to do their thing about God in the films or the study of the American literature in the 1880s from the viewpoint of religion. I think this is valid and good. I think religion in literature is now becoming a discipline in itself. Religion and the film is another master's program. It's very much a part of what you're saying and it's very much a part of the ethos today. I think it's valid because I believe that man is religious and whether or how one expresses this need for religion and religious concepts is important to study. So you could study Camus for example. Although Camus has said he rejected the religion of the Jesuits because it was thrown down his throat as a young boy, if you read *L'Etranger* or any of Camus' works, they're loaded with religion – powerful religion.

MARGARET BEAN: What about the Academy Award ceremony? I don't think you want to leave us with the impression that you think that that part of it is good?

FATHER DYER: There's a good way of doing it and a bad way. I would say that what the media and the American culture are doing is using religion for their own gain.

GERALD CAPLAN: The same way they use sex.

FATHER DYER: Yes, the same way they use sex. I did an analysis of the Academy Award presentations from the viewpoint of ritual and liturgy, and the Academy Awards have all the essentials of Christian religion from the opening hymn, through prayers, through statues, through the passing on to immortality. It had every component element of good liturgy and ritual. This was two years ago when the saint, who embodied the history of salvation of the film, walked up on the stage to give his final blessing – Charlie Chaplin. It was incredible: from the beginning, which was a hymn (in hymnic form) of the history of the films, through the contemporary priests and priestesses mediating values through the advertising media. It was all tied in; the values came from the advertising, they preached the message. The priests and priestesses were all there handing out little statues to one another; those who had passed into immortality were bringing others with them. Then in the end, the Abba, the Father, gave them the final blessing and everybody went home. Another fantastically religious event. I use the term Abba because in the tradition that I come from the charismatic leader is always called Abba, the spiritual father. In the Benedictine community, you call the superior of your house the Abba. It's something that has become habitual with me, so I use it in both a good sense and a bad sense. I should use it only in a good sense, to be faithful to myself.

MARGARET BEAN: We have to stop. I want to thank you very much for coming here. I can't tell you my excitement in discussing these things. It's been very interesting and I've enjoyed it very much.

GERALD CAPLAN: I'll say that I hope you come back, because there's a good deal of unfinished business.

MEMBERS OF THE SUPPORT SYSTEMS SEMINAR, LABORATORY OF COMMUNITY PSYCHIATRY, 1973–1974

Frank Baker, Ph.D.
Margaret Bean, M.D.
Diana Wainman Bitan
Joyce Brinton
Gerald Caplan, M.D.
J. Robert Kagey, Ph.D.
John Garrison, Ph.D
Marie Killilea
Edward Mason, M.D.
Lenore Morrell, Ph.D.
David Paradise, D.S.W.
Robert Patterson, M.D.
Bishop David E. Richards, M.Div.
James Sabin, M.D.
Phyllis Silverman, Ph.D.
David Spiegel, M.D.
Robert S. Weiss, Ph.D.

Matthew P. Dumont

4

Self-Help Treatment Programs

In the last five years there has been a dramatic growth in the number of treatment programs that attempt to deal with a broadening range of human problems without relying on the skills of professionals. This movement toward a peer-oriented self-help approach to caregiving has profound consequences for the future of mental health delivery systems.

Deeply rooted in American traditions of pragmatism and populism, stimulated by the social ferment of the sixties, and sanctioned by the community mental health ideology, self-help programs have come to be seen by many as the primary source of mental health care. The populations served by such programs include alcoholics, drug addicts, the widowed, the overweight, homosexuals, nursing mothers, gamblers, runaway youths, and the mentally ill. There have been occasional reports of one or another expression of self-help programming and a few statements of their common purposes and implications (1-4), but there has been little evaluation of the phenomenon itself. By and large, the acknowledgment of the self-help movement in professional journals is absent, indifferent, or hostile, not unlike the perception by professionals in general. On the other hand, there is an inevitability about the movement based on a confluence of ideological and cultural forces that suggests it is more than a passing fad in the human services.

ROOTS IN AMERICAN TRADITION

Alcoholics Anonymous (AA) is considered by many to be the paradigm of self-help programs; it represents an organized effort by alcoholics to see

---

Reprinted from the *American Journal of Psychiatry* 131:6, 631-635, 1974.

themselves within a spiritual community struggling on a path toward sobriety and righteousness. It began in 1935 in Akron, Ohio, but, as Hurvitz (1) pointed out, its origins were in the Oxford Group, which later became known as Moral Rearmament. The Oxford Group was a spiritual movement which assumed that sinners could be changed through confession and, once purified, had a responsibility to assist other sinners. They aspired to honesty, purity, unselfishness, and unqualified love and relied on a public confessional known as "sharing" as the mode for achieving those ends.

There is an obvious similarity between that ideology and the "12-step" process of AA and the "concept" epitomized by contemporary therapeutic communities for drug addicts. An assumption of sinfulness, a lifestyle of communality, a mode of confessional, and a purpose of spiritual cleanliness and love are deeply embedded in the American Protestant tradition. They characterized the essence of the Puritan theocracy of the Massachusetts Bay Colony in the 17th century, as well as the Quaker communities that emerged from it. Methodism, at the outset, involved weekly experiences of self-revelation by initiates who promised absolute sincerity. This is similar to the encounter group therapy that is the stock-in-trade of most contemporary self-help programs.

The communality exhibited by the self-help movement is characteristically American even apart from its religious and spiritual trappings. Alexis de Tocqueville described us as a "nation of joiners." It would seem that our very heterogeneity and preoccupation with progress induces us to search endlessly for group identifications as a source of cohesion. Erikson (5) theorized that the earliest glimmerings of American civilization were marked by an obsession with neatly drawn community boundaries. There were rituals of inclusion and exclusion that manifested themselves in the persecution of antinomians, Quakers, and witches. Levin (6) and Dumont (7-9) described a recurrent tendency in each generation of Americans to identify an arbitrarily defined group of deviants as a way of affirming a strained and specious sense of communality.

While America may convey from a distance a blended complexion of pluralistic ethnology, a closer look at its metropolitan makeup displays sharply defined clusters of ethnic villages heavily blemished with racism.

The self-help movement manifests the joining instinct in pure culture. The statement "I am an alcoholic" or "I am a junkie" or "I am obese" conveys not merely repentence and a desire for change but a rite of passage to the new community that magically and tacitly infuses identity and pride.

The self-help movement also derives from the main currents of American philosophy. The empiricism and pragmatism of William James and John Dewey are the best expressions of a body of ethics designed for an expansionist industrial society. Truth is what works and no value system is eternally valid. The worst expressions of the same currents come in the form of perennial anti-intellectualism and recurrent fads of smug, healthy-minded, "positive-thinking" optimism. Self-help programs partake of the best and the worst of this intellectual anti-intellectual tradition. They demonstrate a skepticism of established and traditional techniques, which is at best a utilitarian picking and choosing for ones that work and at worst a wholesale rejection of anything that suggests tradition or professional elitism. They generally manifest an optimism bounded only by pure physical exhaustion.

ROOTS IN THE COMMUNITY MENTAL HEALTH MOVEMENT

Self-help programs may not be formally baptized by the community mental health movement but can be said to have the courage of its convictions. Many of the theoretical underpinnings of community psychiatry (10-12) were based on a conviction that social systems had self-healing capacities, that natural caretaking functions were always at work, and that out of crisis new competencies could emerge. Mental health professionals, according to this view, could not be the source of all the caretaking that was required because there would never be enough of them to go around and there was really no reason to believe that their caretaking capacities were profoundly greater than anyone else's. The best that mental health professionals could do was to identify the parameters and interfaces of natural community caretaking systems and to heighten their relief.

The community mental health movement was nurtured by a body of study in social psychiatry that led to the conclusion that social disorganization rather than intrapsychic conflict was at the epidemiological heart of most mental illness. The other salient influence on community psychiatry was the growing evidence that neither the credentialism nor the conceptualizations of psychotherapy was related to its efficacy. The Whitehorn and Betz studies (13) demonstrated that the empirically defined ability of psychotherapists to heal was an expression of personality attributes unrelated to training. There emerged a series of projects designed to demonstrate the ability of nonprofessional therapists in mental health work (14, 15). While the training of nonprofessional mental health workers was rarely programmed outside of pilot and experimental demonstration studies, and while some observers were critical of their success, the presence of indigenous nonprofessionals became increasingly evident in urban mental health centers. Concomitantly, there developed a body of literature, at times rhetorical and at other times scientific, that criticized traditional mental health professionalism for its preoccupation with psychopathology and patienthood and the racial, ethnic, social-class, and sexual bias of its theories and practice (16-21). Some critics became concerned that the increasingly powerful technologies of mental health professionalism might have serious consequences to a free society as their use in the prevention and control of deviant behavior tended to blur the distinctions between health care and social control (22-26).

The essence of the community mental health movement seemed to be that the gap between the people providing help and the people receiving help should not be so vast as more traditional mental health professionals thought necessary.

The order and direction of that movement found a common path with the cultural and historical forces that led to the emergence of the self-help movement. Self-help programs offered an alternative to the theoreticians of mental health care who took seriously the implications of social and community psychiatry.

POLITICAL ROOTS

The self-help movement has a political dimension that more than any of the other influences bearing upon it determines its timeliness, inevitability, and fixedness on the American scene. It articulates and reifies the aspirations, at times muted, at times tortured, of democratic idealism. The Founding Fathers were trying to design a system that was safe from the danger of tyranny. They concentrated on a definition of inalienable individual rights, a balance of governmental prerogatives, and a decentralization of authority consistent with a pluralist, populist, and libertarian structure. In the light of our history, there would seem to be two other kinds of power whose relevance to politics they ignored – money and professionalism. The capacity of economic interests to frustrate the egalitarian purposes of democracy are too obvious and pervasive to discuss in this space. More subtle and more relevant to the self-help movement is the fact that power in this country is increasingly a professional affair. More and more public policies are influenced by such esoteric technologies as systems analysis, long-range plans, simulation models, and program budgeting. Science has become virtually an arm of government; either through direct employment or the sluices of grant funds, government decides what basic research shall be done and what technical problems shall be solved.

At the same time, professionalism itself has become so specialized, so sophisticated, and so arcane that practitioners within the same profession do not share a common purpose, methodology, or vocabulary. The conjunction of this growing reliance by government on professionals and the increasing complexity of professionalism leads to a concentration, authority, and unaccountability of power that would stagger the imagination of the authors of the Constitution. If we have not yet actually seen the abrogation of old-fashioned politics in the face of professionalism, we have witnessed the use of professionalized jargon to sanction policies servicable to vested interests. The power which resides in professionalism is so subtle and so ineluctable that it permits an apparent respect and a rhetorical allegiance to democratic principles while relentlessly frustrating them.

As one example of this, I refer to the revenue sharing concept that the Nixon Administration has put forward as the "New Federalism." Embellished with references to the "Second American Revolution" and "power to the people," the policy appears to take the direction of decentralizing the authority of the federal bureaucracy. A closer look at the actual mechanics of revenue sharing reveals a very different reality (27). Along with bloc grants to states and cities there comes an elaborate array of management information and cost/benefit-accounting equipment that involves a more specific and formidable control than the previous conglomerate of categorical grant funds could ever have. The model seems to have been derived from such multinational corporate giants as International Telephone and Telegraph (ITT), wherein the rhetoric of decentralization and pluralization beclouds strict and authoritarian control from the top in the form of highly professionalized cost-accounting techniques (28). A favored quotation of ITT's president, Harold Geneen, is "I do not like surprises," a statement that epitomizes much of the attitude of Nixonian federalism.

The redistribution of political and economic power is meaningless if the power residing in professionalism is not redistributed as well. In recognition of this, two developments emerged during the last decade that act as countervailing influences on the professionalization of power. These developments, advocacy and consumer control, have largely culminated in the self-help movement. Advocacy involved professionals bringing their skills to the poor and minority populations that could not ordinarily command them. Advocacy planning, neighborhood legal services, and free clinics were examples of that development. However, there continued to be a dependency by the consumers of these services on largely white, middle-class professionals whose commitment to services for the poor was often fleeting or laden with rescue fantasies. In either case, the frustrated expectations and aggravated dependency provoked by such programs led to the more politically sophisticated development of community-consumer control of human services, where accountability was fixed in the clients themselves rather than in the social conscience of those few professionals who deigned to serve the poor. The experiment has not been given the opportunity to be tested out as the vision of the sixties has given way to the more sphinctered mentality of the seventies.

The self-help movement became the repository of the embers of that conception of human services (29) which, when fueled with the activist and youth culture energies from rock festivals and campus protests, became a bright and vigorous network of activity.

THE DYNAMIC OF PEER INFLUENCE

The cultural, historical, and political forces outlined above are not alone in their influence on the self-help movement. There is an intrinsic dynamic to the movement that relies on the salience of peer influence on behavior. The fascinating studies of Asche (30) merely provided a social scientific baptism to the well-known phenomenon of peer group pressures on our response to the universe. By and large, we perceive, conceptualize, and behave the way our peers do; only those who are extraordinary by defect or superiority deviate from peer-determined norms. Despite the enormous variability of the human condition, there appears to be a kind of social entropy at work, a tyranny of roles tacitly but irrevocably defined by peer pressure. Among adolescents in particular, and with such apparently dissocial behavior as the abuse of drugs, peer group influence appears to be the most important factor in the decision to become involved (31, 32). Self-help programs see themselves as acknowledging that influence and presuming that peer pressure may provide not only the hope of a retreat from drug abuse but also a more meaningful socializing activity than schools.

There seems to be some phylogenetic validation for this. Suomi, Harlow, and McKinney, in a compelling article titled "Monkey Psychiatrists" (33), demonstrated a certain universality to the concept of peer-oriented therapy. They summarized the repeated failures to reverse the devastating effects of total social isolation on neonatal monkeys. These unhappy animals were separated from their mothers at birth and placed in isolation chambers where they were deprived of all physical and visual contact with members of any species. There were profound defects in locomotive, exploratory, and social behavior. Sexual responses were absent. They were indifferent or brutal to their own young when artificially inseminated. Aggressive behavior was either self-directed or grossly inappropriate. They spent most of their time in such autistic-like behavior as self-clasping, huddling in corners, and rocking. This behavior would not improve with conditioning techniques or by adaptation to the test situation during isolation. The typical response of normal peers was continual aggression against the isolates. The unfortunate animals appeared to be hopelessly and incurably in a state similar to schizophrenia among humans.

However, the experimenters then exposed them to normal monkeys who were three months younger than the isolates, too young to exhibit aggressive behavior or social interaction more complex than clinging and simple play. Within a week the isolates were reciprocating the clinging; within two weeks they were initiating play behavior; and in several months they were indistinguishable from the "therapist" monkeys.

The authors concluded that social recovery can be achieved in subjects whose social deficits were once considered to be irreversible by exposure to peers whose behavior could be expected to elicit the desired response. "We did not rehabilitate the isolate subjects ourselves, nor is it likely that we could. The actual therapy was performed by our 'monkey psychiatrists.' ... These therapists were not professionals. They had received no formal training, nor were they reimbursed for their efforts by so much as one extra pellet of monkey chow" (33, p. 931).

While it remains for general systems theorists to analyze the elements that conjoin these observations of monkeys with the self-help movement, a recent statement by Gerald Caplan on support systems (4) helps provide a paradigm for what may be a universal sociobiological phenomenon. He quoted the epidemiologist John Cassel, who concluded an exhaustive study linking social disorganization and disease in humans and animals with the statement: "The circumstances in which increased susceptibility to disease would occur would be those in which ... individuals are not receiving any evidence that their actions are leading to desirable and anticipated consequences" (4, pp. 5, 6).

Caplan further quoted Sir Geoffry Vickers as concluding: "So the major threat at every level is the lack of what I have called an appreciative system sufficiently widely shared to mediate communication, sufficiently apt to guide action, and sufficiently acceptable to make personal experience bearable" (4, pp. 5, 6). Caplan then drew upon his own experience to hypothesize that the "quality of emotional support and task-oriented assistance provided by a social network" is the critical intervention in mental health.

Caplan wrote:

> The characteristic attribute of those social aggregates that act as a buffer against disease is that in such relationships the person is dealt with as a unique individual. The other people are interested in him in a personalized way. They speak his language. They tell him what is expected of him and guide him in what to do. They watch what he does and they judge his performance. They let him know how well he has done. They reward him for success and punish or support and comfort him if he fails. Above all, they are sensitive to his personal needs, which they deem worthy of respect and satisfaction (4, pp. 5, 6)

There is no more precise and succinct statement of the essence of the self-help approach.

MENTAL HEALTH PROFESSIONALS AND THE SELF-HELP MOVEMENT

Those mental health professionals who are aware of the self-help movement and who appreciate its significance are concerned about how they can relate to it. Caplan predicted that this field would become a major focus of systematic research during the next decade. In the meantime he saw professionals making their contribution by helping to organize new self-help support systems and offering consultation to key members. To this I would add a sense of urgency. The self-help movement is the result of so many forces that its growth can be said to be overdetermined. It has obvious implications for the planning of mental health care, anticipated manpower needs, and the funding of human services. The more people rely on self-help programs for caregiving the less need there will be for professionals. Unless we can accommodate to and find some common ground with this movement, we will become increasingly cloistered, self-serving, and irrelevant.

The movement itself will grow more extensive and more comprehensive; ultimately it will become confluent. Observers of the self-help phenomenon become aware of new expressions of it with each passing day. The programs themselves are growing in sophistication based on their own accumulated skills and their increasing confidence vis-à-vis professionals. With that sophistication and confidence will come a boldness in confrontation with vested interests of the professional guilds that have assumed hegemony in the acquisition of public funds.

The staffs, review groups, and advisory councils of public funding agencies tend to appear very like the people and agencies that receive the grant funds. Some of us have argued that they are the same people. Once the funding agencies come to represent the interests of self-help programs the competition for scarce resources will become more intense, with professional interests having to justify their prerogatives and salaries in the face of leaner, more energetic, and possibly more effective caregiving systems.

Larger populations will become responsive to self-help methods. In a world where despair, frustration, and isolation seem to be normative, we will become more and more aware of the limitations of our traditionally defined professionalism in alleviating emotional suffering. Consider, for example, the growth in the divorce rate and the numbers of young men and women struggling to raise children, yearning for intimacy, alternating between resentment and guilt, and feeling profoundly alone. Consider the thousands of men whom society has chosen to incarcerate as criminals and then brand for the rest of their lives as enemies of the social order. Consider the millions of middle-aged, unaffiliated women desperately lonely in uncaring cities. Consider the elderly and the unemployed. What have we to offer these people except a randomly assigned diagnostic label and increasingly powerful technologies of behavior control which presume a defect within them? When they reach out to us we call them depressed and when they rebel we call them character disordered. We are most comfortable when we can call their situation masochistic, as if their misery were private, deliberate, and eroticized. If the self-help movement has any relevance to these populations, we would be serving our truest purposes by assisting it.

In any case, the movement is growing stronger and will eventually organize. An indication of things to come is the development of the Massachusetts Association for Self-Help, which grew out of the youth and drug programs supported by the Division of Drug Rehabilitation of the Massachusetts Department of Mental Health. The conference that resulted in this coalition should be described briefly because it illustrates the kinds of energies at work and exemplifies a role that the professional establishment can play in assisting the movement.

A planning committee of more or less arbitrarily selected program directors met regularly for six months, not only to work out the details of the conference but also to work through in miniature form the kinds of social-expressive and political issues that the conference could be expected to engage.

Dr. John Spiegel was asked to serve as consultant and moderator for the conference because of his considerable experience in the mediation of conflict and his transactional wisdom. Both were called upon when the conference finally began in June 1972 on the Brandeis University campus, Waltham, Mass. Representatives from 110 programs spent 3 days and nights together. Each felt that his program was better than any other and was more inadequately funded. They were all anxious about power and equity issues and bitterly resentful of anyone who presumed to speak for them. A black caucus, a Spanish-speaking caucus, a women's caucus, a drop-in-center caucus, and a concept-house caucus emerged. There was verbal abuse, a fistfight, and rumors of weapons. The conference was almost torn apart by a controversy about the alleged presence of marijuana.

There had been an absolute deadline to the conference imposed by the expected appearance of the Governor of Massachusetts. By that time the participants had to agree on a resolution to present to him as well as a constitution and purposes for a statewide steering committee and regional coalitions. Barely minutes before the Governor arrived, agreements on all three were ironed out.

When the Governor appeared, the group rose to its feet and with an exuberance that startled him a bit, shouted and applauded its welcome for a quarter of an hour. There were broad smiles and moist eyes. The room was filled with vibrations of warm energy. The Governor could not have known that the applause was not for him alone but for themselves as well. Coming out of a whole pantheon of vested interests, suspicions, competitiveness, pecking orders, and conflicting ideologies; carrying the baggage of sexual, racial, and social-class descrimination; angry, insecure, and vulnerable, they had managed to do something rare, difficult, and timeless. They had forged a community.

REFERENCES

1. Hurvitz N: Peer self-help psychotherapy groups: psychotherapy without psychotherapists, in The Sociology of Psychotherapy. Edited by Roman P, Trice H. New York, Jason Aronson, 1973, pp 85-141
2. Jaffe D: A counseling institution in an oppressive environment. Journal of Humanistic Psychology 13(4): 25-46, 1973
3. Dumont M: Drug problems and their treatment, in American Handbook of Psychiatry, 2nd ed, vol II. Edited by Arieti S. New York, Basic Books, 1974, pp 287-293
4. Caplan G: Support Systems and Community Mental Health. New York, Behavioral Publications, 1974, pp 1-40

5. Erikson K: Wayward Puritans. New York, John Wiley & Sons, 1966
6. Levin M: Political Hysteria in America. New York, Basic Books, 1971
7. Dumont M: Purification rituals in America. American Journal, May 1973, pp 20-25
8. Dumont M: The junkie as political enemy. Am J Orthopsychiatry 43:533-540, 1973
9. Dumont M: The politics of drugs. Social Policy, May/June 1971, pp 32-35
10. Lindemann E: Mental health and the environment, in The Urban Condition. Edited by Duhl L. New York, Basic Books, 1963, pp 3-10
11. Caplan G: Principles of Preventive Psychiatry. New York, Basic Books, 1964
12. Dumont M: The Absurd Healer. New York, Viking Press, 1971
13. Whitehorn J, Betz B: Further studies of the doctor as a crucial variable in the outcome of schizophrenic patients. Am J Psychiatry 117:215-223, 1960
14. Rioch M, Elkes C, Flint A: A Pilot Project in Training Mental Health Counselors. Public Health Service Publication 1254. Washington, DC, US Government Printing Office, 1963
15. Hollowitz E, Riessman F: The role of the indigenous non-professional in a community mental health neighborhood service program. Am J Orthopsychiatry 37:766-778, 1967
16. Szasz TS: The Myth of Mental Illness. New York, Harper & Row, 1961
17. Goffman E: Asylums. Chicago, Aldine Publishing Co. 1962
18. Hollingshead A, Redlich F: Social Class and Mental Illness. New York, John Wiley & Sons, 1958
19. Agel J (compiler): The Radical Therapist. New York, Ballantine Books, 1971
20. Chesler P: Women and Madness. New York, Avon Books, 1973
21. Rosenhan D: On being sane in insane places. Science 179:250-258, 1973
22. Halleck S: The Politics of Therapy. New York, Science House, 1971
23. Chorover S: Big Brother and psychotechnology. Psychology Today, October 1973, pp 43-54
24. Dumont M: Captain Video meets Super-Ego. Psychotherapy and Social Science Review, May 14, 1973, pp 18-21
25. Dumont M: Technology and the treatment of addiction, in Opiate Addiction: Origins and Treatment. Edited by Fisher S, Freedman A. Washington, DC, VH Winston & Sons, 1973, pp 163-169
26. Dumont M: C.O.D.A.P., the monster masquerading as a windmill. Rough Times (in press)
27. Dumont M: Revenue sharing and the unbuilding of pyramids. Am J Orthopsychiatry 42:219-221, 1972
28. Sampson A: The Sovereign State of I.T. T. New York, Stein & Day, 1973
29. Dumont M: The changing face of professionalism. Social Policy, May/June 1970, pp 26-31
30. Asche S: Interpersonal influence: effect of group pressures upon the modification and distortion of judgment, in Readings in Social Psychology, 3rd ed. Edited by Maccoby E, Newcomb T, Hartley E. New York, Holt, Rinehart and Winston, 1958, pp 174-183
31. Ball J: Marijuana smoking and the onset of heroin use, in Drug Abuse. Edited by Cole JO, Wittenborn JR. Springfield, Ill, Charles C Thomas, 1969, pp. 117-128

32. Dumont M: Why the young use drugs. Social Policy, November/December 1971, pp 36-40
33. Suomi S, Harlow H, McKinney W: Monkey psychiatrists. Am J Psychiatry 128:927-932, 1972

David Spiegel

5

Going Public and Self-Help

Psychotherapists commonly measure the progress of their patients by observing their capacity to have a creative impact on the world which surrounds them: friends, family, job, and the broader community. A person who expands his interest in the people around him is seen as having overcome some anxious or depressive preoccupation with himself. The observations which follow address the hypothesis that this process works in reverse as well. People seem to help themselves as they become collectively involved in broader social and political issues which concern them particularly.

This issue has been studied as part of a more general review of self-help or mutual support groups. They are particularly appropriate to this type of study because they involve collective activity on the part of participants, and they often naturally spend a major portion of their efforts in political directions. Traditional psychotherapy has tended to isolate patients, who are either seen individually with little opportunity to get a sense of their common plight and problems, or are seen in groups and hospital settings, where interchange takes place, but only in the context of strict rules against contact and activity outside the "therapeutic" setting. While these restrictions can often be important to the uncovering of material in therapy as opposed to having it "acted out," they can also be seen as a power operation on the part of the therapists, who retain control over the setting in which the pa-

The following persons contributed generously of their time and thoughts in the preparation and revision of this paper. Their help is gratefully acknowledged: James Amalfitano, Professor Paul Barstow, James Beck, M.D., Ph.D., Rev. Laurence Bernier, Helen Blau, Ph.D., Gerald Caplan, M.D., Matthew Dumont, M.D., Michael Hodas, Marie Killilea, Andrew and Kae McGuire, Richard Savage, Wayne Sherwood, Herbert Spiegel, M.D., and Susan Worgaftik.

tients meet and thus can prevent concerted action on the part of patients in what they perceive to be their own interests.

In mutual support groups, typified by such organizations as Alcoholics Anonymous, drug therapeutic communities, gay liberation and counseling services, and Parents Without Partners, there tend to be stronger horizontal and weaker vertical relationships. The best a patient in a mental hospital can hope for is to be a better patient, or eventually to try to forget he was a patient, as Dumont has pointed out.[1] Let him suggest that he might like to become a psychiatrist and his medication will be increased. In mutual support groups, the leaders are generally recruited from among the successful followers. Authority tends to come from common, not different, experience. More important, what is stigmatizing to the membership is likely to be the same for the leaders. Psychiatrists are commonly characterized as "crazy" but they usually succeed in disavowing the stigma. The leaders with AA begin their talks by saying: "I am an alcoholic." Thus, mutual support groups are easily united in the desire to cope with the social stigma which their position entails, and are more likely to try to do something political about it. Their very existence attests to the reality of a common problem made public, as the paradoxical title "Alcoholics Anonymous" suggests.

In this study, the author observed various aspects of three quite different mutual support groups and interviewed members. The method of research employed could best be characterized as a casual form of participant observation. The author silently observed and recorded at certain regular meetings, was asked to speak at others, and conducted personal interviews with members. The groups studied were not selected in any systematic way and are in many respects quite different. They were chosen because they fell within areas of special interest to the author, and because they were open to involvement in this study. All are mutual support groups, primarily nonprofessional in structure, and are composed of members who possess a common attribute which is considered a stigma by the society in which they reside.

An organizing idea which emerged from this study is the concept that there is a spectrum of behavior ranging from a private concern to the phenomenon of "going public," making an open declaration about a personal attribute, and further to broader political action. Several case examples will be presented in which support group members move along this spectrum from privacy about an attribute through a phase of going public to political action. The study will attempt to explore the personal consequences of such movement. Some individuals engage only in limited public but not political activity. Also, different support groups require and develop varying degrees of public activity among members. Further, the public arena varies tremen-

[1]M.P. Dumont, "Drug Problems and Their Treatment," Section on Adolescent Psychiatry, *American Handbook of Psychiatry* vol. II, revised edition, G. Caplan (ed) (New York: Basic Books, 1974), pp 287-293.

dously – in some groups it consists of a small and supportive membership. In others, the public at large is made aware of the group's presence and membership. Nonetheless, one is impressed by the speculation that groups as well as individuals go through a development from private to public to political activity.

Several cases of differing mutual support groups and a nonrandom selection of their membership will be presented with an exploration of their personal experience, the degree, arena, and personal impact of their public activity, and differences in the nature of the groups, after an exploration of a theoretical framework.

THEORETICAL BACKGROUND

The act of "going public" seems to be a crucial aspect of the success of mutual support groups, in both a personal and a political way. Psychotherapy, as previously described, is largely a private affair, as the strict standards about the confidentiality of information gathered in psychotherapy suggest. Joining a mutual support group involves varying degrees of public affirmation of an aspect of oneself which is generally stigmatized or at best ignored. Some groups, such as AA, take only the member's first name, although meetings are public.[2] On the other end of the private/political spectrum, some militant gay activist groups consist of people who are willing to say publicly: "I'm gay and I'm proud" and who will work for changes in professional attitudes and legislation.

Perhaps the starkest recent example of the significance of public and political affirmation in the service of personal reorientation was the action of the Vietnam Veterans Against the War several years ago in Washington. With tears in their eyes, many of them hurled their decorations onto the steps of the Capitol. Chaim Shatan, a psychoanalyst who has worked closely with the vets, describes the personal significance of this public and political action:

> To men who have been steeped in death and evil beyond imagination, a "talking cure" is worthless. And merely sharing their grief and outrage with comrades in the same dilemma is similarly unsatisfying. Active participation in the public arena, active opposition to the very war policies they helped carry out, was essential. By throwing onto the steps of Congress the medals with which they were rewarded for murder in a war they had come to abhor, the veterans symbolically shed some of their guilt. In addition to their dramatic political impact, these demonstrations have profound therapeutic meaning. Instead of acting under orders, the vets originated actions on their own behalf to regain the control over events – over their lives – that was wrested from them in Vietnam.[3]

[2]M. Bean, Alcoholics Anonymous. *Psychiatric Annuals* 5(2&3): 7-61, 7-57, 1975.

[3]C.F. Shatan, "The Grief of Soldiers: Vietnam Combat Veterans Self-Help Movement," *American Journal Orthopsychiatry* 43:4, July 1973, pp. 648-9.

The meaning of action on the private/public/political spectrum demands exploration. The previous description contains a suggestion by a psychoanalyst that the vets did in public what they could not have done in private. Dr. Matthew Dumont suggests another side to the public affirmation of having a stigma. He points out that in addition to public repentance, the member commits himself to a new community of support:

> The self-help movement manifests the joining instinct in pure culture. The statement, "I am an alcoholic," or "I am a junkie," or "I am obese" conveys not merely repentance and a desire for change but a rite of passage to a new community which magically and tacitly infuses identity and pride.[4]

Thus "going public" is a double move – it involves saying "yes I am this but I am more than this." The member can cushion himself against negative public response to his public action with the often intense solidarity felt among members of a group with a common stigma. He may or may not repudiate certain aspects of himself, but he seems to feel he is confirming his worth as a person at the same time.

There is a large and conflicting literature approaching the complex problem of personality theory. The model I will use is drawn from existential sources and is dialectical. To the extent that it is consistent with the principles of existential phenomenology to describe an "essence" of human personality, it would be "relatedness" – the capacity to relate to oneself and the world around oneself. This theory addresses itself to the constant tension between what is called "subjective" and "objective" reality. Traditional models of personality theory as well as philosophical and religious models fit somewhere along this spectrum, from the Cartesian mind–body dualism which tries to straddle both sides to subjective religious mysticism on one extreme and to something like Skinnerian objective behaviorism on the other.

The dialectical model is an attempt to incorporate all aspects of these conflicting theoretical approaches to human personality. The dialectical formulation is that man is both these objective descriptions of his personality and is more than these. For example, the existential psychiatric literature tends to be critical of traditional diagnostic categories as applied to patients. Many psychiatrists are satisfied that they "know" a patient when they have described him as an "obsessive-compulsive neurotic." Some would argue that the term is totally meaningless. The dialectical position would be that the patient is both the collection of behaviors and thoughts suggested by the term and is more than that.

Therapy on these terms is an attempt to free a man from the learned objective images which govern his life – to help him recognize that clinging to an old image is a choice which he repeatedly makes. However, denial is no more correct than saying "I have no choice but to be what I am." Rather, a patient must learn to live the idea: "I am this but I am more

[4]M.P. Dumont, "Self-Help Treatment Programs: An Overview," *American Journal Psychiatry,* 131(6):631–635, 1974.

than this." In similar terms, Elvin Semrad describes the process of psychotherapy as that of "acknowledging, bearing, and putting in perspective."[5]

Thus, our capacity to relate is what makes us more than any objective description or role. Yet it does not free us utterly from our real existence in body and world, as Descartes and Aquinas had hoped. In addition to the internally generated objective images which come to dominate us and which are so well described by psychoanalysts, we find ourselves the subject of objective expectations from friends, family, co-workers, and supervisors. Finally, we discover ourselves part of various social groupings such as class, religion, nationality, and race which impose complex and occasionally conflicting rules, laws, rewards, and expectations.

It would be useless and painful to deny that we are or have to do with any of these objective roles. The humiliation suffered, for instance, by blacks who tried to be "white" attests to this. Yet the quiet desperation of those who try to absolutely fulfill their roles (which often conflict anyway) suggests that a sense of inner peace does not come from trying to become some set of objective criteria – the alcoholism rate among comfortable, middle-class housewives is suggestive.

Within this framework, the act of going public in a mutual support group seems both subtle and sensible. By asserting that he has a particular stigmatized or unacceptable attribute, the group member is saying "Okay, I am such and such, but see me as a whole person who has rights." The act of joining, and further of taking political action, becomes an act of self-assertion and self-respect. The necessity to hide is humiliating. Harboring a secret is a way of saying "I am unacceptable – to know me is to reject me." It becomes an obstacle to all kinds of self-expression and intimacy. The importance of confession in religion and abreaction in psychiatry attests to the therapeutic impact of making a public statement about a private shame. Energy goes toward moving beyond rather than protecting against.

The liberating personal impact of entering the public and political spectrum within several mutual support groups will be examined. The differing experiences will be related to the contrasting stigmas involved, generalizations about the kinds of people attracted to various mutual support groups, and to differing degrees of personal and group involvement on the public/political spectrum.

The first case example is a study of a member of a mutual support group which operates on a personal, public, and political level.

CASE EXAMPLE: ACTION FOR PREVENTION OF BURN INJURIES TO CHILDREN (APBIC)

This group was founded several years ago by a small number of suburban parents whose children had been the victims of burn injuries, who themselves had

[5]E. Semrad, Personal Communication.

been burned as children, or who were especially concerned about preventing such injury to their children. Their activities have been supportive, educational, and political, as they have grown. The initial meetings soon expanded to include lectures on disposing of dangerous articles in the home and on how to respond effectively should a child's clothing catch fire. Members also lobbied at the State House for legislation requiring flame-retardant clothing for children.

This portion of the study focuses on Andrew, who joined the group several years after it had started. While it is not clear how typical he is of the membership, he is part of a special group within the organization who were themselves burned as children. Such people are particularly effective speakers and visitors to children who have been recently burned. While there is data to suggest some selection factors relevant to those who are the victims of burn injuries as children, such as social class and family turmoil,[6] the notion of a certain character type being burned is less clear in contrast to the ensuing examples of homosexuality and drug addiction. Thus we might expect the group to be more diverse psychologically.

> Andrew, who is now 28, was burned at the age of 7. He was standing near an exposed flame in an old stove in the kitchen on his birthday, and the hem of his bathrobe caught fire. The family reacted well and put out the fire quickly, but his leg was badly burned. The burn was also badly managed, and the skin grafts taken from his other leg were too deep, leaving both legs badly scarred. The family was all the more upset because they had been planning to replace the stove, but had not gotten around to doing so.
>
> Andrew spent long months in the hospital, daily reliving the nightmare of what had happened. He then entered a long period of denial which lasted for most of his teen-age years. He pretended that nothing had happened, but he was not happy.
>
> At age 19, he met Kae, who was later to become his wife. Interestingly, he told her about the burn on their second date, although he rarely talked about it. As he got to know her, he spent a good deal of time mulling over what had happened. He felt that the discussions during this six-year period of his life were unfocused, that they were in some way related to the burn but were leading to "blind alleys."
>
> At age 25, Andrew found himself reliving a different aspect of the incident each day, and he recalled new things about it. He talked with his parents about the burn for the first time in years. While he felt this was helpful, he became somewhat depressed, and after several years he wanted to be past it.
>
> When they arrived in Boston about a year ago, Kae heard about Action for Prevention of Burn Injuries to Children, joined and got her husband involved. Andrew began to speak to groups of mothers about his burns, and to advise them on the handling of those of their children

[6]R.C. Schmitt, and M. Moore, "A Study of the Behavioral and Social Epidemiology of Severe Burn Injuries," unpublished manuscript.

who had been burned. He noted that at about this time his brooding preoccupation with his own burn ceased, and that days would go by when he would not think of it at all. He also realized, and feels that this is related, that his years of trying to deal with what happened to him gave him an advantage in dealing with people who had been burned more recently and their families. Thus he had not merely a burden, but a special kind of knowledge as well.

Several things stand out in Andrew's history. He had gone through a long period of denial about the injury. It seems to be no accident that he uncharacteristically talked about his burn early in his relationship with the woman who was to become his wife. He could deny fairly easily – his burn is not visible when he is dressed. Yet he kept brooding about the trauma and found some relief when he joined an organization – with urging from his concerned wife – in which his unique importance was that he had been burned.

His membership seemed to give some meaning to his suffering. He had been through something, and his journey meant he could teach others. This teaching seemed to give Andrew some peace. He is a thoughtful, introspective, and intelligent man. Yet he came to be frustrated with merely reliving or personally facing the tragedy. He felt that even his confrontation with his parents, while helpful, did less to resolve his feelings than teaching in the group.

The burn had become a permanent part of Andrew's physical life, and he seems to have explored and developed what amounts to a dialectical resolution of the problem. During the recuperation, he was totally absorbed in the injury – he seemed little more than a victim. He then went through more than a decade of attempted denial, i.e., "I am not this." But the denial failed, and he returned to a kind of morbid preoccupation with being a burn victim. Hegel might have chosen Andrew at this stage as an "Unhappy Consciousness ... a doubled and merely contradictory being."[7] He alternated between "being" a burn victim and little else and denying that he was one. The integration and move beyond this state seems to have come with his participation in the group. He was able to add a new dimension to his injury – that of being a teacher, and thus could in effect say: "I am this, but I am more than this." He was neither denying nor dwelling on the injury and felt happier. Further, he was affirming as very important his own capacity to relate to the injury.

An example of the public educational work he and his wife do is the following:

A family had a 12-year old boy who had been burned 3 years previously. He was refusing to get undressed for gym class, and his parents were pushing him to do so. Kae and Andrew told the parents: "Leave him alone – he's got reason to dislike doing that. It's bad enough he is burned – don't make it into an emotional problem as well."

The advice to the parents basically confronted their desire for denial. Andrew stated with the authority which comes of experience that the parents were really asking the boy to act as though he were not burned.

[7]G.W.F. Hegel, *The Phenomenology of Mind*, trans. J.B. Baillie (New York: The Macmillan Company, 1961), p. 251.

The boy was preoccupied, and his parents were in a sense denying. Andrew was pushing the parents toward acceptance with the hope that this would make it easier for the boy to do likewise for himself.

Andrew seems to have moved along the spectrum, from years of personal preoccupation with his injury to going public with friends, to going public within a group of people with similar problems themselves or within their families. More recently, Andrew has become involved in the political development of APBIC and its involvement with the broader community in terms of support and education. In a letter to the author requesting help with a grant proposal, he wrote the following:

> We are asking for (a sum of money) for a 1-year period to make the transition from a volunteer organization to an established ongoing agency aimed at the development of mutual-help groups for victims and their families and the growth of our Speakers Bureau. Basically, we are making the point that both burn research and all the related fields are grossly underdeveloped and underfunded. Also, there now exists *no* group organized to offer support to the burn victim nor guidelines available from psychiatric research in dealing with the trauma of the burn injury.

Along with his organization, Andrew is moving farther into the broad public arena. The tone of the letter is hardly that of a hapless victim, yet it contains no denial about the need for help. The author sounds like someone who feels those who are injured deserve better, not what happened to them, as so many victims tend to feel. It is also a realistic attempt to extract help from available public resources.

Andrew's personal integration of his burn injury seems to have been inseparable from his and his group's increasing public involvement in the cause of those similarly afflicted and their families.

The second case example comes from a group who feel themselves unfairly stigmatized by society as a whole: the predominantly gay members of the Metropolitan Community Church.

CASE EXAMPLE: METROPOLITAN COMMUNITY CHURCH

It is difficult to date the beginning of a movement, but if such is possible for the Gay Liberation Movement, the date would be June 27, 1969, and location would be the Stonewall Inn on Christopher Street in New York City. This bar was a well-known meeting place for homosexuals, and the police made one of their occasional raids for the purpose of arresting those involved in apparent violations of various "morals" statutes. The police had viewed homosexuals as weak and were rough without fear. This night was different, because the patrons of the bar decided to fight instead of submit, and the police were forced to barricade themselves inside until help arrived. What emerged were bruises on both sides, and a sense of surprise and pride among homosexuals.[8]

[8]L. Humphreys, *Out of the Closets: The Sociology of Homosexual Liberation* (Englewood Cliffs, NJ.: Prentice-Hall, Inc., 1972).

A large number of organizations of homosexuals developed in the atmosphere of political ferment of the late 1960's. Particularly notable were the marches in New York commemorating the anniversary of that brawl. Men and women for the first time acknowledged their homosexuality publicly, and reports were common of statements like: "This walk did me more good than 3 years of analysis." Dr. Howard Brown, former Health Services Administrator for the Lindsay Administration in New York City, made a dramatic announcement of his homosexual orientation at a recent professional meeting. He spoke with enthusiasm about the support given him by various gay activist groups, and with disappointment about his years in psychoanalytic therapy.[9] Dr. Brown quickly added political dimensions to his public statement by resigning from his New York City job and organizing the National Gay Task Force, which is being designed to fight for the civil rights of homosexuals and to function as a coordinating and information exchange group for gay people.[10] Dr. Brown, interviewed on the radio, commented that he was quite surprised and pleased at the positive response he had received since his public statement about his sexual preferences, although he was careful to add that he felt his current affiliation with a liberal institution, New York University, within a liberal city, is important.

This change in the public and political activity of gay people provides some insight into a recent change by the American Psychiatric Association. Recently, the Board of Trustees voted to remove homosexuality as a diagnosis under the heading "character disorder" and to substitute "sexual orientation disturbance." This was a major victory for the gay liberation groups, who had been accusing society at large and psychiatrists in particular of persecuting them for what they viewed as a legitimate sexual preference with no pathologic significance. The new ruling meant that a patient with homosexual tendencies would only be given a label of psychiatric illness if he was in some way unhappy about his sexual orientation.

The hypothesis is that in this case the public assertion of a stigmatized attribute led to the beginnings of a broader social reevaluation of the stigma. The author was present at the annual meeting of the American Psychiatric Association in the spring of 1971 in Washington, D.C. At the formal awards meeting, a group of gay people led by a psychiatrist took over the microphone and read an emotional list of demands which included recognition of the rights of homosexuals to their sexual preference without legal or psychiatric discrimination, as well as a demand that the organization record itself in opposition to the Vietnam War. It is hard to tell how great the effect of that emotional confrontation was, but the following year the APA did record itself in opposition to the war, and 3 years later it modified its position on homosexuality. It is unlikely that such a change would have come about without the vigorous public pressure exerted within and outside the organization by those most concerned with such a change: homosexuals. Within the last month, a referendum was conducted within the APA membership on the issue at the insistence of those psychiatrists opposed to the change. By a vote of approximately 58 percent to 38 percent, the member psychiatrists voted to uphold the new position.

In this context of public ferment about the APA decision, the author was invited

[9]"New York City's Former Health Chief Admits He's Homosexual," *Medical World News*, October 26, 1973, pp. 18-19.

[10]"Homosexual Civil-Rights Group Is Announced by Ex-City Aide," *New York Times*, October 16, 1973.

to speak to members of the Metropolitan Community Church in Boston, which describes itself as "a church for all people with a special ministry to the gay community." The parent denomination is the Universal Fellowship of Metropolitan Community Churches, founded 5 years ago by the Rev. Troy Perry, a minister with a pentecostal and evangelical background. The Boston church was founded 18 months ago by the current pastor, the Rev. Laurence Bernier. The author was invited to speak as a psychiatrist about the recent APA ruling.

The congregation is a mixed group in many ways. The church has an active membership of about 50 and another 50 or so on the books. Special efforts have brought female members in as well, and the Rev. Nancy Wilson, a woman, is now the talented assistant pastor. The members of the church had "gone public" in a limited sense by joining. Although some members were straight or as one member put it, "latent heterosexuals," attendance at the least conveyed an interest in the gay world. Some came to the services alone, but many attended in couples. They were encouraged to take communion together, and many embraced and kissed one another during the service. Most of the members were probably not known as homosexuals in the outside world, and thus they took some risk of being "found out" in joining the church. The organizer who arranged for the author's appearance had to interrupt a phone call at one point because he was at his job and feared being found out. However, the church viewed itself as a congregation of believers rather than as a political action group. Many had felt uncomfortable or unwelcome in more traditional churches because of their sexual orientation.

The major complaint which the group lodged against psychiatrists was that, paradoxically, they ignore the real problems of homosexuals. The feeling was that as soon as a therapist learns that a person is homosexual, he drops all other issues and concentrates on returning him to a "normal" sexual orientation. The real problems in living confronted by the person are then ignored. The prayer of one young woman at the service later underscored the need for help with the common problems of living we all face. With her arm around her woman companion, she prayed: "Lord, help me learn to get out of myself and love better."

Surprisingly, members expressed open criticism of gay people. For example, one organizer said: "It's impossible to get queens to come to a meeting on time." Having established their separate identity, they seemed to feel freer to criticize what they perceived as real problems. Similarly, they expected help for what they perceived as the real problems from psychiatric professionals.

The membership seemed to encompass a wide psychological spectrum, from a lawyer who seemed animated, intelligent, active and warm, to one quite disturbed man who called me several days later after having taken a serious but not fatal drug overdose. My impression was that the "healthier" members were more politically active, but that the political repercussions of recent gay rights activity had had a positive impact on most of the membership.

The members at the meeting before the service were intensely interested in the political significance of the changed APA ruling. The response ranged from cynicism to enthusiasm, although there was a general consensus that change was long overdue. On the one hand, a young man stated that the change "isn't worth the paper it's printed on." But an older man, a lawyer, said he hoped that the political experiences would be more important, especially in getting equal employment laws through the State House. He added that he had "fired off" letters to his state representatives as soon as the change had occurred, and that if the membership of the APA reversed the decision (the vote had not been taken at that time), it would "not go well for homosexuals, or for psychiatrists in the eyes of homosexuals."

This lawyer agreed to discuss in more detail his experience of increasing public involvement with the gay community in the Metropolitan Community Church:

Brian, a middle-aged lawyer, had made a point of being open with his family about his bisexuality, although this had not always been the case and never was with his parents. He described difficult years as an adolescent, as he was exploring and attempting to understand his sexual orientation. He was expelled and flunked out of a prep school for a homosexual involvement: "I asked them to choose one or the other reason, but they insisted on both." He was then married briefly, in a relationship which he described as exploitative on both sides: "She was the first girl I was able to make it with and it was a chance for normalcy. For her it offered social advancement. But it was incredibly strained – we came from disparate social and educational backgrounds. I got into psychiatric therapy, got rid of some of my guilt, and later the marriage was annulled."

At this time Brian's sexual orientation was private, and anxiety about being "found out" always remained with him: "You had a nagging sense that if people knew, they would turn from you in horror."

After a period of some involvement with men, Brian fell in love with a woman and decided to marry again. "I was candid about what I had been. I thought we could make it work. I refused to promise that I'd always love her. I felt it was immoral to promise what it might not be in my power to deliver in the future." They were happy for a period of years and had several children. Nonetheless, 10 years ago they agreed to a divorce, and Brian became again involved with people of both sexes. He described their current relationship as amiable: "Most of our friends comment they've seldom seen a happier divorce." They had agreed not to use the children in struggles with one another, and the children passed freely between their respective homes.

Several years ago Brian came out in a public sense by joining MCC. While he had always been religiously concerned, he had not openly affiliated himself with a gay group. A friend convinced him that he had been getting a "free ride" for the work done by the gay liberation movement, and he joined the church. Some time later his teen-age daughters were watching a television program in which some radical lesbians were having a dialogue with "straights," and they were enthusiastically supporting these gay women's point of view. Brian told them that he was thinking of getting involved in "some gay lib stuff." They had known about his bisexuality, but he wondered how they would feel if their friends learned of what he was doing. "Do your thing,"

> they said. "Our friends like you because of who you are as a person. If they don't like you because of that, they're not worth it." "That was pretty heady stuff," Brian commented.
>
> While he admitted to becoming a little tired of public gayness and to turning down invitations to yet another gay rights march, he has quietly become more active. He has been an active correspondent with his representatives over gay civil rights issues, and has recently undertaken a survey about relations between established churches and members of the gay community. He is concerned about possible repercussions at his job, but has decided to go ahead.

Brian acknowledged no particular sense of elation in his growing public affirmation of his bisexuality. Yet he had a lurking fear of rejection once this secret were known, and he felt a clear sense of love and acceptance in his children's support of his public activities. He had been far more open with his second wife, and felt that relationship meant much more to him than his first marriage. He was proud of their continued friendship in spite of divorce, and noted that the MCC has developed a ceremony called a "dissolving" as a means of ending a relationship with less guilt and antagonism. So far, the church has performed about 2 such "dissolvings" and 20 "holy unions."

Like Andrew in the previous case, Brian has experimented in his life with varying degrees of secrecy and public affirmation about an attribute which is quite different but which carries a public stigma. When public acceptance was less, being found out had dire consequences. Yet he found that a marriage designed to be a pretense of normalcy failed. A more open marriage worked better and had provided many satisfactions. He has had a period of intense open involvement in the gay movement, and finds himself wanting to move on, having made the point. Along the way with his increasing public involvement, he has picked up support from his family which he had been afraid he would not get. He seemed to feel freer than he had in the past to be what he is, with less concern about consequences. His growing public involvement has been quite gradual – first with lovers, then with his family, subsequently with friends, then in a quietly accepting religious congregation, and now in his home and professional community. This gradual transition seems to have made the process less frightening and awesome. Interestingly, there is a dialogue within the Metropolitan Community Church about the degree to which they should become more involved in public and political issues and they are planning a large conference around the relationship between the religious and gay communities.

Thus there seems to have been a development toward public and political assertiveness both in Brian's life and in the supportive community which has provided a framework for it. He feels psychotherapy years ago helped him lessen guilt which he feels now was culturally induced, but his public involvement seems also to have enhanced personal self-respect and has elicited support from friends and family.

CASE EXAMPLE: MASSACHUSETTS ASSOCIATION FOR SELF-HELP (MASH)

The relationship between groups which employ the self-help concept in treating drug abuse and the political process is complex. This portion of the chapter deals with a political coalition composed of staff members from various self-help drug treatment programs in the greater Boston area. The focus will be on the impact this group had on the broader public and political arena, and on the personal impact of the group experience on members.

This study concerns the work of one regional subgroup of a statewide coalition of drug self-help programs, recently incorporated as the Massachusetts Association for Self-Help. The association includes "concept houses" (a specialized form of therapeutic community structured to deal with addicted persons); group homes; educational and preventive programs; and emergency, crisis intervention, and hot-line services, among others. The only programs excluded are those which employ methadone maintenance or other chemical approaches to addiction.

The coalition began several years ago, largely through the instigation of Dr. Matthew Dumont, Assistant Commissioner for Drug Rehabilitation in the Department of Mental Health in Massachusetts. He noted that consumer involvement is one of the strongest democratic forces abroad in the country, and realized that drug abusers could hardly form a consumer group in view of the illegality of their activities. He therefore urged therapeutic communities connected with the Department to form a coalition which could press for the rights of drug abusers in particular and young people in general, since both groups tend to be stereotyped as one group anyway.[11]

The coalition started haltingly, but benefited from several conventions, has hired a director, and is subdivided into seven regional groups within the state which are active to varying degrees. This study included participation in the meetings of the Region VI Coalition, which is comprised of therapeutic communities within the greater Boston area. The meetings occurred every 3 weeks on a weekday evening at one of the larger self-help houses. The meetings varied in size, usually between 20 and 30 people being present, consisting of about one-third women and less than one-tenth blacks. A long-time member estimated that about half of those present had used drugs heavily and had themselves been in treatment programs, but another estimate put the portion of former addicts at one-fifth. Several had criminal records. Others in the group seemed to be white college graduates with interests in social issues and undergraduate majors in subjects like philosophy and sociology. The leader of the group, Mike, had such a background, with an interest in organizational analysis as well. He led the meetings expertly and consistently kept to an agenda.

The Region VI Coalition defined its primary function as political. Members were on the staffs of various programs, generally worked hard for low pay, and contributed this political involvement as extra time. Nonetheless, attendance was generally good, and a sense of solidarity and involvement grew over the months. The coalition met with success on several fronts. Members exchanged information about a program to experiment with a new heroin blocking agent at one of the two city prisons. Several members helped create a public controversy by working

[11]M.P. Dumont, Personal Communication.

with reporters and contacting the warden of the prison which resulted in suspension of a program which they saw as dangerous and detrimental to the rights of prisoners.

A major issue was the development of a new federal anticrime program which initially seemed quite repressive to the members. They cited, as an example, funding for people whose function it would be to check up on those who left the program. Nonetheless, considerable amounts of money were involved, and after some initial hesitation and requests for support, one woman in the group accepted the offer of a job developing plans for the project. The members formed a subcommittee which made recommendations and negotiated with people responsible for the project. The regional coalition incorporated in order to be able to legally receive funds, and they now have a contract as a referral agency to member therapeutic communities within this project. They had to compromise and accept a role for methadone maintenance programs and are also working with a university psychiatric clinic, but they now have considerable control over treatment recommendations for people convicted of drug-related offenses in court.

This resolution was not easily come by, but the fact that it happened at all is significant. At the early meetings, those discussing the proposed involvement with the developing referral program were treated with considerable suspicion. One woman had been offered a job helping in the planning phases of the project. This was seen both as an opportunity for input and as a possibility of betrayal. Another woman delivered a none-too-gentle warning: "I'm going to be pissed off if you don't tell me what's happening." The first woman took the job, and the group spent the bulk of many subsequent meetings analyzing the proposals and political maneuvering involved. A subcommittee drew up position papers, and negotiated with officials in the program to have their principles worked into the program. Gradually the sense of suspicion eased, to the point that the group was quite cohesive some 6 months later when faced with some administrative pressure and possible reneging on agreements once the program opened. Newly hired staff members of the program, also new to the coalition meetings, were treated as potential allies and felt they had received a great deal of support in the face of difficult struggles for control of their time and the direction of their work.

Regular members of the group as well as invited guests occasionally spent a good deal of time discussing something of interest to themselves or their own group at the expense of the broader group's agenda. They were generally treated with considerable tolerance and respect, and at times were told by the leader or another member to let the discussion move on. In spite of the diversity of people and programs, there was remarkably little scapegoating. Further, the intense pressures put on the group by the programs with which they dealt were met with a general sense of unity, not division and suspicion.

The coalition achieved some measure of success in having a major input into the anticrime program, in opposing certain chemical treatment programs, and also in becoming recognized. Several self-help programs sent representatives to explain their approaches to the group. A representative from the Department of Corrections came to explain their attempts to work with self-help programs. The group did not meet with uniform success by any means. Members attended State House hearings on reform of the laws against marijuana and came away with the impression that the hearings had been a good show, but that in reality no change was forthcoming. However, the group did turn out a large number of people to lobby against the institution of harsher drug laws, and they were optimistic that they could help maintain present statutes.

Several members discussed their satisfaction at having such a political impact. Some saw it as compensation for the low pay and hard work of dealing with people with complex social, psychological, and drug abuse problems.

One member of the group, Sue, talked about trying to apply what she has learned about political process in her work with residents in her program:

> A woman in another house went to the statewide women's meeting a month ago – it was organized by women in the Division of Drug Rehabilitation. She took nine women from her program there. They came back full of energy and determination and started changing the program. They demanded an equal place in sports – now they played football. They are tearing down Playboy posters, confronting male chauvinist remarks, and have found the process very good for their self-respect.
>
> I have had several revolts in my program which were really good. Once I gave out red and yellow cards, and started talking about something else. But every time someone with a yellow card said something, I said "right," and every time someone with a red card said something, I criticized the comment. They caught on and got angry, and then tore up the cards giving everyone a red and a yellow piece. I accused them of being orange and thus part red. They walked out. I called them back and we had a good discussion on what racism felt like.
>
> These kinds of discussions have a really good effect on the residents. They seem to view everything that happens to them as their fault. They tend not to be connected with the broader political and social situation. When a landlord tells them: "There are roaches because you junkies live in the building," they used to believe it. Now they start asking what kind of tax benefit the landlord gets from having a building that needs repairs.

This woman went on to note a kind of historical process in the involvement of those in the coalition. Initially many of the members had been primarily concerned with the internal workings of their programs. A period of calm ensued, after which many leaders realized that if they did not organize to protect their programs they could lose them – through shifting patterns of drug abuse, funding cutbacks, or by being outmaneuvered politically. The development noted in the previous cases from personal to public to political activity seems confirmed again here. She went on to say:

> I come here because of the people – I like them and I like what we're doing. I don't have to come here professionally.

A man from another program added that he felt the group members, leaders in their own programs, got a kind of support from participation in the coalition not unlike the support residents get within the treatment programs:

> When people get involved politically, they meet others and support one another. What one person does in a therapeutic community talking about his inner problems and his parents, another may do with people politically.

From his point of view the aim was not therapeutic but political. Nonetheless the experience had for him a supportive and affirming quality which is not entirely different from a good therapy experience.

Mike, the group leader, amplified this position, discussing a kind of internal/external dialectic in his participation:

> To me the work in my own program is like dealing with an internal issue – a family. It involves more challenges to authority and less direct and positive feedback. It is crisis after crisis, one step forward and two steps back.
>
> The coalition is an outside group. I feel more rewarded for my work and see more concrete growth.

In the coalition, Mike was viewed as a leader among equals, welcoming a positive response as much as anyone. In his own program, he was seen (he felt) as more of an authority figure, less likely to need a rewarding response. Thus, by involving himself in broader public and political issues he had found a peer group of people in similar situations to his own, generally sympathetic. Equally important, they were able to offer one another real help as a group.

At the final meeting for the year, members congratulated one another on the work done and made plans for the following year. A third statewide Coalition Conference followed, and one of the major pressures was an issue brought up within the Boston area group – participation of clients. A group of "consumers" had attended the conference, were discussing forming relationships of their own among the different treatment programs, and were requesting participation in the political work of the state coalition.

Political involvement by this group seems to have been both effective and helpful to its members. Their identification with the cause of self-help enabled them to obtain certain rights and benefits from a society which is generally critical but fearful of drug abusers. But the majority of the members of this coalition did not seem to be even former drug abusers, although they work with them. Rather, they are leaders of poorly funded, recently developed, and diverse programs aimed at treating a difficult problem. Their membership in the coalition can be seen as an assertion at once of mastery and reliance on help, that is, self-help for program leaders. Their public assertion of a need to work together led to political effectiveness on one side and personal reinforcement on the other, both from group support and a sense of success in achieving goals. The dialectic is one of assertiveness and neediness, and the resolution seems to have been in the direction of personal and program development. This lesson did not pass unnoticed by the clients of the programs, who seem to be reaching in a similar direction.

CONCLUSION

Three case examples have been presented from differing mutual support groups and have been discussed from several perspectives: (1) the spectrum of private – "going public" – political activity, with the speculation that there seems to be an individual and group progression along that spectrum; (2) the differing arenas or audiences before which the public activity occurs and their supportiveness; and (3) the personal impact of such public/political activity in dialectical terms.

The three cases cited all demonstrate examples of activity largely on the public and political end of the spectrum, the MASH group being the most avowedly political. Nonetheless, in all three cases, as the organizations developed, they seemed to grow in the direction of political activism, the Burns group to secure funding and better legislation, the MCC debating how active to be in the Gay Liberation movement and interesting itself in changes in professional attitudes toward homosexuals, and the drug self-help coalition organizing itself to secure funding and clients and to influence legislation after a period of creation and then quiescence in the member programs.

Further, all of the individuals studied showed some personal development in the direction of public and political activity. Andrew had come to it only after years of alternately denying and obsessing about his burn injury. Brian became more publicly and politically active about his bisexuality after discussing more openly his sexual preferences with his family and friends. Mike and other members of the Boston area self-help coalition came to concerted political activity only after a period of building their own programs.

Second, in all of the cases studied, the individuals went through a carefully (if unintentionally) graded series of at first small and relatively sympathetic audiences toward larger and less sympathetic arenas. Andrew broke his decade of silence to discuss his injury with the woman who was to become his wife. It took almost another decade before he presented his experience to a group of concerned and sympathetic people. He has begun to approach the wider community looking for funding. Brian ceased hiding his sexual preferences at first only with friends, then later with family, and then with the guilt stirred by pressure from a friend, he went public in a sympathetic congregation, then with his political representatives, and finally in his home community with a questionnaire about gay people and churches. Mike and others in the self-help coalition began discussing their problems and needs among themselves. The coalition had developed an educational resource branch before it moved on to political activity. With suspicion at first, and then with increasing confidence they negotiated with city, state, and federal agencies. Individual members of the coalition developed as leaders in their own programs before joining together to engage in broader political activity.

The third aspect, personal impact, is perhaps hardest to assess and most interesting. Andrew seemed to find a kind of personal integration and relief in his public activity. He neither denied nor obsessed but rather became something different – a man who had been burned but who had in some sense mastered it and therefore had something to contribute. He acknowledged his problem and at the same time enhanced rather than diminished his self-esteem. Brian did not seem elated by his increased openness, but rather more content. He felt less the lurking fear of rejection if found out, and managed to retain positive aspects even of relationships adversely affected by his sexual preferences. He had some sense of asserting rather than hiding himself, and of demanding fair treatment. Mike and other members of MASH felt beleaguered in many ways – responsible for difficult programs with uncertain futures with little positive feedback. Through the coalition, they found people with common problems – felt less alone. Furthermore, they did something together to ease their collective problems.

The phenomenon of "going public" seems to be an important aspect of the personal growth experienced by many people in mutual support groups. This public assertion of a stigmatized attribute has the paradoxical effect of connecting the person with an aspect of his body, personality, behavior, or role often considered negative, and at the same time asserting that he is a worthwhile person. The very fact that he decides to shun secrecy about this attribute is often a sign of courage. Further, he achieves a kind of solidarity with a group of people with similar problems and amounts of courage.

Making a public statement about possessing a stigmatized characteristic seems to address some fundamental aspects of human personality. Public action avoids the flight into subjective fantasy suggested by sheer denial of a problem on the one hand and the grim acceptance of helplessness in the face of the objective expectations of those around us on the other hand. It is a dialectical action which involves accepting responsibility and moving on. The process of moving on can include an expansion of the public statement into the political arena, where the risks and rewards are greater. The phenomenon seems widespread, as the growing impact of the women's liberation movement and the various groups asserting ethnic pride and identity would indicate.

While this theme of the relationship between public assertiveness and self-esteem is not a common one in the psychiatric and other professional literature, it has been discussed. Rudolph Wittenberg wrote an interesting article in 1948 describing a social work consultation to a woman forming a block organization to deal with local problems. At the end of the study, he notes:

Essentially the value of this experiment seems to lie in release of hostilities and frustrations which, when channelled and organized, can be directed toward modifying the environment. Both individual and group growth seemed possible with this method. There is ample evidence to substantiate the impression that Mrs. Smith has made a better adjustment within herself and toward her children. She gained in self-respect and in status in her own block. She is no longer the bedraggled-looking, hopeless relief recipient. Through release she has become able to free a considerable amount of energy.[12]

The approach used in this case was supportive counseling – a mixture of traditional casework and consultation to a developing group leader. The main result seemed to come more from the public growth than from private insight in the case he reported.

Throughout his devoted and irreverent career, Saul Alinsky maintained that mental health was inseparable from economic and political self-determination:

... many of the psychiatric concepts that apply in your studies and research on individuals apply equally in the field of mass mechanics. Just take my word on it from a general familiarity and discussions with many of your colleagues: When you start talking about guilts, when you start talking about frustrations, when you start talking about ability to handle problems of realistic expectations and so forth, in many cases you are talking precisely of what our organizers are talking about, but using another kind of language.[13]

Alinsky, as a community organizer, sensed that self-esteem was not immune to surroundings, and that a collective movement to obtain power could not help but benefit a person's sense of himself.

Most of the people studied seemed to feel that there is an important place for those who perform traditional mental health services. Brian had benefited from several years of psychotherapy during his early transition from private to limited public assertion of his bisexuality, for example. All of the groups studied actively seek such services in one form or another. At the same time, as was suggested earlier in the discussion of Dr. Shatan's work with Vietnam veterans, something seems to happen in these groups which is different from psychotherapy and which is not duplicated in a professional's office.

In order to assess this difference on a personal level, it might be useful to compare some lessons learned in the public arena with the expectations of good outcomes in psychotherapy. For one thing, involvement in the political process gives one a sense of how complex all political decisions are. They are no longer accepted as wise or necessary but are seen as oppor-

[12]R.M. Wittenberg, "Personality Adjustment Through Social Action," *American Journal Orthopsychiatry* XVIII: 2, April, 1948 p. 219.

[13]S.D. Alinsky, "The Poor and the Powerful," *International Journal of Psychiatry* IV: 4, Oct., 1967, p. 308.

tunities for change. This in the social sphere has some equivalence to the clarification of the common transference distortion in therapy that the therapist is all-knowing and constructs all events in the therapy with some clear purpose in mind. Coupled with the realization that this is not so, the patient finds himself thrown more on his own resources to help himself. For example, the drug self-help coalition found it necessary to set aside simple conclusions about the motivations of the various people in positions of power in order to work out a compromise which gave it some real power.

It is also common in psychotherapy to find a patient feeling responsible for whatever happens around himself, for example, the therapist leaving. This is seen by psychoanalysts as a means of maintaining control in fantasy even though control of the other person is lost in fact. By feeling responsible, the person says to himself, "If only I had not done what I did, this would not have happened." The message from public and political involvement is similar. The drug program staff member quoted earlier noted that drug addicts tend to blame themselves for whatever happens in their lives, and certainly they have much for which to blame themselves. But awareness of political issues helps them sort out the distortions from the realities and see where in fact they are helpless to control their lives unless they work collectively.

Many personal problems can be ameliorated with professional intervention. But evaluation of the best treatment approach must include assessment of all the strengths and weaknesses of each method. A more sophisticated development of insight within traditional therapy may not have more personal impact than a simple public assertion of a problem. Indeed the most effective mutual support groups have emerged among people with problems not well handled by professionals, for example, among alcoholics and drug abusers as well as homosexuals. It would seem that public assertion of a stigma in a setting of mutual support is an assertion of personal worth which can enhance self-respect. It is a request not to be discriminated against because of a given problem. In addition, active participation in such groups can be effective in changing the quality of life for those with problems and for the society as a whole.

Perhaps the most constructive approach would be to view public and political development in self-help groups and traditional forms of psychotherapy as valid alternatives or even companions in an individual's life, depending on that person's desires and opportunities as well as his particular problems. And certain people may require traditional treatment before they could invest themselves in collective activity meaningfully. Others may benefit more from public assertion and mutual support. But the development of public and political assertiveness with a corresponding growth in self-esteem as well as creative impact on our society as a whole seems to be too useful a phenomenon for mental health professionals to overlook.

Ruth B. Caplan

6

Deathbed Scenes and Graveyard Poetry: Death in Eighteenth-Century English Literature.

During the eighteenth century, a minor literary genre developed with its own language and conventions that dealt in descriptions of death. In fiction and nonfiction, poetry and prose, it portrayed an ethos in which death was made a familiar, if awesome spectacle and a focus of social activity that demanded elaborate behavior both from the survivors and from their dying friend. Death was not presented as an isolating and isolated crisis. Rather, it marked the culmination of a social role, a moment within the continuum of life that stretched from birth to eternity, in which the community finally evaluated and benefitted from the moral worth of the dying member.

EMOTIONAL INOCULATION

Among Nonconformists especially, there was an intensification of the Christian doctrine that presented death as the focal point of life. Not merely the prospect of Heaven or Hell, but the moment of death itself, with its attendant pains and terrors, was used by religious writers as the measure against which all of life's actions were to be graded. High Churchmen of an earlier age, like Jeremy Taylor, who was much admired by the eighteenth-century Nonconformists, advised men to weigh every act according to whether its memory would bring comfort or misery at death. As Taylor wrote in *The Rules and Exercises of Holy Dying,* death requires preparation and even rehearsal – in today's terms, emotional inoculation:

> He that would die well, must always look for death, every day knocking at the gates of the grave: and then the gates of the grave shall never prevail upon him to do him mischief....

> But withal, the frequent use of this meditation, by curing our present inordination, will make death safe and friendly, and by its very custom will make that king of terrors come to us without his affrighting dresses; and that we shall sit down in the grave as we compose ourselves to sleep, and do the duties of nature and choice.[1]

We must, Taylor continues, "Provide beforehand a reserve of strength and mercy," since,

> When we come to die, indeed, we shall be very much put to it to stand firm upon the two feet of a Christian, faith and patience. When we ourselves are to use the articles, to turn our former discourses into present practice, and to feel what we never felt before, we shall find it to be quite another thing, to be willing presently to quit this life and all our present possessions for the hope of a thing which we were never suffered to see, and such a thing of which we may fail so many ways, and of which, if we fail any way, we are miserable for ever . . .
>
> Then we shall find, how much we have need to have secured the Spirit of God, and the grace of faith, by a habitual, perfect, unmovable resolution. The same also, is the case of patience, which will be assaulted with sharp pains, disturbed fancies, great fears, want of a present mind, natural weaknesses, frauds of the devil, and a thousand accidents and imperfections. It concerns us, therefore, highly, in the whole course of our lives, not only to accustom ourselves to a patient suffering of injuries and affronts, of persecutions and losses, of cross accidents and unnecessary circumstances; but also by representing death as present to us, to consider with what arguments then to fortify our patience, and by assiduous and fervent prayer to God all our life long to call upon Him to give us patience and great assistances. . . . But this is to be the work of our life, and not to be done at once; but as God gives us time, by succession, by parts, and by little periods.[2]

Rehearsal for the moment of death, therefore, not only required avoiding sin but also the laying down of habits of faith, and familiarity with the idea, even the very feeling of one's own immanent end. These would then become second nature, so that in the crisis of reality, the individual could count on functioning correctly without conscious effort, like a well-drilled soldier under fire, when effort might otherwise be paralyzed by panic or fading reason. Taylor's eighteenth-century successor in this genre, William Law, in *A Serious Call to a Devout and Holy Life,* advised his readers to imagine as they climbed into bed every night that they were being lowered into the grave:

> Represent to your imagination, that your *bed* is your *grave;* that all things are ready for your interment; that you are to have no more to do with this world; and that it will be owing to God's great Mercy, if you ever see the light of the Sun again, or have another day to add to your works of piety . . . .
>
> Such a solemn resignation of yourself into the hands of God every evening,

[1]Jeremy Taylor, "The Rules and Exercises of Holy Dying," *Holy Living and Dying* (London: Duncan and Malcolm, 1839), pp. 368-369.

[2]Ibid., pp. 370-371.

and parting with all the world, as if you were never to see it any more, is a practice that will soon have excellent effects upon your spirit.[3]

As an aid to such meditations, poets like the clergymen Robert Blair, in "The Grave," and Edward Young, in *Night Thoughts on Life, Death, and Immortality,* provided lurid descriptions of the horrors of death and the tomb which give full play to accounts of final agonies, both physical and mental; to the sudden weakness of men hitherto proud in their strength; to remorse striking too late for convincing repentance; and to the decline of the moribund and the decomposition of corpses.

What groan whas that I heard? – deep groan indeed!
With anguish heavy laden; let me trace it:
From yonder bed it comes, where the strong man,
By stronger arms belabour'd, gasps for breath
Like a hard hunted beast. How his great heart
Beats thick! his roomy chest by far too scant
To give the lungs full play. What now avail
The strong-built, sinewy limbs, and well spread shoulders?
See how he tugs for life, and lays about him,
Mad with his pains! – Eager he catches hold
Of what comes next to hand, and grasps it hard,
Just like a creature drowning; – hideous sight!
Oh! how his eyes stand out, and stare full ghastly!
While the distemper's rank and deadly venom
Shoots like a burning arrow 'cross his bowels,
And drinks his marrow up. – Heard you that groan?
It was his last.[4]

The inflated tone and heavy hand in this and similar passages are characteristic. John Locke had argued that knowledge flows in through the senses. Writers on death, therefore, had to link their teachings to familiar feelings, even at the risk of bathos. They labored to paint final agonies in terms that were meant to stimulate the senses through the imagination, so as to make up for the presumed absence of firsthand experience of death in the audience.

RIGHT AND WRONG WAYS TO DIE

The most popular moral novel of the mid-eighteenth century, Samuel Richarson's *Clarissa,* is punctuated by deathbed scenes illustrating the entire

[3]William Law, *A Serious Call to a Devout and Holy Life, Adapted to the State and Condition of all Orders of Christians* (London: J. Richardson, 1893), p. 262.

[4]Robert Blair, "The Grave," *The Poetical Works of Beattie, Blair, and Falconer* (Edinburgh: James Nichol, 1854), Ll. 262-278.

range of right and wrong ways to approach the grave. It draws heavily on what had become by now conventions, so that when her friends enumerate the signs of decay in the heroine – her wasting flesh, her failing sight, her shortened breath – these are not so much evidence of an unhealthy imagination in Richardson as a reflection of an accepted and widely recognized literary tradition which sought to perform a socially useful task by forcing readers to realize and rehearse their own deaths at a safe distance.

Even more efficacious than rehearsing death through a fictional medium was actual presence at a deathbed. The educational benefit of such attendance led John Wesley to take the children under his charge at the Methodist school in Kingswood to watch the neighbors in their final hours. Samuel Johnson described deathbed scenes in *Rambler, 54* as "This school of wisdom for the common man", which

> Is not the peculiar privilege of geometricians; the most sublime and important precepts require no uncommon opportunities, nor labourious preparation, they are enforced without aid of eloquence, and understood without skill in analytic sciences. Every tongue can utter them, and every understanding can conceive them. He that wishes in earnest to obtain just sentiments concerning his condition, and would be intimately acquainted with the world, may find instruction on every side.[5]

Death in eighteenth-century literature is consequently presented as a major social occasion, requiring the presence of many attendants. Those round the deathbed are there not only to take leave of a friend but also to learn – to prepare for their own end by observing a practical demonstration of the fruits of a good or bad life, and by witnessing the actual course of death so that similar sensations in themselves would not prove surprising and therefore paralyzing. By seeing their own mortality reflected in the cases of others, it was thought that they would be sobered and recalled to Christian duty.

In works of this kind, like *Clarissa,* characters are clearly divided between those who have prepared, or are preparing themselves for death, and who consequently make a dignified and peaceful exit, and those who are caught unawares like the fools in Blair's "The Grave,"

> Fools that we are!
> Never to think of death and of ourselves
> At the same time: as if to learn to die
> Were no concern of ours – O more than sottish,
> For creatures of a day, in gamesom mood,
> To frolic on eternity's dread brink
> Unapprehensive.[6]

[5]Samuel Johnson, *The Rambler*, ed. Walter J. Bate and Albrecht B. Strauss (New Haven: Yale University Press, 1969), p. 290.

[6]Robert Blair, *Poetical Works*, Ll. 471-477.

They illustrate Edward Young's warning in *Night Thoughts on Life, Death, and Immortality,* against those who accustom themselves to ignoring death:

> Be wise to-day; 'tis madness to defer;
> Next day the fatal precedent will plead;
> Thus on, till wisdom is push'd out of life.
> Procrastination is the thief of time;
> Year after year it steals, till all are fled,
> And to the mercies of a moment leaves
> The vast concerns of an eternal scene.[7]

At their final hours, these improvident souls disgrace themselves by dying with so little decorum and presence of mind that their eternal fate seems gloomy, and all the thoughtless pleasure of their earthly existence becomes a mockery in retrospect.

Thus, while the 19-year-old Clarissa spends her last weeks preparing for death: composing her will, disposing of her letters and clothes, appointing literary executors, and buying and installing a coffin in her room, which she uses as a writing table, the reader, like the bystanders in the story, is meant to learn from and emulate her composure and marvel at the sanity of her proceedings. The villains of the novel, on the other hand, deny the precariousness of their mortal condition even on their deathbed. They tacitly believe themselves exempt from death, and consequently refuse, even during their final hours, to put their affairs and souls in order. As Young had written, "All men think all men mortal but themselves."[8]

This denial of death is shown to be not only morally reprehensible but also psychologically dangerous, since it reduces the improvident at the time of death to fits of pitiful weeping, hallucination, and incoherence. Just as dangerous, however, is a superstitious preoccupation with evading death, with attempts to fend it off by magical thinking. There is, for example, in *Clarissa,* a vignette of Cousin Larkin, whose psychopathology is complex though her place in the story is negligible. Cousin Larkin had always feared that if she were to make her will, she would die.

> And, one would think, imagined she was under an obligation to prove her words: for, though she had been long bed-rid, and was, in a manner, worn out before, yet she thought herself better, till she was persuaded to make it [a will] and from that moment, remembering what she used to prognosticate (her *fears helping on what she feared,* as is often the case, particularly in the smallpox) grew worse: and had it in her head once to burn her will, in hopes to grow better upon it.[9]

[7]Edward Young, *Night Thoughts on Life, Death, and Immortality* (London: Chapman and Co., 1837), Night the First, Ll. 390-396.

[8]Ibid., L. 424.

[9]Samuel Richardson, *Clarissa, or, the History of a Young Lady* (London: Everyman Library, 1965), I. 330-331.

Driven by her fears, Cousin Larkin does indeed expire shortly after, of what might be called Lockean causes – a pathological association of ideas. A realistic attitude to death was demanded by this literature: one that left the individual prepared and resigned, instead of allowing him, by denial or self-delusion, to cling to a fantasy of immortality.

THE DYING AND HIS SURVIVORS: A MUTUAL SUPPORT GROUP

The educational function of attendance at a deathbed placed a corresponding responsibility on the one who was dying. His behavior was regarded by himself and his society as an object lesson for the beholders, the efficacy of which depended on, and proved his own identity as a Christian. Thus, the ultimate evidence of goodness was to achieve a peaceful end, and to surrender with joy and faith to the Divine decree in a way that would communicate conviction to others:

> We gaze; we weep; mixt tears of grief and joy!
> Amazement strikes! Devotion bursts to flame!
> Christians adore, and infidels believe.[10]

This literature, therefore, held the final earthly test of virtue to be a social one, depending on whether the sight of it could affect and change the morals and faith of others. In the same way, the horrible end of the wicked, marked always by struggle and fear, acted as a caution to the community. During one of his journeys to Ireland, Wesley watched the execution of a party of rebels:

> Four of the Whiteboys, lately condemmed for breaking open houses, were executed. They were all, notwithstanding the absolution of the Priest, ready to die for fear of death; two or three of them laid fast hold on the ladder (of the gallows), and could not be persuaded to let it go. One, in particular, gave such violent shrieks, as might be heard a mile off. O how inexpressibly miserable is that bondage![11]

The dying person was expected not merely to serve as a passive object lesson to his community; he was also encouraged to actively instruct the bystanders. As Jeremy Taylor had written,

> Let the sick man set his house in order before he die; state his case of conscience, reconcile the fractures of his family, reunite brethren, cause right understanding, and remove jealousies; give good counsels for the future conduct of their persons and estates, charm them into religion by the authority and advantage of a dying person; because the last words of a dying man are like the tooth of a

[10]Edward Young, *Night Thoughts*, LI. 682-684.

[11]John Wesley, *The Journal of the Rev. John Wesley, M.A.* (London: J.M. Dent and Co.), III, p. 101.

wounded lion, making a deeper impression in the agony than in the most vigorous strength.[12]

The traditional prophetic role of the dying was cultivated among the Nonconformists; and instruction was particularly prized when it came from the mouths of babes and sucklings. Thus, in Wesley's *Journals,* there are records of small children in their death throes reproving and comforting their elders, and exhorting them, with considerable relish, to give up their vices and to cling to the good life. Thirteen-year-old John Woolley, for example, on his deathbed, recalled his family to faith and sober living, and correctly prophesied the death of his father.[13]

> He added, "I shall die; but do not cry for me; why should you cry for me? Consider what a joyful thing it is to have a brother go to Heaven! I am not a man; I am but a boy. But is it not in the Bible, 'Out of the mouths of babes and sucklings thou hast ordained strength?' I know where I am going; I would not be without this knowledge for a thousand worlds; for though I am not in heaven yet, I am as sure of it as if I was."[14]

In this vein, during her long decline, Richardson's Clarissa,

> Fell into a very serious discourse on the vanity of life, and the wisdom of preparing for death while health and strength remained, and before the infirmities of body impaired the faculties of the mind, and disabled them from acting with the necessary efficacy and clearness . . . .[15]

Similarly, in the nineteenth century, when these traditions had become stylized and saccharine in the retelling, Thomas Hughes' little Arthur, in *Tom Brown's Schooldays,* grows ethereally delicate during an almost fatal fever. From what threatens to be his deathbed, he urges the older Tom, by authority of the younger boy's closeness to death, to lead the Christian life and to stop cheating on his Latin and Greek homework so that God and Dr. Arnold, the headmaster, would be served. Arthur then describes the vision that came to him in illness, in which after nights of despair and anger against God, he learned to accept an early death;[16] and this account of simple piety sobers the thoughtless Tom.

It is in part this didactic role of the dying that surrounds accounts of death, both fictional and real, with conscious, premeditated theatricality. In Methodist and Quaker descriptions of deathbeds, there is often a suggestion of an hitherto unimportant little person who has rarely, if ever, been the center of attention before, and who is taking full advantage of the oc-

[12]Jeremy Taylor, *Holy Living and Dying*, pp. 496-497.

[13]John Wesley, *Journal*, I, pp. 358-361.

[14]Ibid., p. 360.

[15]Samuel Richardson, *Clarissa*, IV, p. 217.

[16]Thomas Hughes, *Tom Brown's Schooldays* (London: Mayflower Books, Ltd., 1971), p. 212.

casion to have a "joyful death" indeed. Rather than being hidden away, so that the spectacle of his death will not disturb the living, the dying person in this literature takes center stage. A principal character, surrounded by grieving family and friends, he seems consciously fulfilling a ceremonial role, accounts of which would be remembered and even published by those who saw the scene.

It is this tradition that enshrines last words with such piety, since the utterances of the good testify to the rewards of faith and virtue. In Wesley's *Journal*, as in Quaker pamphlets describing the last hours of members of a meeting, there is a tone of premeditation about last words, and an often explicit injunction to repeat them to the congregation in order to prove that the individual was a Christian to the end. Thus, Wesley recorded the death of young Benjamin Colley: "Some of his last words were, 'Tell all the Society, tell all the world, I die without doubt or fear'."[17]

It is interesting that last words tend not to be personal prayers for mercy or for reprieve, as one might expect, but rather ejaculations of praise or thanksgiving, Biblical phrases uttered as prophesy, or testimony to the presence of Divinity or of a departed saint, all directed to the bystanders. One of Wesley's followers, for example, cried out at the moment of death, "Do you not see him? There he is! Glory, glory, glory! I shall be with him for ever, for ever, for ever!"[18] A 4-year-old girl, "Spent all the intervals of her convulsions in speaking of or to God; and when she perceived her strength to be near exhausted she desired all the family to come near, and prayed for them all, one by one; then for her Minister, for the Church, and for all the world. A short time after, recovering from a fit, she lifted up her eyes, said, 'Thy kingdom come,' and died."[19]

Another one of the faithful said, "I know . . . that my Redeemer liveth, and will stand at the latter day upon the earth. I fear not death. It hath no sting for me. I shall live for evermore."[20] Yet another cried "Halleluja, halleluja, halleluja!" In this tradition, the dying ideally abandons gradually all selfish concerns, and becomes caught up in the greater identity of the Heavenly choir, speaking from an already elevated, impersonal plane to the community of pious survivors.

The wicked, on the other hand, are denied this memorial; their ends are marked by incoherent and often insane interchanges with the creatures of guilty hallucinations – a chimerical set of deathbed attendants. Thus, Richardson's evil Mrs. Sinclair, the keeper of a brothel in which the chaste Clarissa has been imprisoned, expires in a cacophany of shrieks and groans, while the abandoned rake, Belton, dies mouthing unintelligible confessions, which his friends deduce to be a possible admission of murdering an uncle

[17]John Wesley, *Journal*, III, p. 309.
[18]Ibid., III, p. 273.
[19]Ibid., I, p. 475.
[20]Ibid., I, p. 353.

for his estate.[21] They die, like the wicked men described by Jeremy Taylor:

> We may imagine the terror of their abused fancies, how they see afrighting shapes, and because they fear them, they feel the gripes of devils, urging the unwilling souls from the kinder and fast embraces of the body, . . . exhibiting great bills of uncancelled crimes, awaking and amazing the conscience, breaking all their hopes in pieces, and making faith useless and terrible, because the malice was great, and the charity was not at all. Then they look for some to have pity on them, but there is no man. No man dares be their pledge; no man can redeem their soul, which now feels what it never feared. Then the tremblings and the sorrow, the memory of the past sin, and the presence of some devils, consign him to the eternal company of all the damned and accursed spirits.[22]

Last words are like an epitaph. They are meant to summarize character and identity. Reading accounts of them, one often suspects that they have been composed some time earlier and held in reserve until needed, in order to produce an edifying effect. At times, there is a touch of bathos, when death does not come as soon as expected, and when the words have been squandered too quickly. John Wesley himself seems to have been the victim of such bad timing. For three days, he made final remarks at intervals; and one may sense a growing desperation, and a decline in pithiness, as the strain of topping earlier statements increased. In literature, such mistakes in timing are precluded; Clarissa's last words are in every way suitable to the occasion and to her character. After blessing absent friends, she turns to Belford, the rake who has been reformed by her influence, begging him to forego his sinful course and to consider the fact of mortality that he now witnesses in her. At last, she gasps in the triune form that seems to have been favored for last words: "Bless – bless – bless – you all – and now – and now – (holding up her almost lifeless hands for the last time) – come – o come – blessed Lord – JESUS!"[23]

While the dying person must instruct and move the bystanders, the latter must first help him to assume his new role. They are, as it were, midwives, who help to deliver the soul from earthly entanglements. This was done by exhorting the dying person to fix his mind on heaven and to settle and then forget earthly accounts. It was also effected by praying with the dying, and by asking him a kind of catechism to elicit expressions of faith and to mark the progress of his soul away from the world. In Wesley's *Journals*, for example, key questions included, "Are you prepared to die? If you could live or die, which would you choose?" The "correct" answers expressed an eagerness to go to God, and, in the choice between life and death, an absolute submission to Divine Will.

One of the factors that was held to contribute to a tranquil, "happy"

[21] Samuel Richardson, *Clarissa*, IV, p. 169.
[22] Jeremy Taylor, *Holy Living and Dying*, pp. 386-387.
[23] Samuel Richardson, *Clarissa*, IV, p. 347.

death was readiness in the dying to let go of the world, and a corresponding willingness of the persons around him to release him. If either factor were missing, death would be turbulent and ugly. This literature presented it as an act of particular littleness for the living to cling to the dying. It was not only held to be insubordination to Divine Will but also a selfishness verging on envy which sought to pull the dying back to the frail pleasures of this earth for the benefit of the survivors, away from the solemn glories of Heaven. If the living clung to a dying friend, they would cause him to suffer unnecessary torments. These agonies were illustrated by the story of her husband's death, told to John Wesley in Ireland, by a certain Prudence Nixon:

> In November last, on a Sunday evening, he was uncommonly fervent in prayers, and found such a desire as he never had before, "to depart, and to be with Christ." In the night she awakened, and found him quite stiff, and without sense or motion. Supposing him to be either dying or dead, she broke out into a vehement agony of prayers, and cried for half an hour together, "Lord Jesus! Give me George! Take him not away!" Soon after he opened his eyes, and said earnestly, "You had better have let me go." Presently he was raving mad, and began to curse and blaspheme in the most horrible manner. This he continued to do for several days, appearing to be under the full power of an unclean spirit. At the latter end of the week, she cried out, "Lord, I am willing! I am willing he should go to thee." Quickly his understanding returned, and he again rejoiced with joy unspeakable. He tenderly thanked her for giving him up to God, kissed her, lay down, and died.[24]

It is in part for this reason that the outcast Clarissa resists the offers of her doctor to summon her relatives to her bedside in London:

> But now, doctor, said she, I should be too much disturbed at their grief, if they were any of them to come or to send to me: and perhaps, if I found they still loved me, would wish to live; and so should quit unwillingly that life which I am now really fond of quitting, and hope to quit, as becomes a person who has had such a weaning-time as I have been favoured with.[25]

Once this coveted state of being willing to depart had been achieved, once ties to the world had been cut, it was thought a pity not to die, since this resignation was apt to be ephemeral. Wesley cited the case of a 13-year-old girl, living in constant pain, but full of faith "and loving submission." "O why," Wesley asked, "was she then not taken to paradise? I fear she has now no religion at all!"[26] A German colleague of the Methodists regretted the reprieve at the moment of execution of a soldier condemned to death by his commanders, who had been converted while in prison. When he had recovered from the news of his pardon, the soldier had exclaimed, "Why was I not rather hanged, or even crucified, than pardoned? Why am I thus

[24] John Wesley, *Journal*, III, pp. 228-229.
[25] Samuel Richardson, *Clarissa*, IV, p. 216.
[26] John Wesley, *Journal*, II, p. 447.

stopped in my course? I should now have been with Christ!"[27] Similarly, Richardson's Mrs. Norton writes to her former pupil, Clarissa, regretting the fact that the heroine did not die during a childhood illness, but was saved instead in answer to the ill-considered prayers of then doting parents. Had she died in the midst of innocence and love, she and her family would have been spared the subsequent tragedy recorded in the novel.[28]

DEATH AS THE CONTINUATION OF LIFE

In this literature, death is presented as the "moment of truth," for it destroys all posing and self-delusion. It reduces people to their real scale, exposing their basic identity, and unmasking the hypocrites that were such a popular target for eighteenth-century moralists. As Edward Young had written.

A death-bed's a detector of the heart.
Here tir'd Dissimulation drops her mask,
Through life's grimace, that mistress of the scene!
Here real, and apparent, are the same.
You see the Man; you see his hold on Heav'n.[29]

In the same vein, Samuel Johnson wrote,

> He that desires to enter behind the scene, where every art has been employed to decorate, and every passion laboured to illuminate, and wishes to see life stripped of those ornaments which make it glitter on the stage, and exposed in its natural meanness, impotence and nakedness, may find all the delusions laid open in the chamber of disease: he will there find vanity divested of her robes, power deprived of her sceptre, and hypocracy without her mask.[30]

Consequently, there is a paradox in the treatment of death in eighteenth-century English literature. While death was seen as life's supremely critical moment, at the same time it was minimized as a time of radical change, for its nature was seen as a logical consequence, and continuation of the accretions of a lifetime. In English Protestantism, this position became exaggerated in reaction against Rome. The Catholic belief in the possibility of deathbed conversion and absolution was repudiated and mocked. In his *Rules and Exercise of Holy Dying*, Jeremy Taylor had scorned the Roman deathbed ceremonies as a recent innovation, unsanctified by authority or philosophy. Of Extreme Unction and the prayers for the dead he had written.

> For they make profession, that from death to life, from sin to grace, a man may very certainly be changed, though the operation begin not before his last hour:

[27]Ibid., II, p. 484.
[28]Samuel Richardson, *Clarissa*, IV, p. 49.
[29]Edward Young, *Night Thoughts*, Night the Second, Ll. 641-645.
[30]Samuel Johnson, *The Rambler*, I, p. 290.

and half this they do upon his death-bed, and the other half when he is in his grave: and they take away the eternal punishment in an instant, by a school-distinction, or by the hand of the priest.[31]

On the contrary, Taylor had stressed, a deathbed conversion was suspect.

> A repentance upon our deathbed is like washing the corpse: it is cleanly and civil; but makes no change deeper than the skin. . . . A resolution to repent upon our deathbed, is the greatest mockery of God in the world.[32]

He continued,

> Religion is no religion, and virtue is no act of choice, . . . if we are religious when we cannot choose; if we part with our money, when we cannot keep it; with our lust, when we cannot act it; with our desires, when they have left us. Death is a certain mortifier; but that mortification is deadly, not useful to the purposes of a spiritual life. When we are compelled to depart from our evil customs, and leave to live, that we may begin to live, then we die to die; that life is the prologue to death, and thenceforth we die eternally.[33]

Repentance could only be credible, Taylor insisted, if it began long before death, and its genuineness was probed during the temptations of a lifetime.

The manner of death for English Protestantism was held to be so consistent with the manner of life that the relative saintliness of an individual was proved by the smoothness of his passage through death. As Young wrote in *Night Thoughts*,

> Heav'n waits not the last moment; owns her friends
> On this side death; and points them out to men;
> To vice confusion; and to virtue, peace.[34]

The absence of struggle and horror at the moment of death was a sign of Divine favor toward the Chosen, and of perfect faith in the departing himself, who thereby testified to the reward of true confidence in Christ so that he now faced Judgment with relative equanimity.

A "happy death," as it was called, also proves how little transition there is, in fact, between the good life and Life Everlasting. The earthly saint, who has held aloof from the world, and who leaves it singing hymns of praise, is translated into membership in the Heavenly Choir, where he will continue to praise God for eternity. Thus, Clarissa, who has been called "saint" and "angel" throughout her story, is not changed by dying. Her best friend, Anna Howe, viewing her corpse, sees an angel indeed. The truly wicked also undergo little change. Their death is a foretaste of Hell, mingling physical and mental tortures. Richardson's Mrs. Sinclair, for example, even

[31]Jeremy Taylor, *Holy Living and Dying*, p. 468.
[32]Ibid., pp. 468-469.
[33]Ibid., p. 470.
[34]Edward Young, *Night Thoughts*, Night the Second, Ll. 646-650.

begins to putrify before death in her fatal case of gangrene. For the dead Clarissa, on the other hand, mutability is suddenly suspended. The beautiful and healthy young woman, whose wasting during illness has so shocked her friends, now recovers perfection at the moment of death.[35] When her corpse reaches her family home, Harlowe Place, it is found that the body "was very little altered, notwithstanding the journey. The sweet smile remained."[36] Her family, seeing her now for the first time since they had cast out their once favorite and pampered child, and after she had been tormented and raped, and had wasted away and died in poverty among strangers, all find her unchanged from the Clarissa they remembered: "She was their *very* niece" both uncles said. The injured saint! Her uncle Harlowe. The same smiling sister! Arabella. The dear creature! all of them. The same benignity of countenance! The same sweet composure! The same natural dignity!"[37]

This suspension of change and decay are characteristic of eighteenth-century descriptions of the deaths of the virtuous. John Wesley's *Journals*, for example, are full of such scenes. During his early ministry in Georgia, Wesley was at the house of two sisters, the Boveys, when one of the girls suddenly died. The young missionary commented, "I never saw so beautiful a corpse in my life."[38] A condemned man, who was converted by Methodists in prison, went joyfully to his execution. After hanging, "His face was not at all bloated or disfigured; no, not even changed from its natural colour: but he lay with a calm, smiling countenance, as one in a sweet sleep."[39] A century later, the corpse of Herman Melville's Billy Budd was similarly spared the disfigurations associated with hanging. Another of Wesley's flock, a 16-year-old girl who died in faith, "Resigned her spirit without any sigh or groan, or alteration in her countenance, which had the same sweetness as when she was living."[40] Years later, Wesley buried another pious girl, the 14-year-old Abigail Pilsworth,

> When we went into the room where her remains lay, we were surprised. A more beautiful corpse I never saw: We all sung:
>
> Ah lovely appearance of death!
>   What sight upon earth so fair!
> Not all the gay pageants that breathe,
>   Can with a dead body compare![41]

And, of Wesley himself, a witness of his death at the end of the century wrote,

[35]Samuel Richardson, *Clarissa*, IV, p. 347.
[36]Ibid., IV, p. 398.
[37]Ibid., IV, p. 399.
[38]John Wesley, *Journal*, I, p. 35.
[39]Ibid., II, p. 90.
[40]Ibid., II, pp. 200-202.
[41]Ibid., IV, p. 346.

His corpse was placed in the New Chapel, and remained there the day before his interment. His face during that time had a heavenly smile upon it, and a beauty which was admired by all that saw it.[42]

This tradition of the beautiful corpse is particularly exploited in American literature. Nathaniel Hawthorne, for example, in "The Birthmark," seems to invoke it. Aylmer, a scientist, has an exquisite wife, Georgiana, whose only flaw is a birthmark in the form of a tiny red hand. Revolted by the mark, Aylmer develops an elixir to remove it and persuades Georgiana to drink the potion. She reluctantly obeys: "As the last crimson tint of the birthmark – that sole token of human imperfection – faded from her cheek, the parting breath of the now perfect woman passed into the atmosphere, and her soul, lingering a moment near her husband, took its heavenward flight."[43] At the moment of death, and only at that moment, human perfection reaches its height. The full beauty of the body is revealed only when it is at last unsullied by passions and by the threat of mortality and when it is unable, theoretically, to rouse the forbidden or repressed passions of the bystander. At death, the "human shape divine" may be appreciated in all its glory – a convention that seems to have been developed further by Edgar Allen Poe for his own dark ends, when he removed the exemption from sexual arousal even from the observer of the dead. In the earlier, Enthusiastic tradition, death is both sexualized and simultaneously desexualized. It provides a situation in which it was perhaps safe for young John Wesley to exclaim over the beauty of a suddenly dead girl, when he had been forbidden by social convention from remarking on her attractions in life.

The suspension of mutability in the dying saint raises another issue. While death is explicitly described as a liberation of the spirit from all earthly entanglements – the perfection of a lifetime of effort to escape the desires of the flesh and the lures of earthly ease, riches, and pleasures – implicitly, death for many of these writers means taking possession of those very luxuries of the earthly condition. The beautiful woman, whose face is the epitome of corruptible vanity, remains most beautiful in death; and the deceased continues in some measure to direct his earthly affairs through his will, a document whose importance was stressed by moralists. One sees this phenomenon in the seventeenth-century *Pilgrim's Progress*, where Heaven is suspiciously like Vanity Fair; where saints wear beautiful robes, shining crowns, and ride through golden streets in equipages. Similarly, the dead Clarissa, who has renounced her clothes and jewels during her last few weeks, selling them for a pittance to pay for a few last necessities (thereby dying poor, although actually an heiress, and so escaping the fate

[42]Ibid., IV, p. 525.

[43]Nathanial Hawthorne, "The Birthmark," *The Complete Novels and Selected Tales of Nathaniel Hawthorne* (New York: Random House, Inc., 1937), p. 1032.

of the rich who have such difficulties climbing into heaven) returns in state to Harlowe Place to a pompous funeral and an imposing tomb.

IMAGERY OF DEATH

The fact that a deathbed scene was regarded as an integral part, and a continuation of earthly existence was fostered by the language and imagery surrounding death in Enthusiastic writing, and by the use of the very word "death" itself. In Wesley's *Journals*, for example, great ambiguity about the word is achieved by a set of interlocking images. The "Dead" are those who have not yet grown aware of their own sinfulness and who have not achieved faith. Congregations who resisted revivals were referred to as "dead and cold," like the community of Bandon, Ireland: "I . . . found the Society much lessened, and dead enough"[44] or that of Burslem, Staffordshire: "The Society in general was cold and dead, and only two were converted to God in a whole year."[45] Similarly, an individual may be a "lifeless backslider,"[46] before permanent conversion.

In order for these "dead" to "rise again," to be "awakened," they had to undergo an often convulsive episode. That "dead" person who signaled that he had reached the point of dawning conviction of sin and grace, was described as displaying signs of agony, and of thrashing about as though in the death throes so lovingly treated in Graveside Poetry and *Clarissa:*

> I met the Society at St. Ives, where two women, who came from Penzance, fell down as dead.[47]
>
> J--n H. then beat himself against the ground again; his breast heaving at the same time, as in the pangs of death, and great drops of sweat trickling down his face.[48]
>
> While I was speaking, one before me dropped down as dead, and presently a second and a third: five others sunk down in half an hour, most of whom were in violent agonies.[49]
>
> Great numbers, feeling the arrows of conviction, fell to the ground, some of whom seemed dead, and others in the agony of death, the violence of their bodily convulsions exceeding all description.[50]

Round these thrashing bodies, other members of the congregation clustered to pray each soul through its moment of trial, but also to hold the convulsed body down. Preachers like Wesley described with wonder contor-

[44]John Wesley, *Journal*, III, p. 99.
[45]Ibid., III, p. 110.
[46]Ibid., III, p. 93.
[47]Ibid., I, p. 432.
[48]Ibid., I, p. 190.
[49]Ibid., I, p. 206.
[50]R. A. Knox, *Enthusiasm* (Oxford: Clarendon Press, 1950), p. 527.

tions so superhumanly powerful, that it took half a dozen strong bystanders to hold a single penitent.[51]

This process of conversion, in which those "dead in sin" are resurrected into faith after confronting their own identities as sinners, is likened both to the agonies of death and, simultaneously to the agonies of birth:

> On several evenings this week, and particularly on Friday, many were deeply convinced, but none were delivered from that painful conviction. "The children came to the birth; but there was not strength to bring forth."[52]
>
> Some received remission of sins, and several were just brought to the birth.[53]

And the role of the bystander is again that of a midwife, guiding and controlling the laboring friend, who is about to be reborn as a Christian.

Once the process of conversion has begun, the person who is now "alive," is still dead since he is tied to the flesh and hence to sin,

> I had much conversation with a very noted person (in Ireland): but I found none in town who expected that any good could be done to such a sinner as him! Such a sinner? Why were we not all such? We were "dead in sin," and is he more than dead?[54]

The sinner is not freed from "death" until the moment of physical dissolution, when the virtuous "fall asleep" and awaken to life everlasting. If the dying person is a confirmed sinner, however, and has spent his life "dead in sin," his physical death leads to death indeed, in the fires of hell. But to further confuse the imagery, fire is also linked to conversion, to the process of "awakening," when individuals and communities are undergoing revival, "I rode to Dublin, and found the flame not only continuing, but increasing."[55] John Manners, another Methodist minister, reported, "The people are all on fire."[56] "Our joy is quite full. The flame rises higher and higher. Since Saturday last, eight sinners more are freely justified, and two more renewed in love."[57] And in America, the area where revivals were rife during this period was known as the "burned over territory."

The virtuous person during physical death, who "falls asleep" to awaken to life, is also described, like the sinner, in the course of conversion, as undergoing a process of rebirth, where he is simultaneously the laboring mother and the child who is entering a new world through "the narrow way that leadeth to life."[58] As Young wrote,

[51]John Wesley, *Journal*, I, p. 196.
[52]Ibid., III, p. 84.
[53]Ibid., III, p. 108.
[54]Ibid., III, p. 98.
[55]Ibid., III, p. 103.
[56]Ibid., III, p. 104.
[57]Ibid., III, p. 107.
[58]Ibid., III, p. 460.

Strong Death, alone can heave the mossy bar,
This gross impediment of clay remove,
And make us embryos of existence free.[59]

The people round the deathbed work to comfort the sufferer and to deliver the soul from the body, thus freeing the spirit to live an independent existence away from its former home. In this connection, one may remember that Clarissa, as she lay dying, was suspected by the villainous Lovelace and the Harlowes of being pregnant, and to this both parties of her persecutors ascribed her last indisposition.

SEXUALIZATION OF DEATH

The processes of conversion, death, and birth were identified with each other by a community of images. These processes were all linked by other metaphors to sex. Conversion in Enthusiastic literature was often likened to rape. A young girl, piously educated, suddenly realized that she was a self-righteous sinner, "The Lord then, while I was on my knees, stripped off all my fig-leaves."[60]

God as rapist alternates with the devil in the same role, trying to seize the resisting soul: "One [member of the congregation] was carried away in violent fits. I went to her after the service: She was strongly convulsed from head to foot, and shrieked out in a dreadful manner. The unclean spirit did tear her indeed."[61]

More peaceful sexual language was applied to the conversion of a congregation: "I preached at Wintanburn, on the foundation of a new preaching-house. There was much rain before I began, and a violent wind all the time I was preaching; yet some of these I trust did come to the marriage."[62]

Richardson's description of Clarissa's rape, where she thrashes and screams, falling from one convulsive fit into another, only to be held down by Mrs. Sinclair's prostitutes, becomes a diabolical parody of conversion. Lovelace, the serpent, the reembodiment of Milton's Satan, thinks of the rape in remarkably spiritual terms, as a way of tearing down a superior soul by corrupting and humiliating Clarissa's will. He becomes indeed the "unclean spirit" trying to possess another subject both for Mrs. Sinclair's hell, and for the devil's territory. Moreover, the first concerted, though aborted attempt to rape the heroine takes place after a fire has burned through an upper room at Sinclair's, like the fires of hell, the fires of passion,

[59]Edward Young, *Night Thoughts*, Night the First, Ll. 126-128.
[60]John Wesley, *Journal*, II, p. 372.
[61]Ibid., III, p. 168.
[62]Ibid., IV, p. 411.

but also the fires that rage through revivals. Moreover, the rape drives Clarissa to reassess the state of her own soul, and to acknowledge the pride, self-righteousness, and vain self-confidence in her own judgment which first exposed her to dishonor. Thus, the rape, like a conversion experience, awakens the subject into the need to reevaluate her own identity.

Finally, the rape leads to Clarissa's death, and it is in death that sexual allusions are most common in Richardson and throughout deathbed literature: "In the afternoon I buried the remains of Judith Perry, a lovely young woman, snatched away at eighteen. But she was ripe for the Bridegroom, and went to meet him in the full triumph of faith."[63] The girl who had felt stripped of her fig leaves by the Lord, said on her deathbed

> My Saviour will come today, and fetch his bride. She afterwards asked [the minister] "If I saw no more appearance of death in her face yet?" When I told her there was, she begged I would indulge her with a looking-glass; and looking earnestly into it, she said with transport, "I never saw myself with so much pleasure in my life."[64]

The same language is used for men: "Full of unutterable peace and joy, [he] went to him whom his soul loved."[65] A condemned criminal was carried to execution, "Enjoying a perfect peace, in confidence that he was 'accepted in the beloved'."[66] A Moravian pastor said of one of his people, dying of consumption on the ship that was taking the young Wesley to America, "He will soon be well; he is ready for the bridegroom."[67] And the erotic possibilities of death were demonstrated by William Blake's illustrations for Blair's "The Grave," in which souls hover over bodies in suggestive poses.

Death in *Clarissa* owes much to these erotic conventions, which, like the other traditions of orthodox dying, is burlesqued in Lovelace's false deathbed scene. Waking in the midst of his fever at M. Hall, and finding his relatives, medical attendants, and the local clergy praying round him fervently, Lovelace exclaims, "God be thanked, my lord! said I, in an ecstasy. Where's Miss [Clarissa]? For I supposed they were going to marry me."[68]

Clarissa's own dying takes on the quality of a bride in preparing for her wedding. As she writes to her former governess, Mrs. Norton, repudiating the idea of marrying Lovelace, "I am upon a *better preparation* than for an earthly husband."[69] When these preparations for death are completed, she writes, "My wedding garments are brought."[70] And the buying and

[63]Ibid., IV, p. 333.
[64]Ibid., II, p. 370.
[65]Ibid., II, p. 239.
[66]Ibid., I, p. 88.
[67]Ibid., I, p. 27.
[68]Samuel Richardson, *Clarissa*, IV, p. 114.
[69]Ibid., IV, p. 2.
[70]Ibid., IV, p. 303.

decorating of her coffin is spoken of as furnishing a house. Her funeral is like a wedding procession, as she lies in her coffin, dressed in white, strewn with flowers, while six virgins carry her into Harlowe Place. Lovelace, with unconscious prophesy, characteristically turns the matter into a joke when at the expense of the staid fiancé of Clarissa's best friend he suggests, after Clarissa's escape from Sinclair's house, that she is improperly entertaining a rival suitor.

> I tell you, believe it or not, that she refuses *me* in view of *another* lover.
>
> Can it be? . . .
>
> 'Tis true, very true, Mr. Hickman! True as I am here to tell you so! And he is an ugly fellow too; uglier to look at than me. . . . The wretch she so spitefully prefers to me is a misshapen, meager varlet; more like a skeleton than a man! Then he dresses – you never saw a devil so bedizened! Hardly a coat to his back, nor a shoe to his foot: a bald-pated villain, yet grudges to buy a peruke to hide his baldness: for he is covertous as hell, never satisfied, yet plaguy rich. . . .
>
> Ay, sir, we have all heard of him – but none of us care to be intimate with him – except this lady – and that, as I told you, in spite to me. His name, in short, is DEATH! DEATH! sir, stamping, and speaking loud, and full in his ear; which made him jump half a yard high.[71]

NO LONELINESS IN DEATH

Just as the deathbed becomes a social occasion, so the experience beyond death is portrayed as far from lonely. The grave, albeit dank and moldering, is for Blair a vast bustling concourse,

> The appointed place of rendezvous, where all
> These travellers meet.[72]
>
> The shivering Icelander, and the sun-burnt Moor:
> Men of all climes, that never met before:
> And of all creeds, the Jew, the Turk, the Christian.[73]

Or, as Young wrote,

> How populous, how vital, is the grave![74]

Little Arthur in *Tom Brown's Schooldays*, after nights spent in terror over the prospect of being closed into a lonely tomb, has a vision of the multitudes that await his company after death:

> I saw men and women and children rising up pure and bright, and the tears

[71]Ibid., III, pp. 494-495.
[72]Robert Blair, *Poetical Works*, Ll. 6-7.
[73]Ibid., Ll. 491-493.
[74]Edward Young, *Night Thoughts*, Night the First, Ll. 116.

were wiped from their eyes, and they fell away. And beyond were a multitude which no man could number, and they worked at some great work. . . . And I saw there my father, and the men in the old town whom I knew when I was a child; many a hard stern man, who never came to church, and whom they called atheist and infidel. . . . And as I looked I saw my mother and my sisters, and I saw the Doctor [Headmaster Arnold], and you, Tom, and hundreds more whom I knew.[75]

In this literature, the fear of isolation is further reduced by perpetuating the conventions that allow the dying in some measure to maintain their ties with living friends. Psychologically, deathbed scenes and funerals impress on the survivors beyond rational doubt the fact that their friend is actually dead. In Christianity, the finality of the parting is softened, and the common psychological techniques for denying death – by imagining that the friend is absent only temporarily, that he will awaken or return at any moment, and that the gap in their own lives need not therefore close behind him – are sanctioned and ritualized.

In eighteenth-century literature, the ties between the dead and the living are emphasized and harnessed to draw the affections of the survivors away from their own earthly state. At the end of the century, for example, Wesley quotes with wonder a dying child who tells his sister that he hopes to be permitted to return to earth to watch over her. In his later years, Wesley collected instances of spirits returning to advise those left behind. It is interesting that the most typical form for such a visitation is a substitute deathbed scene. The survivor, often in bed himself in the middle of the night, is visited by a friend whom he has reason to believe is on the high seas or serving in a distant army. The friend is distressed and may appear dishevelled. He takes leave of his host, often silently, with marks of grief and reluctance. Later, the puzzled survivor learns that his friend had been dying, far away, at the hour of the vision. Thus, the need for a proper deathbed scene was so ingrained that when it was physically impossible to achieve, a psychical substitute was found.

Nevertheless, denial of parting, while qualified, is not entirely condoned in this tradition. There is a promise of ties maintained in some diaphanous way to be eventually renewed, but these are held within rigid bounds. Parting is final for the moment, and the survivor is obliged to content himself with a "joyful grief," marked by submission and eager anticipation of his own end.

What is presented in deathbed literature and Graveyard poetry is far more than a precursor of Gothic horrors – a collection of conventionally horrid images which are meant to raise a frisson of delightful terror. Behind the waving cyprus trees, the moldering ruin, the hooting owl in the lonely churchyard, the dank vault, and the sobbing wind at midnight, there is a message of moral and psychological significance. A twentieth-century cler-

[75]Thomas Hughes, *Tom Brown's Schooldays*, pp. 213-214.

gyman once remarked to this writer, "Everyone dies, but everyone dies alone." The eighteenth-century writers on death sought to dispel that loneliness. In their writings, only villains die alone. The good are lapped about with company. They are helped, even drilled to face their own end, and in support of this, they have helped others to die. Whatever the actual truth may have been about life and death in the eighteenth century, the ideal presented in this literature was one of a population schooled to regard death not as something apart from life, but as an integral stage in human existence, a culmination, not a negation of all the experiences of a lifetime. It was in an individual's performance on his deathbed, under the gaze and with the support of his community, that his identity was finally fixed. This was the moment at which he proved a lifetime of moral worth or failure, at which he could become a shining legend for his circle or be remembered as a hopeless sinner. He was shown to be motivated, therefore, even at a time of greater stress, to muster as much dignity and composure as possible. And the more composed he was, the easier it was for his circle to witness the proceedings, to remember the departed hopefully, and to contemplate, with a measure of calm resignation, their own end.

REFERENCES

Blair R: The Grave, in The Poetical Works of Beattie, Blair, and Falconer. Edinburgh, James Nichol, 1854

Hawthorne N: The Birthmark, in Pearson NH (ed): The Complete Novels and Selected Tales of Nathaniel Hawthorne. New York, Random House, Inc., 1937

Hughes T: Tom Brown's Schooldays. London, Mayflower Books, Ltd., 1971

Johnson S: The Rambler. Bates WJ, Strauss AB (eds). New Haven, Yale University Press, 1969

Knox RA: Enthusiasm. Oxford, Clarendon Press, 1950

Law W: A Serious Call to a Devout and Holy Life, Adapted to the State and Condition of all Christians. London, J. Richardson, 1893

Richardson S: Clarissa, or, The History of a Young Lady. London, Everyman Library, 1965

Taylor J: Holy Living and Dying: Together with Prayers: Containing the Whole Duty of a Christian. London, Duncan and Malcolm, 1839

Wesley J: The Journal of the Rev. John Wesley, M.A. London, J.M. Dent and Co. (Publication date not recorded)

Young E: Night Thoughts on Life, Death, and Immortality. London, Chapman and Co., 1837

Robert S. Weiss

7

The Contributions of an Organization of Single Parents to the Well-Being of its Members[1]

Gerald Caplan has recently discussed the importance to individuals in crisis of what he terms "support systems" (Caplan, 1972). By a support system he means "an enduring pattern of continuous or intermittent ties that play a significant part in maintaining the psychological and physical intergrity of the individual over time." This paper discusses support systems provided by Parents Without Partners to individuals who are rearing children on their own.

PARENTS WITHOUT PARTNERS

Parents Without Partners is by far the largest and best known organization of single parents. Its aims and program are described in a number of sources. (Harris, 1966; Guild, 1968; Clayton, 1971. Egleson and Egleson, 1961, describe the founding and original intent of the organization.) Although not all potentially eligible individuals find the organization attractive, often because they believe the organization is too much a dating market, or because they believe themselves in some way different from members,

---

Reprinted with permission from *The Family Coordinator,* vol. 22, no. 3, July 1973, pp. 321-326.

[1]Work on this study was supported by a grant from the Department of Health, Education and Welfare, Social and Rehabilitation Service, C-R-D 294 (2) 7-245 and from the National Institute of Mental Health, Research Scientist Development Award, 5-RO-1-MH 15428. The author's colleague in the study was Professor Carroll Bourg. Appreciation is expressed to Dr. Donald Klein, Mr. Paul Hochberg, and Mr. Alex Seidler.

or for still other reasons, the organization has flourished. (For ambivalent reactions to PWP see Hunt, 1966, 88.) The organization reported itself in 1971 as having 70,000 members and growing rapidly (Clayton, 1971).

This discussion of the contributions of the organization to its members is based on a year's work with one chapter of about 600 members. During the year we attended most meetings of the board of directors, a good many of the frequently held discussion groups, some dances and other social activities, and a few informal parties. We also discussed the organization with many of the more active members and held formal interviews with a small number of current members and former members.

Not all the individuals whose names were carried on the PWP membership roster were active within the organization. According to estimates made by leaders, only about half of them participated in more than one or two meetings or activities. Even among the active members there was great variation in needs and interests and, therefore, in pattern of participation. Some gave a good deal of time to administrative work, while others restricted their participation to attendance at discussion groups and still others were primarily interested in social activities or in programs for children.

The pattern of an individual's participation might well change over time. A number of new members were at first interested primarily in the discussion groups or social activities but later became more involved in administration. Many members were quite active for a time and then lapsed into relative inactivity.

The organizational provisions which single parents utilized could be divided into those which were responsive to the marital loss itself and those which were responsive to the defects of life as a single parent. Some new members had only recently separated from their spouses or, less frequently, had only recently been widowed. These individuals were coping primarily with loss. They often wanted most to be able to talk to understanding and sympathetic listeners about their feelings, their concerns, and their plans. Perhaps most useful for them were discussion groups limited to individuals in similar situations, the opportunity for occasional conversation with others in the same boat about shared problems, and for some, therapy groups led by professionals. Other members, on the other hand, seemed already to have made the transition from marriage to life on their own, but to have found life on their own unsatisfying. The lives they had organized contained relational deficits, i.e., distressing absences of important relational provisions. The organization seemed to take cognizance of these dissatisfactions as well as the disturbances of loss. Its program could be seen as responding to four potentially continuing sources of distress: (a) the absence of a sustaining community; (b) the absence of similarly placed friends; (c) the absence of support for a sense of worth, and (d) the absence of emotional attachment. In what follows I will describe PWP's provisions of new resources and relationships that may reduce each of these deficits.

A Sustaining Community

Many members seemed to feel that PWP offered an accepting social setting rich in engaging, or at least interesting, activities which they could attend alone without feeling odd. A number of members saw PWP as their only alternative to social isolation. In recognition of this leaders attempted to schedule events for times ordinarily marked out for social activities, when PWP members might otherwise have been especially likely to feel themselves marginal to their community: weekend evenings, Sunday afternoons, holidays. Events were not restricted to those times, but an effort was made to insure that something was scheduled for each of them.

An extensive roster of activities was available to members. In one typical winter month events included dance classes, musical groups, Sunday afternoon cocktail parties, a skating party for children and adults and another for adults only, a lecture by a psychiatrist on the problems of the single parent, a holiday dance, and several discussion groups. Administration of the organization was another activity with which idle time could be filled: many members attended more than one of the several meetings held to plan future events or to decide matters of organizational policy. In addition, many of those who had been in the organization for some time had become part of friendship networks whose members sometimes had dinner together or met one another at large informal parties. Members could easily establish an extraordinarily busy social life entirely within the organization.

Friends in the Same Boat

Women, but not men, tended to find PWP valuable because it provided them with the opportunity to form friendships with same-sex others who were in situations similar to their own. Many women seemed to have relinquished friendships they had made during their marriages because of differences in schedules and in concerns, unwillingness to visit in the evening when husbands were home, envy of the married friends, or belief that the married friends feared that they might just possibly seduce the friends' husbands. For these women PWP friends became almost their only friends.

Within PWP friendships seemed most likely to be established by women of similar age and socioeconomic status who lived near enough to one another to be able to visit occasionally and to exchange such favors as babysitting. Not all women were able to find potential friends in PWP, just as PWP was not equally attractive to all single parents who looked it over. Among women who attended a few meetings and then dropped out the most frequent explanation was that they had not found other women in PWP sufficiently like themselves: the women they had met were the wrong age or too loud or too aggressive or widowed rather than divorced or divorced rather than widowed.

Friendships among a number of women living in the same neighborhood gave rise to cliques. Loyalty to cliques tended to be strong because they often constituted the individual's most important social network. If cliques became rivalrous with one another, as might happen in connection with the competition of members of different cliques for desirable positions in the organization, loyalty to one's own clique might demand antagonism to the rival clique. The chapter was sometimes threatened with schism as a result of this phenomenon.

Male friends of clique members tended to be included in cliques as rather marginal members, although at gatherings they might be shown deference and special attention. It was the female members of the cliques who kept in touch with one another, scheduled parties, and decided on guest lists.

Some men in the organization formed cross-sex friendships which were similar in their qualities of loyalty, affection, and exchange of favors to the same-sex friendships of women. Nevertheless these were largely friendships of convenience. Both the man and the woman in such a friendship seemed generally to recognize that the relationship would fade if either developed a more intense cross-sex relationship elsewhere. In the meantime the friendship gave the man a home he could visit where, as one man put it, he could feel a part of a family for a time, and provided the woman with a masculine presence and with someone who could serve as an escort for an occasional evening out.

Men in the organization exhibited little interest in forming friendships with one another. Leaders in the organization had learned from experience that an all-male activity, such as an evening of poker or a bowling tournament, would be sparsely attended. Men who were in administrative roles in the organization sometimes developed a sense of comradeship – when they were not actively rivalrous – but they would meet only when required to do so by their organizational responsibilities. When they did meet they often discussed personal as well as organizational issues.

Support for a Sense of Worth

Both men and women sometimes found that contribution to the organization through service in administrative or planning roles supported their own sense of worth. Leaders referred to this phenomenon by saying, "The more you put into PWP, the more you get out of it." There were at least three ways in which individuals benefited through their contribution to the organization. First, they established a place for themselves in the organization and so facilitated further participation. A woman who was chairman of a dance committee remarked that it was only because she had been in charge that she had had the courage to attend. Second, the effective management of an organizational task reassured those members whose marriages had ended in separation or divorce that they remained capable of success in at least some of their efforts. In addition, administrative effort was rewarded by both formal and informal praise. Successful performance together with its recognition could help restore damaged self-esteem. One woman, just elected to an important office, said at the installation dinner, "I can say what PWP has given me in just one word: worthwhileness."

Perhaps because it was recognized within the organization that administrative responsibility could be therapeutic for many members, the organization maintained almost two dozen administrative divisions. "Cultural programs," "recreational programs," and "children's activities," for example, each constituted its own division, responsible for its own schedule of activities. This administrative fragmentation made it possible for an administrative position to be offered to almost any member who wanted one, if not as a director of a division, then as a program coordinator or other functionary within one.

Contributions to the organization were generally acknowledged in the monthly bulletin. The bulletin carried many stories praising, congratulating, and at the least naming, members who had in any way distinguished themselves. Members felt slighted if contributions they believed themselves to have made went unrecognized, but generally leaders were careful, even in informal conversation, to allocate credit appropriately.

The same needs which led to the importance among members of recognition for service led to great sensitivity to criticism. Unfortunately, organization members seemed unusually likely to find fault with one another's administrative performance, partly as an expression of clique rivalries, but partly for reasons that seem more obscure and may have to do with the emotional tensions they were experiencing. Every year determined and angry criticism led to resignations from the board of directors. One year, it was reported, half the original board resigned.

Nevertheless the benefits of leadership were believed to outweigh the risks involved. The benefits were thought to be especially great for men. Virtually every man who appeared reasonably competent was pressed to accept an administrative position. Women had to display more initiative. One woman said that it had taken her almost a year to get the organization's inner circle to allow her to direct the discussion group program. But it is noteworthy that despite the initial reluctance of the leadership she was ultimately permitted to assume responsibility for an important organizational activity.

A New Emotional Attachment

Most members, even those who had voluntarily ended their marriages, experienced loneliness prior to joining PWP. It was widely believed in the organization that hope of respite from loneliness was the primary motive for members joining the organization. For most members this meant establishing a cross-sex emotional attachment, a relationship more emotionally intense than the cross-sex friendships referred to above.

The friendships among women and collegial relationships among men that PWP sponsored seemed to mitigate, but not to dispel, loneliness. Speaking of the slight value of friendships for dealing with loneliness, one woman said:

> Sometimes I have the girls over and we talk about how hard it is. Misery loves company, you know.

For most members only cross-sex attachments seemed effectively to fend off loneliness. Many of those who came to the organization at least in part to escape loneliness hoped eventually to establish such an attachment, to find someone to date and to become involved with.

Despite this, the organization was presented forcefully to the public and to new members as not concerned with helping members deal with loneliness. The following description of the organization's goals, given by an officer in an orientation meeting for prospective members, was typical of such presentations:

> This is not a lonely hearts club.... This is primarily so we can discuss problems about raising children. And if you can contribute and become a worker, then you will get so much more out of it.

In another orientation meeting a prospective member who said that he hoped that he might find dates in the organization was sharply reproved with the statement, "If you are here for dating, this is not for you."

Nevertheless the chapter sponsored dances and parties which seemed primarily designed to provide members with opportunities to meet possible dates. The parties were generally restricted to members and their guests, but single men not members of the chapter were invited to dances since otherwise the four-to-one preponderance of women in the chapter would have left many without dance partners. Indeed the opportunity to meet someone whom one might date was implicit in every PWP activity that involved both men and women. This was well recognized by members; even in the most routine business meeting members might joke about possible sexual interest in one another and would be alert to any indication of genuine sexual or romantic interest, in themselves or in others.

Almost all men who had been with the organization for longer than six months seemed at some point to have dated a woman within the organization. From comments made in discussion groups it appeared that more than a fourth and perhaps as many as half of the female members who had been in the organization that long had dated men who were members. These are uncertain impressions but it did seem to be the case that there was a good deal of dating within the organization.

Nevertheless leaders of the organization adamantly refused to acknowledge that the organization provided members with possible dating partners. Dances and parties were rationalized as necessary recreation. Leaders insisted that most members were not yet "ready" to get involved with others, despite their knowledge that many were actively seeking just such involvement and some had achieved it.

Why the dissimulation? Why did leaders of the organization refuse to acknowledge that much of its program was directed to providing settings in which members might explore the possibility of establishing emotionally significant cross-sex relationships?

One important reason was the belief held by leaders that only if PWP insisted that it did not sponsor dating could it attract respectable individuals to membership. An ex-president of the organization suggested that before there was public acceptance of the sobriety of PWP's mission there were penalties attached to membership and, especially, leadership:

> I wouldn't accept the presidency for years. There was a stigma attached to it because of this lack of understanding of PWP in the community. You used to say Parents Without Partners and they would giggle.

Leaders were less concerned with actually discouraging dating than with preventing the promotion of dating becoming identified as an organizational aim. Dating among members that was handled with circumspection might produce interest, but not censure; it was essential, however, that the couple not display their relationship while participating in organizational activities. So long as dating could be treated as non-organizational it was tolerated; and so long as it was understood that any consequent involvements were non-organizational, dances and other events could be held even though they might seem designed to facilitate meeting potential dates.

On another level it was important for many, though not all, individual members to be able to claim that they had joined PWP for reasons other than hope of finding a new emotional involvement. Men could in this way defend themselves from any suspicion that they were insufficiently attractive or resourceful to have found dates on their own. Some, indeed, insisted that they had been fully occupied before joining PWP and after joining had made it a practice not to date within the organization. Many women in the organization, although they might in private frankly discuss their loneliness, did not want to appear to be aggressively searching for someone. A minority of women, especially widows, had sincerely repudiated the possibility of forming another attachment. Organizational dissimulation was in different ways useful for all these members.

CONCLUSIONS

PWP provides a complex of support systems responsive to the special problems of single parents. Some of these, including discussion groups where individuals can seek the support and advice of others in the same situation, are responsive to the pain and confusion of marital separation and bereavement. Others are responsive to inadequacies in the on-going lives of single parents. The alternative community which PWP makes available, complete with its own events, activities and problems of government, the opportunities for friendship and for responsibility and service to others the organization provides, and the dating relationships it facilitates, all may be seen as responsive to needs which are peculiar to the situation of the single parent.

It might be noted that there are certain difficulties in an organization attempting, as PWP does, to respond directly to the needs of its members rather than act as an instrument through which the members may achieve goals elsewhere in the society. Because responsibility is defined as a potential benefit as well as an organizational requisite, efficiency sometimes suffered, both because of difficulties of coordination of the unnecessarily diffuse leadership and because of a high rate of turnover. Because friendship networks were sponsored among organization members, conflict within the organization sometimes took on the quality of a feud between families. The desire of leaders of the organization to maintain the organization's respectability while yet responding through programming to the loneliness of many members was a chronic source of discomfort. A more usual goal-oriented organization would surely have been less conflicted in refusing to provide so troublesome a staff benefit.

That the organization has survived, and indeed is prospering, attests to a demand for its services. Yet this should not be taken as demonstration that PWP holds the answer to the problems of all single parents. Actually only a tiny proportion of the over four million individuals eligible for PWP are members.[2] Some undoubtedly feel no need for it: perhaps their work brings them an adequate sense of community and an adequate basis for feelings of worth, and they may in addition have managed loneliness in other ways. Some single parents are in the wrong social class for PWP, which for the most part appeals to middle income groups. Many undoubtedly have not heard of PWP despite its extensive publicity. And some, we know, simply do not want it. What part of this enormous population of single parents not in PWP experiences the same difficulties and deficits as those displayed by members of PWP? And where do they turn for help? We have no information regarding these issues.

Nor is it easy to decide the sorts of individuals for which PWP will

[2]This estimate is based on data contained in Table 5, "Presence of parent, by marital status of parent, for persons under 18 years old living with only one parent, March 1971," U.S. Bureau of the Census, *Current Population Reports,* Series P-20, No. 225, "Marital status and living arrangements March 1971." If we assume three children per family we find 4.7 million individuals who fit PWP eligibility requirements. A similar, though slightly smaller, estimate can be derived from data in Tables 11-2 and 11-25 of Donald J. Bogue, *The Population of the United States* (New York: Free Press, 1959).

prove helpful. Some members described the organization, with some exaggeration, as having saved their lives. Other single parents, whose needs would appear to have been similar, came to only one or two meetings and afterwards said they had been repelled by it. Much may depend on whether the prospective member feels comfortable with the people already in the organization, and they, in turn, with him or her. The organization's ideology would require its members to welcome all those who are eligible, but in practice members respond more warmly to some than to others. Even after there has been initial acceptance on both sides, much may depend on how the new member responds to the contributions and the problems of the organization, and whether he or she can benefit from the one without being overwhelmed by the other.

REFERENCES:

Caplan G: Support Systems. Address to Conference of Department of Psychiatry, Rutgers Medical School, June 1972. Unpublished working paper of the Laboratory of Community Psychiatry, Harvard Medical School

Clayton PN: Meeting the needs of the single parent family. Family Coordinator, 20: 227-336, 1971

Egleson J, Egleson JF: Parents Without Partners. New York, Dutton, 1961

Gould EP: Special Report: The Single-Parent Family Benefits in Parents Without Partners, Inc. J Marriage Family 30: 666-671, 1968

Harris ET: Parents Without Partners, Inc.: A Resource for Clients. Soc Work 11: 92-98, 1966

Hunt M: The World of the Formerly Married. New York, McGraw-Hill, 1966

Henry Wechsler

8

The Self-Help Organization in the Mental Health Field: Recovery, Inc., A Case Study[1]

The past decade has witnessed the growth of a relatively new form of activity in the mental health field: the self-help group of former mental patients. Forty-two such groups are currently in existence, the majority established in the past five years. The largest and perhaps the oldest of these groups is Recovery, Incorporated: The Association of Nervous and Former Mental Patients. Recovery reports over 1,800 dues-paying members, and a total regular attendance of over 4,000 individuals. It officially recognizes 250 local groups in 20 states, located mainly in Illinois and Michigan. Other self-help groups in the mental health field tend to be small and have relatively short life-spans, while Recovery has exhibited a significant growth. However, despite this growth, Recovery has as yet failed to make any perceivable impact upon professionals in the mental health field. Prior to this report, no extensive study of the structure, functioning, and therapeutic potential of this organization has been attempted.

For the purposes of this study, information about Recovery was obtained from a number of available sources:

1. The Recovery literature.
2. Visits to various groups by the author, and four consultants.
3. A questionnaire study of the membership.
4. A questionnaire survey of psychiatrists' opinions about Recovery.

Reprinted with permission from *Journal of Nervous and Mental Disease,* 130: 4, 297-314, 1960.

[1]This report is based upon a study conducted as a special project of the Joint Commission on Mental Illness and Health under a grant from the National Institute of Mental Health.

HISTORICAL DEVELOPMENT

Recovery was founded in 1937 by the late Abraham A. Low, M.D., a neuropsychiatrist on the faculty of the University of Illinois College of Medicine. Originally, the organization was limited to patients at the Psychiatric Institute of the University. In 1942, the organization and the Institute severed connections, and Recovery secured private offices in Chicago. Under Dr. Low's leadership, Recovery acquired a specific method of self-help and after-care aimed at the prevention of relapses and chronicity among the mentally ill. Group meetings were conducted as part of Low's treatment procedure, and Recovery members were drawn mainly from patients in his private practice.

During the early days of the organization, Low kept in close contact with the activities of the groups. He received regular reports from the leaders, and personally attended the larger discussions at which he presented the final interpretations of the subject matter. Gradually, as the organization grew in size, Low's direct control over group activities of necessity decreased. Finally, in 1952, he withdrew his objections to the expansion of Recovery on a national level, in effect placing the direct control of the widely scattered local groups in the hands of his former patients who had become group leaders. With Low's death in 1954, the transition of Recovery from a professionally supervised adjunct to psychotherapy to a lay-run form of self-help became complete.

Recovery is incorporated under the laws of Illinois as a non-profit organization, and is financed through annual membership dues, the sale of literature and records, and individual "good will" donations. The national headquarters of Recovery, Inc., is located in Chicago. The organization is run by a Board of Directors, a councilors committee, and organizational officers. The councilors and directors are elected annually by the dues-paying members, and the officers are appointed by the Board of Directors. There are no formal criteria for membership, other than that of being a former mental patient or "nervous person." Essentially then, any individual who perceives himself to be emotionally disturbed may join. Furthermore, an individual may start a new group if, in addition to qualifying for membership, he studies the Recovery method, receives at least one week's formal leadership training, and obtains authorization from the Board of Directors.

THE RECOVERY METHOD

Recovery utilizes exclusively the techniques, principles, and terminology described in its official text, *Mental Health Through Will-Training* (3). The member is expected to read this book, learn Dr. Low's system, utilize the system in his everyday life, and obtain practice in its application by attending weekly group meetings. The book does not present an overall systematic formulation of a theory of mental health, but rather each chapter is intended to illustrate one or more principles through the use of examples.

In order to present most accurately the Recovery method, it was necessary to outline its major basic assumptions and concepts. In each case, the reader is referred to the page in the textbook where a more complete statement may be found. The following analysis is not intended to serve as an exhaustive treatment of the system, or as a detailed statement of the official Recovery position, but rather as a way to acquaint the reader with the essence of the method. The method will be presented without any attempt to evaluate the validity of its assumptions or the effectiveness of its techniques. These points which follow will be discussed in a later section.

1. The returned mental patient and the psychoneurotic both suffer from similar symptoms (3, p. 18).
2. The psychoneurotic or postpsychotic symptom is distressing but not dangerous (3, p. 112).
3. Tenseness intensifies and sustains the symptom; and thus should be avoided (3, p. 135).
4. The psychoneurotic and postpsychotic patient are particularly susceptible to the arousal of tenseness because of their excessive irritability (3, pp. 86, 88).
5. The use of free will is the basis of the Recovery method and the solution to the nervous patient's dilemma.
   (a) The life of the individual is governed by free will (3, p. 185).
   (b) The psychoneurotic or postpsychotic patient can attain mental health through the use of his will (3, p. 19, p. 145, p. 209).
   (c) The function of the will is to accept or reject thoughts or impulses (3, p. 132).
6. Mental health should be the supreme goal for the mental or nervous patient (3, p. 384).
7. The "physician" is the supreme authority on all matters pertaining to mental health (3, p. 24).

In summary, these assumptions state that when the physician diagnoses a condition of a psychoneurotic or postpsychotic patient as a nervous symptom, the patient should realize that, although the condition is distressing, it is not dangerous. The patient should accept the diagnosis of the physician, and should attempt to employ his will in order to eliminate the tenseness which sustains and intensifies the symptom.

The situation is to be restructured in terms of the following Recovery principles, and the individual is to act within this new cognitive framework:

1. *Spotting:* When a symptom, impulse or thought appears, it must be "spotted" for what it is. The individual must see that there is no danger involved. Spotting is a form of introspective relabeling of various

components of the situation.

2. *The Recovery Language:* When an individual restructures the situation, he must employ the basic tool of the method, the Recovery Language. The use of Recovery Language is intended to change a situation from one that is felt to be beyond the control of the individual to one that can be coped with.
3. *Differentiation between External and Internal Environment:* An individual's life space is composed of the external and internal environment. The external environment consists of the "realities" of the situation, and can seldom be changed. The internal environment consists of various "subjective" components, such as feelings, thoughts, impulses and sensations. These can be controlled, restructured or reappraised.
4. *Avoidance of Judgments of "Right" or "Wrong":* For any given life situation, an evaluation of "right" or "wrong" is merely an opinion, or a subjective judgment. The Recovery member should refrain from making such evaluations as they serve only to produce temper, which in turn increases tenseness and contributes to symptoms.
5. *The Average versus The Exceptional:* The member should consider himself to be an average person, and should strive to be average. He should realize that his symptoms are no worse than anyone else's symptoms, that he is no sicker than anyone else. Each situation is average as it has been and will be encountered by numerous other individuals.

Once the situation has been restructured in accordance with these principles, it remains for the individual to act. Recovery guide lines for action can be characterized broadly by the term *control.* In essence, the individual is told to control those aspects of his internal environment which serve to propagate tenseness. The primary condition that is to be controlled is *temper.* Two types of temper exist: fear and anger. Temper is a combination of feelings with an evaluation that the self or the other person is "right" or "wrong." The individual is to control temper, to reject and suppress thoughts and impulses which result in tenseness. He is to force himself to bear the discomfort of doing that which he fears. In situations which are not dangerous, the individual must act despite the subjective anguish which his symptoms may be expressing.

The individual must constantly *endorse* himself for each effort at the practice of Recovery, no matter how minute. Self-endorsement is a basic principle of Recovery. It is a way in which the member can congratulate himself, not necessarily because he was successful, but because he tried to utilize the method. Low believed that, eventually, each effort will entail less work; each attempt will be more successful. The restructuring of the situation will become automatic and will require little or no conscious application. With each success, the individual's self-esteem will be increased, and he will eventually come to believe what he has been told: that he can, through the use of his will, achieve mental health.

THE RECOVERY GROUP MEETING

At the present time, meetings of Recovery groups are intended to serve the purpose of providing members with the opportunity to practice the techniques of Recovery. Groups are usually composed of between 11 and 30 members. Meetings follow a rigid schedule in order to assure conformity with the methods and beliefs of Recovery. It is the leader's function to guide the meeting along the pre-arranged format. Each meeting is divided into four parts.

1. Reading from the Textbook

The first part of the meeting is usually devoted to the reading of a chapter from the textbook. The leader may call on members to read short paragraphs. A technique widely used in some groups is to call on members who are hesitant about reading in public. This may serve the function of encouraging newcomers to join in the activities of the group. At the conclusion of his paragraph, the reader is quite often asked whether he had any symptoms during the reading. He is then "endorsed" for having the "will to bear discomfort," the "courage to make mistakes," and for being "group minded" by doing what he "feared to do." Thus at the same time that the newcomer is encouraged to participate in the meeting, he is also given a practical demonstration of the Recovery method at work in reference to his own reading. This is frequently an important first step in motivating the curious newcomer to become a Recovery member. The most obvious purpose of the readings is to expose the members to the contents of the book, and to encourage them to continue the reading at home. Sometimes one of Dr. Low's records or tape-recordings is substituted for the readings. This portion of the meeting usually lasts for 30 to 45 minutes.

2. The Presentation of Examples

Rules for Presentation

The leader introduces this portion of the meeting by stating that only members who have read Dr. Low's book may participate. Newer members who as yet have not read the book are asked to listen quietly, and to save their questions and remarks for the question period. The participants form the "panel" and are usually seated face-to-face around a table.

The leader informs the group that all examples have to be taken from "trivial" everyday occurrences, and, since Recovery is a lay-run non-medical organization, it cannot help individuals with major problems. This is often qualified by stating Dr. Low's belief that such "trivial" incidents comprise the bulk of a nervous patient's problems. The leader then asks one of the members to read a portion of the official outline (4) for the presentation of an example. The outline divides each example into four parts:

a. A detailed description of an event.
b. Description of the symptoms and discomfort that the event aroused.
c. Description of the utilization of Recovery principles to cope with the event.
d. Description of the reaction which the member would have experienced before joining Recovery.

The Nature of the Examples

As a result of the rigorous regulations for the presentation of panel examples, there is very little variation as to the type of examples given at the meetings. In addition to the actual rules, the "model" examples included in Low's book also serve to set the tone for the members' examples. In general, the examples presented at Recovery meetings may be characterized by:

a. *Familiarity.* Only commonplace everyday events are usually discussed. The events have usually taken place in the very recent past.

b. *Concreteness.* Very literal, extensive descriptions of these events are given. Specific times, places, and individuals are usually mentioned.

c. *Uniformity of Symptoms.* The same symptoms are usually mentioned by most of the panel participants. These symptoms are almost always identical to the symptoms cited in the textbook. It is as if the textbook is used as a basic symptom list, from which members may choose the symptoms most appropriate for them.

d. *Somatization of Symptoms.* In addition to the uniformity in the symptoms, there is a tendency to present symptoms in somatic terms. This, too, is probably influenced by the type of examples discussed in the textbook. The most frequent types of symptoms discussed are: air hunger, heart palpitations, perspiration, and tremors.

e. *Exclusive Use of Recovery Concepts.* In nearly all cases, examples are presented in terms of Recovery language. If an occasional term such as "projection" or "identification" is introduced, it is soon withdrawn by the speaker.

f. *The Testimonial.* The majority of examples serve as testimonials, since they refer to the success obtained through the use of the Recovery method as compared to the failures encountered previously. Success is not a prerequisite for the presentation of an example, since an individual is to be endorsed for each attempt in the use of the method regardless of its result. However, the form in which all examples must be constructed is conducive to the presentation of testimonials. Occasionally unsuccessful examples are also given, but they are in the minority.

3. Group Participation

After the speaker has finished giving an example, the meeting is thrown open for comments from the panel. This is called "group spotting" and involves an analysis of the example through the use of Recovery concepts. The leader usually starts the discussion and calls upon volunteers. Comments must be phrased in Recovery language, and must pertain to the example under consideration. The leader immediately stops any discussion not in accordance with this rule. Comments may be classified as either positive or negative in nature. Positive comments are usually predominant, and consist of enumerations of the Recovery principles that were utilized by the person who gave the example. The leader praises him for utilizing these principles. Some negative comments are also included, consisting mainly of instances in which the individual failed to apply certain Recovery techniques. The individual who has given the example is free to accept or reject the comments and criticisms of the panel. The tendency is for him to accept all comments, and to agree with the group. In cases when negative comments are made, the group congratulates the individual for the Recovery methods utilized, and for being able to present an example not fully successful in nature. In addition, the individual is told not to attempt to be too perfectionistic by always expecting total success. Thus, both successful and unsuccessful examples are praised. The tendency is not to permit any example to pass, regardless of how successful the narrator may have thought it was, without adding additional Recovery concepts that may be applied to it. In this way, the panel is constantly reminded that no one can practice Recovery perfectly, and that everyone can always learn more, and benefit from practice before the group.

4. The Question and Answer Period

At the conclusion of the panel presentations, there is a brief question and answer period, which usually lasts no longer than 15 minutes. Anyone may ask questions about the examples that were presented. Newcomers are particularly urged to participate. Comments must be limited to the examples, and at no time may one question the Recovery method itself, except to obtain clarification of a term or concept. No discussion of other psychological theories or systems is permitted. If a new member brings up a possible disagreement between the Recovery system and what his doctor may have told him, he is quickly told that the panel is not qualified to discuss such an issue since it does not relate to the example.

5. The "Mutual Aid" Social Meeting

Nearly all the members remain after the formal part of the meeting has been concluded. Refreshments are usually served, and individual members may talk to each other and to the leader. The designation of this period as "mutual aid" refers to the fact that this is an opportunity to discuss problems and to obtain advice from others. There is an attempt to keep this informal discussion within the bounds of the Recovery method, and to utilize only the techniques and concepts of Recovery, Inc. A rule of thumb is that all discussions of problems should be limited to five minutes, so as not to leave time for self-pity and complaining. During this part of the meeting the leader and the veteran members usually speak to newcomers in order to interest them in Recovery.

Recovery provides an additional mechanism through which a member may obtain help from other members during a time when no meetings are being held. A member who is experiencing difficulties may telephone a veteran member or leader. The problem must be presented and discussed in the same way as any panel example.

THE RECOVERY MEMBERSHIP

In order to obtain information about the personal characteristics of the Recovery members, questionnaires were sent to the Chicago headquarters and to the state leader in Michigan, to be distributed to the members. Of the 1,875 questionnaires that were distributed, 779 were completed and returned. The answers seemed to present a rather clear picture of the typical Recovery respondent, although general interpretations should be made with some caution. Since there was no control over the distribution of the questionnaires, and since it cannot be assumed that the non-responders would have answered in the same way as the respondents, the characterization which follows may not apply to the entire Recovery membership. It does, however, describe in general terms at least 779 members.

Background Factors

The modal Recovery respondent appears to be a middle-class, middle-aged, married woman. She has had at least some high school education, and may have attended college. Her husband is employed in a non-manual occupation and the yearly family income is approximately $6,000.

The typical Recovery respondent has one or more dependent children. She is active in community and church affairs, belongs to one or more voluntary community associations, and attends church services weekly. She takes part in various leisure time activities, *e.g.*, hobbies, and visits or entertains her family, friends, and neighbors. Thus she is an individual who appears to be integrated into her community and who, at least on the basis of certain socio-economic criteria, appears to hold an average or perhaps better-than-average status.

Reasons for Joining Recovery

Most of the respondents had originally learned about Recovery in the lay press, and had joined at the suggestion of a relative or friend. Only about a tenth of the respondents stated that they had joined on the advice of a physician.

The respondents reported that they entered this activity because they believed that they had one or more symptoms usually associated with a nervous or mental disorder. The major reasons for joining were given as follows:

(a) psychological symptoms, such as fears, delusions, and "nerves;"
(b) psychosomatic symptoms, such as tremors and heart palpitations;
(c) curiosity about whether the organization could help.

History of Hospitalization and Treatment

The respondents reported relatively few extensive histories of treatment for nervous or mental disorders prior to joining Recovery. Half of the respondents reported no hospitalization, and about one-fifth reported no professional treatment of any kind before joining Recovery. Among the respondents who reported hospitalization, there was little indication of chronicity, since the majority indicated very few hospitalizations, and of very short duration.

Extent of Participation in Recovery

For most of the respondents, Recovery appears to be a regular and long-term activity. Such obligations of membership as regular attendance and participation in the panels are conscientiously fulfilled. It is apparent from statements made by these individuals that membership in Recovery is treated as a vital, significant activity.

Approximately one-third of the respondents had been in Recovery for less than one year, one-third for one to two years, and one-third for three years or more. Almost all of the respondents reported that they attended meetings weekly.The length of membership, high frequency of attendance and high level of participation are of interest in view of the observation that over a third of those answering the questionnaire stated that they no longer need to attend meetings in order to function adequately.

The Special Case of the Leader

Of the 779 questionnaires, 112 were returned by leaders or assistant leaders of local Recovery groups. In general, the leaders displayed the same characteristics as regular members, with only a few minor exceptions. Leaders tended to be of a slightly higher socio-economic level. They reported more activity in church and community groups, and they displayed slightly more extensive histories of previous treatment for nervous or mental disorders.

THE ROLE OF THE MEMBER

The distinctive philosophy and method of Recovery facilitates establishing a particular type of role for the member. The first aspect of this role relates to the fact that the individual is a member of a group which meets regularly in order to provide mutual aid. Each member has certain obligations toward his fellow members and in return has certain expectations about their behavior toward him. He is expected to show concern about the condition and progress of other members, to provide them with support and acceptance, and to help them in the "correct" application of the Recovery method. He has expectations that others will act toward him in a similar manner. Because of the mutual aid quality of Recovery, the group feels helped by any individual's successes or harmed by any individual's failures.

By joining Recovery, the participant formally admits to himself and to others that he is "a nervous patient," and that he is formally associating himself with a group of nervous and former mental patients. The individual is to view himself, and in turn is to be viewed by others, within the context provided by membership in such an organization.

The term "nervous patient" may be a strange one to apply to the members of an organization completely lay run and directed, since "patient" usually implies treatment by a physician or other professional. However, the Recovery members do refer to themselves at meetings as "patients," and can be said to assume the nervous patient role. Of itself this role has a number of implications.

The Recovery Nervous Patient Role is Voluntary

Adopting the nervous patient role is completely voluntary: the individual has the choice of joining or not joining. For some people this may be merely a formalization of a role status which has already been in existence. Such individuals may have formerly been hospitalized, or may have previously been under treatment for a nervous or mental disorder. Through the utilization of various mental health facilities, they may have already identified themselves as nervous patients. However, according to data obtained with the questionnaire survey, a sizable segment of the Recovery membership has had no contact with such mental health facilities. For these individuals, the act of joining Recovery seems to imply a voluntary acceptance of a role that may be highly devalued in contemporary American society, and a consequent exposure to the stigma that is often associated with this role.

The Recovery Nervous Patient Role is an Acceptance of "Difference"

Membership in any specialized group may result in the perception of the self as different from individuals who do not belong to the group. In certain groups, the feeling of difference may be extremely vague and unstructured, but in Recovery the theoretical framework is seen specifically to outline the nature of the difference. The member is told that he is different from the average person in that he is more prone to the development of tenseness, and that he cannot tolerate as much tenseness as the average person. Thus, the Recovery member is cautioned to control and avoid actions which may be completely permissible to the average person.

The Recovery Nervous Patient Role is an Acceptance of "Similarity"

At the same time that the Recovery member may accept the assertion that he is different from other "healthy" individuals in the community, he may be also impressed with the fact that he is similar to the nervous patients within Recovery. The Recovery method stresses that all nervous patients are "average," and that no nervous patient is sicker than any other nervous patient. The members are thus provided with an in-group which experiences the same problems, practices the same method, and utilizes the same terminology.

The Recovery Nervous Patient Role Provides a Cognitive Framework from Which the Individual Must View His Actions

The Recovery member must evaluate his actions from the point of view that he is a nervous patient. He must not exhibit temper, because he is told that this will increase his symptomatology. He must carefully judge all of his behavior in relation to what bearing it will have on his mental health. Thus, when the Recovery member is shoved in the subway or caught in a traffic jam, he must act according to Recovery principles, even if it means inhibiting a spontaneous reaction.

The Recovery Nervous Patient Role is Generalized to All Aspects of Life

Since a member must apply the Recovery method to all phases of his life, particularly to all trivial, routine, everyday occurrences, the nervous patient role assumes *maximal generalization.* The role is not limited to the individual's behavior within Recovery, but pervades all spheres of his activity: his job situation, his home life and his recreational pursuits.

Participation in Recovery Serves to Reinforce the Nervous Patient Role

The nervous patient role is constantly reinforced through membership in Recovery. The repeated application of the method serves to reinforce the role, as does the perception of success in utilizing the method. Even partial failure in applying the method may serve to reinforce the role, as the individual may feel that he has more to learn, and must try harder. Secondary rewards such as group support, recognition, and encouragement may also serve to reinforce the Recovery nervous patient role.

No Formal Mechanism Exists for the Termination of the Recovery Nervous Patient Role

Low required patients to attend classes and meetings for at least six months. He did not set any general termination date for membership, but it can be assumed that this was managed on an individual basis. Currently there is no one to suggest to a member that he is ready to end his membership and to surrender the nervous patient role. In view of the fact that one of Recovery's major aims is expansion, it would seem very unlikely that anyone would be urged to leave. Secondary gain may be sufficient motivation for many individuals to remain in Recovery, even though continuation of the nervous patient role may no longer be necessary. Barring the operation of other factors, there appears to be an in-built tendency within Recovery for long-term continuation of membership.

THE SPECIAL ROLE OF THE LEADER

Like the member, the group leader assumes the role of a nervous patient through the act of belonging to Recovery and through the utilization of its method. In order to participate in panel meetings an individual must give examples concerning his own problems and symptoms. Leaders are not exempt from this, and in fact usually present numerous examples in order to keep the meeting active. The role of the leader, however, has certain additional features which deserve comment.

The Leader as an Expert

Perhaps the major function of the leader is to serve as an expert in the utilization of the Recovery method. Leaders are perceived by the group to be sophisticated in the use of Recovery terminology and concepts. Because of their position, they are able to control the agenda and content of the meeting, and serve as the major interpreters of the method. Most leaders stress that the Recovery method is not open to interpretation, and must be employed as it is written. However, a leader's comments at the panel meeting are usually more highly valued by the group than those of any other individual.

The Leader as a Guardian of the Method

The leader may control the meeting by deciding whether an issue under discussion is in accordance with Recovery regulations. A leader may terminate comments which he considers not pertinent to the example under discussion. A leader's decision in such matters is almost always considered final, and is seldom challenged. To be sure, any interpretations or decisions on the part of a leader may be brought to question by the group. Individual leaders determine for themselves how strongly they may wish to utilize their authority, some being more permissive than others. Since membership in Recovery is voluntary, leaders must allow the group certain degrees of freedom in order to motivate members to remain in the group. A completely authoritarian leader might alienate his members through arbitrary decisions and actions.

The Leader as a Role Model

Recovery leaders tend to be viewed by the members as possible models for their own behavior. The role model qualities of the leader may not only include his knowledge of Recovery techniques, but also his behavior during the social part of the meeting, as well as his general level of "health." Although leaders may not be necessarily any "healthier" than the members, they may be perceived to be freer from difficulties, and their behavior may be emulated. The type of panel examples that the leaders present often influences the type of examples presented by the group. In this way the apparent level of mental health of a leader may set the tone for his group. For example, in one group a leader was observed to present examples that did not reflect severe problems and difficulties. This appeared to influence the group in such a way that almost all examples presented were of the same general type. In other groups where leaders spoke of very severe psychological difficulties, examples given by members were of the same order.

BASIC FUNCTIONS OF RECOVERY

Undoubtedly Recovery helps to satisfy some of the needs of its members; otherwise it would cease to exist. In response to the questionnaire survey, almost all of the members indicated satisfaction with the organization. They reported that they had been helped, and were particularly enthusiastic about the group aspects of Recovery.

The functions the organization may serve for its members may be separated into two major categories: the functions of the Recovery method, and the group functions of Recovery.

BASIC FUNCTIONS OF THE RECOVERY METHOD

Ordering the Psychological Field as a Means of Reducing Anxiety

The Recovery method is characterized by a search for order amidst a labyrinth of complex psychological problems and processes. Personal experiences are restructured within the cognitive framework provided by Recovery so that events which may be anxiety-promoting and unfamiliar may be translated into a more familiar and understandable form. Examples are presented in such a way that complex psychological problems tend to be treated as tangible symptoms of a somatic nature. Since examples must be about trivial incidents, they tend in the main to entail familiar everyday experiences. Symptoms appear to become standardized, and somaticized, almost exclusively adhering to the type cited in the textbook. In this manner a degree of certainty is introduced into the psychological realm, since even the most threatening emotions may be viewed as conforming to a set of universal regulations.

In addition members are given a simple routine to counteract the anxiety-producing uncertainty associated with their problems. This is done by imposing a rigidly standardized procedure characterized by repetitiveness. The meetings assume the characteristics of ritual and may serve to reduce anxiety in the same manner as the ritualistic ceremonies described by Malinowski (5) in his study of primitive religions. Each member is provided with a set of simple semantic labels to be used as tools for restructuring subjective experiences. The tools are available to all and may be manipulated with relative ease, once the Recovery method has been learned.

Introduction of Controls to Strengthen Defenses Against Anxiety

The basic component of the Recovery method is the belief that an individual can and must exercise control and self-discipline in all matters that affect his mental health. The will is to be trained to achieve this desired end through the continuous application of Recovery techniques. It is as if an attempt is made to strengthen the defense mechanisms of the Recovery member and to provide him with new controls and defenses against anxiety.

Control is to be first introduced at the simplest and most basic level. The individual must learn to walk when he is tempted to run, to lie down when he is agitated, to make decisions in the simplest situations. Eventually, control is to be extended to the more complex processes, such as the suppression of temper and the rejection of anxiety-producing impulses. Self-discipline is to be gradually generalized to all spheres and levels of activity. The Recovery meetings themselves assume the characteristics of exercises in self control. Impulses to speak must be checked. The individual must first raise his hand, and must make his comments in accordance with the strict procedural regulations.

Inspiration and the Power of Positive Thinking

The continuous reporting of successful examples at Recovery meetings may provide inspiration for the members. If one hears that other members are successfully coping with their problems, he may begin to believe that he too can do the same. In line with the inspirational aspects of Recovery meetings is the stress upon what may be designated as "the power of positive thinking." The member is constantly told to employ positive thoughts and to reject negative ones. The Recovery theory is presented in such a way that all psychological difficulties appear to be manageable. It is almost as if the nurturing of positive thought is believed to lead to positive results.

This aspect of Recovery resembles a once-popular form of psychotherapy based on auto-suggestion, devised by Emile Coué. In effect, the members are to tell themselves that "every day I get better and better." It is hoped that such auto-suggestion will lead to actual success in the elimination and suppression of symptoms. However, there appears to be a basic contradiction which may affect the operation of this form of positive thinking. The Recovery member is not only told to have positive thoughts, but he is also told that he *must* have them because he is a nervous patient and can only afford to have positive thoughts. All positive thoughts, therefore, are based on the assumption that the person is a nervous patient. The acceptance and maintenance of this basic assumption may keep the self-fulfilling prophecy from operating.

Maintenance of Activity and Satisfaction of Dependency Needs

Recovery on the one hand implies a passive acceptance of the authority of the founder of the method and, on the other hand, the belief that mental health can only be attained through active effort. Recovery requires that the members accept the authority of Dr. Low, as embodied in his writings and their presentation by the leader of the group. The new member passively puts himself in the hands of Recovery, forming a dependent type of relationship with the leaders, the members, and the basic authority of Dr. Low's text. In return, he is given a method and told what to do. Through the acceptance of the group's authority, the newcomer may obtain gratification of his basic dependency needs. He may feel that if he obeys the rules and regulations of Recovery, he will be taken care of.

However, counteracting this trend toward dependency and passivity is the stress in Recovery upon self-help. The Recovery method must be actively practiced. The member is told that progress can only come through continual effort and work. The individual can receive help from others, but in the long run it is his own effort which will produce progress. The combination of the passive dependency and active self-help elements in Recovery may serve to fulfill the individual's dependency needs without lulling him into passive inactivity. Salvation in Recovery may be obtained only through work, but the work must be done along the lines prescribed by the organization and by Dr. Low.

Cathartic Value of the Recovery Confessional

The group confessional aspects of the meetings may aid the individual in removing some of the anxiety associated with his symptoms. The mere act of publicly admitting the symptom may serve to disassociate some of the affect with which the symptom is labeled. Guilt and stigma associated with the attempt to hide the presence of symptomatology may be eliminated. Getting the symptom "off one's chest" may provide at least temporary relief. In addition, when one individual confesses his symptoms, others may learn that the symptoms which they have are similar.

The Semi-Religious Nature of Recovery

The Recovery method and its practice at panel meetings is clearly reminiscent of various elements characteristic of certain organized religions. The method involves faith and acceptance of regulations handed down by a higher authority. The method stresses self-discipline and the volitional aspects of human nature. This type of approach is more amenable to certain religious beliefs than is the Freudian and Darwinian notion of man as an instinct-driven animal. The emphasis on the power of positive thinking and on inspiration is also clearly analogous to some religious tenets.

The analogy between Recovery and religion may be extended further. Recovery has a bible, the textbook of Dr. Low. Hero worship of Low sometimes assumes the proportions of making him almost appear a god-figure. The leaders assume the role of disciples. In certain Recovery groups, the desire for expansion and for national recognition is analogous to the missionary zeal in religious groups. In addition, the repetitive ritual-like panel meetings resemble certain forms of religious ceremonies.

THE GROUP FUNCTIONS OF RECOVERY

Current organizational policy is to de-emphasize the social nature of the organization and to concentrate on the method. However, the importance of the group atmosphere is not neglected. Members take part in extra-curricular social activities such as outings and parties. A social period of "mutual-aid" has become institutionalized as part of every meeting. Individuals come to meetings early and remain until the late hours of the evening to spend additional time with their fellow members.

Membership in Recovery involves more than the practice of a particular method of self-help and aftercare. It also entails membership within a community of individuals who have joined together because of perceived mutual problems and goals. Members form interpersonal relationships with one another, are affected by and in turn affect each other. The Recovery method serves to increase the solidarity of the group. The uniqueness of the Recovery language allows it to serve as a badge of membership which can be used to distinguish the in-group member from the outsider. The agreement upon basic goals also serves to strengthen group feeling.

The Recovery group provides the individual with significant others with whom he may interact. For the social isolate this, in itself, would constitute an important motive for membership. For the members who have other opportunities to interact in the community, certain special aspects of the Recovery group setting may be particularly attractive.

Recovery as a Sheltered Social Environment

Recovery differs from other types of organizations because of its distinctive composition and general goals. All members are perceived to be in need of help, and are encouraged to discuss their symptoms freely. No one is stigmatized for having psychological problems. The members need not conceal the nature of their difficulties in order to obtain group acceptance. It is almost as if Recovery provides its members with a sheltered social environment in which everyone is treated as being equal, despite the level of his mental health or the nature of his symptomatology.

The Recovery group exhibits a greater tolerance for deviant behavior than other organizations. Individuals are generally accepted by their peers despite behavior that might be considered abnormal in other groups, as long as these persons adhere to the basic regulations of Recovery. The over-all atmosphere is supportive, since members have joined together to help each other. Within such a group environment, the person whose concern over his symptoms might have previously interfered with his social interaction may find it easier to relate to other group members. He may also be able to test various patterns of behavior, and to abandon those which are inappropriate.

The individual may learn that other people are confronted with similar difficulties and problems. In this way, he may change his previous perceptions of his particular situation as unique. He may identify with other members of the group, and lose the feeling of isolation and sense of stigma imposed upon him by his symptomatology.

The Group as a Source of Secondary Rewards

Inherent within the Recovery framework is a formal reward system designed to motivate participation at the meetings. Individuals are to be endorsed for reading from the textbook, for presenting examples, and for appropriate comments and questions. The reward system covers almost all behavior that goes on during the meeting. If an individual is not as yet able to present an example, he may be endorsed for not feeling forced to give one, or for just listening. As a consequence, the mere presence of an individual at a meeting warrants some form of endorsement. Continuous endorsement is intended to raise the level of self-esteem of the members. Besides the formal reward system, the individual obtains other rewards in exchange for his membership. He is provided with a social group which will accept him, and give him support and recognition. These social rewards are not contingent upon the degree of success or improvement that may be obtained through the method. To be sure, apparent successful utilization of the method may result in a higher level of social reward, but a certain amount accrues to all members.

It may be that the social rewards which had previously served as a means to an end, have become functionally autonomous, and may serve as ends themselves. A member may join to receive help for his particular difficulties, but because of the social rewards may remain in the organization even if he has not obtained sufficient help to alleviate his symptoms, or if he has obtained enough help to be able to function adequately without further attendance at meetings.

The Group as a Controller of Behavior

The group may serve to control behavior through the manipulation of rewards and sanctions. Control is applied primarily to assuring conformity to the doctrines of Recovery. Thus, the individual must use the accepted vocabulary, must provide appropriate examples, and must conform to the various regulations. The group socializes each member. He must learn to control his impulses by speaking only after raising his hand. He must refrain from autistic verbalization which could prevent him from utilizing the method appropriately. He must sit still when not participating, so that he does not disrupt the meeting. If his behavior is anti-social he is a threat to the group and must be controlled. Very few sanctions are applied by the group, but perhaps the simplest and most effective one is to ignore completely the non-conformer. If he does not adhere to the method, his comments are cut off by the leader and his remarks are ignored by the group.

Recovery as a Cause

In many local groups there is the tendency for Recovery to be a cause in itself. The member may not only identify with his fellow group members, but also with all Recovery members. This act of identification may extend the person's ego boundaries in such a way that the success or failure of the organization is perceived as the success or failure of the self. The member becomes totally involved in the organization, and serves as a missionary whose desire it is to convert the non-believing world to Recovery's cause. Identification with Recovery may enable the individual to transcend his immediate problems and difficulties. Recovery becomes a cause to be preached to all who will listen. In this way, the individual may remove a great quantity of libidinal energy from his symptoms and utilize it in missionary activities. This zeal can take many directions. It may be used to build up Recovery membership and to gain national recognition for the organization. It may also be employed to foster anti-professional attitudes, and to foster the belief that it is "Recovery against the world." The exact nature that this may take depends upon the individual and the climate of opinion in his group.

POTENTIAL PROBLEMS ARISING FROM MEMBERSHIP IN RECOVERY

Although Recovery is the largest self-help group in the mental health field, its membership comprises only a small segment of the potential number of former mental patients and emotionally disturbed individuals. Alcoholics Anonymous, founded at the same time as Recovery, reports that in 1956 it had 5,000 groups in 60 countries with a total membership of 150,000 (2). In addition, while A.A. has received widespread professional and lay recognition for its efforts, Recovery has yet failed to do so. Although the problems of alcoholism and mental illness may not be similar, the differences between the two self-help organizations may be indicative of certain limitations of the Recovery approach.

When a survey of opinions about Recovery was made among members of the American Psychiatric Association in Detroit and Chicago, certain important qualifications concerning the effectiveness of the organization became apparent.

In general, the psychiatrists felt that Recovery is a helpful and valuable tool because of its group aspects. They felt that the group meetings satisfy the needs of some ex-patients for various forms of group support. However, they were concerned that the organization is not under medical or professional supervision, and that there is no systematic screening of members and no thorough selection and training of leaders. Some psychiatrists were particularly wary of the particular method that Recovery utilizes. Criticisms of the method included statements like the following.

(1) It offers magical-omnipotent-authoritarian-unrealistic solutions.
(2) It is superficial, limited and prevents or hinders insight.
(3) It is regressive, fixes defenses, forces adjustment at a low level of maturity.
(4) It creates complacency about the problem of mental illness.

These criticisms illuminate two major potential problem areas in the functioning of Recovery: problems relating to the absence of professional supervision, and problems arising from the Recovery method itself.

PROBLEMS RELATING TO THE ABSENCE OF A PROFESSIONAL

The transition of Recovery from an adjunct to the treatment regimen of Dr. Low to a lay-run self-help organization has left a number of unresolved problems. The Recovery method specifies that the physician is the primary authority in all matters pertaining to mental health. Only he is qualified to make a diagnosis, and the patient must follow his directions if he is to get well. At present, there is no physician associated with Recovery. As a consequence, certain functions that may have previously been fulfilled by Dr. Low now are either relegated to the lay leaders or no longer performed.

Selection of Members

At present, the Recovery method is to be used by all the members, regardless of the specific nature of their disorders. Originally, members were mainly patients of Dr. Low. It may safely be assumed that he had some control over their selection. Current Recovery membership, of course, includes many people who were never treated by Dr. Low, and some who have never received any professional treatment for psychiatric disorders. There is real doubt as to whether the method is appropriate for all of these individuals.

Recovery, it should be remembered, is a voluntary organization, and participants are free to leave at any time. An individual who feels that he is not receiving adequate help, or that he is being harmed, will probably drop out. However, it is possible that secondary social rewards stemming from membership in the group may motivate some persons to continue as members even if the Recovery method is inappropriate for them.

Selection of Leaders.

Recovery also has no formal criteria for the selection of leaders. In view of the crucial position of the leader within the organization, this may constitute one of the organization's greatest weaknesses. When the founder was guiding the activities of the Recovery groups, he was in the position to exercise a strong influence in leader selection. At present anyone may become a leader if he takes the short-term training course and gains the approval of the Board of Directors. Thus, there is the real possibility that mentally ill persons may become leaders and may manipulate the group in accordance with their own needs. This is a high order of potential danger since the leader may serve as a role model for the behavior of others.

Leaders, however, must present examples about their own personal problems and difficulties. They must be able to operate in a group, and must be sufficiently fluent verbally to utilize the method. These requirements may eliminate certain types of mentally ill individuals from leadership roles. In addition, since Recovery is a voluntary organization, the leader must be able to motivate the members to remain in the group. Although these factors may serve as partial safeguards against poor and unhealthy leadership, they by no means eliminate the danger completely.

"Graduation" Policy

Recovery does not have any specific policy for the "graduation" of its members. When Dr. Low was present, he may well have advised certain members that they no longer needed to attend meetings. Without this type of advice, members may remain in the organization after they no longer need to, or when they are not receiving sufficient help from it. Many individuals who have been in the organization for three years or more still attend meetings frequently. Others still attend meetings regularly despite feeling that they no longer need to. Because Recovery is in a state of expansion and desires to build up its membership, it is highly unlikely that any member will be asked to leave, even when such a course would be beneficial to him. Of course, for certain individuals, continued membership, perhaps even on a lifetime basis, may be instrumental in the obtainment of necessary support.

Control over the Contents of the Meeting

Dr. Low was in the habit of making the final summaries and interpretations after all examples had been presented at the panel meetings. He reserved the right to modify or to correct any statement he considered to be inappropriate. At present, there is no qualified professional who fulfills this function. The group may misinterpret the method or may provide inappropriate advice in areas where lay persons are not competent. It is equally possible, under improper leadership, for discussion at meetings to range beyond the limits of the Recovery method. Surely all of these potential difficulties are possible, and others as well, but the method is so structured as to tend to minimize these dangers. All discussion at the meetings must be presented within the framework of the Recovery concepts and must deal only with trivial examples. The member can also always disregard inappropriate advice.

Relation to the Network of Traditional Aftercare Services

Recovery has no formal connection with any facilities, agencies, or professionals in the mental health field. Because of its relative isolation from other potential sources of help, Recovery is in the position of providing a limited range of services to its members. It may not be able to refer a member to other sources of help which may be necessary. A potential consequence of such isolation may be the development of anti-professional attitudes, and reluctance on the part of the members to obtain professional help when it is necessary. Anti-professionalism need not always be a characteristic of a lay-run self-help organization. Alcoholics Anonymous, which is completely lay run, appears to have good relations with professionals and in many instances has cooperated with professionals in order to provide maximum help for the alcoholic.

Control of Deviancy

An important problem arising from the utilization of lay-run groups for emotionally disturbed individuals involves the possibility of their becoming channels for deviant behavior. Groups like Recovery, because of their unique composition, may foster bizarre and maladaptive behavior on the part of the members. Such groups may be tolerant of behavior which elsewhere would be considered deviant, and may produce deviant group norms. In this sense, such groups may become "fringe" or "crackpot" types of organizations.

The possibility of this kind of development, however, appears to be minimal. The survey of membership has strongly suggested that the organization is not composed of marginal individuals, but rather is made up of persons of solid middle-class status. Observation of group meetings has not uncovered unusually predominant manifestations of abnormal or unacceptable behavior. The philosophy of Recovery, rather than being deviant, resembles in certain respects the general ethos of middle-class American society. The value placed on salvation through work and effort is strongly reminiscent of the Protestant Ethic. The focusing of the Recovery method on concrete symptoms can be compared to current pragmatic and behavioristic ideologies. Finally, the inspirational nature of Recovery is in line with the current fashionableness of "positive thinking." If Recovery is a deviant organization, it is not deviant because of its philosophy or because of the type of members that it attracts; it may be deviant, however, in the sense that it stands outside of the network of traditional rehabilitation and aftercare services.

PROBLEMS RELATED TO THE RECOVERY METHOD

The Rigidity of the Recovery Method

The Recovery method is to be literally applied to all examples presented at the panel meetings. The method is viewed as a perfected, finished system of self-help and aftercare. No provision is made for any changes in the Recovery concepts and techniques, nor is such change viewed as desirable. Questioning of the basic assumptions of the method is not permitted.

The great concern displayed by Recovery leaders and members over the faithful application of the method prevents individualized consideration of each member's problems. The tendency is to change each panel example so that it fits the method, rather than to modify the method so that it applies to the example. As a consequence, appropriate consideration of an individual's problems may have to be rejected in order to maintain the Recovery method intact.

The Recovery outlook contrasts sharply with the position of Alcoholics Anonymous. Although A.A. has a basic set of "Traditions" and "Steps" which in certain respects are similar to the Recovery method, they are not so literally and rigidly employed in all instances as is the Recovery method. A.A.'s position, briefly stated, is as follows. "Nobody invented Alcoholics Anonymous. It grew. Trial and error has produced a rich experience. Little by little we have been adopting the lessons of that experience, first as policy and then as tradition. That process still goes on and we hope it never stops. Should we ever harden too much, the letter might crush the spirit. We could victimize ourselves by petty rules and prohibitions; we could imagine that we had said the last word. We might even be asking alcoholics to accept our rigid ideas or stay away. May we never stifle progress like that!" (1).

Of course, the rigid application of the Recovery method may also have certain advantages. The schedule of the meeting may prevent discussion from extending into areas in which the members may not be qualified. The method prevents the giving of advice to members outside of the context of Recovery terminology, and serves to control the content of discussion. In addition, the feeling that the method is perfect and can help all members is in line with the inspirational aspects of the organization.

The Stress Upon Control

Recovery emphasis upon control may provide members with defenses against anxiety, and may help them to cope with their symptoms. However, the basic concern over emotional control may serve to neglect the provision of adequate mechanisms for the release of affect.

Some release of emotion may be a by-product of the catharsis ensuing from the public presentation of a behavioral example, but this kind of release is not a major concern of Recovery. Recovery appears to stress a denial of affect, rather than a release aimed at the establishment of new insights. For the individual whose basic problem is the expression of feeling rather than its control, such a method may be unsuitable. Individuals with over-rigid systems of defenses against anxiety may be harmed by increments arising from the Recovery method. Despite the problems which may arise from the lack of inclusion of a "release" mechanism in the Recovery method, the omission may also serve as a potential safeguard. If emotional content was released at the meetings, it is doubtful whether lay persons would have sufficient skill to cope with such material.

The Superficiality of the Method

The Recovery method does not attempt to probe for the etiology of symptoms. The major concern is the treatment of an individual's problems as they exist at the present. Problems are viewed in the form of symptoms, usually presented in a highly concrete, somaticized form. Dynamic interpretations are not permitted, as they are outside the realm of the method. The total effect may be the temporary suppression of the symptom rather than recognition and management of underlying cause. This suggests that any help that the Recovery method provides for a person may be temporary. Symptoms which are suppressed in one form may reappear in altered context. Observation of panel meetings has indicated that although members tend to report successful coping with symptoms, such symptoms persist from meeting to meeting, changing only slightly in form.

The Regressive-Infantilizing Aspects of the Method

Although the Recovery method places much emphasis on self-help and individual initiative, it nevertheless encourages the member to submit to a higher form of authority. The member must unquestioningly accept the Recovery method in its entirety, with the image of Dr. Low as the supreme authority. The method leads the individual to reduce complex psychological problems to concretized somatic symptoms. The participant is given certain basic tools of a highly ritualized nature, which are to be used in warding off anxiety-producing situations. The new Recovery language which is supplied to the individual creates the appearance of verbal labels which are to be manipulated. For certain people, the employment of these aspects of the Recovery method may tend to force adjustment at low levels of psychological maturity. The individual is placed in the situation of a child who must obey a father figure and use certain semi-magical rituals. He is to gain salvation through complete obedience. Individuals capable of deeper insights into the meaning of their problems may be forced to regress to obtain psychic equilibrium.

Dealing Only with Symptomatology

Recovery provides help for an individual only in reference to his symptomatology. It does not deal with such areas as his potential for growth and development. Its focus is limited to maladaption in effect to the "unhealthy" facets of the participant. There is no clear conceptualization in the Recovery method of what the healthy person is like. All members must constantly present examples of their problems and difficulties. The leaders, who serve as role models for the newer members, present these types of examples most frequently. The majority of Recovery group meetings are concerned with the various symptoms individuals in the group may experience. As a consequence, the group appears to be at all times concerned with illness. For the individual with a potential for growth beyond his immediate symptoms, the great concern in Recovery over symptomatology and illness may well be over-restrictive. As a consequence, for some persons psychological growth may be impeded.

There are certain safeguards within the Recovery method which to some extent serve to counteract this preoccupation. All examples and problems must be discussed within Recovery terminology. A time limit is placed on all discussion, and descriptions must be of an objective, concrete nature. These features of the method may prevent the degeneration of the panel examples into "gripe sessions." However, they may not eliminate completely the basic preoccupation with illness which is shared by the members.

Emphasis on Inspiration

The focus upon inspirational aspects in Recovery may prevent individuals from obtaining a realistic appraisal of the severity of their illness. Certain members may be given a false sense of complacency as to the actual nature of their problems. Because of Recovery's emphasis on inspiration and the belief that the problems of all members can be successfully coped with through this simple method, persons on the verge of acute episodes may be prevented from obtaining necessary professional help.

Cost of the Nervous Patient Role

An earlier section of this report has discussed the type of nervous patient role which membership in Recovery may imply. This role may lead to certain basic problems. It may stigmatize the member by formally defining him as different from other persons who are not emotionally disturbed. It may force him to view all of his behavior from within the cognitive framework provided by the role of a patient. As a result, he may have difficulty in perceiving himself in any other way. This may tend to reinforce his feelings about his illness. The role may be a permanent one: there are no mechanisms for a formal termination of it. The individual's integration into community life may be significantly impeded. If maintenance of the role permits the individual to remain outside of the hospital, to be reasonably productive, it may serve a positive function despite its limitations and relative permanence. And the group to which he is attached by the role of patient may provide him with a certain amount of support that could not be found elsewhere.

REFERENCES

1. Bill W: A. A. Tradition: How It Developed. New York, Alcoholics Anonymous Pub., Inc., 1955
2. Is A. A. For You? New York, Alcoholics Anonymous Pub., Inc., 1956
3. Low AA: Mental Health Through Will Training. Boston, Christopher Publishing House, 1950
4. Low AA (Mrs.): How a Panel Example Should Be Constructed. (mimeo) 1956
5. Malinowski B: Magic, Science and Religion. Boston, Beacon Press, 1948

Robert S. Wiess

9

Transition States and Other Stressful Situations: Their Nature and Programs for Their Management[1]

Mental health specialists have in recent years given increasing attention to situational distress; i.e., reactions that are so much the product of exposure to a particular situation that they are displayed by almost everyone in the situation. Examples of situations that are almost invariably upsetting are bereavement, marital separation, and, although the upset they produce may be less intense, residential uprooting and long-stay hospitalization. Commenting on the uniformity of symptons among individuals in situations such as these, Tyhurst has written, "If symptom incidence is not close to 100 percent ... this is probably because the survey has been incomplete in some way or the memories of informants were faulty" (Tyhurst, p. 161). In each case, not only do the great majority of those exposed to the situation manifest some sort of upset but also reactions to the situation are similar from individual to individual. (See Glick, Weiss, and Parkes; Weiss; Weissman and Paykel; Richardson.)

Typical responses to these stressful situations include depression, restlessness, and tendencies toward impulsive and irrational behavior. These reactions are similar to symptoms whose sources are neurotic or psychotic emotional organizations or other forms of character disorder. However, symptoms of situational distress should be recognized as indicative of a distinctly different condition, justifying a different therapeutic response (see Lindemann 1944; Parad and Caplan 1965; and Rapoport 1965). Whereas the proper treatment of characterological difficulty might well be an attempt

[1]This is a revision of a paper presented at the 1975 meetings of the *American Orthopsychiatric Association* under the title, "An Approach to Helping Individuals Who Have Entered Unfamiliar Life Situations."

to produce character change, the proper treatment of situational distress should be help in coping with the disturbing situation.

There are three distinct forms of stressful situation. The first is a severely upsetting situation of limited duration in which an individual's resources must be hastily summoned to cope with threats to his or her emotional and social stability. Examples are an intense marital quarrel or the news that one's spouse is threatened by a serious, possibly fatal, illness. Although "crisis" has been used by Lindemann and Caplan as a term for the upset of individuals exposed to any form of disruptive situation, it seems particularly appropriate when used to refer to a situation that is of sudden onset, of limited duration, and of considerable severity in the stress it imposes on those exposed to it.

Crises often begin with a brief period in which the individual's emotions seem to be suspended. The situation is recognized by the individual as intensely threatening, yet the individual appears separated from the implications of the threat, as though the threat were to someone else (see Tyhurst; and also Glick, Weiss, and Parkes). Accompanying this suspension of feeling is a mobilization of energy in response to the crisis situation. While the crisis holds, the individual can give attention to little else; the crisis must be managed, everything else must wait.

A crisis ends in one of two ways: by a return to the preexistent situation or by a persisting disruption of that situation. Should the first occur – should the marital quarrel be forgotten and the marriage continue as before, or the threat to the spouse prove a false alarm – the individual will return to his or her previous emotional organization and relational arrangements. But should the crisis end instead in change – should the marital quarrel lead to separation, or the illness require that the spouse be hospitalized – the individual's emotional organization and his or her other relational arrangements must also undergo change. In addition to having to cope now with new problems, the individual must find different ways of dealing with upset, tension, or fatigue, and find new sources of support for security, for feelings of worth, and for other components of well-being. Some previously maintained relationships may fade because they no longer seem appropriate, while others may be modified to respond to the individual's new needs, and relationships not previously existent may now be developed. The individual's concerns and aims may change and with them the individual's sense of self. This period of relational and personal change constitutes the second form of stressful situation, one I will call a "transition" or "transition state." (This term was used by Tyhurst (1957) to refer to situations characterized by disruption of preexisting social equilibria, a class of situations that includes those I would characterize as crises as well as those I would characterize as transitions.)

Parkes has recently drawn attention to the desirability from a community health standpoint of giving special attention to transition states. He rightly argues that they occur frequently, that they are productive of intense upset, and that the way in which they are managed may affect the later course of the individual's life (see Parkes, 1971). Individuals within transition states seem remarkably accessible to being helped. Simply in terms of return on therapeutic investment it would seem desirable to provide services to help individuals deal with transition.

The transition state ends with the establishment of a new stable life organization accompanied by a new stable identity. The new life organization may be adequate to the individual's needs, or it may in some way remain insufficient. Should a relational provision important to well-being, such as the sense of personal worth that comes from caring for dependent children, be unobtainable in the new life organization, the individual may be said to have entered into a "deficit" situation. As an example, many single parents seem to live in a deficit situation in that the absence of a second adult with whom they can share the tasks of child care gives them too much to do, too much for which to be responsible, and too little opportunity to escape the emotional demands of the children. In addition, the absence of a cared-for fellow adult whose accessibility is assured leaves many single parents vulnerable either to loneliness or to the anxieties associated with unreliable intimate relationships.

In addition to crises, transitions, and deficit situations, there are undoubtedly other stressful situations: those Hill has called "crises of accession," for example (Hill 1949). "Crises of accession" occur on the introduction into a stable situation of a new individual for whom a role must be found. But the triad of crisis, transition, and deficit are especially important among stressful situations since they so often represent the sequelae of loss. Crisis occurs on first awareness of the imminence of loss. If the loss cannot be avoided, then transition ensues. The transition may in turn give rise to a life organization which is in some respect deficient.

INTERVENTIONS IN CRISIS, TRANSITION, AND DEFICIT

Although no systematic information is available on helping people in crisis, unsystematic observation suggests that almost the only useful form of help is *support.* Support is furnished by a helper (who may or may not be a professional) who is accepted as an ally by the distressed individual. It consists of the communication, sometimes nonverbal, by the helper that the helper's training, experience, and understanding are at the service of the distressed individual as the latter struggles to regain equilibrium. It is support in this sense that C.S. Lewis refers to when he remarks that the mere presence of others seemed to make more bearable the grief he experienced after the loss of his wife:

I want the others to be about me. I dread the moments when the house is empty. (Lewis, p. 7.)

Support appears to be useful in all distress-inducing situations – in transition and deficit situations as well as in crises. Few who find themselves in such situations can be sure that their resources are adequate to the demands being made on them. People in crises seem able to use no form of help other than support. They have too little free energy with which to engage those who would offer something more. Lewis follows the quotation above with the comment: "If only they would talk to one another and not to me."

People in transition states can profit from other forms of helping in addition to support. Orientation, guidance, and access to an accepting community are all likely to be useful to them.

In transition states, because patterns of managing have been disrupted, individuals are likely to be confronted by difficulties for which they have no ready solution. The newly separated man, for example, may never before have had to furnish an apartment or maintain an independent social life. Indeed, people in transition may have difficulty in even identifying their problems: so extensive may be the disruption of their previous ways of life that they may not know where to begin rebuilding. And, to the extent that their sense of themselves has come into question, they may be uncertain how they want to rebuild.

Because confusion and unpreparedness are so prominent among the difficulties of transition, a helper can be useful to an individual in transition by providing that individual with a framework which orders and explains the individual's experiences and responses. In addition to cognitive materials that help make sense of the individual's observations of his or her reaction to the situation, other sorts of cognitive materials may also be useful: for example, reports of the experiences of others in similar situations, descriptions of the devices others have used for managing, and discussions of the risks and benefits of various strategies.

People in transition are likely to discover that their new situation is unshared by friends and kin and that the problems they face have become distinctly different from those occupying other members of their community. They may develop a sense of marginality to their community and, with this sense, feelings of social isolation. In consequence, they may also find it useful to have available to them a temporary community of others in the same situation, for whom their experiences will have meaning and who can fully accept them.

Individuals in deficit situations have different needs. Their lives have stabilized again. They are no longer beset by confusion; they know well the conditions under which they live. In addition they are likely to have reestablished a network of friends, some in the same boat as themselves, which provides them with a more or less adequate community. Their need is apt to be for help in dealing with the problems that result from the inadequacies in their life organization. The single mother, for example, may need someone to talk to about the problems of adolescents who complain that their one-parent home provides an insecure base from which to move to independence. Or she may need someone to help her think about ways of relieving or at least tolerating her own loneliness. Time-limited help may not do in relation to deficit situations. It is characteristic of such situations that problems recur; indeed, it may seem that one problem is no sooner resolved than another develops. In consequence, individuals in deficit situations seem to require a continuing, problem-focused support system.

HELPING PEOPLE DEAL WITH TRANSITION

I and my colleagues at the Laboratory of Community Psychiatry have developed a program, "Seminars for the Separated," aimed at helping people with the transitional situation that follows marital separation.[2] We are currently developing a similar program for the bereaved.

The ending of a marriage – whether through separation or bereavement – disrupts relationships in almost all sectors of life: friendships change in character and may fade entirely; kin relationships become troubled as relatives question the way in which one is managing; job difficulties may develop because of the preoccupation with the loss and its sequelae; relationships with children are likely to undergo fundamental revision (Glick, Weiss, and Parkes 1974; Weiss 1975). These disruptions of former relationships give rise to a number of difficulties. I have already noted the feelings of marginality associated with the fading of friendships, and the disorientation and confusion that occur when formerly relied-on structures are no longer available. In addition, people in transition often report the following.

1. *Obsessive review.* Their thoughts are absorbed by the events that brought about the new situation, though other concerns may demand attention. They may want to end their dwelling on the past, even feel it to be oppressive, and still find themselves returning to it again and again.
2. *Anger, guilt, and related emotions.* Distress leads to a search for its author. Others may be blamed for having brought about the disruption of the person's life. So may the self. Blaming others is likely to be

[2]I would like here to acknowledge the contributions of Drs. Ralph Hirschowitz, Bernard Fisher, Maurits van Nieuwenhuysen, and my wife, Joan Weiss. Each helped in the program's design. Mr. Justus Fennel and Mr. Gerald Brocklesby demonstrated that the program could be conducted with success by others.

accompanied by feelings of anger, blaming the self by guilt and feelings of unworthiness. Even if there is no one to blame, individuals in transition may feel resentful of those who have been spared similar stress.

3. *Uncertainty regarding the self.* Along with the weakening of earlier definitions of goals and commitments, there may be a weakening of self-definition. The relationships that served as anchors to identity have been lost, and the new identities can in consequence easily be assumed. But this leaves individuals in transition liable to impulsive redefinitions of their commitments and goals. In addition, they may be unusually suggestible and thus vulnerable to pressures brought by others.
4. *Tendency to false starts.* New modes of dealing with the discomforts of transition repeatedly suggest themselves, and sometimes are acted on. Some are almost certain to prove impractical or unsatisfactory, and thereupon to be dropped, though with concomitant dismay at failure to carry through plans, however briefly adopted.
5. *Self-doubt and loss of self-confidence.* People in transition recognize their own tendency to false starts, impulsivity, and constant redefinition of their selves. They, like others, are apt to view their ineffective or self-defeating actions as demonstrating serious imperfections in character. Self-doubt increases, and there is further loss of self-confidence. Their already high level of anxiety may be increased by their seeming inability to settle down and function properly.

Howard Becker has written (1967) that when the effects of marijuana were little understood many people upon smoking marijuana for the first time became frightened of their response to the drug but, as new users learned from their friends and from the mass media what to expect, panic attacks became rare. People in distress-inducing situations are like those who were unprepared for the effects of the drug: their lack of preparation for their own reactions makes them vulnerable to secondary distress. Because they can neither control nor understand their responses, they become fearful that there is something fundamentally wrong with them.

To help people in transition manage this set of difficulties, we have sought to develop programs that will provide cognitive materials, support, and an assured place in a temporary community. The cognitive materials – based on research and on our further understanding as we work with individuals in a particular transition situation – are presented within a lecture series that forms the core of the program. Support is furnished by the staff and by participants themselves. All participants become aware that it is an aim of the staff, and eventually of most participants, to help all who attend return to effective functioning. Finally, a number of devices are used to enhance the participants' sense of membership in a community. It is possible for participants to meet with one another for coffee – which we supply – before and after the formal program, and in this way develop a sense of membership in a social group. The basis for feeling this group to be a community lies in each participant's recognition of the extent to which experiences and concerns are shared by all, and in each participant's feeling that he or she has a secure place in the group.

A SUCCESSFUL PROGRAM: SEMINARS FOR THE SEPARATED

Seminars for the Separated, our only fully developed instance of this approach to helping people in transition, has been conducted by our group seven times and by other groups using our model many more times.

In our first few series of seminars, we repeatedly changed both format and materials in an effort to make the seminars more effective. In the format we settled on after several series, the seminar met once a week for 8 weeks. Each meeting began with a lecture of about 45 minutes on some aspect of separation. After each lecture, discussion groups of five to eight people were formed, each with a staff member as leader. These discussion groups usually met for an additional hour and a half, during which they might review material presented in the lecture or take any other direction which the group desired. All participants had been provided with an outline of the program before the first meeting.[3]

The first lecture series dealt with the emotional impact of separation: the distress that follows loss of a spouse or any other attachment figure, even one ambivalently regarded. We described the apprehensiveness and tension associated with loss of an attachment figure, the pining for return of the figure, and the intense anger often directed at the figure as a result of feelings of abandonment or betrayal. We also described the guilt that may accompany separation, especially if the individual accepts responsibility for it, and the confusions that must accompany so inconsistent a set of feelings. Turning to problems associated with loss of support for identity, we discussed, among other issues, susceptibility to mood swings and the likelihood of false starts.

The second lecture dealt with the extremely ambivalent continuing relationship with the former spouse, and the process that produced this ambivalence. We discussed at this time specific issues likely to create conflict between separated spouses in the areas of property division, support, custody, and visitation. In the first few series of seminars we had given attention at this time to the processes of marital breakdown, but this material, although interesting to participants, seemed to be less useful to them than material dealing with problems in their current situation.

In the third lecture, we focused on the impact of separation on rela-

[3]The outline for one of the later series is presented as an appendix to this chapter.

tionships with friends, kin, in-laws, and others in the individual's social milieu. In the fourth, the impact of separation on the individual's relationships with his or her children was discussed. Here we talked about the structure of the single-parent family and also about the fundamentally changed relationship with his or her children of the parent who relinquishes custody. The fifth lecture centered on the problems of starting over. In an early series, we talked about dating at this time, but in later series we postponed detailed discussion of dating to the next meeting and first talked in a more general way about the problems of building a new life organization and new identity. We here considered the promises and risks of alternative strategies for reorganizing one's life. In an early series, we discussed new committed relationships in the sixth lecture; in later series, we discussed dating as well as new relationships at this time.

In the seventh meeting, we considered sources of help, described what we hoped our program had given to participants, and contrasted the aims of our program with those of psychotherapy. In this meeting we also discussed the values and limitations of supplementary communities, including those that develop in connection with interest groups (church organizations, dramatic societies, evening classes, and the like), and those established for individuals whose marriages have ended, such as Parents Without Partners.

In the eighth meeting, we reviewed and evaluated the series. At the close of the eighth meeting, we held a wine-and-cheese party to mark the series' end.

Many of the participants in the second and third series proved unwilling to relinquish the weekly meetings at the seminars' formal ending even though they recognized that there was little more to cover. We accepted their request for a group leader who might help them move into a more therapeutic mode. But when both continuations of the seminars ended abruptly after a few weeks, we decided that continued access to the seminars community was what was wanted, rather than therapy. We thereupon established the practice of scheduling a "reunion" to be held about 6 weeks after the last meeting. This promise that the community would not be irretrievably lost seemed to make ending more manageable. By the time of the reunion, the seminars community was no longer so important, and there was no need for further reunions.

We monitored the seminars in several ways. After each meeting, we telephoned participants to ask them whether they thought the seminars had been useful to them and how the seminars might be changed to make them more useful. Each participant was phoned at least two or three times over the course of the series. As might be expected, participants talked during these calls not only about their reactions to the seminars but also about other significant events in their lives. Some participants treated the telephone calls as an integral part of the program and were disappointed if they were not called when they expected that they would be.

We also collected evaluations of the program in the final meeting of each series, and again at the reunion meeting. About a year after the end of one series still further evaluative information was collected by interviews with a small sample of people who had not attended the seminars because places were already filled when they called and a sample of people who *had* attended the seminars.[4] Attention was given to ways in which recovery from separation might have been affected by attending the seminars.

The most immediate benefit of attending the seminars appeared to be reassurance that emotional distress following separation was a normal and indeed almost universal reaction. The lecturer's explanations of separation distress, including his excursions into theories of attachment and loss, helped participants view their own reactions as acceptable. In addition, the lecturer's estimate of the time necessary for movement through the various phases of recovery gave participants some sense of where they were in the process. The result of the first lecture was sometimes a dramatic reduction in anxiety. One man said:

> If you have a terrible pain in your side, and you don't know whether you have cancer or a muscle pull, you can go through an awful lot of emotional anxiety until you find out it is only a muscle pull.

It was possible for people to function more effectively once the difficulties of the situation were made explicit. Participants could learn to tolerate their upset and to reduce the impulsiveness of their behavior. A woman said:

> I began to realize how abnormal your thinking and behavior really is when you are going through this, and I began to just take things a little bit easier about everything.

One woman, in particular, was able to restrain herself from acting on her persisting attachment to her former husband (with whom she had been unhappy for years) because the materials of the seminars gave her a better understanding of her feelings:

> In the second meeting, one of the things Dr. Weiss was talking about was that you are in the strange phenomenon where when you are with your separated spouse, because he or she is nearby, you find yourself comfortable and complete. A week ago I had a conference with my husband and his lawyer and my lawyer. Afterwards I told my lawyer that I was not going to do that any more. Because I felt that as long as my husband was in the room I felt protected, and that it was just the two of us, not the lawyers. I had not eaten all day because of it. That evening I was sitting in bed, eating vegetable soup, my first meal of the day, and I thought to myself, "I could call him up and say, 'What a colossal mistake we've made; I only feel together when I'm with you,'" And I thought, "My God, that's what Dr. Weiss was talking about!" And how fortunate I was to recognize that thing at once.

Membership in a supportive discussion group was a second important contribution of participation in the seminars. The support of the group could

[4]This study was conducted by Mrs. Dorothy Burlage of the Laboratory.

be trusted partly because other members so clearly understood the nature of one's own emotional state. A woman said:

> The group was supportive ... First of all, everybody else is separated ... And they understood me in a way that nobody else who knows me would. A stranger might be taken in by my laughing and joking, but people who know you better don't get taken in. And there is acceptance.

Another woman reported that membership in the community of participants helped to fend off feelings of marginality and loneliness. She said:

> When I first pulled up to that rickety-tickety old building, I thought, "What the hell am I doing here?" And when I walked in, and all these people were sitting in this sleazy livingroom ... I wanted to run away. Then I started to recognize that I had the same problems and could relate to these people. Because I wasn't relating to anybody at that point, I was so screwed up: the only thing I did was cry all day ... I felt desperately lonely at home but I didn't feel lonely in that group.

The comparison of individuals who had not participated in the seminars with those who had participated turned up yet another way in which the Seminars were helpful. Those who had not participated seemed still – a year or more after their separation – to want to review why it had occurred. Those who had participated tended to treat their separation more as past history.

Most of those who had participated viewed the seminars as valuable, perhaps the most helpful single experience of their separation. A few participants felt the seminars had made the difference between recovering and failing to recover. One woman, doing well when interviewed about a year after the end of the series, said:

> I think the seminars got me over the suicidal hump.

A PROGRAM STILL IN DEVELOPMENT: SEMINARS FOR THE BEREAVED

After developing Seminars for the Separated to a point at which the program seemed effective, we turned to the development of a similar program for the bereaved.[5]

Having completed research on the processes of recovery from bereavement (Glick, Weiss, and Parkes), we anticipated that we could integrate this material into a program of lectures and discussions like those of Seminars for the Separated. On the basis of two series of meetings in what we have come to call Seminars for the Bereaved, however, we now feel that there

[5]I want to thank Mrs. JoAnne Westfall, Professor Sophie Lowenstein, Professor Lisa Peattie, Mrs. Jan Tomasello, and Mrs. Joan Weiss for their contributions to this project.

are great differences in the nature of the loss in the two situations, that the two transition experiences impose different stresses on those exposed to them, and, in consequence that a program of helping the bereaved must differ in significant respects from a program for the separated.

Our first discovery was that discussing with the bereaved the nature of grief was of mixed value. Whereas the separated had found discussion of the nature of separation distress helpful in many ways, the bereaved found discussion of the nature of grief provocative of a good deal of pain. It was useful, to be sure, to reassure the bereaved of their essential normality, to give them a sense of where they were in the process of recovery, and to provide them with a setting in which their grief could be revealed without others withdrawing from them. But while the distress that follows marital separation is a confusing, and sometimes bewildering, condition, the grief that follows bereavement ordinarily is not. The bereaved had little need for explanation for why they sorrowed. True, the intensity of their restlessness and loneliness could be frightening to the bereaved as well as to the separated, but the cause of the condition is less difficult to understand. In addition, whereas the separated generally want desperately to overcome their distress, the bereaved tend to be more ambivalent about their grief: they too want to return to effective functioning, but they also feel that their grief testifies to the depth of their feelings for their spouse. Finally, whereas the separated often have several ways in which they can soften the pain of loss – for example, by disparaging the spouse and telling themselves that the separation was for the best, by contacting the spouse if they become unbearably lonely, or by maintaining fantasies of reconciliation – the bereaved generally view their loss as without compensation and must accept it as entirely irrevocable. Some among the bereaved do attempt to promise themselves that they will see their spouse again in an afterlife. My impression is that the promise is not believed – or, if it is, doesn't matter.

During our first series of Seminars for the Bereaved, we recognized that it was usual for the bereaved to maintain as a defense against constant pain a "distancing" of their loss: they pushed awareness of the loss to the peripheries of their mind; they forced themselves to think of something else; they kept busy and tried not to think at all. Just talking with them about grief was ordinarily enough to penetrate this defense and subject them to pain. Although making it possible for participants to forego the defense now seems to be one of the contributions of the Seminars for the Bereaved, we are attempting to develop methods that will minimize the pain they must endure.

This is far from the only way in which we have been required to reconsider, in our work with the bereaved, the approach we had taken in our Seminars for the Separated. Almost every topic we introduced had to be dealt with differently, because the nature of their loss causes the bereaved to view themselves differently. The separated tend to define themselves as misunderstood, betrayed, stigmatized, and perhaps personally flawed. The bereaved are more likely to view themselves as both victim and survivor: a victim in comparison with other wives or husbands; a survivor, perhaps illegitimately so, in relation to their spouse. Compared with the separated, the bereaved appear less self-doubting, more hurt: in consequence they more quickly resent awkward or clumsy attempts to help.

Our very selection process proved to need modification when we shifted to work with the bereaved. Whereas we had been able to accept into Seminars for the Separated virtually anyone who was eligible in terms of length of separation, it appears as though participants for Seminars for the Bereaved must be selected much more carefully. The bereaved seem less able to tolerate fellow participants whose situation is decidedly different, for example, a woman who had been separated from her husband before he died. Nor are the bereaved as willing as the separated to tolerate group members whose mode of participation is burdensome, for example, someone who almost compulsively dominates discussion.

We had found in our Seminars for the Separated that it was useful for each discussion group to have within it at least two men and two women. The only way in which some participants could be brought to understand the point of view of their spouse was by having that point of view expressed by a member of the group with whom they had learned to identify. Thus a man who had previously refused to accept his wife's report that his children were harder to manage after a visit with him would be able to understand how this might happen when it was described by a woman in his discussion group. And having more than one woman and more than one man in the group meant that no single individual was responsible for representing an entire sex. In our work with the bereaved, however, we discovered that it is of little value to have both sexes in the same group. Although there may at first be some appeal in participating in a group in which the other sex is also present, discussion soon reveals that the mourning experience of widows is quite different from that of widowers, and there is, therefore, little basis for matching of experience across the sexes. Widows and widowers both develop deep grief, but they differ in their ways of expressing and recovering from their grief. Nor is it the case that a widow can learn to understand her spouse's viewpoint from a widower, or a widower from a widow, as is true in the analogous situation among the separated. In the groups we have organized that included both widows and widowers, the widows began talking to one another, and the widowers became a mostly silent audience.

Despite the problems we are encountering, Seminars for the Bereaved still seems to be a promising approach. Most of the participants in the two series we have thus far held have indicated that the program helped them return to effective functioning. Unfortunately, it appears that the only way we can develop an effective program for the bereaved – or, indeed, for those in any distress-inducing situation – is by trial and error. Our assumptions and anticipations are too often imprecise or mistaken for us to develop an effective program from them alone. For example, in our first series of Seminars for the Bereaved, we were uncertain about whether to schedule a party for the last meeting. Participants in Seminars for the Separated valued the wine-and-cheese party that ended the program; not only did it seem to them to be an appropriate way to take leave of one another, but for some of them it also constituted a kind of rite of passage into postmarital life. We were hesitant about scheduling a similar party for our group of bereaved because we thought that many of them defined themselves as still within that period of mourning when gaiety is prohibited. But we tried the party in the first series anyway and discovered to our surprise that participants brought to it an excitement that appeared in none of the separated groups: there was a good deal of eager planning for it; some of the women came to it in formal dresses. On looking back, one might guess that they had interpreted the party as establishing their right to reenter the social world, but we could never have guessed that this is what the party would mean; we had to try it and see.

SOME GENERALIZATIONS REGARDING HELPING IN TRANSITION

It appears to us at this point that every program intended to help people in transition will have to be responsive both in content and in format to the character of the particular transition with which it deals. I would assume, therefore, that a program to help foreign students adapt to the American educational scene would require the same development process, the same modification of initial presumptions as experience is gained, that we have completed with our Seminars for the Separated and are in the midst of in our Seminars for the Bereaved.

The staff must be prepared to proceed without the security of an established, well-understood program and must be prepared to make mistakes. There will inevitably be times of great stress for the staff, when participants drop out because the program is not right for them, or complain of retrogression rather than advance because of the program, or attack the staff for errors of omission or commission. The staff may require access to supportive supervision that can help them identify what is going wrong, develop appropriate modifications, and help them sustain their morale despite criticism and apparent error. Supervisory support and guidance may be required only infrequently, but it seems important that it be available.[6]

It seems to us that a good transition program should provide three kinds

[6]I want to thank Professor Gerald Caplan for providing supervision for the efforts described in this chapter.

of helpers. One is the *expert,* an individual who has studied the problems of the particular transition and, perhaps, the nature of the loss or other event that gave rise to it, and can speak about them with authority. Our lecturer played this role. A second kind of helper is the *veteran,* the individual who has been through the transition and so is able to draw on his experience in discussing issues, and to demonstrate in his own person that recovery is possible. We have tried in all our work to include at least one veteran among our staff: if the lecturer was not himself a veteran, then the telephone evaluator or one of the discussion group leaders would be. *Fellow participants* constitute a third kind of helper. Whereas experts can describe what is known, and veterans can report how they themselves responded to the situation, fellow participants can offer the immediate understanding that comes only from being in the same boat.

It is important for all who act in a helping role – experts, veterans, and fellow participants alike – to recognize that the aim of help in transition is to strengthen individuals as they struggle to establish a new emotional equilibrium and a new identity. This can only be done by respecting the character structure, the outlook, and the goals of each individual participant. We establish as an understanding in all our programs that no helper is entitled to criticize any participant or, indeed, to attempt to change that participant's habitual mode of dealing with challenge. The aim of our programs is simply to help the individual master the challenges of distress-inducing situations. We respond to distress whose etiology is situational by providing help whose focus is situational.

APPENDIX: OUTLINE FOR SEMINARS FOR THE SEPARATED

An outline similar to the following was sent to all prospective participants in Seminars for the Separated.

Format for each meeting will be about the same. Dr. Weiss will lecture for 45 minutes or so on an aspect of separation. There will be a brief opportunity for questions, which probably should be mostly requests for clarification, evidence, qualification, or the like, since discussion can be better managed in the small groups to follow. Small groups will include no more than 11 persons in addition to the group leader. They will meet for discussion for about an hour and a half.

There will be eight meetings.

Telephone Calls

We may call individuals by phone to learn whether the meetings seem helpful and, if so, in what way, and in what way they seem disappointing or insufficient. We will say more about this in the first meeting. In the past this has been our primary means of feedback.

Topics

Meeting One

The emotional impact of separation

1. *Why is there grief and loneliness after a marriage breaks up?* Most, although not quite all, feel deep sadness after a marriage ends, even one they would not willingly return to. Most feel lonely in the absence of the spouse. How does this come about? To answer this question, we will have to consider the nature of "attachment," a feeling of being "all right," "at home," more or less secure, in the presence of the other.
   (a) *Attachment feelings:* Where they come from and how they are expressed in marriage. When a marriage sours much of what we think of as "love" disappears – the husband and wife no longer idealize one another, perhaps no longer trust one another. But they may miss one another when they separate: Why?
   (b) *Loss of attachment is experienced as abandonment.* The separation can be seen by each member of the couple as the other's fault: if he or she had only been different, it need not have happened.
   (c) *Loneliness as a response to the absence of an attachment figure,* and reasons why loneliness isn't helped by being with married friends.
   (d) *Physical expressions of feelings of abandonment:* tension; vigilance; restlessness; sleeplessness.
2. *Other reasons for self-questioning.* There are many reasons for self-questioning to develop. There are feelings of guilt, fault, and failure because of complicity in a failed marriage. There may be a tendency to identify with the rejecting other in viewing the self. There may be a feeling of diminished social standing.
3. *The search for the cause.* One of the reactions to loss is obsessional review: a constant playing over in one's mind of what happened. This can become associated with the hope that if one can find the cause in oneself, or demonstrate that the cause was in the other or in the interaction, the future can be faced with more confidence.
4. *Problems associated with loss of anchors for routine and identity.* The decrystallization of identity and its consequences: ability to set new goals, but ability too to change goals according to what seems to be impulse; difficulties in getting going; problems of judgment.
5. *Euphoria.* The nature of feelings of euphoria: the sense of new freedom; of a new and more effective self; of a richer, more gratifying world. Some psychological processes that may be responsible for euphoria. The ability to take in stride certain kinds of setbacks while euphoric, and the vulnerability of euphoria to setbacks that make one lose confidence in oneself.
6. *Volatility.* Susceptibility to wide mood swings, from depression to eu-

phoria and back again with hardly an intermediate stop. Accident-proneness, impulsivity, and problems of emotional control.

Meeting Two

The continuing relationship with the former spouse

1. *Separation as an event in a relationship.* The continuing relationship of the separated couple that is likely if there are no children, virtually certain if there are children: a relationship of intense ambivalence.
   (a) We will already have discussed *continuing attachment.* We might note here some ways it may be expressed: a desire to keep in touch, a tendency to search for the other, feelings of warmth, responsibility.
   (b) We should now consider the intense anger that is also likely to be present: the other is seen as responsible for one's distress; there are very likely to have been experiences of betrayal; there are reality conflicts involving money and custody or visitation.
      (i) The other as responsible for one's distress – if only he or she were different!
      (ii) Betrayal – and why infidelity is the deepest betrayal of all.
      (iii) Disputes over real issues: property settlements, visitation, custody, and support.
2. *Unravelling the marriage.* There are a good many bonds in marriage. What happens to each?
   (a) What happened to love? Where did that idealization go, that feeling of wanting to make the other happy, that identification, that trust?
   (b) What about companionship? What happened to all the things that were held in common?
   (c) The division of labor, and being dependent on one another for running a home and family together. How odd that coordination should have taken so much time and energy and turn out to have been so little necessary: you really can manage by yourself (except that it is harder to deal with the kids alone).
   (d) The vows that were made. Are they so easily jettisoned? Probably not.
3. *How does ambivalence express itself?* How can it be managed?

Meeting Three

The impact of separation on relations with kin, friends, and others

1. *The impact of the separation on kin.*
   (a) The problems separation poses for kin: obligations of loyalty; disruption of own relationships; for parents, disappointment.
   (b) Problems posed for women. How to accept the help of kin without

thereby losing autonomy. Should one return home and what would happen if one did? How much help can sisters give? Can a brother serve as a masculine figure for one's children? What does separation do to one's standing in the family?

   (c) Problems posed for men. How much should one tell one's kin? What about one's kin's desire to maintain a relationship with one's children; how to let them know that this is all right? What does separation do to one's standing in the family?
   (d) In-laws. Men tend to lose touch with their in-laws, but women, partly because they have custody of the children, sometimes do not. Nevertheless in-laws sometimes do manage to retain good relationships with a son's former wife, less often with a daughter's former husband.
2. *The impact of separation on friends.* Relationships with married friends seem to go through three phases: first the friends rally around someone in trouble; then the friends react to the individual as someone abandoning another or being abandoned, and each friend has his or her own way of dealing with this; then there is a gradual fading of most, though often not all, former friendships. Almost always, separated individuals stop participating actively in the friendship network of their married friends. Neighborhood friends and old friends respond differently.
   (a) Problems of social isolation; ways in which social isolation may be experienced by women and by men.
   (b) A note on holidays. The family holidays of Thanksgiving and Christmas can be difficult for the separated to manage. So can the children's birthdays. Some comments will be made on the experiences various people have had and on ways they managed.

Meeting Four

The impact of separation on children and on the parent's relationships with them

1. *A review of research on the effects of growing up in a one-parent home.* Most children return to developmental progress, but short-term upset is to be expected.
2. *Helping the children deal with the separation.* The kind of help children may respond to may vary with their ages. Young children need to feel the continued commitment of a caring, competent, figure. Older children may need other supports as well: in school, with peers. Adolescents may need to focus their energies on their own lives and to feel permitted to be "selfish."
3. *Impacts on the relationship of the mother and the children.* The mother's relationship does not change in fundamental respects, but it becomes stressed inordinately. Some issues:

(a) Going from a two-parent to a one-parent family. Changes in roles, relationships.
(b) Managing responsibility for discipline; the difficulty in retaining one's temper, dealing with closeness in the family.
(c) Tendency to see in the children aspects of one's own early family, of one's self, of one's spouse.

4. *Impacts on the relationship of the father and the children.* The father's relationship with his children does change in fundamental respects. He is no longer a member of the children's household and his household roles disappear. But these were critical to his previous relationship with the children. Men therefore have the task of developing a new relationship.

Meeting Five

Dating

1. *The attractions and discomforts of dating.* Reassurance of worth and attractiveness; remission of loneliness; sexual gratification and the reassurance that pleasure remains possible; substitution of action and excitement for anxiety; means for relief from daily responsibilities; means toward social integration. On the other hand, a return to adolescence, attacking one's self-esteem, indeed one's essential sense of self; a feeling that one is involving oneself with people one hardly likes, perhaps hardly knows (and, among women), that one's vulnerability is being exploited; the sense (especially among men) that one is becoming obligated to a commitment one does not want.
2. *General understandings about conditions in which it is appropriate for a relationship to be sexual.*
   (a) If there is emotional attachment.
   (b) For some individuals, under some circumstances, if there is hope of an emotional attachment developing.
   (c) The issue of respectability, and alternative strategies in relation to uncommitted relationships when respectability is important and when it is not.
   (d) The manipulation of expectations and understandings in dating; why both men and women may strive to simulate the beginnings of attachment and how they may get trapped by their own simulation.

Meeting Six

Forms of new relationships in which attachment is an element

1. *Going together, living together, and remarriage:* similarities and differences.
2. *How real is fear of repetition?* Does one necessarily make the same

mistakes again? There are three subordinate questions: Is one attracted always to the same sort of person? Does one express the same sort of personal difficulties? Does the relationship necessarily follow the same course?

Meeting Seven

Approaches to helping

1. *What kind of help have we offered?*
   (a) Experts and fellow-experiencers; where is the profit in interacting with each?
   (b) The theory of helping individuals deal with new situations; of helping individuals manage crisis.
2. *What can one expect to get from therapy, or other supportive or directive relationships?* From participation in "single people's communities" such as Parents Without Partners?
3. *The natural desire to continue to meet, and a discouraging comment regarding its likely actual value.*

Meeting Eight

Another separation

In this last meeting the lecture will be brief and will focus on reviewing what has been discussed and on suggesting what may be the time required before things really settle down.

Discussion groups will take place as usual.

There will be a wine-and-cheese party after the discussion groups.

References

Becker HS: History, culture, and subjective experience: An exploration of the social bases of drug-induced experiences, J Health Soc Behav 8: 163-176, 1967

Glick IO, Weiss RS, Parkes CM: The First Year of Bereavement. New York, Wiley–Interscience, 1974

Hill R: Families Under Stress: Adjustment to the Crises of War Separation and Reunion. New York, Harper and Row, 1949

Lewis CS: A Grief Observed. New York, The Seabury Press, 1961

Lindemann E: Symptomatology and management of acute grief, Am J Psychiatry 101: 141-148, 1944

Parad HJ, Caplan G: A framework for studying families in crisis, in Parad HJ (ed): Crisis Intervention: Selected Readings. New York, Family Service Association of America, 1965, pp. 53-74

Parkes CM: Psycho-social transitions: A field for study. J Soc Sci Med 5: 101-115, 1971

Rapoport L: The state of crisis: Some theoretical considerations, in Parad HJ (ed): Crisis Intervention: Selected Readings. New York, Family Service Association, 1965, pp. 22-31

Richardson HB: Preliminary comments: A family as seen in the hospital, in Glasser PH, Glasser LN (eds): Families in Crisis. New York, Harper and Row, 1970, pp. 222-240

Tyhurst JS: Individual reactions to community disaster: The natural history of psychiatric phenomena. Am J Psychiatry 107:764–769, 1951

Tyhurst JS: The role of transition states – including disasters – in mental illness, in Symposium on Preventive and Social Psychiatry. Washington: U.S. Government Printing Office, 1958, pp. 149-169

Weiss RS: Marital Separation. New York, Basic Books, 1975

Weissman MM, Paykel ES: Moving and depression in women, in Weiss RS (ed): Loneliness: The Experience of Emotional and Social Isolation. Cambridge, Mass., M.I.T. Press, 1974, pp. 154-164.

Phyllis Rolfe Silverman

10

The Widow as a Caregiver in a Program of Preventive Intervention with Other Widows

One of the primary problems programs of prevention face is how to seek out people who have not asked for help. There is the question of who is the appropriate caregiver for such a population (3)? The Laboratory of Community Psychiatry confronted this dilemma when it tried to develop a program that would prevent emotional illness in a population of bereaved people. In this instance the target population with the high risk of developing serious emotional distress consisted of younger widowed people. A caregiving group had to be defined that would be acceptable to them. This paper describes the caregiving group chosen, their special qualifications as interveners, and discusses the kind of intervention they provide.

The caregiving group consists of other widows who have recovered from their bereavement. It was hypothesized that if another widow reached out to the new widow she would be accepted as a friend because she was someone who understood since she had been there herself (2). Does experience bear out this notion that the recovered widow is an appropriate and accepted helper? The material that follows presents data which provide some answers to this question.

THE WIDOW TO WIDOW PROGRAM

The Widow to Widow Program, as this demonstration in preventive intervention is known, has been in operation for three years. Five widows have reached out to over 400 new widows under the age of 60 in this time (4).

Reprinted from *Mental Hygiene*, 54:4, 540-547, October, 1970.

The widow caregivers, called aides henceforth to distinguish them from the widow recipients, all live in or near the community they serve. They have all been widowed about three years, are for the most part in their mid-forties, and have no more than a high school education. While their husbands were alive, they devoted themselves to raising their children and keeping house. Two of them did help their husbands in his business. After his death they all had to think of supplementing their income, which came largely from social security and pensions.

Each of the aides had become involved in community activities subsequent to their becoming widows. It was through our contact with these community organizations that we were able to recruit them. Until now they had never thought of earning their living helping people in this way. All of them could talk about their bereavement, the very difficult time they had and the current problems being widowed still created for them. They had only one reservation about the program as it was described to them. They wanted to be sure that service, not research, was the main purpose of what they would be doing.

In order to assure that their experience as widows would be utilized to the maximum no attempt has been made to supervise their work. At weekly group meetings people they visit are discussed, and they used each other as well as myself for consultation about what they have done and about how they might proceed. Most frequently they chart an independent course of action which seems right for them and the new widow they have visited.

They quickly corrected our notion that within one year, or less, a widow has recovered from her bereavement. They feel that although by then she *may* be over the acute stage of her grief, she is not recovered, and may even be depressed by her growing awareness of what the loss means. They say a widow never recovers but rather learns to adjust to the situation. They thought this took about two years to accomplish. It involves an ability to repattern her life without a husband, to find new friends, new interests, and sometimes a new career. It also means learning to live with loneliness.

INITIAL REACHING OUT AND SERVICE OFFERED

How is their experience translated into their work? Their first task is to establish their credentials as an appropriate caregiver; that is, as someone the widow will accept and see as potentially helpful. The new widow first learns that the aide, too, is a widow in the letter of introduction she receives. The stationery has the names of the three religious groups sponsoring the program on it.[1] In the letter the aide tells the new widow that she will visit

[1]The program is sponsored by the Archdiocesan Council of Catholic Women, the Mt. Bowdoin YM and YWCA and Temple Beth Hillel. These are community based agencies traditionally involved at the time of a death in the family.

at a given time on a given day. She gives her home phone number and invites the widow to call if for any reason she does not want the aide to visit.

The aides do not feel that a visit before three weeks would be useful to a new widow. At the moment of acute bereavement they do not feel that a new widow can identify with another widow, because she still thinks of herself as a married woman.

Several things influence the widows' response to this letter. One is their willingness and readiness to consider that they are now widowed. Some women thought this was a "terrible thing to call me" and threw the letter away.[2] Others thought they were "already on a mailing list, now what do these people want?" Still others were impressed with the fact that someone cared, and were reassured by the names of the religious organizations on the letterhead. Some of their reactions were colored by who else was available to talk to.[3] Some women, therefore, called and told the aide not to come; others chose to let her visit because they lacked the energy to call and refuse the visit. Some simply weren't home when she arrived, but most looked forward to the visit. Many widows subsequently became involved with the program although their initial response to the aides' offer to visit was negative.

Once they sensed there was no ulterior motive in the aides' interest, the fact of the aides' widowhood was the important thing that made it possible for them to become involved. The aide mentions it in her letter but it always comes up early in the actual encounter, either in a face to face visit or on the telephone.

The fact of common widowhood is often discussed through the aides' attempt to clarify how the widow is managing financially. They talk about social security, VA pensions, and the like, and the aide will describe her own experience and clarify for the widow what benefits she is entitled to and how to be sure of getting them. One widow saw this discussion about money as an

> affirmation of life. It makes you think about what is needed to go on living and reminded me that that's what I have to do.

The aide's willingness to answer questions about her own widowhood seems to give the widow permission to unburden herself.

SHARING COMMON PROBLEMS

The fact of the aide's widowhood seems to make it easier for the new

[2]This may be why organizations of widowers and widows chose names such as NAIM Conference of Chicago and THEO (They Help Others) in Pittsburgh.

[3]Many felt that their family and friends sufficed for their current need only to come to an awareness later on that they did not really understand, and were inappropriately impatient with them to recover more quickly than was possible.

widow to accept her, to talk to her, to ask for advice on problems related to her own widowhood, and to feel as if she can still be part of the mainstream of life – that is, she is not so alone and the only one to whom this could happen. Another widow said:

> Since you are a widow too, when you said you understand I knew you meant it and that was so important. I can't stand sympathy and that's all anyone else could give me."

Pride and an unrealistic wish to be independent seem to get in the way of a relationship between widow and non-widows. The new widow finds the latter's efforts to be helpful clumsy. Often they find themselves providing reassurrance rather than being reassured. This does not happen with the aide. The aide is using her own experience as a human being and as a widow to guide her in her encounter with the new widow; she appreciates the real need that exists but never takes the widow's initiative away from her. If the widow becomes dependent on the aide, it does not seem to bother either of them at this point in the encounter. This most often will take the form of frequent phone calls, or the aide will drive the widow to the social security office and the like.

The widow explores the common problems of widowhood with the aide.

One woman was worried about her child, who took out his father's picture and talked to it. And another was upset because her daughter wasn't doing well in school anymore. The aide could talk about not knowing how to help a child, could honestly normalize the behavior in the knowledge that with time the child does makes an adjustment, but also recognizing the child's need to mourn which the widow doesn't always see. In the words of one widow:

> I tried not to cry in front of my children. I wanted things to be as normal as possible for them. Then my little one stopped working at school. The teacher said he was depressed. The children felt it wasn't right that things should be the same if their father was dead. They thought I didn't care about him.

As a result of talking to the aide the widow started to show the children her true feelings and her boy's studies began to improve. The aides could talk about their own children, the problems they had now as well as when their husband died and how they saw their husband's death contributing to them. They reported what worked for them and what didn't work, and were receptive of the widow's suggestions for solutions as well. They established with the widow the fact that widowhood is lonely, frustrating, that there is often a bitterness which accompanies it; that you really don't get over it, but get used to it. By so doing they seem to take the fear and worry out of mourning and give the widow a context for her behavior which she can accept and understand. They see normal grief as extending over time, and counsel patience to the widow.

Often, the aides report that the widow tries to be strong and feels she must avoid being excessively dependent and is inadequate if she requires assistance. This feeling is fostered by people such as her doctor to whom she may complain. She is usually told she will get over it and be strong. The aide, on the other hand encourages the widow to return to get a physical check-up to verify that her symptoms are indeed just "nerves." If the doctor prescribes tranquillizers, the aide encourages the widow to use them and not to feel that she is weak and defective for needing this "crutch" in order to get through this period until she learns to find her way in her new circumstances. Over and over again the aide is told:

> You understand the void in my life.

The aide sees this as meaning that it is not always necessary to talk about it because they indeed do know.

The aide is not trying to make the widow into what she is not nor does she want her to act as she, the aide, did, but rather to accept the fact that she is going through hell to be more accepting of herself and her own needs at this time. This is something that the widow reports she does not learn from her immediate family or friends. If she does, it is because there are widows among them.

LEARNING TO LIVE AS A WIDOW

The aides talk of the needs of the widow to change from seeing herself as married to thinking of herself as widowed. This they see as the first step to recovery.

The aides identify three themes in this process. First is the need to learn to make decisions independently or unilaterally, that is, without the guidance and help of a husband:[4] *"The biggest decision I ever made was what loaf of bread to buy."*
The second theme is the need to learn to be alone: *"What do I do after the children are asleep? I can't stand the empty silence, and I can't watch another T. V. program."*
The third theme follows on these two in that there is a growing need to make new friends and be out with people: *"I don't get invited out by our couple friends anymore. I'm not always comfortable with them. It makes me feel even lonelier."*

As far as decision making is concerned, the aide is primarily helpful in two ways. She is not afraid to give direct advice if it is needed. She seems more willing to do this early in the contact when the widow seems confused

[4]Mrs. Ruth Abrams, research social worker in the Conjugal Bereavement Study at the LOCP has observed that in the first months after her husband's demise the new widow leans heavily on his wishes and her memories of him, and tries to do things as he would have wanted. Recovery, she observed, begins when the widow can "give up her husband's ghost," which means she is able to learn to make decisions based on her current reality.

and needs direction about for example, money, children, selling the house and so forth. In the latter phase of accommodation she is more apt to offer encouragement, ideas and support; though she is often quite pointed in telling the new widow she needs to act for herself. For a woman who has seen herself, for most of her adult life, as a partner in a marriage, this is not always an easy transition to make. We begin to differentiate between those widows who respond to this encouragement, get a job, learn to drive and begin to repattern their lives, and those widows (a small minority) who have difficulty. This latter group seems to cling to the past and to be searching for a replacement for their deceased husband who will make their decisions for them. Often they try to put the aide in this role but at this point in time she seems to instinctively repel this effort while not rejecting the widow herself. The program is too young to know how the aides can help this latter group of women pass this stumbling block (2).[5]

To fill the loneliness of any empty evening is not easy. The aide in part helps by being available, if only on the telephone, to talk and to empathize with the problem which she, too, is experiencing. Some widows run away from this by never being home, others put all their energy into taking care of the children. The aide tries to help find a middle road. She acknowledges aloud for the widow that the consequence of running is that one day she will suddenly have no place to go and then she will be really depressed. The problem for the aide is to offer real alternatives for the widow. This brings us to the third theme which involves helping the widow expand her resources and repeople her life differently. Out of this the widow can create for herself alternatives with which to cope with her aloneness and her loneliness.

The aides have helped in two ways: They have helped the widows find other groups of "single" people where they might find common interests. There are several kinds of single groups. One such group is being formed by widows who have been served by the program. They met at several large meetings arranged by the aides to discuss the problems of widowhood. Several cookouts were also planned. These group meetings have attracted women who initially refused to see the aide or spoke to her only on the telephone. Once they came to a meeting they returned because they found:

> It helps to talk to others in the same situation. Sometimes when I get home and think about what other women have said I learn something new about myself. The only reason I came in the first place was because I was embarrased to refuse (the aide's invitation) again. If I had realized how friendly and nice everyone is I wouldn't have been so reluctant.

[5]In a survey of psychiatric clinic records I noted that most widows who appeared for treatment, came for the first time two years after the death of their husband. These patients may come from this group, and it may be that the effort now, at the end of the first year of bereavement, may have the greatest payoff to prevent a serious emotional disturbance from developing.

Another group of women have sought out single people clubs where it is possible to meet men. These women have relied on the aide to inform them about such groups and have asked her to take them to a meeting to overcome their initial shyness.

The second way of helping has been to get these widows to reach out to other widows in their immediate neighborhood who have refused to see the aide, or who are so physically disabled that they cannot leave home. This provides the widow with an opportunity to do something for someone else as well as to make new friends. Some widows seem ready for this by the end of the first 18 months of their bereavement; and the aides are eager to share with them their role as caregiver.

As the widows move out into the role of caregiver it seems appropriate to consider ways of making them more responsible for the ultimate life of the widow to widow program. The next phase of new activity should involve the widows served in the workings of the program. As they were helped so they can help others and thus give the program continuity and a permanent status in the community.

We are only beginning to understand the unique role of the widow caregiver. At this point, however, it is possible to say the evidence seems to support our initial hypothesis that another widow is the appropriate intervener in a program of preventive intervention where the client group did not ask for the service.

DISCUSSION

The purpose of any program in preventive intervention is to prevent emotional breakdown in a vulnerable population. While, at this point, we cannot demonstrate that we are achieving this goal in the Widow to Widow Program, it becomes clear that the aides are indeed being very helpful to the widows they reach and that in good part their ability to do so is a consequence of their being widowed themselves.

To better understand the special quality of the aides' helpfulness, two basic problems facing a new widow need examination. The first problem is that of facing the fact of widowhood; that is, accepting their changed marital status and all this involves. The second problem is to learn to manage their own lives, and to demonstrate to themselves and others that they can be and are independent.

Many women see widowhood as a social stigma. They see themselves as marked women, different from everyone else, even carrying this so far as to see themselves as defective, that something must be wrong with them if they lost their husbands. In addition, all widows report they experience a growing social isolation as time passes after their husband's death. They no longer belong with their married friends, who they find gradually withdrawing from them. They can no longer conform to standards which society calls "normal" and they become people in a "special situation," that is, with a stigma. Goffman (1) describes this phenomenon but it is beyond the scope of this paper to explore all its ramifications for understanding the problems of widowhood. He, however, describes the function of the veteran of this role in helping the newly stigmatized person accept his lot. This is exactly the work of the widow aide. Goffman points to the need of the stigmatized individual to feel that:

> he is human and 'essentially' normal in spite of appearances and in spite of his own self-doubts....The first set of sympathetic others is of course those who share his stigma. Knowing from their own experience what it is like to have this particular stigma some of them can provide the individual with instruction in the tricks of the trade and with a circle of lament to which he can withdraw for moral support and for the comfort of feeling at home, at ease, accepted as a person who really is like any other normal person (1).

Goffman further notes that the veteran serves as an example of someone who can successfully live with his stigma. In addition he functions as a bridge person to the outside world helping them to normalize and be more accepting of people in this category. First, however, they must help the new member accept his own membership in the category. The aide understands instinctively the new widow's reluctance and resistance to accepting this status. The widow is not unique in this. Goffman notes the difficulty the alcoholic, the deaf, and so forth have in accepting their assignment to a special category. However when they do so, their hope for "normalizing" their life is increased and adjustment or recovery can be achieved. In accepting help from another member of the category they take the first step toward accepting their own membership. By the very nature of the problem then, the veteran, in this case another widow, is best equipped to help the new member. She is first a bridge to accepting the role of widow and then to helping the widow find a place for herself in the larger community. In addition, the veteran has a privileged communication with the new member which no outsider can have. The aide can say things about being a member of the category: about feelings (positive and negative), about problems it creates which if mentioned by a non-member would be considered an intrusion or an impertinence. Intervention becomes the work of the members of the category and we begin to understand the success of such self help groups as Alcoholics Anonymous and Parents Without Partners.

There is also a progression in the organization. The members move from initially being recipients of service to becoming providers of service. As a provider of service he develops a sense of independence and adequacy which brings him well on to the road of recovery, accommodation, or adjustment. This is the second need a widow has and as she in turn becomes a caregiver she develops a new sense of independence and worth. Insofar as the Widow to Widow Program can do this, it should be able to accomplish its goal of preventing emotional breakdown in a new widow.

The self help group has several important characteristics. Primary among them are: that the caregiver has the same disability as the carereceiver; that a recipient of service can change roles to become a caregiver; and all policy and program is decided by a membership whose chief qualification is that they at one time qualified and were recipients of the services of the organization. The prototype for self help groups has been Alcoholics Anonymous, run by alcoholics for alcoholics. This program has assiduously remained independent of the formal health and welfare system, using professionals only as occasional consultants, never to make policy or direct a program.

What I am advocating is the development of a self help organization. It may be that this kind of organization is best suited to do the work of preventive intervention. What problems arise for a self help group begun in a Laboratory of a Medical School? Are these problems different for such a program started in a Community Mental Health Center or clinics.

Many mental health agencies have attempted to replicate some aspects of the success of these self help groups by employing so called "non-professional indigenous workers." Unlike A.A. these non-professionals are usually given extensive training and supervision so that they begin to adopt professional values and emulate professional techniques. If they were following the self help model, they should be making policy, developing their own techniques for helping, and the consumer of their services should be able to move into their role of caregiver. In the average agency setting this would be difficult to achieve since it would mean that the professionally trained caregiver could be displaced by his former client. He could also potentially lose control of policy as well as of practice. This would be inappropriate and inconsistent with the mandate an agency has from the community supporting it. The goal, as I see it, should be a partnership between independent self help groups and the formal agency whose special expertise is utilized as needed.

The Laboratory of Community Psychiatry at Harvard Medical School is a research and training center and has no commitment to serve a particular population. Nor is it an agency committed to any particular technology. It does not have a staff who would be offering an additional or competing service and whose position would be threatened if clients became caregivers. It is therefore feasible for the Laboratory of Community Psychiatry to experiment in sponsoring a self help program staffed by non-professionals who meet all the requirements for being potential recipients of the service themselves. Here is a unique opportunity to learn how to stimulate the development of such organizations to do the work of prevention, to learn what form an on-going organization can take in the community, and to experiment with different forms of collaboration between the formal agency and the emerging self help group.

UPDATE ADDENDUM

The experimental phase of the Laboratory of Community Psychiatry's Widow-to-Widow Program of outreach to new widows in a defined Boston community lasted several years. It was supported in part by the National and New England Funeral Directors Associations and in part by a National Institute of Mental Health Research Grant (MH-03442) which also included other projects.

As the Widow-to-Widow experiment was coming to an end, a hot line was developed to see if it was possible to reach more people in a wider geographic area in Massachusetts. It was called the Widowed Service Line. It was manned by widows and widowers who volunteered their time. Some of these individuals had been helped in the Widow-to-Widow program and now wanted to help others. Dorothy MacKenzie, Elizabeth Wilson, and Mary Pettipas, who were widow aides in the original experiment, ran the Line, and educated and consulted with the volunteers. The Line reached primarily a different population of widowed individuals – those who were widowed a number of years and were looking for opportunities to extend their social network. Ruby B. Abrahams reports on the styles of caregiving offered by the widowed volunteers in the next chapter in this book.

In response to many requests for information from widowed people around the country who had expressed an interest in setting up similar programs to help themselves in their own communities, Silverman and the original widow aides convened a workshop in Boston in 1971 for about 100 widows and widowers from 19 states. A separate workshop was held for clergymen, funeral directors, and mental health specialists who work with the bereaved. The material from the workshops has been collected in a book edited by Silverman et al., *Helping Each Other in Widowhood,* Health Sciences Publishing Corp., New York, 1974, in order to communicate basic information about bereavement, widowhood, and mutual help as a preventive intervention strategy to a wider lay and professional audience. The Widow-to-Widow program is being copied in communities throughout the country where widowed individuals are interested in developing mutual help programs to serve others like themselves who become widowed every day. Many widowed organizations that had been primarily social in emphasis are now incorporating this service model which involves reaching out to the bereaved and not waiting for them to ask for help.

The Film Program, a unit under the direction of Edward Mason, M.D. within the Laboratory of Community Psychiatry, has produced a black and white, 41-minute film available for rental or purchase, *Widows,* in which several women frankly describe their experiences after a husband's death. The film is intended to be helpful for sensitizing professionals of all fields to the problems of widowhood and for mobilizing community resources for the development of preventive services.

REFERENCES

1. Goffman E: Stigma. New Jersey, Prentice-Hall, 1963
2. Silverman PR: Services for the Widowed During the Period of Bereavement, Social Work Practice. New York, Columbia University Press, 1966
3. Silverman PR: Services to the widowed: First steps in a program of preventive intervention. Community Ment Health J 3:1, Spring, 1967
4. Silverman PR: The widow to widow program: An experiment in preventive intervention. Ment Hyg 53:3, July, 1969

Ruby B. Abrahams

11

Mutual Helping: Styles of Caregiving in a Mutual Aid Program — The Widowed Service Line[1]

Mutual help groups have formed among people who share the same disability or stigma and consequently find themselves outside of the social system. Goffman (1963) discusses ways in which such people help each other to define their situation, to accept their new status as stigmatized people, and to develop new roles enabling them to reenter the system. Widowhood is one situation where disengagement from a pattern of social relationships is sudden and traumatic. Lopata (1970) points out the failure of American society to provide means of helping the widowed adjust to their new role and become reengaged in the system. The widowed no longer fit into the prevailing "couples society." After the funeral, relatives and friends go back to their families and the widowed person is increasingly left alone and left out. Caplan (1964) suggests that the crisis situation experienced after any loss can be a turning point toward or away from emotional disorder. During crisis, the individual experiences increasing tension which motivates him to seek help from others, and also makes him more susceptible to the influence of others. The help offered at this time may have a major effect in determining his choices of mechanisms for coping with future crises.

The Widow-to-Widow outreach program (Silverman 1969, 1972) and the Widowed Service Line were established as demonstration programs in which widowed volunteers, who felt they were ready to reach out and help other widowed people, were enabled to do so. Lennenberg and Rowbotham (1970) state that the "essence of mutual help is exchange": from this ex-

[1]The Widowed Service Line is an outgrowth of the Widow-to-Widow Program, directed by Phyllis Silverman, Ph.D., under the general direction of Gerald Caplan, M.D., Laboratory of Community Psychiatry, Harvard Medical School. The research was made possible under grant No. 09214 from the National Institute of Mental Health.

change the helper develops his role and self-image as a helping, valued person and acts as role model to the recipient of help, who in turn may eventually become a helper. The dynamics of mutual helping are constantly fluid and both helper and seeker of help move into new roles and find opportunities for healthy personal growth.

This chapter focuses on the nature of the mutual interchange between helper and recipient of help and attempts to identify some differences in helping styles. Observation of the volunteer helpers on the Widowed Service Line suggested that as helpers' inputs to the mutual process varied, so did their expectations and the kinds of satisfactions sought from the process. The widowed volunteers entered the mutual help program at different stages in their adjustment and growth process. They brought to the caregiving task not professional training, but their own life experience. The kinds of adjustment achieved to the widowed situation reflects the individual's personality and life-style. Experience, personality, life-style, needs, and the seeking of varying satisfactions are inputs to the mutual help process. According to differing needs, satisfactions or rewards of the process vary among the helpers. An analysis of these varying inputs and rewards in the helping process can serve to clarify some of the differences in caregiving styles.

THE WIDOWED SERVICE LINE

The Widowed Service Line was a "hotline" telephone service organized by widowed people to help other widows and widowers in the Boston area. This program grew from the Widow-to-Widow Service, an outreach program for newly bereaved widows which, at the inception of the "hotline," had been operating for 3 years in one of Boston's inner city communities. The success of widow-to-widow mutual helping had been demonstrated in the outreach program (Silverman 1970); the Widowed Service Line was set up to extend the support system for widowed people throughout the Boston metropolitan area. Staffed by a team of widowed volunteers, the telephone model provides a relatively inexpensive method of covering a wide area and reaching a large number of the widowed. The service was publicized by television, radio, metroplitan and local newspapers, and church bulletins; at the height of the publicity about 150 calls were received each month.

Two of the five widow aides who worked in the outreach program became coordinators of the Widowed Service Line. These aides, during their 3 years with the Widow-to-Widow program had become highly skilled helpers, effective both in crisis counseling and in long-term helping relationships. On the Widowed Service Line, the coordinators moved into supervising, training, and organizing roles. Increasing responsibility and personal development are a vital part of the mutual helping process which offers opportunities for growth both to helpers and those who seek help – a principle well documented by Reissman (1965) and others. The two coordinators were assisted by a team of 18 volunteers (13 widows and 5 widowers). Calls from the widowed seeking help were received by an answering service; these names and telephone numbers were passed on to the coordinators, who fed them out to the volunteers.

Most of the volunteers had full-time jobs and families to care for; therefore, the return telephone calls were usually made in the evenings from the volunteers' own homes. These men and women were mainly in their 40s and 50s, with no more than high school education. They were recruited in various ways. Some had been helped in the Widow-to-Widow program and moved into helping roles when this new phase of the service opened. Others heard about the program through the media and offered their services. Some heard about it from friends, who had already been accepted as volunteers. The two coordinators screened all the volunteer applicants. For selection into the program, the widow or widower had to be sufficiently over his/her own grief to be ready to reach out and help others; other criteria included sensitivity, perceptiveness, and indications that a sufficient commitment would be made to the program. The widowed callers to the hotline ranged in age from 24 to 80, the majority being in the 40s and 50s. They presented a wide variety of problems and differing needs (Abrahams 1972).

THE MUTUAL HELP PROCESS: EXTENT OF EMOTIONAL SHARING

An important input in the mutual help process is the extent to which the helper feels the need to share his feelings with the recipient of help. The helper sets his own limits on how much he will discuss his feelings with the caller. Helping styles range along a varying continuum of social distance, as indicated in Fig. 11-1.

At one end of this range, the social distance maintained between helper and recipient approximates that of the professional/client relationship. At the other end of the range, as social distance diminishes, the mutual help relationship approaches that of friendship. Blau and Scott (1962) emphasize the affective neutrality of the professional orientation to the client. Weiss (1970) characterizes the professional/client relationship as one "where the professional has an impersonal, usually confident and authoritative attitude, whereas the client is perplexed and deferential." Friendship (Weiss 1969) is characterized by "intimacy which provides an effective emotional integration in which individuals can express their feelings freely and without self-consciousness." Characteristics of the caregiving styles of the 18 widowed volunteers ranged between these two extremes. Four distinct types of helping have been identified along this range.

The social distance maintained by the helper limits the extent to which

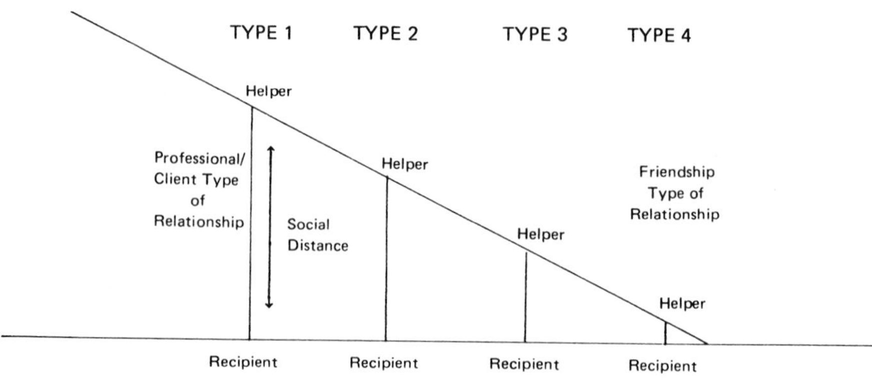

Fig. 11-1. Helping relationships along the continuum from professional/client to friendship type of relationship.

emotional sharing is a major part of the helping style. Along the same continuum, Fig. 11-2 shows how the area of emotional sharing may increase as part of the helper's input. Theoretically, we are assuming that the extent of the helper's total input into the helping relationship is constant, but the area of emotional exchange is a varying proportion of that input.

In Fig.11-2, type 1 represents the situation in which the volunteer has little need to verbalize and share his own feelings as part of his helping input. This again approximates the professional/client relationship, where

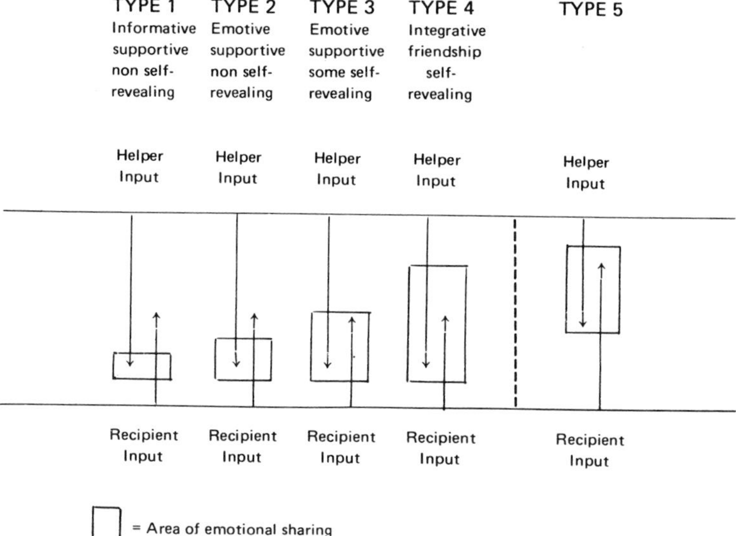

Fig. 11-2. Sharing of feelings in the mutual help relationship.

the helper strictly limits the sharing of feelings.[2] The helping inputs developed by types 2, 3, and 4 show an increasing amount of two-way sharing of emotion and experience. Type 4 approximates a friendship relationship where the recipient is admitted as an intimate. Type 5 represents a situation that can occur when the volunteer feels he is being more helped than the recipient (the recipient's input is greater). Such a situation indicates that the volunteer is not suitable or not ready for the helping role and should be removed to some other role in the program.[3]

THE MUTUAL HELP PROCESS: HELPER INPUTS AND SATISFACTIONS

In order to define further the four suggested helping styles indicated in Figs. 11-1 and 11-2, the following helper inputs and satisfactions are considered.

A. Helper's Inputs	B. Helper's Satisfactions
1. Previous helping experience 2. Widowhood adjustment experience 3. Life-style, as it relates to reaching out to others 4. Type of commitment to helping others; needs involved in this commitment 5. Knowledge of communty resources and innovativeness in suggesting such resources 6. Emotional input, need to express own emotions	1. Type of satisfaction sought 2. Meaning of this type of satisfaction in total life-style 3. Satisfaction from degree of involvement with caller 4. Confidence and self-image 5. Frequency and extent of follow up calls 6. Growth and personality development from the mutual help process

Analysis of the volunteers' inputs to and satisfactions from the helping process suggests that these volunteers could be clustered into four groups,

[2]Eliminating overt and verbalized sharing of feelings in the professional/client relationship does not mean that the helper approaches the seeker of help without feelings of caring and warmth. In any helping relationship, the communication of caring takes place primarily at subverbal, subliminal, or subconscious levels.

[3]These classifications of helping types do not imply any evaluation of helping effectiveness (except in the case of hypothetical type 5, Fig. 11-2). Such an evaluation would require a detailed follow-up study of the recipients of help, which was outside the scope of our research. In the absence of such a study, we are assuming that the four types of helping, though different, are equally effective. Our task here is to describe, not to evaluate helping styles.

each of which has a different focus that distinguishes the helping style. The four types[4] of helping are identified as:

1. Informative-supportive (non-self-revealing),
2. Emotive-supportive (non-self-revealing),
3. Emotive-supportive (some self-revealing),
4. Integrative-friendship (self-revealing).

Styles of Helping

Helper Type 1: Informative-Supportive (Non-self-revealing)

Inputs and satisfactions

Typically, this volunteer has been involved in many volunteer activities and may be a leader in community work. Social satisfactions are derived mainly from relationships in organizational settings. Life is centered around task performance and relationships involved with tasks. Personal life may lack closeness; these are people who can live alone, without unbearable loneliness. They are sustained by feeling needed in their helping tasks. They perceive themselves as helpers and leaders and are practiced in the processes of reaching out to help others. When asked about reasons for joining the program, the typical response involved the notion of "being qualified" to help:

> I felt I was equipped to do this. . . . I had had a hard time working it (widowhood) through for myself, but I felt I learned something and could help others make that adjustment. . . .

Of all the volunteers, type 1 expressed the least need to share their feelings with callers:

> I have no need to unload my feelings. . . . I am through that. . . . I tell them just enough so they can find some relationship with me. . . .

These volunteers find their major life satisfactions in their helping activity, which is a solution to their loneliness. They enjoy problem solving, and this was mentioned as a major reward for volunteer activities:

> I enjoy finding solutions for lonely people who are hemmed in by their situation . . . it is a challenge to me. . . .

In contrast to the other volunteers, type 1 helpers did not emphasize their own growth as a major result and reward of participation in the

[4]These are types used in Hempel's (1952) sense of "classificatory types," which he considers essentially as a device useful in the early stages of concept building. No individual fits exactly into any ideal type scheme, but these classifications serve to clarify some helping foci.

program. They felt that they had already arrived at an equilibrium of adjustment. Their growth had occurred at an earlier period in overcoming their bereavement and rebuilding their lives. They did not perceive the helping process as a means of ongoing personality growth.

Style of helping

Given these inputs and satisfactions from the mutual helping process, the helping style of these volunteers was the nearest approximation to the "professional/client" style. From previous community work, these helpers brought a fund of knowledge about community resources and were highly innovative in suggesting ways of using these to their callers. They researched extensively the programs and services available in each caller's community. The focus of their helping is in giving information, finding new resources and helping the caller to utilize them. They offered ideas for new activities and ways of finding new roles and relationships to rebuild the life after the losses of widowhood.

> I find many of these callers will go and do things, if you tell them exactly what to do, where to go, what to expect, and how to get there. Then they will go . . . but they can't seem to do it on their own. . . .

Type 1 volunteers are self-assured in their role as helpers, expressing positively their confidence in the help they have given their callers. They are able to listen to other people's feelings, but rather than dwelling on emotional problems, they focus more on activities:

> Some of them will cry on the phone . . . but I don't oversympathize, or let them wallow. I try to get them on their feet. I get hold of the common sense in them and work on that . . . .

These are active, outreaching, busy people who are not looking for friends among their callers; they preserve the social distance of the professional relationship. They were able to handle a larger number of callers than the other volunteers, dealing efficiently and to their own satisfaction with most of their callers in two to four telephone conversations. However, they were well organized in selecting a few cases for longer, more intensive follow-up and were conscientious and reliable in following through where needed. Of all the volunteers, type 1 were the most committed to the program and the most likely to stay with it over time and move into roles of further responsibility.

Helper Type 2: Emotive-Supportive (Non-self-revealing)

Inputs and satisfactions

These volunteers are exceptionally warm, outgoing people, for whom involvement with others is a way of life. This involvement has often placed them in a helping role, though not necessarily in formal settings or volunteer programs. These people have always reached out beyond the circle of family and close friends and can easily open up to and help those they encounter who need help. Their personalities attract others to them, and they stand out in their local communities and networks as leaders and helpers. Rarely are such people living alone. Even after widowhood, their need and capacity for close relationships will bring them into living situations with family, close friends, or remarriage. They continually expand their lives outwards, which has helped them to recover well from their own bereavement experience. Unlike type 1 helpers, who felt that they struggled alone through their bereavement, type 2 volunteers feel that they were helped by others, and they want to repay that debt to any other widowed person. Their reasons for volunteering were typically expressed in terms of reciprocity. This was often translated into spiritual feelings involving an interpretation of life as a process of giving and receiving:

> I believe we are in this world so that we can help others . . . we have to give back in life . . . to serve is a need. . . .

Since these volunteers were actively involved in many social networks in their communities, they were aware of resources useful for their callers and were innovative in suggesting new activities. Their knowledge of such resources derived more from personal contacts and experience than from systematic research, as with type1. They are much concerned with "feelings" but they are not looking for emotional involvement with the callers.

For these volunteers, the main reward from the helping process was perceived as their own growth and development:

> I am not realizing myself as a human being unless I am being helpful to others.... It helps you to grow and you have to grow all the time. . . .

Like type 1 volunteers, the type 2 helpers also enjoyed a challenge, but they perceived their challenges in terms of difficult people rather than difficult situations. They felt most rewarded when a caller, who was initially unresponsive, opened up later after many telephone conversations.

Style of helping

In comparison with type 1, this style of helping is focused more toward feelings than activities, but these volunteers have no need to unload their own feelings as part of their helping. They preserve a social distance from the caller, which places their helping relationships closer to the "professional/client" than to the "friendship" end of the continuum. Their concept of helping emphasized listening:

> I think helping is to listen, be receptive, hear them . . . let them get their feelings

and frustrations out . . . and let them know that someone cares . . . .

A personal approach was used in putting callers in touch with other widowed people. Often a widowed friend or personal acquaintance was suggested and the type 2 helper would be there to make the initial introductions. These volunteers often met their callers face to face, had a meal with them, or took them personally into social groups or clubs where they might meet other widowed people. They preferred to work more intensively with fewer callers and enjoyed most those callers who needed long term follow up.

All of the type 2 volunteers in their own lives were moving into new roles and relationships. They were integrating their bereavement experience and moving forward to new life-styles. They came into the program at an appropriate time to help other widowed people; they were helpful and were helped themselves in reaching a deeper understanding of their own options and directions. These people move forward continually to new forms of activity in their quest for self-development. Their stay in the widowed helping program was of limited duration, but while they were there, they were dynamic and constructive members of the helping team.

Helper Type No. 3: Emotive-supportive (Some Self-revealing)

Inputs and satisfactions

These volunteers had not participated in formal helping activities before they joined the program. Their life-styles were primarily involved in kin networks. At the time of their own bereavement they were helped by a widowed friend (in two cases, this help came from the Widow-to-Widow program), and discovered then how widows can help each other. At this time, they also found that the members of their close family circle, upon whom they had always relied for their social support, were unable to help them meaningfully with the bereavement experience. As one type 3 volunteer stated it:

> You have to talk to an outsider ... the family just try to joke you out of it ... but if you talk to a stranger and another widow, she can listen and you can get it off your chest . . . .

Help received from another widow has sensitized these volunteers to the needs of the widowed and gave them the self-confidence to reach out beyond their kin network.

> I volunteered because I knew people needed help and I had learned that only another widow can give that help . . . .

They had not previously thought of themselves as capable of reaching out to "strangers," but through the program they experienced the satisfactions of expanding their social contacts and being valued by a wider circle of persons beyond the family. Lopata (1969) found that widows dependent on kin for social interaction frequently had not acquired the interpersonal skills to create new life-styles after widowhood and were ill-adapted to handle their losses. The mutual aid program can be a first step in moving out of the kin network and developing the interpersonal skills required by the realities of a mobile society (Foote and Cottrell 1955).

Since the life experience of type 3 volunteers was narrower than that of types 1 and 2, they were less knowledgeable about community resources and needed more help from the program coordinators in developing such knowledge. Their life-style has provided less opportunities than that of types 1 and 2 for moving into new roles since widowhood and they have farther to go in the process of adjustment. They still have a need to talk about their own feelings since bereavement and this will become part of their helping style. The loneliness of widowhood is still with them and will be relieved by their relationships with other widowed callers.

Mutual sharing and reaching a greater understanding of the common problems of widowhood are reported as major rewards for type 3 helpers:

> It has helped me because you realize others are in the same situation ....

Involvement in the program has developed self-confidence and a new self-image for these volunteers; they are increasingly defining themselves as helpers. The feeling of being appreciated was also mentioned as a major satisfaction:

> I enjoy the older people ... they are so grateful ... you feel you are doing something ....

Type 3 helpers were finding that the activity and involvement with others in the mutual help program had broken the cycle of depressions that often follow bereavement. Insight was gained into these depressive cycles by following others through the same experience:

> Sometimes you get a really depressed one ... you help them and they come out of it for a while, then they are back in it ... it goes in cycles .... but I'm too busy now to get into these depressions ....

In sharing the experience with others, they are working through their own feelings and learning that outreaching activity is a way out from depressive anxiety.

Style of helping

The type 3 style of helping is farther from the "professional" style than that of types 1 and 2 and nearer the friendship end of the continuum. Social distance between helper and recipient is reduced as the helper's own need for emotional input into the helping relationship increases. However, the life-style of type 3 volunteers was still closely involved with kin relationships, and these volunteers were not looking for friends among the callers. They focused on helping callers to unload their feelings, to express their sadness and despair. At the same time, these helpers may talk about their own feelings and how the cycles of depression have become less frequent. They were less innovative than types 1 and 2 in suggesting activities and new roles for their callers, although they learned to use adequately the resources suggested in the program's resource file. They spent many hours listening helpfully to the depressed, sharing their insights into their own emotional fluctuations. Their newfound awareness of the value of reaching out offered a helpful role model to those callers who were just beginning to move into the recovery stage after bereavement. The closeness of their own current experience to that of their callers may heighten the encouraging effect of the role model.

Type 3 volunteers were like type 1 in dealing with a larger number of callers, averaging two to four conversations with each one. They helped the caller over a depressed period, but did not follow through with the intensity of either type 1 or 2 in finding ways of rebuilding the caller's life. They have farther to go in the struggle to rebuild their own lives. The availability of type 3 listeners for the unloading of feelings has its own value for certain callers at certain times. The callers who especially need a listener function are (1) the more recently bereaved and (2) the elderly (Abrahams 1972).

Type 3 volunteers are likely to stay with the project for some time, as the new experience of reaching out beyond the family is helping their own recovery. As their confidence in helping increases, they become more committed to the program. It is conceivable that in time, some type 3 helpers may develop helping styles more like types 1 or 2.

Helper Type 4: Integrative-Friendship (Self-revealing)

Inputs and satisfactions

These volunteers had not previously been involved in helping roles in the community. They were more isolated from kin than type 3 and were feeling acute loneliness at the time they joined the program. Their joining was usually not self-initiated, as they had not defined themselves as helpers at that point; they were mostly recruited by friends already in the program. Their life-style prior to widowhood had been centered in the nuclear family, and therefore widowhood left them in a state of extreme isolation. They were motivated to volunteer because of their loneliness, rather than by any conscious decision to help others:

> I volunteered because I thought it would fill up some of my time ... and take my mind off my own troubles ....

I didn't know what I wanted to do ... I think I like to be in a group of people ... I didn't realize that I could help anybody ....

The main input of these volunteers into the mutual helping process results from their own emotional needs for friendship and relationship. They had little knowledge of community resources, but learned of these from the program's files.

For type 4 volunteers, the rewards from the helping process were extensive in terms of their own development toward reintegration and adjustment. They had the farthest to go and the most to receive from the mutual help program. They were rapidly gaining confidence in their new self-image as helpers. From feeling lonely and outcast, they now felt needed and valued. They were basically friendly people who were ready to move into new roles. The fact that they had not done so was due to situational rather than emotional isolation. This is in contrast to the widowed who are isolated but still emotionally disturbed and not suitable, or not ready, to become helpers.

Style of helping

Type 4 volunteers developed a helping style most nearly approximating the "friendship" relationship, where there is equal give and take between the two individuals, who can express their feelings freely. In offering this kind of relationship to their callers, they were effective helpers. Their concept of helping focused on sharing:

I think the most helpful thing is having someone to talk to ... just to know there is someone else there .... Certainly your own feelings come out ... it made my life easier because I had someone to talk to ....

Type 4 volunteers, in developing friendships, made the most frequent follow-up calls of any of the volunteers. Calls were often being made every other day. It is not suggested that these volunteers tried to make friends with every caller, but they were looking for friendship and where the caller was appropriate for this relationship, it was likely to develop. They often arranged meetings with their callers, invited them home, and personally took them to the widowed clubs.

In addition to the friendships developed, type 4 volunteers followed through frequently on other lonely callers, such as the elderly, the handicapped, and the sick. They did not work as intensively as types 1 and 2 in efforts to help these individuals build a new life, but their frequent calls and emotional interchange let the other person feel that someone cared.

Prior to joining the program, these were the most isolated of the volunteers, but their participation and responsiveness to the program helped them dramatically and they were moving rapidly into new relationships and rebuilding their lives in new directions. As they become increasingly involved in other roles and activities, they may move out of the program, when it no longer fulfills their needs. This is to be expected of some helpers in a mutual aid program and in no way detracts from the value of their service while they are involved.

Summary and Implications

The persons who select themselves and are selected by the mutual help program have certain qualities in common, such as sensitivity, concern for others, and the desire to share helpfully with others what they have learned from their own experience. However, the style of helping that each volunteer may develop varies according to his own needs and the satisfactions he seeks from the mutual helping relationship. Variations in styles of helping range from a style approximating the professional/client type of relationship to a style approximating friendship, as social distance diminishes between helper and recipient of help and as the area of mutual two-way sharing of emotional input increases.

We have identified four styles of helping, each with a different focus and varying inputs. Style 1 has as its major focus the exchange of resource information from helper to recipient, together with step-by-step encouragement and support to help the recipient utilize the information in order to rebuild a new life. Style 2 has a major focus on skillful, empathetic listening, together with a warm, personal approach to the client, often using personal contacts to help the recipient begin to use new resources for becoming reengaged. Style 3 involves more two-way emotional sharing than styles 1 and 2; it is characterized by supportive listening and sharing of problems of readjusting. Style 4 approximates a friendship relationship, in which there is equal sharing of emotions and experience. Helper types 1 and 2, whose life-styles encompass extensive resources for self-growth and development, may serve as role models for the widowed who call for help. Types 3 and 4 are in the course of developing new resources for themselves, and in terms of readjustment are closer to the recipient and offer the support of a closer sharing. They function in a different way as role models in process of change. The feedback we had from callers and the extent of return calls indicate that these were all valid ways of helping.

It must be emphasized that "classificatory types," as used in this chapter, are essentially a device for developing concepts to clarify our understanding of the helping relationship. There are more than four types of helping and possibly no one helper exactly fits the description of the four styles outlined. Furthermore, the mutual helping process is dynamic and constantly fluid. Recipients of help move into helping roles, and helpers may change their styles of helping as their own adjustment and growth progresses.

A closer understanding of the helping process has implications for any kind of mutual help program. It may be possible to devise a means of matching helpers with recipients in order to maximize the helping relationship. In helping programs, this is sometimes achieved informally. It is common experience with both professional and nonprofessional caregivers that they are able to help some people more than others. Sometimes a case is referred to another worker who "specializes in" or has been successful with a certain kind of problem or personality. Within the framework of any given program, the possibility exists for a systematic matching of helpers and recipients, taking account of the needs and satisfactions of each in the helping relationship. Case conferences, or volunteers' meetings, might be one place where a better matching of helpers and recipients could be discussed and effected.

The helping experience fosters self-growth at differing rates and in different ways for the helper, which again has implications for his future in or outside the program. The mutual help program has to accommodate both the volunteers who through time are likely to become more committed to the program and those whose self-growth will move them out to other interests and activities. For the volunteers who stay in the program, opportunities must be created to enable them to move into new roles and responsibilities as time goes on. At the same time, the program must also allow for constant turnover as those who develp new interests move on. Mutual helping involves a fluid process which motivates the participants to become reengaged in various ways, and the program must be flexible enough to accommodate this process.

Mutual help programs offer opportunities for healthy personality growth to both helpers and recipients of help after some traumatic loss experienced by both. The helping experience not only provides a way out from loneliness and anxiety but also a new satisfaction in reaching out to others, expanding commitment beyond the primary group circle, and building meaningful social ties to the community. These programs provide a means of developing new forms of social roles that are much needed in a society where social isolation and alienation are widely experienced. This study has indicated some of the varying ways in which such roles may be developed.

This exploratory observation of helping roles among volunteers of the Widowed Service Line suggests the need for further research and evaluation of caregiving styles. It was not within the scope of this investigation to undertake a follow-up study of the callers to the Line, who are the other half of the two-way mutual helping relationship. In future studies of the helping process, it would be valuable to record motivations, inputs, and rewards on both sides of this helping relationship. By this method, some evaluative formulations might be developed.

All the helpers involved in the Widowed Service Line had reached a certain level of adjustment after bereavement but their needs in the helping process varied considerably. There was some indication that helpers may best help those recipients whose needs at the time of seeking help are closest to their own needs at that time. Any helper/recipient matching system would have to allow for constant fluctuation in the pattern of needs, as both helpers and recipients move forward in their widowhood experience and recovery.

Further studies of the mutual helping relationship in different types of mutual aid programs are required for more clarification of the dynamics of this complex two-way process.

REFERENCES

Abrahams RB: Mutual help for the widowed. Social Work 17: 5, Sept 1972

Blau PM, Scott WR: Formal Organizations. San Francisco, Chandler, 1962

Caplan G: Principles of Preventive Psychiatry. New York, Basic Books, 1964

Foote NN, Cottrell LS: Identity and Interpersonal Competence. Chicago, U. of Chicago Press, 1955

Goffman E: Stigma. Englewood Cliffs, NJ, Prentice Hall, 1963

Hempel CG: Symposium: Problems of Concept and Theory Formation in the Social Sciences, Language and Human Rights. Philadelphia, U. of Penna. Press, 1952

Lenneberg E, Rowbotham JL: The Ileostomy Patient. Springfield, C. Thomas, 1970

Lopata HZ: The social involvement of American widows. Am Behav Scientist 14: 1, Sept-Oct 1970

Lopata HZ: Loneliness: Forms and components. Soc Prob 17: 2, Fall 1969

Riessman F: The helper therapy principle. Social Work 10: 2, April 1965

Rogers C: Client Centered Therapy. Boston, Houghton Mifflin, 1951, ch. 4

Silverman P: The widow to widow program. Ment Hyg 53: 3, July 1969

Silverman P: The widow as caregiver in a program of preventive intervention with other widows. Ment Hyg 54: 4, Oct. 1970

Silverman P: Widowhood and preventive intervention. Family Coordinator 21: 1, Jan 1972

Weiss R: Helping relationships: Relationships with social workers, priests and others. Soc Prob 20: 3, Winter 1973

Weiss R: The fund of sociability. Transaction, July/August 1969

David E. Richards

12

Peer Consultation Among Clergy: A Resource for Professional Development

During the past decade much attention has been given to the role and function of the clergyman in our society. While this was true in the preceding decade as well, there is a marked contrast between the way in which attention was called to the clergyman in the post-World War II decade and what has been happening since the mid-1960s. Immediately following the war, churches enjoyed a remarkable period of rapid growth. Membership and income increased, and enrollment in theological seminaries and schools of Divinity suddenly grew. The booming churches needed professional manpower. The clergyman was valued because his role and function was an essential part of what seemed to be a massive return to institutional religion. The occupational identity of the ordained clergyman seemed clear, largely because the institution he served was busy, prosperous, building and growing.

This favorable condition changed suddenly and quite radically during the 1960s. Membership declined, budgets fell off, new buildings became burdensome. The positive attention that had been called to the clergyman began to change, the things that received attention now tended to be negative. By the mid-1960s, some clergymen were under heavy criticism for behaving in what was seen as a nontraditional manner with regard to social, political, and economic issues. For their part, clergy frequently became critical of institutional religion. The unusual number of admissions to the ministry of the 1950s was balanced by a remarkable number of demissions during the 1960s. This trend is now diminishing, and there is some evidence that a healthier perception of both the theory and the practice of parish ministry is beginning to develop. Nevertheless, as a professional group, clergymen must continue to cope with changed attitudes toward religion and the church and must continue to persevere with the impact that these changes have upon the way society perceives their role and function. In a recent study of the relatively new phenomenon of secularly employed clergy, Bonn and Doyle make the following observation.

> The occupational identity of the ordained clergy, once well established in American Society, is currently surrounded by uncertainty and caught up in a process of social change. . . . Miller (1971) reports a considerable drop in income of clergymen relative to other occupational groups between 1939 and 1959, and the lifetime earnings of clergy are considerably less than those of elementary school teachers and about the same as carpenters and truck drivers. . . . Perhaps even more revealing is the ambiguity surrounding the minister in today's society. . . . From an occupational standpoint, the real threat to the authority of the clergyman's role stems from other occupations taking over the social functions which once belonged to clergymen. Teaching, administering aid, counseling, advising the young, healing and even politics are all roles which have fallen into the province of other specialized occupational groups. Few skills remain, over which the clergy maintain a monopoly and clergymen profess little unique knowledge (Haystrom 1957). (1:326) (1).

While this situation may be changing somewhat, the role and function of the clergyman can still be described as an "occupational conglomerate," and it is to this "occupational conglomerate" that we now seek to relate a particular method and resource for professional development. The method considered here is best described as dyadic peer, or coequal status, consultation in which the roles of consultant and consultee are regularly reversed according to a previously agreed upon schedule. The goal is mutual or shared support and strengthening.

The concept of consultation dyads of peers actively engaged in the same field emerged in the Episcopal Church from two sources (2). An example of the first source was a program of rather traditional mental health consultation offered by the Laboratory of Community Psychiatry of the Harvard Medical School to the clergy of the Episcopal Diocese of Massachusetts. Over a period of years, this allowed a number of clergy to have the experience of receiving group consultation in regard to the management of their parish affairs and the work of providing pastoral care both in the parish and community. The initial popularity of this program indicated that clergymen both needed and wanted ways of enriching their own understanding of their role and function. As consultees, they learned how to assess their own perplexing situations and how to appropriate and apply the help that was made available to them through professionals in the related fields of psychology and psychiatry. The group consultations were led by the faculty and fellows of the Laboratory of Community Psychiatry. The structure and ambiance of the group allowed the individual clergyman to benefit from the perplexities and new learnings of his peers. In the group process, consultees learned how to solicit and accept help for themselves, and from time to time they gave help to one another in a highly professional way. Within the context of this experience, they were learning the role of consultee and from time to time practiced, under the example and tutelage of the group leader, the role of consultant.

The second source from which the concept of role-reversing dyads emerged was, again, a fairly traditional mental health consultation model in which the director of the Laboratory provided individual consultation to the Bishop of the Diocese of Massachusetts whose clergy in the meanwhile were engaged in group consultation with the faculty and fellows of the Laboratory. The Bishop utilized his consultation opportunity as a way of increasing his own competence and comfort in dealing with the mixed task of administering diocesan affairs, providing pastoral care to clergy and to parishes and representing the Episcopal Church in the community. He found this experience so valuable that he urged consideration of its wider use throughout the Episcopal Church. Various contracts have now been made between bishops and mental health professionals.

However, the idea of one-to-one consultation for bishops went through another stage of development when the Committee on Pastoral Development of the House of Bishops decided to examine the possibility of establishing an in-house consultative resource designed especially for new bishops. The experience of becoming a new bishop was looked at from a fresh point of view. Stereotypical expectations were analyzed, and it was seen that exaggerated and unreal assumptions were made about the ease with which parish priests made the transition from parochial work to diocesan leadership. Insight was developed regarding some of the crisis points which normally existed in this transition and questions were asked about how help could be provided so as to facilitate the transition, relieve the emotional, professional, and social strain engendered by such a transition, and reduce the isolation which often accompanies the promotion into a post of greatly expanded responsibility and prestige. While one-to-one consultation with a behavioral scientist was good for solving some of the problems encountered, it was thought that some of the transition needs might best be met by a peer who had experienced the change and who possessed the compassion and the skill to assist a fellow bishop just beginning the transition.

The program of providing collegial support to new bishops was advanced by stages. The first stage was to gather together a group of experienced bishops from various locations and from dioceses that differed in size, constituency, and tradition to explore realistically the need and readiness for such a plan. The existing model of mental health consultation was examined and the essential characteristics of the consultant and consultee roles were analyzed. Definition was given to these roles and a disciplined form of professional interaction was described. It was soon concluded that if a bishop were trained in this disciplined form of interaction and if he were prepared to accept and follow it, he could in fact provide valuable consultation without having to develop any further mastery in the behavioral sciences. The textbook upon which the training was based was Gerald Caplan's *Theory and Practice of Mental Health Consultation* (3). Both the theory and the practice were adaptable, and the bishops who were present for the first study seminar enthusiastically endorsed the idea of developing an in-house consultation service.

The second stage was to secure sanction from the president of the House of Bishops. This sanction took two forms. First, he approved of the plan in general and went on record as endorsing the concept. Second, as each new bishop was elected, he personally recommended that he accept the offer of assistance made to him when he was invited to establish a consulting relationship with an experienced bishop for the first 2 years of his episcopate.

The third and continuing stage commenced when the first group of experienced bishops attended the first training seminar for developing consultation skills. This 3-day seminar was conducted by Dr. Caplan. At its conclusion, participants indicated whether or not they were ready and willing to take on responsibility for offering consultation to a new bishop. Each year this seminar is offered to a new group. After 5 years, approximately 40 percent of the bishops of the Episcopal Church have received this training, and 70 pairs of dyads of bishop colleagues have been formed.

Maintenance of the program is provided by myself as a bishop who bears specific responsibility, as director of the Office of Pastoral Development, for arranging for training, matching consultants and consultees, and interpreting, evaluating, and refining the program.

The dyads meet in accordance with the schedule that each dyad sets for itself. Major importance is attached to the initial meeting in the consultee's diocese. Subsequent meetings occur at times when bishops meet in convention or conference, in the consultant's diocese, or at a convenient location midway between the two dioceses.

The important point is that for the first year or two of a new bishop's career he has an experienced colleague outside his own immediate system to whom he can turn in complete confidence for help, guidance, support, and the opportunity to explore the broadest possible range of options with regard to any problem or dilemma he may face. This makes available to him a reservoir of professional experience and is a major step toward reducing the professional and social isolation that sometimes besets persons who are promoted to positions of greatly increased responsibility and prestige.

Touching the lives and influencing the functioning of bishops in this way is considered a plus factor in the life of the Episcopal Church. However, bishops – while representing a major influence – actually represent a numerically small portion of the total clergy of the Church.

The previously described group consultation for priests and parish ministers is one way of providing guidance, help, and support for clergy other than bishops. However, this method of group consultation has some requirements that limit its applicability. Sanction and cooperation must be granted by a group; proximity and congeniality are factors in establishing such sanction and cooperation. The availability of a qualified and interested mental health professional is required. Costs are involved in engaging the time and services of such a behavioral scientist. Scheduling meetings for busy and heavily committed persons is always a problem. Much profit accrues from such group work for parish clergy, but profit might also accrue from the work and interaction of peer dyads.

If it worked for bishops, it was postulated that it could also work for priests and parish ministers. It was worthwhile to ask the question: How can we match parish clergy in a helping, supporting relationship so that with maximum ease and minimum strain they too can be available to one another and lend guidance, support, and help in the accomplishment of a task which is mutually understood?

An experiment was then conducted in which clergy who had previously participated in group consulation in Massachusetts were invited by Gerald Caplan and myself (then a Senior Fellow at the Laboratory of Community Psychiatry on sabbatical) to attend seminars at the Laboratory in order to explore how the roles of both consultant and consultee could be defined for them in a dyadic relationship. Once again it was observed that the commitment to "a disciplined form of professional interaction" was absolutely key to a successful and rewarding consulting relationship.

The unique aspect of this form of relationship was the plan for role reversal. Rather than establishing a continuing role for one person as consultant and the other as consultee, the arrangement called for the planned exchange of these roles from the beginning. For the first hour, one person served as consultant. For the second hour, this same person presented his dilemma and became the consultee. This is the role he had previously "learned" in the group consultation setting. From time to time as a participant in the earlier consultation groups, he had shared the consultant role with the outside consultant as the group struggled to help a member with his pastoral problems, but during the dyad-preparatory seminars he had an excellent opportunity to explore further what it meant to be a consultant. When the role-reversing dyads were formed, he had the prized opportunity to enjoy and practice both roles.

Dyads were formed partly by mutual consent, but sometimes by planned arrangement. Ease of access to the other was important but, in order to promote confidentiality and autonomy, geographic propinquity in the same or contiguous parish was not encouraged. A maintenance function was required in order to keep the dyads going. Once again, specific responsibility had to be assigned, this time to a diocesan staff person whose functioning in this role was approved by the diocesan bishop. Periodic meetings of all the dyads with Dr. Caplan and myself to share experiences helped to sustain the enthusiasm and to refine the discipline.

After preparing for and practicing role-reversing consultation over an extended period of time, some of the dyad members were asked to meet to assess the concept and to identify the essential ingredients of this type of professional interaction. They agreed upon these three conclusions: (1) in order to fulfill the consultant role it was essential to have experienced and learned the consultee role; (2) the maintenance function was important because it reinforced the sanction from the diocese and because it encouraged the participants to remain faithful to the discipline which they had accepted; and (3) the success of the process required that the dyads meet together as a group from time to time so that each individual dyad could be strengthened by participation in a reference group. These group meetings provided opportunities for reviewing the theory and for exchanging experiences and information.

Caplan has pointed out that in a given population only a percentage will be open to and will take advantage of consultation. Consequently it always remains optional, but in order to maximize the acceptance and use of this resource, there is need for a great deal of general education, interpretation, explanation, and, where appropriate, persuasion. People have to be aware of what it is and is not in order to decide to accept or reject it. The following list of points elaborates on the form and quality of the professional interaction which is the goal of role-reversing peer dyadic consultation:

1. This style of consultation partakes of the one prime characteristic of all good consultation in that it is free of judgmentalism. Participants in the dyads stated this as the most appreciated aspect of their consulting experience. In this regard, it differs completely from supervision and allows participants to remain free of defensiveness and the fear of being put down by a colleague. This factor in itself fosters healthy openness and enables the consultation process to deal with very complex issues. The tendency, conscious or unconscious, to hide, cover, withhold, or dissimulate does not seem to be present.
2. Current problems can be dealt with at the time that they are pressing down on the consultee. Since there is no need to wait for a stated meeting, dyad participants can seek one another out either by phone or in conference at the very point of crisis. This means that troublesome problems can be dealt with without a long waiting time. Consultation can move quickly from topic to topic. A great deal of meaningful exchange can take place at frequent intervals.

   Pastor A (the consultee) describes an occurrence that was extremely threatening to both his professional and personal status. After a number of years as rector of a strong and well-organized parish he was "called upon" by several of his vestrymen who challenged him regarding his leadership style. While one can appreciate the candor involved in such a confrontational meeting, at the same time one can understand how upsetting this meeting must have been. The vestry members desired a change in style. Even though this may have been a reasonable desire and perhaps advantageous for the parish, the confrontation suddenly faced the rector with such questions as: "What have I been doing wrong? Why do my people not like me? Do they really want me to leave? Am I inadequate for this task?"

Where does a clergyman go when he needs to deal with these questions? In this case Pastor A was able to go quickly to his consultant. This is how Pastor A describes the help he received through consultation with Pastor B.:

> In the winter I had a rather serious occurrence. Three members of my vestry asked to come to talk to me. They felt that I was too much of a leader and not enough of an enabler. We had very different expectations and visions of the role of a Rector. I felt somewhat threatened and challenged by this experience. Pastor B as my consultant helped me work through my feelings of anger, guilt, hostility, and self-doubt that came as a result of this experience.
>
> I have thought many times that I don't think I could have gotten through this past winter without this weekly consultation.

Whatever the outcome of this situation may have been, if Pastor A had not had access to a peer consultant, he might have suffered an exaggerated sense of isolation and rejection. However, by having speedy access to someone who could help him objectify and deal with the criticism involved, he was able to extract positive and beneficial results from the experience.

3. Because there is training provided for learning the disciplined form of interaction, the consultation process need not spill over into ventilation. That is, it does not invite the expression of associated feelings. It keeps the focus on the problem. Because the consultee has accepted the discipline, this means that he is required to think out the problem in an orderly way. As he tells it to the consultant he is telling it to himself, and in the telling he knows that he must trim away the associated emotionality which may in fact be distorting his preceptions and his ability to act. This distortion and paralysis may not be clearly understood and the picture may remain fuzzy until he is required to put the facts in order. Simply ventilating his despair and frustration may keep the picture fuzzy, but disciplined consultation on the subject makes way for clarification. When the consultant takes an objective position he helps the consultee to do the same. This provides an opportunity for supportive reflection on a hitherto insolvable problem. The consultee is allowed to postpone his decision until the assessment is completed. He secures time to explore neglected aspects of the case and to turn up possible solutions that may not come readily to mind.
4. Some clergy discovered that after learning this style of consultation they were able to use it helpfully, in regard to certain subjects, with

some of their parishioners. They observed that this required a high degree of trust between pastor and parishioner. Without such trust, the parishioner could misconstrue the objectivity to be practiced as a lack of genuine interest and concern over the problem. The danger of seeming coldness might inhibit creative pastoral interaction if the problem relates to a deeply personal matter of the parishioner. However, the more objective consultation style can prove extremely helpful in assisting a congregant in the accomplishment of a task that has to do, for instance, with parish organization or program.

5. Dyadic consultation does not open up issues that cannot be dealt with. Since it is the consultee's responsibility to name the issue to be discussed, he is never required to abandon his defenses. This means that he sets the pace and no one else can force him to confront unresolved emotional conflicts. By definition, boundaries are established; encounter and confrontational techniques have no place in the consultation relationship. The consultee is allowed to feel safe by knowing that his privacy will not be invaded. The emotional content of a task-oriented, job-related problem is dealt with indirectly as help and relief is provided directly to the work dilemma.
6. When systematic reflection on the problem is encouraged, this dissipates the usual worry over the problem that is triggered by pressure, anxiety, and puzzlement or uncertainty about the outcome. Focusing on the problem with a colleague in a constructive way provides the feeling that one is actually doing something about the situation. Participating in a time of shared concern reduces worry, thus increasing the possibility of a less panicky solution.

   The value of systematic reflection with a colleague as a help in reducing anger and anxiety is demonstrated by this instance in which one clergyman was able to help his colleague manage and resolve some of the agitated feelings that developed in regard to the consultee's relationship with the assistant minister on his parish staff. The relationship between rector and assistant had deteriorated and become a source of great anxiety to the rector. This fact in itself was burdensome, and the poor relationship threatened to interfere with the fruitfulness and progress of the work of the parish staff. Pastor A (the consultee in this case) brought the matter forward in consultation, seeking help from Pastor B. In describing this situation, Pastor A writes:

   > In the two years that Pastor B and I have been consulting with each other, a great degree of trust has built up between us. We have been more and more dealing with our relationships to people in our parishes who have been quite difficult for us. Pastor B has been a great help to me in regard to my assistant. I have discovered a lot of reasons why we have not had the best working relationship, and it has made my lot somewhat easier to have Pastor B to talk to when I have felt angry or upset with my assistant. Pastor B has asked

many probing questions, and I have had to look at myself and my assistant in a new light many times.

In this instance, peer consultation has led to analysis and discovery – the resolution of angry feelings and the increase of insight.

7. Regular peer consultation helps to overcome both personal and professional isolation by reducing the sense of competition or rivalry that may exist among peers. It removes the tendency to compare one's functioning with the functioning of other colleagues. Dyads are out to help each other, and since the contract is bound by complete confidentiality, each member knows that there is no point in being out to impress anyone with either his brilliance or his stupidity.
8. When the discipline of the consultative process is followed, the alternative solutions, the options available to the consultee, are increased in a way that one could not generally do by himself.
9. Since the consultee retains the responsibility for choosing which option to employ, the decision and the action are distinctly his own. This in turn affirms in the consultee that he is not helpless – he simply is temporarily stuck. This means that his identity is not damaged by asking for help nor have his dependency needs been catered to in such a way as to increase his dependency and lower his self-esteem.

   Complex situations that drag on over a long period of time can be very debilitating and discouraging to the pastor who may come to feel somewhat helpless in the face of such complexities. Pastor A describes an involved problem pertaining to the parish day school. It had to do with a dominant school principal who apparently operated very aggressively and constantly placed her own personal needs and goals above those at the school. The rector was responsible for the school, but the organizational structure did not allow him to intervene. He made this long-term problem a matter for consultation and this is how he describes it:

My dyad partner, Pastor B, and I met regularly until last Lent. During our many meetings we discussed a problem I had with the church's Day School, and it was very helpful to see the problem from all angles.

Our Director of the Day School became sick with a back ailment. She continued teaching for about a year and then was absent for 9½ months of the following school year. During this time she called in to the teachers the program for each day. Gradually she did not seem interested in trying anymore, but insisted that her salary should be increased, while the teachers had to take a cut to balance the budget. She absolutely refused to let the Day School committee talk to the teachers. This led to an untenable situation. The teachers threatened to quit.

The real crunch came when the public schools started their kindergarten program and our school suffered a drop in enrollment of 50%. In order to make the school pay we had to do something. The Director became very

> hostile and did not want to make any changes, especially when it meant a reduction in staff or in her salary. Any suggestions made by the committee were totally rejected by her. The net result was that five members of the committee quit, and in fact left the church. She tried to bring a suit against the school and the church and did everything she could to upset our Day School. She tried to open another Nursery School, but this failed through lack of enrollment.
>
> I am happy to say we survived this episode; and our Day School, and now a Nursery School, is doing very well.
>
> Pastor B, my consultant, was very helpful to me in seeing this problem through. We discussed each alternative as it came up. Although we do not meet as often now, both of us know that if we have a problem we can discuss it with the other. If any problem comes up, all you have to do is telephone. The dyadic program has been good for us.

Apparently the solution to the problem described above had many choice points. Examining the alternatives and making the right choice was an ongoing process until finally a permanent settlement was achieved. Having an outside person to help objectify the situation and analyze the various options made choosing and deciding easier for Pastor A.

10. Peer consultation places high value on mutuality and thus reduces the importance of personal status. In the dyads, the possibility of one person coming through as rescuer and the other person coming through as the rescued one is obviated. Generally, both wish to derive benefits, and both welcome the opportunity to offer and receive assistance.

SUMMARY

Planned role-reversing consulting dyads of peers offers a type of supportive interaction. It is worth consideration because of the easy access it provides to the securing of professional help with one's task and the very low – even nonexistent – monetary cost that is involved. It personifies a statement made many years ago by Professor Bigg in his introduction to *The Imitation of Christ:*

> Men are bound together in this world in very singular ways . . . Life is so constituted that we need reservoirs of every kind of excellence of intelligence, of knowledge, of practical ability, of morality. No man is sufficient for himself. At every turn he must borrow and he must lend (4).

Peer dyadic consultation is a process of borrowing and lending. From this process of interchange of ideas, abilities, knowledge, conceptualizing skills, and workable schemes comes a mutual enrichment which enables both parties to face their respective tasks with increased enthusiasm, optimism, and confidence. It is in fact a process probably as old as man himself, but each generation needs both to explore and exploit this excellent resource. Men in every age need to learn for themselves of the benefits and support to be enjoyed by freely giving and receiving. The world somehow becomes safer when one knows how to practice the concept of mutual responsibility and interdependence. In a culture and society in which persons, and especially males, are given to distancing themselves from one another, it is important to be conscious of the values and the essential characteristics of healthy and productive professional interactions. This is precisely what planned peer consultation seeks to provide when it describes and offers assistance in developing, between two persons, a disciplined form of interaction with stated goals and specific limits.

REFERENCES

1. Bonn RL, Doyle RT: Secularly employed clergy. *J Sci Stud Religion* 13, 3:325-343, 1974
2. Caplan RB: *Helping the Helpers to Help: The Development of Mental Health Consultation to Aid Clergymen in Pastoral Work,* in collaboration with Caplan G, Richards DE; Stokes AP Jr. New York, Seabury Press, 1972
3. Caplan G: *The Theory and Practice of Mental Health Consultation,* New York, Basic Books, 1970
4. Bigg C (trans): *The Imitation of Christ* (ed 5), Thomas à Kempis. London, Methuen, 1908

Gerald Caplan

13

Organization of Support Systems for Civilian Populations[1]

This chapter deals with the methods to be used by community intervenors who seek to organize support systems for civilian populations in times of war and disaster. The intervenors may be community mental health specialists, social scientists, community organizers, or other specialists who are accepted by the populations and their leaders as competent to help improve the ways people deal with the human burdens and challenges of a catastrophe.

My remarks are based on 35 years experience in military and civilian psychiatry in Britain, Israel, and the United States; on my research in the fields of crisis theory, mental health consultation, and community mental health practice methodology; and, in particular, on my experience in Israel during and after the Yom Kippur War, when I helped organize services for the families of war casualties.[2]

The theoretical base of this chapter is crisis theory, as it has been developed over the past 20 years by our Harvard University community mental

[1]Lecture delivered, in part, at the International Conference on Psychological Stress and Adjustment in Time of War and Peace, Tel Aviv, Israel, January 6-10, 1975.

[2]My views have been much influenced by my Israeli colleagues, many of whom may recognize in my proposals ideas that they first suggested to me, or that they developed themselves. I acknowledge my debt to them collectively; it is not feasible to trace each of the ideas to its individual originators. I wish to single out for special mention only Batya Vashitz, M.S.W., Acting Director of the Department of Family and Community Service of the Jerusalem Municipality who, at the request of Mayor Teddy Kollek, was the main sponsor of my program during the Yom Kippur War; and also Mica Katz and her colleagues, the psychologists of the Adler Institute in Tel Aviv, whose work with widows and bereaved parents under the auspices of the Rehabilitation Department of the Israeli Ministry of Defence was a particular inspiration in my efforts.

health research group, and particularly our recent formulations of the theory of support systems.[3] In the latter, we have focused on the powerful contribution of social aggregates, consisting of continuous or intermittent links with significant individuals, networks, groups, or organizations, in fortifying and augmenting the adaptive capacity of persons and families exposed to acute life crises or long-term privations and burdens. We have been especially impressed by nonprofessionalized natural person-to-person supports that are common in most communities and that usually involve the three linked elements of (a) helping the individual exposed to stress mobilize his psychological resources and master his emotional burdens; (b) sharing his tasks in dealing concretely with his predicament; and (c) providing him with extra supplies of information, money, materials, tools, skills, and cognitive guidance to improve his handling of his situation. This has led us to explore avenues and methods whereby community professionals may stimulate the development of such natural supportive links among members of a population exposed to acute or long-term stress, and whereby we may build collaborative programs with already existing nonprofessional support systems so that we may help these spread their contributions to wider segments of the population.

Despite its obvious relevance and importance, space will not permit me to deal here with the treatment of civilian casualties in war or natural disaster or with the organization of services to prepare for this. Nor will I deal with the crucial methodological issue of how community intervenors build and maintain among community leaders and the population at large sanction for their helping operations. This has been discussed in a recent book, *Theory and Practice of Mental Health Consultation.*[4] In connection with our present topic I may just mention that whether the community intervenor comes in from the outside on a temporary basis during the emergency, or whether he is a long-term member of the community with a specialist status, there is value in his having preexisting relationships of mutual trust and respect with community leaders or with people they know, which may act as the basis for a rapid negotiation of sanction for his intervention efforts during the actual crisis. In any event, without current local sanction based on trust and respect, a community intervenor will not get far in implementing the recommendations discussed in this chapter.

TARGET POPULATIONS

I have found it of value to differentiate supportive organizational efforts in relation to three subpopulation categories: (a) families of casualties, (b)

[3]G. Caplan, *Support Systems and Community Mental Health: Lectures on Concept Development* (New York: Behavioral Publications, Inc., 1974).

[4]G. Caplan, *Theory and Practice of Mental Health Consultation,* (New York: Basic Books, Inc., 1970).

families of potential casualties, namely military or civilians personally exposed to conflict or catastrophe, and (c) dependent and needy individuals, such as those who are pregnant, sick, or frail.

Families of Casualties

This category includes the families of those who have been killed, who are reported missing in action, who are prisoners of war, and who are wounded.

General Principles of Intervention

These apply to all cases.

Convene and link

A primary mission of the intervenor is to ensure that the family members who are centrally involved become quickly linked with significant others – kin, friends, neighbors, and supportive representatives of the larger community. In most cases, this occurs spontaneously because of the natural biosocial arousal produced by the national emergency; but intervenors may need to stimulate and foster the process in the case of families who are isolated as a result of being newcomers to an area or because they may for various psychosocial and cultural reasons be alienated from their social milieu. Intervenors may also have to ensure that the helpful interactions continue after the acute phases of the crisis have passed, when the volunteering spirit usually dies down, but when the needs for continuing support by the stricken families may continue or even increase as they struggle to adjust to the long-term consequences of their tragedy. The purpose of the linking is to provide emotional support, cognitive guidance, and concrete help with crisis-related tasks.

Maintain a "watching brief"

This legal term is a useful motto in guiding our intervention efforts. The numbers of people involved both in the acute crisis and in its continuing adaptational sequels are likely to be so great that not only is direct intervention by the specialist in all cases not feasible but continuing systematic intervention even by other community caregiving professionals in all cases would overtax available resources. Moreover, most of the sufferers are likely to master their predicament with the help of their kith and kin and to feel that they would be weakened by being forced into an overly dependent status by too much involvement of community professionals in what they may well feel is their private predicament. In only a small proportion of cases are the spontaneous and natural supports likely to be inadequate, and even in these the picture will be patchy; extra support may be needed only during especially difficult phases of their adjustment process. Therefore, both from the point of view of the families and also because of the need to conserve limited community resources, professional intervention must be kept to the absolute minimum. On the other hand, when it is needed, it must certainly be provided, and it must be provided immediately, because if people are left to struggle without help on their own with overpowering problems, maladaptive and maladjustive responses may quickly occur; once the wrong path has been chosen, the bad results tend to become chronic and difficult to reverse.

All this leads to the conclusion that a primary goal of our planning must be to ensure continued monitoring of the reactions of families. This monitoring must be tactful and unobtrusive, and it must be part of a community caregiving structure that will energize immediate intervention when this is indicated. The pattern of the monitoring will obviously vary in accordance with local sociocultural conditions. Its elements will consist of a central or neighborhood decision-making group that includes or has access to a specialist in human relations; a network of community caregivers, such as doctors, nurses, educators, police, welfare workers, and religious leaders, who are in continuous routine contact with the afflicted; and a communication system which ensures that messages are passed without delay from the caregivers to the specialists when a family's behavior arouses the suspicion that it is not coping adequately on its own or with the spontaneous help of its normal social entourage. These messages should immediately lead to specialized investigation or to planned intervention. The human relations specialist must communicate to the community caregivers the patterns of possible maladaptive responses, so that they will recognize the early signs of these in the families with which they are in routine contact. He must also make himself available as a consultant to discuss questionable cases with any caregiver who is in doubt; and in special cases he should be willing himself to talk with family members. The latter should be avoided as much as possible because irrespective of the outcome of such a contact, the fact that it takes place at all increases the possibility that the family may label itself deviant or may be so labeled by others.

Avoid labeling

The last point is a special example of a more general, and very important, issue. The capacity of people to struggle actively against the difficulties of their predicament, to persevere in confronting confusing and frustrating situations, and to master emotional and cognitive stresses and challenges is much influenced by their self-image. Self-respect and a feeling of pride and autonomy, buttressed by awareness of the respect of significant others, are a major source of the courage and fortitude needed to master crisis and privation. These attitudes are eroded if persons involved in life's difficulties, who are naturally upset and confused during their adaptive struggles, are labeled psychiatric or psychological cases, or are categorized as deviants.

Even though the people who affix these labels do so with good intent as a signal that rescue efforts should be focused on the sufferers, and even though the labelers themselves are not intending to stigmatize and dehumanize – in fact, the contrary – many of those who are so labeled, as well as many of the bystanders, will feel that to be a "casualty" or a "case" means to be perceived as weak and ineffectual, and to be expected to fail unless given specialized assistance. This is apt to lead to a self-fulfilling prophecy. If everyone expects a person to be passive and dependent on others, he tends to become so, particularly during crisis when his self-image is in any case confused as he struggles with a predicament that is for the time being beyond his available problem-solving skills, and when he is in a state of increased susceptibility to the influence of significant others.

We must also realize that in wartime or in a similar situation of communal disaster, we helpers have difficulty differentiating our own status from the persons we are helping. We are all potentially in the same boat, and it is difficult to preserve control and poise and not to identify with their helpless and hopeless feelings. This puts a great strain on our capacity to maintain sufficient distance so that we may empathize rather than identify, and to maintain our usual special therapeutic role of objective concern. Categorizing and labeling them is one method of handling our difficulty. By seeing the other person as a "case," we can differentiate him from ourselves, and thus keep ourselves psychologically separate from him so that we do not get infected by his overwhelming feelings of impotence and despair.

We must, however, beware lest in trying to maintain our own professional poise so that we can effectively fulfill the demands of our role, we weaken him by our labeling. If a person is in fact sick and comes for treatment to a physician, we can expect him to pay the price of accepting the patient role with its inevitable label and its attendant weakness and passivity, because in return he can expect to get the rewards of diagnosis and treatment, backed by the traditions and knowledge of the medical profession and its powerful institutions. Accepting the label is, as it were, part of his admission fee, and by the time he comes for treatment he has experienced sufficient discomfort that he may be willing to pay this fee as the price of curing him. We, on our part, accept a commitment to follow through on whatever treatment will be necessary. In contrast, intervention in the life of a fellow citizen whose son, for instance, has been killed in combat and who is naturally distraught and, for a time, incapacitated by grief is a quite different situation – particularly if the intervention is relatively uninvited by him and is carried out by a generalist professional agent of a solicitous community rather than by a staff member of a health care institution where he is a patient. Since there is no physician–patient contract we cannot be sure that he will allow us to follow through on a treatment plan; nor can we ourselves validly accept such a commitment, since the essential prerequisite, his expressed willingness to accept our systematic diagnostic investigation, is also likely to be missing. Under such circumstances we cannot expect to receive our usual fee, including his agreement to accept our professional labeling. Also, we cannot be as sure as if he were a patient that our intervention will help him. We surely intend to do our best for him, despite all the constraints of our lack of knowledge and the absence of a traditionally accepted role, and we hope we may do him some good. But, at least, let us be certain that we do him no harm – and that means that we must avoid labels in our communications with him and with those in his social environment. We must deal with him not as a "problem *case*" but as a "human being with problems."

The labeling problem is less serious if the intervenor is not a physician or some other type of clinician, but a social scientist or an educator, because labels in the latter fields are often less debilitating than those of clinicians; but in my experience, the families of casualties are themselves so aware of their own upset and their difficulty in maintaining psychological and social control, that they are often worried that they may be becoming emotionally disturbed or sick, and are therefore sensitive to any possibly stigmatizing label – as one young widow put it in a newspaper article after the Yom Kippur War, "Do not turn me into a problem! It is true that I am overcome with grief because my husband has been killed. But I am still myself. I am still an ordinary person. I refuse to be changed into a dehumanized category by being called a 'case.' I want people to relate to me as a normal individual and not as a stereotyped 'war widow'."

Use volunteers as intermediaries

Labeling often occurs automatically just because an intervenor who contacts a family carries his own professional label, and everyone assumes that the person he is dealing with must occupy the usual complementary status. Thus if I, as a psychiatrist, visit a family, people will take it for granted that one of the family members is, or may become, my "patient." I can try to persuade people that this is not so or not necessarily so, but I am not likely to succeed if the family I am visiting is manifesting the emotional upset of a crisis. Attempting to hide my professional identity is a hazardous strategem; if it fails, matters will be much worse. The situation is similar, even if less pronounced, with a social worker. Irrespective of her attempts to behave differently from her usual professional mode, many people will take it for granted that the persons she is dealing with are her "cases"; In Israel, for instance, there has been reluctance among families of military casualties to have dealings with social workers from the local welfare offices, lest they be stigmatized as "welfare cases."

In some parts of Israel, psychologists who have for years worked as counselors in school systems have become generally accepted as a part of the educational system that deals with normal people, and they may therefore be in a better position to intervene directly without stigmatizing those they contact. In a culturally heterogeneous population, however, even this may not be uniformly reliable. Certainly, the psychologists of the Adler Institute in Tel Aviv have reported some initial reluctance among bereaved families to participate in discussion groups they have organized, even though these meetings take place in the homes of other bereaved families and not in a clinical setting.

This automatic and inadvertent labeling as deviant is much less likely if the professional who intervenes in the family is a familiar community caregiver, such as a public health nurse, a schoolteacher, a family doctor, a clergyman, or a staff member of a community center. The expected complementary status of the usual clients of such professionals is that of an ordinary person who may be struggling with some life difficulty, but who is likely to master it with a little routine help, guidance, and encouragement. Everyone in the population, and not just the deviants and incompetents, is expected to have dealings with such caregivers from time to time during inevitable life crises or predicaments.

A further step along this parameter is taken if the intervenor is a nonprofessional – a friend or neighbor, or else a member of the community who has volunteered to help those who are suffering because of the universal emergency. The universality of the emergency puts everyone in the same boat in sharing its potential dangers and burdens; not only does the nonprofessional status of these intervenors mean that the people they help are not likely to be automatically assigned some form of weakening client label but it is also likely that the offer of help will be perceived as part of a natural mutual obligation system in which the helper and the helped are bound together as collaborators in jointly facing the national tragedy, rather than the helper giving charity to an unfortunate sufferer out of pity for his individually determined plight. The essential basis of the interaction may be seen as reciprocal – that is, "at this moment you have been the target, so I am obliged to help you; but it is possible that in the future, I will be the target, and then you will equally be obliged to help me. We both can expect this help from each other as a right and not a favor, because we are both members of the same community, all of whom are equally exposed to this tragedy."

During the Yom Kippur War, I was much impressed by the relaxed atmosphere of mutuality that characterized the attitude of many families of casualties toward their volunteer helpers. It was as though the ordinary boundaries of family privacy had opened up, and strangers were temporarily accepted as adopted family members, bound together by kin ties of mutual obligation that were not dependent on individual likes and dislikes. Some volunteers, on the other hand, had a more difficult time accepting this situation. Since they were personally less directly involved in the crisis than the people they were helping, they felt some reluctance to enter what would usually be the private domain of another family. This varied according to ethnic subculture; also, I had the impression that the more a volunteer was involved vicariously in the crisis of a family because, for example, he himself had sons in the front line or had lost a son in a previous war, so that he could identify more easily with the family of the casualty, the less he was likely to feel himself to be a trespasser.

Irrespective of the validity of these conjectures, there is no doubt that my experience during the Yom Kippur War repeatedly demonstrated the value of nonprofessional volunteers as direct intervenors with the families of casualties. And in many places the specialized community intervenors quickly discovered the merits of organizing such volunteers as a network of intermediaries who had direct contact with families under their professional direction. The Adler Institute, for instance, found that bereaved parents opened their doors more freely to nonprofessional volunteers than to psychologists, even those labeled "educational" psychologists, and that once a volunteer had quickly built up a positive relationship with the parents, she[5] had no difficulty bringing them along to a discussion group directed by a psychologist. After the bereaved parents had begun to relate to the other members of the group and also to the psychologist, the volunteer could drop out and the parents would continue to attend on their own.

Obviously, there is also a logistic benefit in organizing a system of nonprofessional volunteers, not only as intermediaries in dealing with the families of casualties but also in fulfilling other wartime community demands. An inevitable aspect of war or natural catastrophe is the likelihood that large numbers of casualties will occur during a short time. No peacetime level of professional resources can be expected to cope directly with the immediate intervention demands. The mobilization, recruitment, and development of a large number of volunteers from the almost inexhaustible pool of the civilian population may therefore fill a service gap that would otherwise be impossible to handle.

Organize mutual help groups and networks

An important goal for an intervenor is to move the families of casualties as quickly as possible from a passive to an active pattern of behavior in dealing with their troubles. During the preliminary phases of reaction to a sudden stress, especially if it is unexpected, passive dependency is a natural response. Afflicted people should be provided with the opportunity to regress and withdraw for a time with impunity into confusion and depression by protecting them and taking over or sharing with them their essential life tasks. The optimal length of this withdrawal period will vary according to subculture and personality as well as to the demands of the life situation.

[5]Because of the wartime situation, most of the volunteers were women.

An intervenor should ensure that the psychological withdrawal does not lead to social isolation, but takes place within the context of increased social nurturance, as long as the latter does not interfere with the sufferer's natural defensive patterns. I will deal with this point later. However, it is equally important that the intervenor ensure that as soon as the family members can bear it, they should begin to mobilize their energies in actively struggling against the painful and frustrating elements of their predicament and return to active social participation.

One way of achieving this is to involve them as soon as possible in joining forces with other persons who have been similarly afflicted in order to help each other, particularly those who are currently in greatest need.

The sufferers thus become helpers and move from the passive victimized role to the active role of mastery, with the added benefit derived from sharing the power of numbers in their organization. Of course, when a family has just experienced a trauma of the type with which we are dealing, it is unrealistic to expect them to start helping others within the first few weeks; but it is possible to build around them a network of expectations that this is the path that they will soon begin to follow – and the best way of starting them thinking along these lines is not by words but by exposing them to role models with whom they may identify. I refer to the intervenor organizing links between the families of casualties and those who previously had a similar experience. Such veterans have a special contribution to make. As indicated earlier, they are likely to feel sufficiently identified with the plight of the newly afflicted that they will have less inhibition than ordinary volunteers about penetrating the usually private domains of other families. They will, by the same token, be more acceptable to the families of casualties.

Veterans will derive special personal benefit from helping someone else deal with a situation that in the past incapacitated them, because by contact and identification with the present-day victim they will reexperience their old suffering, but in an attenuated form and in a situation where their activity consolidates and validates the idea that they have mastered their own fate. As indicated in a previous publication,[6] there is a characteristic pattern of reciprocity between helper and helped in such a situation. Not only can the current sufferers more readily accept help from someone who himself has experienced their predicament without eroding their pride and self-respect as much as if the helper were a volunteer drawn from the less directly involved population, but also they can identify with the veteran who acts as a model demonstrating that mastery of the predicament is realistically feasible. At the same time he communicates nonverbally the merit of the active helping approach.

There are many possible patterns in organizing mutual help contacts between veterans and recently afflicted, as well as among the latter. In some instances, especially in the early days and weeks, a dyadic or small network

[6]Caplan, *Support Systems*, pp. 15-16.

approach is best. Later on, or in certain subcultures almost from the beginning, a group approach is acceptable (for example, the groups organized for war widows and also for bereaved parents by the Adler Institute). Intervenors should freely explore a variety of patterns and discover what seems to work best in the local situation; they should guard against narrowing their options because of cultural preconceptions. For instance, in our Harvard work with civilian widows, we originally took care to build widow-to-widow networks and groups on a homogeneous basis – we tried to match race, religion, and social class, thinking that each of these factors might introduce communication blocks in a heterogeneous dyad, network, or group. As our work progressed, we no longer paid as much attention to this, except for contacts with widows in the earliest stages of bereavement. The psychologists of the Adler Institute, on the other hand, have reported that in their work they have experienced no significant difficulty in stimulating free communication among bereaved families in groups drawn from different ethnic and socioeconomic classes who happen to live in a particular geographic region; the problems and reactions of the families of war casualties seem to have enough of a universal human quality that the shared experience overpowers obstacles to free communication that might exist in other settings.

Support the supporters

This is a crucial element in the mission of a community intervenor. War and natural catastrophe are obviously stressful for everyone and although those who are not directly victimized and who are able to be active in rescuing and nurturing the afflicted are better off than the rest of the population, they too are loaded down with heavy cognitive, emotional, and concrete burdens. The constant intimate involvement with the sufferings of afflicted families involves them in the danger of emotional depletion because of prolonged psychological arousal and possible contagion. Since the helpers are not able to change the reality of the tragedies and can only hope that by their efforts they will to some extent cushion the blow and contribute to a better adjustment, the results of which will only become evident in the future, it is hard for them to judge whether they are doing anything really helpful. So, even well-trained and experienced professionals who are able to work hard and continuously without undue fatigue in their familiar peacetime roles are apt to get tired and dispirited in such wartime work. This is all the more likely if they have close relatives in the front lines and realize that they themselves are in constant danger of joining the ranks of the families of casualties.

These problems of the professional helpers are aggravated by the fact that the emergency usually disorganizes the community institutions, so that the security of normal boundaries,. supervisory structures, role definition, and availability of administrative and technical supports may be reduced. Moreover, war and catastrophe produce novel problems that civilian professionals have usually not been trained to understand and handle. I remember vividly the reply of the chairman of a mental health organization, a highly competent psychiatrist with many years experience as a psychoanalyst, when he was asked by a colleague, during a meeting that was convened to plan emergency services, whether he could provide specific information about the expectable reactions of family members to the news that a relative had been killed in action. He said very honestly, "We psychiatrists are accustomed to dealing with pathology. We really don't know very much about normal people and about the range of expectable reactions in such a situation. Nor can we be sure that the techniques we have found useful with our patients will be helpful and not harmful when applied to ordinary people struggling with personal tragedy."

Many civilian professionals do not have this psychiatrist's insight or ability to admit ignorance. They find out the hard way – and so do the people they are trying to help – that it may not be useful to extrapolate theories and practices from the usually highly skewed samples of their clinical practice to the demands of normal people caught up in a national catastrophe. Whether the awareness of ignorance results from thinking the matter through ahead of time or from the experience of failure, it usually leads to a feeling of helplessness, especially among professionals who are accustomed to basing their operations on clear-cut concepts and techniques validated by science or by their guild traditions.

Nonprofessional volunteers are in a worse situation. Although they are not likely to be unbalanced by finding that old conceptual models and techniques do not work, they enter the helping situation often with pronounced feelings of inferiority. Unless they can base themselves on previous personal experience, they are likely to believe that they completely lack the knowledge and skills to help others deal with so complicated a human tragedy; if they do not begin with this feeling of inferiority, they may quickly develop it as they identify with the sufferings of the afflicted and feel helpless to change their reality-based situation. Moreover, their lack of professional "armor" makes them vulnerable to intense personal involvement in the crisis reactions of the afflicted families, and they may become upset themselves as they share the emotional turmoil.

It follows that the community intervenor must devote particular effort to supporting the supporters, both professional and nonprofessional. In fact, throughout the six weeks I was in Israel during and after the Yom Kippur War, most of my own time was spent on this task. My main approach was to stimulate the convening of meetings, during which I provided the Israeli workers with cognitive guidance and with an opportunity to share their experiences, express their feelings, and support each other.

Basing myself on principles derived from many years of practice by our Harvard group, particularly in the fields of group consultation and crisis intervention, I took care that these meetings should be quite structured and task-oriented. Despite the high level of emotional tension in all concerned, I did not allow discussion to become explicitly abreactive, nor did I accept the role of group psychotherapist by focusing on the personal feelings of an individual participant or making uncovering interpretations about the group. I was, of course, sensitive to the complications of group process and dynamics, but I hardly ever drew attention to these. Rather, I made use of my understanding of what might be going on under the surface in order to maintain the "emotional temperature" of the group within bounds that facilitated our task of increasing our understanding of the reactions of the people we were trying to support and of working out promising ways to help them.

Most of these meetings began with a short presentation by me that was focused on the expectable issues in dealing with the target population. Initially, I built my presentations on my past studies of crisis intervention, and eventually I modified and enriched them on the basis of my own and others' experiences of the Yom Kippur War. My presentation was followed by participants' reports of their own current work. These often took the form of interchanges with me, in which I drew from them examples of the difficulties they had encountered and how they had struggled with them. I then elicited from other group members that they too had faced similar difficulties and we discussed alternative ways of dealing with them. I would usually try to link these issues to my initial conceptual framework and then develop a discussion of a range of options in handling the problems, which I built on the suggestions of group members and on my reports about what other Israeli workers had found valuable.

Since, unlike the chairman of the mental health organization whom I quoted earlier, much of my own research and practice during the last 30 years has focused on the reactions of ordinary people to life stress, I was able to communicate much relevant information about patterns of crisis response and techniques of crisis intervention, particularly techniques that do not demand a highly sophisticated professional training but are of the "human helping-hand" variety, that can be rapidly learned by professionals and nonprofessionals alike. But I had the feeling that an equally important supportive contribution in these groups came from my legitimating, as a high status outsider, what the helpers would in any case have been inclined to do, guided by their human sensitivity and their common sense; I dignified their operations by defining and categorizing them and by linking them with my professional conceptual models.

The director-general of one of the government ministries with which I was involved said to me at the end of my visit, "I hope you won't be insulted, but the other day I told one of my senior officials, 'The merit of Professor Caplan's lectures is that he talks in ordinary understandable language about what most of us would intuitively think of doing in helping a fellow human being in a predicament. But he is a famous professor from Harvard, who has spent a lifetime doing research in this field, so if he advocates these approaches, it gives us more confidence in continuing along these lines.' I believe that if, on the other hand, any of us were to say the same things nobody would pay attention!" I told him that far from being insulted, I felt that he was paying me a great compliment.

Of course, the question arises whether the kind of reassurance to which the director-general was referring, comforting as it may well be to the caregivers, is sufficiently significant in improving the level of their operations to merit all the time and effort involved in the meetings. If that was all that went on, I am not sure the answer would be positive, even though I believe that workers who are not buttressed by this or some similar means are likely to falter in their helping efforts or to embark on what may seem to be more sophisticated clinical types of intervention that may be ineffective, as well as increasing the danger of debilitating labeling. But although I used simple terms and advocated homespun remedies in my lectures, and although I was pleased that the impression I was apparently creating was as reassuring as the director-general reported, I was in fact seriously trying to deepen and broaden the understanding of my audiences, and I was not just telling them that whatever they were doing was fine. I was also increasing their range of options for action, not only by communicating those already known to me but also by behaving as a communication bridge so that they could pool information from other members of their group.

The very convening of those meetings was important, as was my own presence. Even had I said nothing especially insightful, the fact that I had interrupted my affairs in the United States and had come on an emergency basis to Israel to share in their struggle was an important source of support, not only by me as an individual but also as one of their fellow Jews overseas. The feeling of being part of a larger collectivity than just those one sees every day is a powerful source of strength. These meetings also brought helpers together who might otherwise have operated in isolation and thus with less feeling of strength and confidence.

Another contribution that I consider to have been significant was in linking workers from separate institutions and organizations, so that they learned to collaborate in dealing with problems that overlapped professional and institutional domains. This was much easier to accomplish than it would have been in peacetime because the emergency produced a general opening of boundaries and a willingness to work with almost anyone in pursuit of superordinate goals. I had the feeling that much individual and institutional energy was mobilized for the communal good that had previously been misspent on interpersonal, interprofessional, and interjurisdictional conflicts. Of special importance was the building of effective communication between professionals and nonprofessionals. I will deal with this issue later in more detail, but at this point I would just mention that a special feeling of communal solidarity seemed to emerge from meetings where professionals and nonprofessional volunteers met to explore how they might best work together. My own mission vis-à-vis my professional colleagues on such occasions was to act as a role model of a mature professional who was obviously highly respectful of the especially valuable potential contributions of nonprofessionals in our joint venture. On the other hand, in relating to nonprofessionals, I emphasized the importance of effective organizational structure to ensure implementation, follow-through, and feedback, as well as to articulate effectively with the professional caregiving network.

Another issue that my Yom Kippur War experience convinced me to take seriously is that of providing individual helpers with opportunities to see and feel how each of them is fitting in to the total picture of community effort. At 6:00 P.M. each day during the war, I took part in an Emergency Staff meeting at the Jerusalem Municipality. There I heard systematic reports from the heads of city and government units dealing with such essential services as food supply, fuel, transportation, education, health, and sanitation. And there we made plans for immediate action to maintain the life of the city and to bolster its morale. When I first arrived in Jerusalem, Mayor Teddy Kollek somewhat hesitantly asked me if I wanted to attend these meetings. He said I might find them rather boring and a waste of time because they focused mainly on technical matters. In fact, I rapidly discovered that these meetings were the high point of my day, even though it was often difficult to get to them in the blackout from other parts of the city where I was busy with my discussion groups. The Emergency Staff meetings gave all of us a daily picture of the ongoing life and problems of the city, of how different services meshed with each other, and of how the operations of each of us contributed to the total effort. A spirit of comradeship pervaded our deliberations; in many years as a consultant I have never experienced the attentiveness and the receptivity that I enjoyed on the occasions that I made some small contribution to the proceedings when we discussed such issues as morale, the organization of volunteers, or our services for families of casualties. In my own subsequent meetings with professional and nonprofessional caregivers, I reported what was happening in our Emergency Staff; I was thus able to share with many others an overview of the pattern of our total community effort, so that each caregiver could see his own work in perspective.

Another means of achieving this goal was by convening gatherings of representatives of different caregiving units, departments, or organizations, such as the council of social agencies and joint meetings of education, welfare, health, and mental health units, or of public health and welfare workers in the different regions of the city. The ostensible reason for these meetings was for me to give a lecture about some aspect of the emergency; but the main goal, and I felt that it was often achieved, was that each participant should gain a concrete picture of the larger whole of which he was an integral part, and that he should carry this message back to his home unit.

In addition to my work as a convenor, educator, and consultant to groups and organizations, I spent some time offering consultation to individual caregivers and to such small caregiving units as public health, social work, and guidance teams in schools who were dealing with some special problem in a client that was linked with the wartime situation. And on occasion I personally intervened in sample cases, as part of my consultation efforts, and in order to collect firsthand material for my lectures. In retrospect, I am surprised at how little demand there was for individual consultation and intervention, even though I had let it be widely known that I was always available for this purpose. Many individuals talked to me briefly about their work predicaments before or after meetings, as always happens; but it seems that the wartime situation evoked a group response rather than an individual response – and certainly this was in line with my own philosophical bias.

I have discussed supporting the supporters on the basis of my own experience during October-November, 1973. I believe that despite idiosyncratic elements linked with my personality and background and with the local situation during the Yom Kippur War, the picture I have painted has general validity. I hope I may be excused if I end this section on an even more personal note, which may also have general validity. Who supports the supporters of the supporters? In my case, I came to Israel without a team of fellow intervenors who can usually be expected to support each other. I obtained some support from the city and government officials, with whom I worked most closely in organizing lectures, and from members of the Emergency Staff. But my main support came from the feedback from the caregivers with whom I was dealing. During those six weeks, I probably worked harder than at any previous time in my life; and although, of course, I usually felt tired at the end of a long day of meetings, I really did not experience undue fatigue. I believe the reason was that the tension aroused in me, as it was in everyone else in Israel, because of our concern for the existence and well-being of the state and for the casualties and their families, was continually being dissipated by my great activity, which I felt was productive and helpful in mastering the crisis. My feeling that I was being productive was validated by the response of the caregivers with whom I was talking. The warmth of their acceptance of my contribution was an important personal reward. Just before I left, I said to one of my sponsors who was expressing gratitude and also apologizing for working me so hard, "You don't have to thank me. I have to thank you for giving me such an opportunity to serve. What we have done together has been important, and I feel that it has been my great privilege to have been allowed to participate. The harder I worked, the bigger was my reward." Those words were spoken in complete sincerity. On the other hand, since I am using my own case as a vehicle to improve our knowledge of generally applicable principles of intervention in stress situations, I must also record that although I returned from my visit to Israel with a deep feeling of personal satisfaction and psychological mastery I lost eight pounds in weight during the six weeks; five days after my return home I developed a streptococcal infection of my throat which put me to bed with a high temperature for a couple of weeks – a more severe illness than I have had in many years. So it seems that without being at all aware of it, I had been seriously depleting my somatic reserves during the emergency. This raises some important questions regarding pacing of intervenor efforts during wartime and the need to work out hygienic rules for adequate rest periods or "tours of operation" for civilian supportive workers just as for combatant personnel. And once again we are reminded that the arousal and release of emotional energy carries a somatic price even if the excitement is subjectively felt to be satisfying and to lead to mastery.

Specific Intervention

Families of fallen soldiers

Notification of death. There is no perfect way of bringing such bad news, but it is worth trying not to make matters worse. The Israeli Army's current practice is not altogether free from the latter hazard. A death notification is supposed to be made by a soldier in dress uniform who has a similar rank to the casualty and who reads the official notice in a ceremonial way to the family in their own home. He must, wherever possible, be accompanied by the family's doctor or some other neighborhood physician, usually from Kupat Cholim (the Workers Sick Fund), and by a mental health professional. There is a special notification staff who operate out of the office of the Town Major, the officer in charge of army personnel movements and records for the area. The reason for the physician is that during the Six Day War, a few people died of coronary thrombosis or stroke when they received the news; so the physician, who is supposed to examine the medical records of family members beforehand to see whether anyone has a history of cardiovascular or other major disease which would increase vulnerability, is present to provide whatever emergency treatment might be immediately necessary to prevent serious medical complications. The mental health worker attends in order to deal with possible adverse psychological reactions to the shock.

Certainly, the idea of a formal notification ceremony by a uniformed soldier, who salutes and then stands at attention while reading the death notice, may be an appropriate way of demonstrating the respect of the army and the nation for the casualty and his relatives; it is probably appreciated by some families, particularly those with a tradition of national service that includes army experience in previous wars. It may also be supportive to many other people in that moment of shock to have the imposed structure of a standardized and dignified ceremony. But to some Israelis, the ceremony may be seen as cold and unfeeling rather than helpful; the sight of a strange soldier in dress uniform, accompanied by a doctor and a psychologist, moving up a street where almost every family has one or more members at the front is likely to strike terror into the hearts of everyone, lest the procession should be en route to their address. In Jerusalem, and I imagine it happened elsewhere too, the army regulations were quickly modified in practice to conform with the usual human situation. The Town Major's staff visited the stricken families in civilian clothes, or in army fatigue uniform that was inconspicuous, and they made their announcements in an informal way which they individualized in accordance with the character of the people they were visiting.

The communication of such evil tidings with human sympathy in case after case placed a great strain on the Town Major's notification staff; their capacity to gear their operations to the needs of family members of different subcultures and remain warm and supportive instead of protecting themselves by becoming cold, unfeeling, and withdrawn depended on the morale of their own group. The Jerusalem group bitterly named themselves "The Angels of Death," and some of them voiced concern that people would recognize them in the street and turn away from them because of their grisly task. A few tried to relieve the strain of their role by frequently indulging in gallows humor in talking to each other. The Town Major's medical officer, who sometimes accompanied the group on their rounds, did an excellent job in supporting them by convening frequent staff meetings to discuss their impressions of the needs of families. He also arranged discussion groups with a volunteer psychologist; but this project quickly lapsed due to the resistance of the notification staff to confront and analyze their feelings about their burdensome work, probably because they felt this would endanger their defenses.

The most promising way of ensuring the maintenance of warmth and sensitivity among members of such a death notification squad is to make it easy for those who cannot bear the job to move on to other duties without loss of face, and to arrange for frequent rest periods, both routine and in response to signs of individual strain. Candidates for this task, like those for such other intensely burdensome roles as burial details or hunting for corpses on the battlefields, should be chosen from those with strong religious or other ideological commitments. However much external support is provided, these men are likely to need a good deal of internalized support, buttressed by continuing contacts with a powerful reference group, in order to maintain their motivation and humanitarian effectiveness.

Although I do not have much to suggest in improving the operations of the Town Major's staff in handling their inescapable difficulties, I certainly applaud the policy of the Israeli Army in delivering death notices personally to the family in its own home, rather than sending them by mail or telegraph as is the custom in some other countries. But I do have serious reservations about the Israeli arrangement that a physician and a mental health specialist should be a routine part of the notification team.

I think it is a good plan for the Town Major's staff, before they make their home visit, to talk with the family doctor on the basis of a review of his medical records. Such a discussion provides important details about the family that enables the group to individualize their approach. It also provides an opportunity to contact other potentially helpful local caregivers, such as the public health nurse, the neighborhood rabbi, and school personnel. They can also plan the notification visit at a time when the entire family is likely to be at home, or perhaps circumspectly to break the news first to some supportive members of the extended family so they can arrange to be there. On one occasion, for instance, I was present when the Town Major's officer, who had ascertained from the family doctor that the dead soldier's mother had a severe heart condition, broke the news first to her husband at his work place, contacted her brother and an older daughter, and then collected them all in his automobile and took them to their home to inform the mother.

I also approve of the physician being present in the small proportion of cases where a family member has a medical history of increased vulnerability. But to bring a physician in routinely, especially a doctor who probably has had no prior opportunity to learn what he is expected to do, since he has been contacted on an emergency basis without previous briefing, involves the risk of possible medical activity that may be harmful. A doctor who takes time out of his busy day to go with the Town Major's officer will probably feel called upon to do something active for a family member in order to justify his presence, and not just to stand passively by in case some medical emergency should occur – a rare eventuality. In Jerusalem, what many physicians tended to do was to take along a hypodermic syringe loaded with a powerful sedative or tranquilizer, and as soon as the announcement had been made and one or more family members had reacted with a dramatic emotional outburst, the doctor would give them an injection and put them to sleep. This appeared on the surface to be a valuable medical contribution, and by interrupting a screaming fit it was apt to exert a calming effect on the other family members, and almost certainly on the Town Major's officer and on some inexperienced mental health workers, who might themselves be disturbed by the intensity of the "hysterical" reaction.

Other mental health workers, and I agree with these, complained that the doctors were "too quick on the draw" with their hypodermics; before a bereaved wife or parent could clearly appreciate the tragedy and begin to react to its immediate impact, they were rendered unconscious. Moreover, when they awoke after the effect of the drug had begun to wear off, their capacity to grapple with their crisis was usually reduced because of residual symptoms of the sedation. If these difficulties were then dealt with by further drugging, the adjustment of the bereaved was likely to be significantly hampered. Chemical insults were being added to the injury of their tragedy and were interfering with their natural psychological and social adaptive mechanisms.

I discussed this problem with the Jerusalem Town Major's medical officer. He agreed that many physicians were operating along these lines. He believed that this was partly based on their not having a professional definition of their role in that situation, and possibly in some cases on a wish to retreat quickly and gracefully from what was for them, too, a harrowing scene. On the other hand, he emphasized the difficulty of his doing anything effective about it because doctors in Israel (as elsewhere) are rather sensitive about outside interference in their treatment of their patients. They would certainly not be likely to listen to the suggestions of the notification staff or the psychologists – mere laymen – and he himself could not hope to offer guidance to the total population of general practitioners in Jerusalem, which he would need to do in order to reach those many doctors who might be called in to participate in the death notifications. He also pointed out on the basis of his own experience in many notifications, that in several subcultures it was expected behavior for a widow and bereaved parents to wail, scream, tear their hair, and throw their bodies about dramatically as a sign that they really loved the dead person. After such behavior had continued for some time, the bereaved began to feel exhausted and, left to themselves, they would have quietened down and regained control; but they could not do this lest their friends and neighbors blame them for demonstrating a lack of proper feeling. At such times a doctor's pill or injection could legitimate the bereaved person's withdrawal into a quiescent state because he would be defined as a patient who had received therapy. The dose of tranquilizer or sedative could be quite low, since it operated mainly on the symbolic plane. So, clearly, it would not be valuable to advise doctors not to use drugs as a general rule, even if they would be willing to pay attention to such advice.

The medical officer suggested that I might write an article in an Israeli medical journal to guide physicians on how to deal with death notification situations; whether or not this would be an adequate mode of communication to those who might most profit from it, it was clear that this was not a plan that would lead to early results. Nor did we think we could persuade busy Jerusalem doctors to come to a meeting with me to discuss the issue. Eventually, we decided that the medical officer should, in the name of the Town Major, produce a one-page list of guidelines to be distributed to every Jerusalem physician and also be handed out by the notification staff whenever they invited a doctor to go with them on a home visit. The notice would define the doctor's main function as the prevention of cardiovascular and other serious complications of psychological shock; would emphasize the rarity of such reactions; and offer guidelines for the use of tranquilizers and sedative drugs – including warning against premature injections of large doses of sedatives and recommending the prescription of small amounts of tranquilizers on demand to prevent exhaustion, as well as a mild sedative for a few nights to help the bereaved get some sleep. The notice, as a whole, should encourage physicians to keep their pharmacological intervention to a minimum so as not to interfere with the natural defenses of the bereaved and their supportive network. I hope this notice improved matters, but I have no follow-up data to validate it. On the whole, I feel that it would be better to change Israeli Army policy so that it would require a physician to go to the home with the notification staff only when his medical records contain information indicating a significant danger of a serious bodily complication, and in other cases for the doctor to be prepared to dispense a mild tranquilizer or sedative if a family member comes to his office and asks for such help.

From my previous discussion of labeling, it will be clear that I am quite opposed to the routine presence of a mental health specialist on the notification team. Irrespective of what such a worker may do, his presence implies the expectation that the emotional upheaval of family members may be, or may become, a form of mental disorder, instead of being a completely natural human response to an unnatural event. Moreover, the likelihood of a clinical diagnostic label being wrongly attached to a family member's normal reaction of crisis upset is increased in the case of ethnic subcultural groups with whose norms the mental health specialist may not be familiar. Behavioral reaction patterns to the impact of stress, which most people are inclined to believe to be either universal or molded by idiosyncracies of an individual's personality and experience are in fact powerfully molded by his subculture and are promoted and maintained by reciprocal reactions and expectations of his immediate social milieu. The range of patterns is great, from the sophisticated Western European, who is likely to receive the bad news with apparent unfeeling coldness and behavioral control, to the Easterner who rolls frenziedly on the floor, shrieking and tearing out his hair in handfuls. There are probably underlying similarities in all cases, namely a conscious and unconscious attempt to ward off the realization of the calamity by confusion, cognitive clouding, feelings of unreality, denial, etc., but the details of how this is accomplished vary widely. As long as the afflicted person receives the news within his own cultural group, everyone around will understand his reactive behavior and will foster it and protect him. If his self-damaging efforts involve real danger, for example, if he not only tears his hair and scratches his face but tries to enucleate an eye or jump out of a window, the bystanders will stop him; and if he bangs himself on the furniture too much as he thrashes about on the floor, someone will hold him down for a while.

It is therefore important to ensure that the bad news is communicated in the presence of a group of supporters of the same subculture; I would like to see the Israeli Army's regulations changed to replace the physician and the mental health specialist by some local formal or informal leader, such as the neighborhood rabbi or one of the community elders or wise men, who would be likely to convene an appropriate supportive group of neighbors and "landsmen," and who could also be relied on to contact a physician or the Emergency Center of the local authority if they identified signs of deviancy indicating the need for specialist intervention.

Another reason for my opposition to the routine presence of a mental health worker, particularly one without training and experience in crisis intervention, is that during the expectable confusion and upset of the initial reaction to the death notification, relatives are usually incapable of assimilating verbal communications, expecially those coming from a stranger who is not familiar with their semantic framework. At such times the messages that have a chance of getting through to them are mainly communicated by the behavioral nonverbal patterns of those around, by concrete familiar words, by tone of voice, and by bodily contact. I have been present when well-meaning mental health clinicians, accustomed to the verbal mode of abstract communication in their psychotherapy and counseling of middle-class psychoneurotic Western patients, have attempted to "reason" with family members who appeared to be reacting irrationally to the shock of the bad news. Their communications just did not get through. I do not think they did harm, but the obvious frustration of the clinician certainly did not improve the already tense atmosphere; in view of the great need during the emergency for constructive work by all the human relations specialists of the community, I felt that the mental health worker could have been more productively occupied somewhere else.

Help with adjustment to bereavement. This is a vast subject on which several books have already been written, some of them by our Harvard group; and I do not have space here even to summarize the core issues. I will therefore deal only with a few points that have special significance in the wartime situation, particularly those that came to my attention during my Jerusalem visit.

Support during the initial stages of bereavement was usually adequately supplied by the extended family, friends, neighbors, and the local community, especially if the bereaved were religious and followed traditionally prescribed mourning rituals and practices. In such cases, there was rarely any need for specially organized intervention.

In the case of some newcomers to Jerusalem, or others who had little prior contact with the people of their neighborhood, and in the case of nonreligious families who did not adhere to standardized mourning practices which prescribe supportive behavior by others in the form of condolence calls, participation in prayers during the Shiva[7] and first year of mourning, etc., it was important to be particularly careful in ensuring adequate monitoring and not infrequently to organize neighbors and community caregivers to come in and help.

Our Jerusalem Emergency Staff instituted an effective service along these lines. We organized teams, consisting of a recognized community leader (usually a member of the City Council), the neighborhood rabbi, and a municipal official, who paid a formal condolence call on every bereaved family at least once during the first days of its Shiva, or its equivalent in nonreligious homes. They expressed the sorrow and support of the Mayor and the City Fathers, and they offered to arrange for whatever help the family might feel it needed. The teams routinely reported back to our Emergency Staff headquarters, where I and a core staff of the social work department debriefed them and recorded indications for further intervention. On the basis of this information, we organized emergency medical, social work, and volunteer assistance, and we also reported urgent special needs to the Rehabilitation Department of the Ministry of Defense that is responsible for the continued handling of all cases, but whose workers were so loaded down in meeting the heavy demand of the emergency period that they often could not systematically make initial contact with bereaved families until several days later.

In many cases, the acute needs that demanded emergency intervention were not primarily related to the bereavement; they involved medical, economic, or housing problems of family members – especially of children or aged relatives – that had antedated the tragedy, but had been precariously kept under control in the past. The bereavement upset this uneasy equilibrium, and it brought the family's urgent needs to our attention and led to an increase in priority in regard, for example, to the institutional placement of a retarded child, medical care of a grandfather, admission of a child to a day-care center, or provision of a homemaker to free the mother to get treatment for a chronic medical difficulty. In the case of young widows with many children, we not infrequently provided lay volunteers to take over the care of the children for part of the day so as to give the mother a rest. And the pressure of the increased salience of the general demand for child care led us to organize several new day-care centers and kindergartens, at first staffed by lay volunteers and later continued on a more professional basis.

The main task of dealing systematically with the continuing social, educational, and psychological needs of the bereaved was entrusted by the Israeli Government to the Rehabilitation Department of the Ministry of Defense. In peacetime, this unit had a skeleton staff that dealt with disabled veterans of former wars and with war widows, orphans, and bereaved

[7]Shiva is the name given to the first seven days of deep mourning prescribed by the Jewish religion; the mourners sit at home and are continually visited by friends and neighbors.

parents. The pressure of work in the Yom Kippur War led to the recruitment of a large additional staff of volunteer social work and mental health professionals and lay helpers, who worked under the supervision of the core staff of the department, which was gradually enlarged over the following year. I acted as consultant to the Director of the Rehabilitation Department and to his headquarters staff in Tel Aviv. In particular, I advised them to recruit core staff and temporary professional volunteers on a part-time basis of 2 days service a week and not fulltime, both to lighten the emotional load on each worker and to ensure integration with local caregiving systems where workers would be employed for the rest of the work week. I emphasized the need for adequate technical supervision and in-service training of workers drawn from ordinary social work and mental health practice in regard to the very special needs of normal bereaved people, and in particular the avoidance of routinely labeling them as disturbed. And I also emphasized that adjustment to bereavement, although characterized by a number of acute crises, is usually a long, drawn-out process, the major problems of which take at least 2 or 3 years to resolve; which means that follow-up monitoring and intermittent intervention demands the continuing availability of a large staff. Since a small country such as Israel has only limited professional resources, the latter issue implies the recruitment and deployment of lay volunteers on a large scale, in order to be able to satisfy anticipated service demands.

In addition to issues raised elsewhere in this chapter, I found that in training and consultation sessions that I conducted for the staffs of Rehabilitation Department units and other professional caregivers dealing with the bereaved, the main point to which I returned time and again was that we must respect the native patterns and timetables of the adjustment process in the people we are trying to help, and we must not force them to conform to our preconceptions of what constitutes "healthy grief work." In the past, specialists such as Erich Lindemann and the psychoanalytic investigators of the bereavement process, myself included, had written about the normal mourning process in what we today realize to have been an oversimplified way. Our recent Harvard research,[8] for instance, has shown a wide variation in the ways widows handle the expectable problems of the first year of mourning which all correlate with a healthy outcome. Open expression of feeling, the amount of weeping, willingness to focus on the irrevocable reality of the loss, for instance, have proved not to differentiate widows who eventually adjusted well psychologically and socially from those who did not. Even signs such as continuing awareness of the presence of the dead spouse and imaginary conversations with him, which indicate denial of the reality of his death, have turned out not to be predictive of a poor outcome.

So my advice was that we should not interfere with defensive behavior

[8]I. Glick, R. S. Weiss, and C. M. Parkes, *First Year of Bereavement* (New York: Wiley-Interscience), 1975.

that the bereaved were utilizing to keep the level of their confrontation of their problems to a bearable intensity, if the defensive pattern was idiosyncratic and even more so if it seemed to be culturally determined. Rather, we should adopt a nonspecific supportive approach; offer what help the bereaved requested; and wait patiently in suspicious cases until we saw signs of real pathology before deciding on therapeutic intervention. The important point was to maintain contact and a trusting relationship with the caregiver, offer help on concrete issues, and ensure continued links between the bereaved person and his social surround.

I found one major difference between the psychological situation of those bereaved by war and the civilian cases that have been the subject of our past bereavement studies. In the peacetime situation, the mourners are usually preoccupied in the early weeks with repetitive memories of deathbed and funeral scenes. Details of the last illness, of what the corpse looked like, of their interaction with the doctors and nurses, and the like, form the basis of ruminations that are usually burdensome but nevertheless provide a concrete structure for the working out of the bereaved's turmoil, and eventually for coming to terms with negative feelings. Our studies have shown that despite the added psychological and physical burdens of nursing the deceased in his last illness, such personal involvement seemed to give an advantage to mourners who had this experience that was absent among widows whose husbands had been killed when they were on their own in some distant place in a road or plane accident. On the other hand, even in those cases, there were usually memories of the corpse being brought home, and of the funeral, which could act as a concrete personal reference point in initially trying to come to terms with the catastrophe. The relatives of battlefield casualties are usually in a worse situation. They have no personal experience of the event, nor can they have direct contact with the corpse. When they get the news they usually get no reliable information about what happened, nor can they go to where the body is. They have to fill in the details with fantasy – and this is not only productive of self-torture but also deprives them of the concreteness and certainty that usually act as an anchor point in trying to come to terms with unacceptable reality.

During the Yom Kippur War, the bodies of fallen soldiers were immediately buried in military cemeteries close to the battlefronts. Notification of the family did not take place until several days later and included minimal details about the circumstances of the death. The fact that the absence of these details would be particularly burdensome to the family was intuitively recognized by the casualty's army friends and officers; in many cases members of his unit, who were present when he was killed, took time off as soon as possible to visit the family and describe what had happened. Junior officers, who in the Israeli Army are often particularly close to their men, seemed, in my experience, to spend most of their available leave time during the first few weeks after the fighting stopped in visits to the families of casualties.

In the absence of such eyewitness reports, widows and bereaved parents not infrequently continued for weeks, and sometimes months, to doubt the truth of the notification of death. They clung to the hope that there had been some mistake and that their loved one had been taken prisoner and had not been killed. In certain pathetic cases, a bereaved father would travel to his son's unit, and even to the battlefront, to search for him, or at least to look for eyewitnesses. In some instance, matters were made worse because well-meaning but foolish members of a casualty's unit who became aware that he was missing, but who had not been present when he was killed, would phone his family to reassure them that they had seen him alive and well after the date when the army authorities said he had been killed. Sometimes this happened quite innocently, because soldiers at the front who could not get to a telephone would often ask a buddy who was moving to the rear to telephone their family and tell them that all was well. Because of the unaccustomed disorganization of the battlefront in the early days of the war, and the normal difficulties of telephone communication in Israel, messages often were delayed, and when the soldier eventually managed to reach a phone that worked and to call the list of wives and parents of his friends, he might easily make a mistake in the date when he had received a particular message.

In view of these phenomena, it became a high priority matter for every supportive group to try to make sure that as soon as possible there should be a communication link between the bereaved and eyewitnesses of the death. In addition, it became an issue of great importance that families should visit the temporary military cemeteries where the war dead were initially buried. The Army understood the significance of this and made arrangements for such visits about a month after the war. Our Emergency Staff, as one of its last acts before disbanding, organized transportation for the bereaved families to the burial places. I tried hard to arrange that each family should travel separately, accompanied in one or two taxis by close friends and community representatives, so that they might have some privacy and individual assistance in their mourning, but it proved logistically impossible to organize the visits that way. Instead, the families, together with community caregivers, such as neighborhood rabbis, city leaders, and representative officials, traveled in a procession of buses. This was a harrowing experience for all concerned, particularly because of the propinquity of disparate subcultures, so that those whose traditions prescribed demonstrative wailing traveled side by side with those whose culture demanded a stiff upper lip and behavioral control.

And yet with all its burdens and sociocultural complications, this visit to the military cemetery was probably psychologically useful to most mourners – certainly many of those with whom I had direct or indirect contact reported an easing of their tension after the event.

Another opportunity for a kind of personal involvement with the deceased and with the concrete reality of his death came 10 months later when the corpses were moved from the distant burial grounds to cemeteries close to the homes of the bereaved families. It is interesting that the Army initially proposed that this reburial should be quietly organized by night as a crash program, and only afterwards would families and friends be invited to individual or collective ceremonies at the final gravesides. This plan was apparently rejected by representatives of the bereaved families, who demanded that each corpse should be transported separately and should be reburied in an individual funeral. This was what happened. For weeks, during August and September, 1974, burial parties in separate command cars, each carrying a coffin with a guard of honor, could be seen on the main roads of the country transporting the more than 2500 bodies to their hometown military cemeteries. Each day the newspapers carried funeral announcements for the individual casualties. And each day several separate funerals took place. I attended one in Jerusalem and found myself among several hundred mourners in a simple, dignified, and moving ceremony during which the main eulogies were given by a military chaplain and by a fellow officer of the dead man, who spoke in the names of his army friends, and who described how the deceased had lived and died. I had not known the man personally but went to the funeral with my wife because we are old friends of the bereaved parents. It was interesting to me that although we did not talk to our friends at their son's graveside because so many people were clustered around them, when I happened to meet them in the street a few days later, they thanked me most sincerely for coming to the funeral; so it seems that they were intensely aware of every one of the hundreds of their well-wishers who had been present and from whose presence they appeared to have derived some strength and consolation in their tragedy.

Many people have condemned this reburial program because they feel it added a further unnecessary burden to the heavy load of the bereaved families, coming as it did before the Yahrzeit, when, in any case, anniversary reactions would be expected to turn the iron once more in the wounds. But in the light of the foregoing, I feel that it was a valuable aid to healthy mourning, and I have so far heard no reports of unfavorable effects.

Problems with young children were a frequent cause of concern for war widows, as they usually are for widows in general. In many of my discussions with caregivers, I was asked for advice in this area, and I urged active guidance for widows, for child-care workers, and for school personnel in helping them provide a supportive environment for the children whose fathers had been killed. Widows often needed help in choosing the right words to tell their children about the tragedy in terms that were geared to the child's age. Mothers, as well as child-care workers and teachers, were frequently upset because children did not seem to appreciate what had happened, used excessive denial, and behaved unfeelingly; they felt that the children should be mourning more openly and actively. Some of the adults were taken aback when younger children persisted in asking when daddy would be coming home as though they believed that he was still alive. And, at the opposite pole, some mothers who were trying hard to maintain emotional control were upset when their own defenses were endangered by a child's persistent weeping, loss of appetite, enuresis, night terrors, excessive clinging, and continuing laments for the dead father.

I advocated that at least one of the local caregivers such as a public health nurse, a social worker, or a pediatrician should offer ongoing counseling and supervision to every widow with young children, which should include being available on demand to deal with her questions about intercurrent crises. I also emphasized the importance of trying to mobilize the help of a male relative to support the mother, especially in dealing with older sons; if such a relative was not available, to recruit a male volunteer who might act as a "big brother," a "proxy uncle," or a "proxy grandfather."

Teachers needed guidance on how to deal with the child whose father had been killed, both during Shiva and after return to school. I suggested involving the other children in the class by having some of them visit during the Shiva or by the class sending a letter of condolence, and by taking steps to make the bereaved child feel welcome when he returned. It was important both to extend consolation, love, and sympathy, but also to expect that the child would be reabsorbed into the ordinary educational framework and not continue to be singled out for dependency-inducing coddling, or separate himself into some stereotyped "orphan-victim" category.

I also helped teachers understand the importance of allowing children to move at their own pace in coming to terms with their bereavement, and not trying to force them to give up their defenses of denial and evasion until they felt ready to do so. The goal of the teacher should be to maintain a nurturing relationship with the child and to give him the opportunity to come easily to talk about his sorrow if he felt like it but not to press him. It was also important for the teacher to initiate visits to the mother and to keep her informed about how the child was performing in class, as well as learn how he was behaving at home. Only if there were clear indications of incapacity, such as deterioration in learning or social alienation, should the school nurse, doctor, or mental health worker be called in – and then only for a discussion with the teachers about the child in the first instance, rather than referring the child in person for special investigation that would entail the risk of labeling him as sick.

I conducted some of the educational and consultation discussions with school personnel myself, but my main thrust was to distribute this function so that such discussions were organized on a school, regional, or neighborhood basis by the school psychologists and the other mental health workers of the community. I felt that it was in this arena rather than in routinely visiting homes with the Town Major's notification staff or with the Ministry of Defense rehabilitation teams, that the mental health specialists could make their most valuable contributions; I constantly urged that, wherever feasible, the specialist should deal with a widow and her children indirectly, namely through the intermediation of those caregivers with whom the latter were regularly in contact – nurses in well baby clinics and schools, kindergarteners, teachers, school social workers, pediatricians, and family doctors. The goal should be that all community agencies and professionals who might have contact with a war widow and her children should pool their information about them and work together in being sensitive to, and satisfying, their changing needs during the initial mourning and later adjustment phases. The mental health specialists should stimulate this coordination by contributing information about expectable problems in the reactions of a mother and her children to the death of the father, and should make themselves available as consultants whenever they might be required, to help the other caregivers deal with whatever difficulties might occur as the process unfolded.

Families of soldiers missing in action

Of all the categories of casualties, this turned out, not unexpectedly, to be the most harrowing to families. In the early stages of the war, matters were made worse because Israel had had no previous large-scale experience of losing trace of its soldiers in battle; the country is small, and in past wars either the Army was advancing, or if a unit happened to be overrun there would usually be survivors who could report what had happened. On this occasion, especially on the Suez Canal, almost the whole line was initially engulfed, and communication was interrupted for days, so that entire units disappeared practically without trace.

Because of the unprecedented nature of this situation, the Army and the Ministry of Defense had no established policies regarding spheres of responsibility in handling the problems of the families; this led to understandable administrative confusion and delays in notifying families. Eventually, procedures were worked out: notification was done by the Town Major's staff just as for those killed in action, and continuing care of the families was allotted to the Rehabilitation Department of the Ministry of Defense. In Jerusalem, our Emergency Staff dealt with the families of these cases along lines similar to the families of those who had been killed.

The initial administrative confusion aggravated the dominant issue in this group – the torture of uncertainty in the minds of relatives. They did not know whether their loved ones were dead or prisoners of war, with all the horrible possibilities of the latter situation considering the savage customs of the Arabs. Also they had no religious or culturally based traditions of how they should behave, nor did their friends and neighbors know how to behave toward them. Some families tried to escape the torture of uncertainty by deciding that their relative had been killed and by beginning actively to mourn him – but their religion did not permit them to sit Shiva nor would their social surround allow this. Some families tried the opposite escape route of saying that they were certain that he was a prisoner of war; they roamed the country and combed the hospitals searching for someone from his unit who would corroborate this. The Egyptians and the Syrians, as part of an organized campaign of psychological warfare, or just because of their traditional approach, refused to publish names of their prisoners of war or to give lists to the International Red Cross; but they frequently paraded prisoners at triumphal press conferences or television programs, and photographs of individuals and groups therefore began to appear in Arab and international newspapers. This provided further material for the searchings of relatives.

In a basement office in Tel Aviv, some of the families of the MIAs organized exhibitions of these photographs of prisoners of war; this room was constantly thronged by distraught relatives searching for evidence that their loved one was alive. One evening, an Israeli television program showed some scenes of this place; in one episode two women could be seen fighting with each other about the identity of a prisoner, half of whose face was portrayed in a particularly vague photograph that could barely be deciphered with a magnifying glass. One woman was sure that it was her brother because he appeared the correct height; the other woman was equally convinced that it was her husband because of the shape of his jaw and the tilt of his cap. They almost came to blows.

We did our best to help in this agonizing situation, by urging the families of MIAs to stay at home initially and not tire themselves out by urgent searchings that most probably would be fruitless, while at the same time we tried to link them quickly via the Town Major's office and other communication channels to the missing man's unit in order to obtain possible authentic information. We also mobilized local caregivers, particularly the rabbi, and community leaders, friends, and neighbors to visit the family in its home – a watered-down functional equivalent of Shiva behavior – so as to provide continual social interaction as a framework for them to talk over their concerns, ventilate their feelings, and whenever possible, distract their attention by talking about other matters. After the initial shock was over, we encouraged productive activity among families by linking them with others in the same boat to develop mutual help groups that campaigned for better organized search programs.

The Army and the Ministry of Defense responded by establishing a central search service that monitored all possible sources of information about prisoners of war and accumulated its own complete collection of photographs from newspapers and television programs, which it compared systematically with photographs of the MIAs.

Mercifully, the turmoil of the families of MIAs in Israel did not last as long as in the United States during the Vietnam War; after a couple of months the truth was revealed in most cases, although 18 months later, 56 bodies of soldiers, believed killed in action but not finally accounted for, have still not been recovered on the Suez front. I hope that all the families of these men are continuing to be actively supported by their relatives, friends, and neighbors, and by the caregivers of their local communities. I also hope that most of them are members of mutual help groups that to some extent combat their feelings of helplessness by providing ongoing mutual support and by concerted action in collaborating with governmental authorities in conducting investigations and maintaining international pressure on the Arabs to permit searches of the battlefields that may uncover possible traces of the missing.

Families of prisoners of war

Many families graduated into this category after passing through the purgatory of MIA. Some families were relatively "lucky" – they were quickly informed by the Town Major's staff that their relative had been taken prisoner. Some families initially received no official notification from the Army, but began to suspect that something was wrong when the man's communications from the battlefront ceased and neither he nor any of his friends telephoned or wrote to them; their reaction was to haunt the Town Major's office or try to communicate directly with the man's unit in order to seek information. Since the Town Major had a limited staff and rather cramped office space geared to peacetime demands, the sudden pressure of frantic families trying to ascertain the fate of their relatives during the confusion of war was particularly burdensome, both administratively and emotionally. If this burden resulted in lowering efficiency, it would not help in providing answers to the questions of the families, even in cases where valid information might be obtainable.

One of the most important contributions of the Jerusalem Mental Health Association during the war was to organize rosters of volunteers, both professional and lay people, who spent their time in the waiting rooms and offices of the Town Major's department and helped his staff deal sympathetically, patiently, and effectively with these families. This was a situation where the fact that the volunteer happened to be a mental health clinician was no drawback – he was obviously operating vis-à-vis the family members not in his professional role but as a public-spirited citizen to help out the Town Major's staff, who were shorthanded in coping with the extra load of information seekers. And vis-à-vis the Army personnel, the professional status of the volunteer helped quickly build a collaborative relationship of trust and respect so that the burden of the work could be shared more easily.

As soon as a family found out for certain, or almost for certain, that their relative was a prisoner of war, a new phase in their ordeal began. They now had to try and discover where he was and if he had been wounded or not. They also began, quite naturally, to imagine what his life was like in an Arab prisoner-of-war camp, and to be burdened by fears that he was being tortured or otherwise ill-treated. Those whose relative was a prisoner of the Egyptians felt a little better than if he had fallen into the hands of the Syrians, particularly after it was discovered that the Syrians had tortured to death and mutilated a group of Israeli soldiers they had captured on the Golan. But even the families of POWs in Egypt could not feel tranquil because they were certain that the Egyptians, too, would not abide by the rules of the Geneva Convention, as evidenced in the early weeks by their refusal to give lists to the International Red Cross or allow official representatives of that organization to visit. In fact, as it subsequently transpired when the POWs were released, the Egyptians had indeed savagely beaten and in many cases tortured most of their Israeli prisoners, and had behaved almost as inhumanly as the Syrians.

Our supportive endeavors for families of POWs took two main forms. Especially during the initial phase of acute uncertainty, but also throughout the process, we stimulated a rallying round of friends, neighbors, community representatives, and caregivers. In one instance, for example, my wife and I visited for several weeks on a daily basis some old friends of ours whose son was initially reported MIA and then a POW in Egypt. Whenever we visited their home we found other friends there; people came in and sat for a while chatting and expressing solidarity almost as though it was a house of mourning. Most of the talk was about the absent son. The parents reported over and over again the cumulative pieces of information they had been able to glean from a variety of sources about the last known movements of their son and his unit. We helped them put these bits of information into perspective, we fortified them in bearing the burden of their terrible uncertainty, and we helped them cut down their fantasies about all the worst possible things that might have happened to him. When someone found an indistinct press picture of the boy among a group of POWs in Egypt, we too examined it with a magnifying glass and corroborated that it looked like him. When the Town Major reported that the Army authorities were now convinced that the boy was a prisoner of the Egyptians, we shared the relief of the parents; over the next few weeks we did our best to help them keep a tight rein on their imagination in regard to the possible ill treatment he might be suffering, and maintain their hopeful expectations that it was only a matter of time before he would be returned safe and sound. (In fact, when he eventually was released, we discovered that he had been cruelly tortured, and he is still receiving medical treatment for his injuries; but it would have done his parents no good, and certainly would not have helped him, if during that period we had agreed with the impulse of the parents to immerse themselves in hopeless imaginings of what might be taking place.)

The second approach to families of POWs was to catalyze the organization of mutual help groups. These groups rapidly moved into the arena of political action and began organizing public demonstrations and sending deputations to persuade the Israeli Government, international organizations, and world opinion to force the Arabs to publish lists of their POWs and to adhere to the terms of the Geneva Convention by allowing visits of inspection by the International Red Cross. At a later stage the political action groups of POW families campaigned to hasten the release of their relatives by insisting that this should be the first goal of Israel in any military disengagement agreement.

I am sure that this campaign helped maintain the morale of the families. Those who were most active, and even their co-workers and the family members who stayed at home but participated vicariously by identification, probably felt less helpless because they were doing something active on behalf of their relatives in the Arab prison camps. It may even be that some of the prisoners were treated less cruelly by their captors when the latter realized that world public opinion was being focused on this issue, and that there would probably soon be international inspections of prison camp conditions. On the other hand, as is not unusual when political campaigns are developed on an *ad hoc* basis in mutual help groups by people without political experience, led by men whose leadership may be based more on their capacity to give public expression to emotional reactions felt by their followers than by demonstrated wisdom and effectiveness, I feel that the objective results of this activity were of questionable value, and at times may even have been counterproductive. The Israeli authorities really needed no prodding by POW families in placing this issue at the top of their priorities in negotiations with the Arabs. Nor did Israeli public opinion need to be persuaded. On the other hand, the Arabs probably interpreted the emotional demonstrations to be an indication that this was a point of weakness in the Israeli character, and I think they tried to take advantage of it, perhaps more than if the demonstrations had not occurred, by using the POWs as a central instrument of psychological and political warfare against Israel.

Since I am a psychiatrist and not a political scientist, I am not able to resolve this question professionally in my own mind; but in any case, I feel that it was important from a mental health point of view that this campaign was organized by the families of POWs and that it obtained the wholehearted support of Israeli leaders and public opinion. This national solidarity not only fortified the families but also buttressed the nation's determination to stand up forcefully against its enemies on behalf of its citizens rather than quietly submit, as Jews had sometimes been obliged to do in past history when they had gone unresisting to the torture chamber and gas chamber and incinerators. In an extreme situation, defiance of the adversary and public moral protest fortify the capacity of people to overcome their difficulties and also proclaim the eventual triumph of the human spirit over adversity, a faith that is of supreme importance for those who are in the midst of the struggle as it is for the rest of mankind.

A further distressing complication was added for the families of POWs in Egypt. The Egyptian authorities began a series of radio broadcasts, in the style of the North Vietnamese, in which the "interviewed" Israeli POWs, after giving personal details about themselves and their families, made allegedly voluntary statements condemning Israel and justifying the Arab war effort. Because names of POWs had been withheld, many Israelis listened regularly to these broadcasts in order to discover friends and relatives who were in Egyptian hands. The effect on a family of hearing their son voicing anti-Israeli sentiments was often devastating. Instead of being able at least to reduce their pain at his captivity by thinking of him as some kind of national hero, they suddenly felt that he was betraying his country and that his treachery was being widely publicized. If they tried to lessen their shame by maintaining that everyone would realize that he was being forced by his captors to make these statements, they would have to confront the likelihood that he was being brainwashed or tortured, and even in that case they would feel upset that he had not shown the heroism to resist and to refuse to turn renegade, whatever the punishment. This shame was made all the worse because young people in Israel are brought up on stories of national heroes who chose to be tortured to death rather than betray their comrades or their nation.

We dealt with this problem by organizing increased local support for such families, and by arranging for mass media programs to report and condemn the malevolence of the Egyptians and to solicit public sympathy and support for these POWs and their families. In these programs it was naturally emphasized that the "freely volunteered" anti-Israeli statements by the POWs were obviously authored by the Egyptian propagandists who had forced their captives to read them, and that the Egyptians clearly underestimated the intelligence of the Israeli public if they thought this transparent strategem would take anybody in.

I had personal contact with one distressed POW family whose son had been compelled to read a statement condemning the Israeli Government, and in particular Defense Minister Dayan, for starting the war by launching an unprovoked attack across the Suez Canal. The family asked me to listen to a tape recording of the radio program, and I was able to point out to them that their son, however much he may have suffered when he was being "persuaded" to collaborate in this melancholy episode, was still in sufficient control over himself to have subtly turned the tables on his captors. He had answered all the initial identifying questions about himself and his family in a normal tone of voice and at his usual talking speed, but when he was asked what he felt about the Israeli war effort, his tone of voice became monotonous, he changed his speed, and he occasionally stumbled over a word, so that it was obvious that he was reading from a document written by somebody else. I told the parents that I thought he must have been in good shape physically and mentally to have been able to accomplish this, and I also pointed out that the tone, content, and wording of the statement were obvious low level Arab propaganda and would be recognized as such by any Israeli listener of average intelligence. The parents, who had asked me to listen to the tape as a friend and not in my professional capacity, were obviously reassured by what I said, but even more by the fact that I clearly identified with their son in his miserable predicament and showed no trace of condemning him or them.

The most important support for these families came from scores, and in some cases hundreds, of letters that each of them received from strangers all over the country who had listened to the broadcasts, from which they had obtained their name and address. These men, women, and children wrote spontaneously to tell the family that their son was alive and well, and to congratulate them on this, as well as to express hope that he would soon be returned to them and would quickly forget his tribulations in Egypt. Not one of these letters, to the best of my knowledge, in any way criticized the prisoner for making anti-Israeli statements. On the contrary, whenever the statements were mentioned, it was within the context of condemning the Egyptians for their inhumanity in forcing a prisoner-of-war to behave like this, and of deriding them for imagining that any Israeli would be deceived by their obvious propaganda.

Families were so exhilarated by receiving these letters that many of them collected them into albums, which they kept to give to the POW when he returned as a sign of the identification with him of the Israeli population. One father said to me, "I want him to know when he comes back that he was not on his own when he was suffering, and that our people did not forget him during his trouble in that foreign land."

Families of wounded

The Israeli Army, in a characteristically humane provision, arranged that wherever possible a telephone should be brought to the bedside of wounded soldiers, as soon as possible after admission to hospital, so that they could personally tell their family what had happened to them and give immediate reassurance about their condition. In other cases, the information was relayed through the Town Major's office, and family members were invited immediately to visit the hospital where the soldier was being treated. Our Emergency Staff, backed up by the Municipality Social Work Department, made contact with the family of each seriously injured man and arranged for transportation to the hospital, which was often in some distant part of the country, and, if necessary, for volunteer homemakers and baby-sitters to free wives and parents to make the journey without having to take small children along with them. Volunteer drivers with their own cars were available on a 24-hour basis for the emergency transportation of families to visit their wounded relatives; it is of interest that many of the people who volunteered for this duty were disabled veterans of previous wars, who did yeoman work, not only in transporting the relatives but also in providing them with support and guidance, and in demonstrating that it is possible to master the aftereffects of even major war wounds.

Our group also organized a volunteer program to help people from other parts of the country who came to visit their wounded relatives in Jerusalem hospitals. We spent much time and effort recruiting local families who were willing to offer home hospitality to the visitors, believing that people would prefer the quiet amenities and privacy of a home to staying in a noisy, busy hotel. For those who preferred the anonymity of the latter, we arranged with a number of local hotels to provide rooms free of charge or at nominal rates, and in each hotel we arranged a club room where relatives might sit, have light refreshments, and relax in between visits to the hospital. In each club room there was a volunteer hostess, who was prepared, if requested, to help cater to the needs of the visitors. We asked each hospital to appoint a liaison worker from its social work staff to contact our organization if there was anything needed by one of its visitors.

Our program was well organized, but it was hardly used at all. First, we quickly discovered that relatives of severely wounded soldiers refused to leave the hospital until they went home after the acute treatment phase was over. They stayed at the bedside or in the adjoining corridor, and no amount of persuasion would induce them to move. The hospital authorities were forced to provide stretchers for the relatives to sleep on, unless they had available beds in wards that had been emptied to prepare for casualties that had not appeared. The visitors were fed in the hospital cafeterias, and whatever social needs they had were dealt with by the hospital volunteers. All hospitals dealing with military casualties were overflowing with wartime volunteers, in addition to their usual lay volunteer organization. Some of the hotel space we had arranged was used by the visitors, but nobody seemed interested in home hospitality, the feeling apparently being that they had too much to worry about already without having to be bothered by being guests in the homes of strangers, however well intentioned.

Supporting the Families of Soldiers on Active Service

Our main contribution to the welfare of wives and parents of soldiers was to advocate that they should keep busy at their usual duties in the home and at work, and that those who had available time should do wartime volunteer work. It was our experience that most people managed to master their continuous anxiety regarding the dangers to which their loved ones were exposed if they had enough work to do that they defined as productive, so that they could feel that they too were actively contributing to the war effort. True, many of them showed signs of tension and excessive fatigue, and there were difficulties with appetite and sleeping; but on the whole, people quickly adjusted and maintained control, even though, of course, their mood was grim. The feeling that the whole nation was in the same boat led to a general lowering of interpersonal barriers, and Israelis of different classes and ethnic groups became considerate and polite to each other, which is not at all their usual behavior, but a manifestation of the spirit of comradeship with those with whom they felt they were sharing common dangers.

It is of interest that the few complaints I heard from management personnel during the war about nervousness, "hysterical" outbursts, and loss of efficiency among their workers all related to unmarried women or widows who had no husband or son in the Army. Although they did not suffer from the everpresent anxiety of the others, they must have felt to some extent left out, and they did not have such a need to maintain emotional control. My general advice to supervisors and administrators in such cases, and also in regard to those with relatives at the front who showed irritability and reduced control, was to be selectively inattentive to signs of strain and to refocus the individual onto meeting the demands of his job, while communicating the expectation that although we were all going through a difficult time we must persevere, do our duty in maintaining the essential life of the country, and eventually we would emerge successfully, as we had in the past. I also used my influence as a community mental health specialist to dissuade people from engaging in uncovering and abreactive operations which might weaken normal defenses instead of supporting and strengthening them, although I must admit that I was not successful in persuading some of my clinical colleagues in this matter. They could not see the essential difference between the situation of a soldier suffering from a battle neurosis, where immediate abreaction is an important precondition to rapid return to duty because of the acute overpowering and disorganization of defenses caused by his major traumatic experience, and a civilian who is managing on the whole to cope with his much lower level of stress, apart from temporary uncertainty at peak periods or when he gets unduly fatigued. In the latter instances, the appropriate treatment is to strengthen defenses, for instance, by communications through his expectational network, since the defenses are substantially intact and have not been swamped.

Some of my colleagues could not understand that if they published articles in the daily press and spoke on the radio about the increased need for specialized services to treat the psychological symptoms produced by worrying about the dangers of war, and if they advertised "hot lines" and "talk centers" to deal with the increased anxiety of the population, they were building an expectational climate that would facilitate a weakening of defenses and seduce some people to take the route of dependency who might otherwise struggle actively to stand on their own feet, despite their discomfort.

During the war, the daily newspapers started publishing a list of emergency telephone numbers and addresses. I am sorry to say that on the occasions I looked at this list I found that more than half of the items carried some kind of mental health or mental illness label. The effect on many members of the public must have been to persuade them that we expected large numbers of psychiatric casualties in the population. In fact, less damage was probably done than I feared because the Israeli public has in general a low opinion of the mental health movement; their dominant attitudes under stress were in the direction of task orientation rather than emotional uncovering. I understand that most of the people who responded to the invitations to discuss their wartime troubles on the emergency telephone line or at advice centers and clinics turned out to be chronic neurotics or psychotics who had become accustomed over the years to being patients.

Although I believe that the contribution of a community intervenor to supporting the adult members of families of soldiers may not be very significant, I feel that he does have an important role to play in regard to children, whose ego structure has not yet developed to the full its capacity to master stress. In my contacts with school personnel, I was often asked for advice in this area, although I am glad to say that the need for my intervention was lessened by the excellent way this issue was being handled by the school psychologists and the policy makers of the Ministry of Education. During the war, the Ministry put on a television program portraying the procedures it advocated in schools for dealing with children whose fathers were in the Army, and this was completely in line with my own ideas and with the advice I gave to educators who solicited my help.

Our approach was two-pronged. First, we emphasized the importance in fostering and maintaining a sense of security in the child population, of continuing to maintain the familiar educational structure and the demands and challenges of a curriculum focused on inculcating values, knowledge, and skills designed for long-term benefit. This would apply particularly to children who might have a tendency to be unsettled because of worries at home about the safety of their father or brothers in the Army. For them, the continuation of school work in its familiar mode and setting would provide the assurance of abiding structure in an uncertain world; and the demand on them to preserve discipline, to focus attention, and to fulfill tasks would strengthen their ability to keep their anxieties under control.

The second aspect of the program was of equal importance. Educators must systematically provide their students with structured opportunities to deal safely and constructively with the emotion-laden topics of the present day. This should be accomplished not by a psychotherapeutic approach of focusing in class directly on the idiosyncratic concerns of individual children, except in passing and as illustrative material, but by the educational method of learning about the expectable human issues involved for most people, and developing emotional and cognitive tools for understanding and dealing with them. Time should be regularly set aside, in accordance with the age of the child and the demands of the rest of the curriculum, for the class to focus on the current war situation, its human and material dangers and opportunities, including how people can be expected to react in the light of how they have behaved throughout history. There should be a chance for free expression – in lower grades via spontaneous drawing and painting and imaginative games and story-telling, in the higher grades through verbal discussion and debate – so that each child might make his individual contribution to the common theme and express his feelings within a controlled and constructive framework. The teacher should direct the attention of the class to significant current events drawn from newspaper and television accounts of the war situation and the home front and from the personal experience of the students. If the father or brother of any of the children should become a casualty, the class should discuss this issue openly and work out how best to help their friend master his tragedy. Such class discussions should not only involve expression of feeling and understanding of processes but should also lead to the planning and implementation of constructive action, such as the development of organized volunteer projects like helping to paint automobile headlights for the blackout, running errands for old people, cleaning up the environment, baby-sitting to allow overburdened housewives to go shopping, etc.

This two-pronged general approach should be supplemented by educators watching for signs that a small number of individuals with special needs based on their home situation or the absence of their father and brothers in the Army may be under particular strain. A teacher should tactfully make himself more available to such children so they can talk to him if they so desire and should pay a "routine" visit to the home in order to collaborate with the mother in lessening the strain. If he uncovers a situation that he feels is beyond his competence, he should seek consultation from the school nurse, social worker, or psychologist, who may advise him how to deal with it on his own or in collaboration with them, in line with what should be customary procedure in the school in peacetime as well as during a war.

Dealing with the Dependent and Needy Population

During a war, the civilian population continues to have its usual service needs. Some of these can be temporarily pushed aside so that caregivers can concentrate on dealing with issues that are war-specific; but it is important not to neglect the core needs of medical, surgical, and obstetric emergencies, plus the needs of aged and chronically dependent people which previously were satisfied by men who are now away from home on army service or by caregivers who are occupied in dealing with military casualties. Also, the dangers and anxieties of the times, the blackout, and the shortage of public transportation, etc. are likely to disturb many old and chronically sick people, especially those living on their own, who in peacetime managed to maintain themselves in precarious equilibrium, but who now may not be able to continue to feed and take care of themselves and interact with others without outside assistance.

In Jerusalem, our Emergency Staff, in collaboration with the city social work department, focused special attention on this problem. We had a 24-hour telephone switchboard that received and acted on calls for service assistance from anyone in the population including medical, surgical, and obstetric emergencies and requests for help in family, housing, and social predicaments. We also organized a screening, planning, and implementation service in the social work department that pooled information from this switchboard, from our network of professional and volunteer caregivers, and from the other community agencies that came into contact with the population. The head of the department was in charge of this central decision-making and coordinating group and she distributed the requests for service among her own staff and related agencies, and arranged for follow-up to ensure that plans were implemented. She also recruited a small army of volunteers, drawn mainly from the regular membership of community, educational, welfare, and cultural organizations such as the League of Academic Women, the Women's Zionist Organization, and the Gold Institute for Overseas Youth Leaders, to whom she allotted such tasks as taking care of a woman's home and children when she went into the lying-in hospital or for a few days after she came home with her baby, transporting patients to the hospital, helping the elderly do their housework or their shopping, or taking them out for a drive or a walk. Each of the groups of volunteers was organized with its own informal leaders, drawn from the officers of their association or institution, who were responsible for making sure that the allotted tasks were accomplished; each group was linked with a professional caregiver such as a public health nurse or a social worker who was responsible for any professional work that might be needed. The director and I met from time to time with these groups of volunteers within the framework of their parent organizations, in order to increase their understanding of the human issues involved and in order to maintain their motivation and morale by communicating our appreciation of the importance of their contribution. We also made it clear both to these volunteers and to the community professionals that to get the best results from volunteers in wartime they must be plugged in to the professional caregiving system, because the civilian field is so burdened by novel problems, because there is so high a level of tension, and because communication and transportation channels are so heavily loaded, that confusion and disorganization are an ever-present danger. Unless caregivers are well led and tightly organized and supervised, whether they are professional or nonprofessional – but the hazard is greater in the latter case – much effort will be wasted, and they will tend to run around in ineffectual circles.

ORGANIZATIONAL IMPLICATIONS

Below are some of the many lessons I learned from my experience during the Yom Kippur War.

It would be useful to have a Central Planning Group (CPG) in each city or population center, which would accept responsibility for planning and coordinating support services during a war or other communal emergency. If none exists, its immediate formation should be one of the first goals of a community intervenor when he begins his emergency activities. The main functions of the CPG are to predict and keep abreast of the changing needs of population groups; to organize new services or to coordinate existing services to cover these needs; and to develop appropriate communication links and feedback mechanisms so that follow-through can be assured and so that resources can be quickly redeployed in the light of the changing situation.

The CPG should be small, consisting of three to five members, so that it can meet easily and frequently during the emergency. It does not need to be a governmental unit or to wield power directly. Its influence may operate through the personal connections or the high status of its members. Each member should be a key person in one or more of the main service organizations or institutions of the area and should have wide personal connections and good relationships with the rest. The group as a whole, or its convenor, should act in an advisory capacity to the mayor or other executive authority of the area, through whom necessary decisions can be implemented and essential connections with other key people can be quickly developed when the exigencies of the emergency situation demand it.

The group should meet frequently during the emergency, daily if possible, in order to pool information and decide on short-range plans. The best way of ensuring this is for its members to be part of the Emergency Staff, so that they can get together before or after its daily meetings. It would be useful for the CPG to be appointed by the Emergency Staff as its Subcommittee on Support Systems, which would thus automatically link it officially with all the local services. For instance, if the CPG needs quick access to the mass media, as we did in order to deal with the Egyptian misuse of POWs for anti-Israel propaganda, this is relatively easy to achieve via the public relations or information officer of the Emergency Staff. The CPG is also in a position to keep the Emergency Staff, and in particular the mayor and governmental leaders, informed about problem issues and population groups with vulnerable morale, so that the community leaders can pay special attention to them.

The CPG should continually monitor the human needs of the entire population and locate categories and subpopulations currently in most urgent need. It should ensure that these are dealt with through existing services; if the latter are not adequate, it should itself organize or stimulate the organization by other bodies of stop-gap services until more systematic programs can be developed. In a confused and overburdened service field, this may be done by drawing to the attention of existing organizations circumscribed emergency needs and persuading them to accept new responsibilities and to redeploy their own forces in accordance with these; or by recruiting volunteers, both professional and lay, to develop an emergency structure to fulfill a particular mission on a temporary *ad hoc* basis. In the case of all volunteers this means drawing them out of their existing task situations, and the CPG must be alert to the danger that this may lead to hiatuses. For instance, if professional caregivers are mobilized to deal with the families of casualties, they will necessarily have less time to handle their usual tasks, and people with ordinary emergency health and welfare needs may thus be neglected; and if housewives spend too much time as volunteers, for instance in hospitals or child-care centers, their homes may become disorganized and their own children may suffer.

A major function of the CPG is to ensure the effective mobilization and deployment of such volunteers. In wartime or in any major communal emergency, recruitment of volunteers is not a significant problem. Many people rush to volunteer, either because of a sincere desire to help others or because they are too nervous to sit at home. Both categories should be welcomed; there is likely to be work for everyone.

The main problems are organizational and logistic, and these are the ones on which the CPG should focus. In the expectable confusion of an emergency, the CPG must be prepared to develop a simple structure so that volunteers are quickly put to work on essential tasks that they can accomplish with preexisting skills; so that they can be appropriately led, supervised, and supported; and so that information generated by their work may be quickly pooled, screened, and communicated to energize other services, if these should be needed, as well as to help the CPG keep in touch with the changing needs of the population.

Most of the volunteers will be nonprofessional and the biggest danger is to try and train them to operate as watered-down professionals. Such training will not succeed, except in confusing and frustrating the volunteers. It is also unnecessary, because in the support system field ordinary people, if properly motivated and briefed, and if supported themselves, can immediately fulfill important tasks both by person-to-person human influence and by taking over chores to lighten the burden of those victimized by the emergency.

I believe that leadership and implementational supervision (namely, following through to make sure that allotted tasks are accomplished) should be in the hands of the nonprofessionals. The easiest way of doing this is to utilize existing associations and organizations, which should be recruited *en bloc* for emergency volunteer work, and which may use their own organizational structure and officers. In taking this route, it is important for all to remember that since the new mission is different, new leadership may be needed. In my experience, the required influentials quickly emerge in an association of people who know each other. Each subgroup task force should have its convenor, who distributes tasks to individuals, makes sure that everyone knows what he is expected to do, keeps in touch with them to ensure that it has been done, and transmits messages to higher levels of the organization, and eventually to the CPG, about accomplishments and needs for additional services.

Since, in an emergency, administrators are in a constant state of communication input overload, this vertical system will be inadequate, and it must be supplemented by a horizontal system, so that requests for additional service as well as planning decisions about individual predicaments can be maximally decentralized. A good way of accomplishing this is to articulate the nonprofessional volunteer services with the professional caregiving services of the locality and also with the neighborhood community organizational services. In Jerusalem, for instance, our analog of the CPG linked volunteer task forces both with local professional caregivers, such as welfare workers and well baby clinic staffs, and also with neighborhood citizens' councils and community centers.

The two other crucial elements in organizing an effective emergency volunteer service are *briefing* and *support.* The responsibility for these lies with the CPG; although, as with the rest of its work, it may distribute specific tasks for implementation by others. Both briefing and support should be undertaken by caregiving professionals, unless they are confident that this can be properly accomplished by the nonprofessional leaders of the volunteer organizations.

By briefing, I mean the allottment of a mission to the volunteer organization; the subdivison of the mission into categories of population to be dealt with and description of their needs; the location of the needy persons; the types of help to be offered; the nature of the desired collaboration with the local professional caregivers and communal institutions, together with a description of their organizational framework; and indicators for calling in supplementary assistance. The briefing tells the volunteers what we want from them and it orients them to the people they will be helping, as well as to the overall supportive structure within which they will be operating. *It does not tell them how they should accomplish their tasks.* That is left to their own initiative and ingenuity, with the stated or unstated expectation that every individual volunteer will go about his work in his own way, on the basis of his own personality and past experience.

Of course, in a large volunteer organization the main briefing can be done by the CPG with the leaders, and the latter can then distribute the necessary detailed information to their followers. I usually feel more secure, however, if a caregiving professional is present at all such initial briefing sessions to make sure that the field of responsibility is defined so as to articulate adequately with the operations of the professional caregiving network.

By support, I mean the regular convening of local and central meetings of the volunteers together with the relevant echelon of the professional caregivers, including members of the CPG in order to accomplish the tasks of guidance and emotional buttressing previously outlined in this paper.

It is the responsibility of the CPG not only to promote and organize services to cater to people's needs but also to prevent infringing on their human rights during an emergency, when the normal protections of privacy and jurisdictional barriers are reduced, and when well-meaning individuals and groups may inadvertently weaken rather than strengthen the afflicted by such procedures as public labeling, expectations of dependency, and influencing them to deviate unduly from their natural defenses and styles of coping.

Finally, a Central Planning Group should ideally, at the end of the emergency period, evaluate its experience and use this evaluation to plan for the next time when its services may unfortunately be needed. This may include improving its lines of communication with key authority figures, institutions, and organizations; training its own members and the caregivers of the community in the fields of crisis intervention and the theory and practice of support systems in an emergency;[9] preparing such printed materials as guidelines for physicians and for volunteer organizations; and trying to modify relevant policies of governmental agencies on the basis of the lessons it has learned, for instance, persuading the Army to change its casualty notification procedures and the Ministry of Defense to alter the personnel practices of its Rehabilitation Department.

[9]By chance, I was involved in an educational project in Jerusalem during the summer of 1973 that paved the way for my intervention program during the Yom Kippur War. I conducted a faculty seminar on Crisis Theory and Techniques of Crisis Intervention at the Paul Baerwald School of Social Work for the supervisors of students' field work assignments. The participants were 20 social workers in key positions in the Jerusalem health, education, and welfare systems, including the person who directed the city social work department during the war, the chief social worker of one of the general hospitals that served casualties, and key members of the Jerusalem Mental Health Association. Over a 2-month period we studied together the theoretical and practical issues of providing services for people in emergency situations, especially some of my latest ideas on support systems and the value of nonprofessional person-to-person help; we developed friendly personal relationships and a common language. In effect, we built a network of key workers and a reference group in the Jerusalem area who shared or understood each others' values and philosophy. This network was immediately energized when the war started; and the invitation for me to come to Jerusalem as a community intervenor to help them practice what I had preached was one of the consequences, as were many of the service innovations that emerged.

Index